Thank you for picking up *Haikyu!!* volume 4!! And!! Guess what?! I'm running out of ideas!! About what to write here!!! So I'm just gonna!!! Fill up space!! With a whole lot of "!"s!! !!!!!!!!!

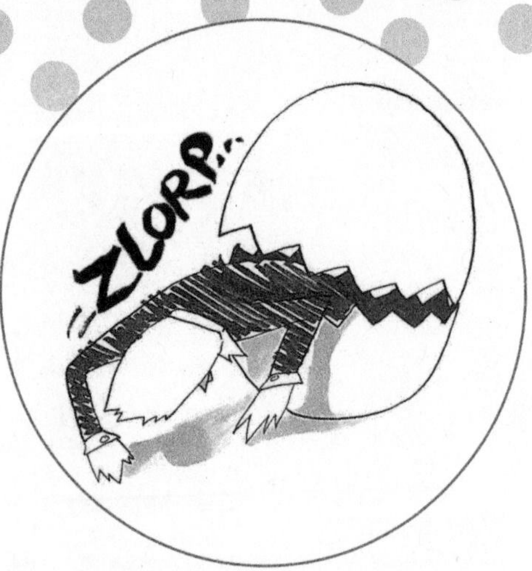
ZLORP...

HARUICHI FURUDATE began his manga career when he was 25 years old with the one-shot *Ousama Kid* [King Kid], which won an honorable mention for the 14th Jump Treasure Newcomer Manga Prize. His first series, *Kiben Gakuha, Yotsuya Sensei no Kaidan* [Philosophy School, Yotsuya Sensei's Ghost Stories], was serialized in *Weekly Shonen Jump* in 2010. In 2012, he began serializing *Haikyu!!* in *Weekly Shonen Jump*, where it became his most popular work to date.

HAIKYU!!

VOLUME 4
SHONEN JUMP Manga Edition

Story and Art by
HARUICHI FURUDATE

Translation **1** **ADRIENNE BECK**
Touch-Up Art & Lettering **2** **ERIKA TERRIQUEZ**
Design **3** **FAWN LAU**
Editor **4** **MARLENE FIRST**

Printed in the U.S.A.

Published by VIZ Media, LLC
P.O. Box 77010
San Francisco, CA 94107

10 9 8 7 6 5 4 3 2 1
First printing, October 2016

www.shonenjump.com

www.viz.com

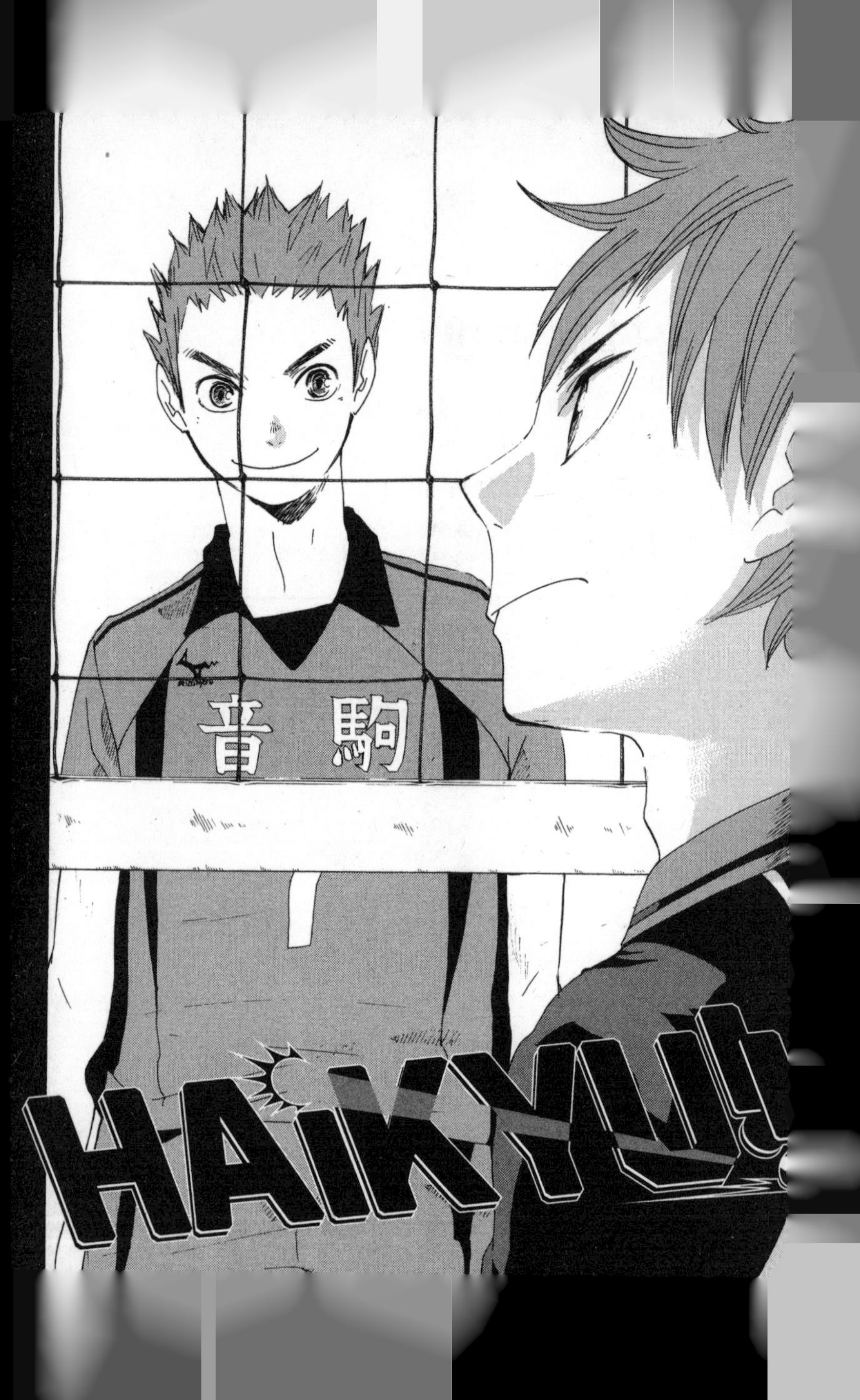
音駒
HAIKYU!!

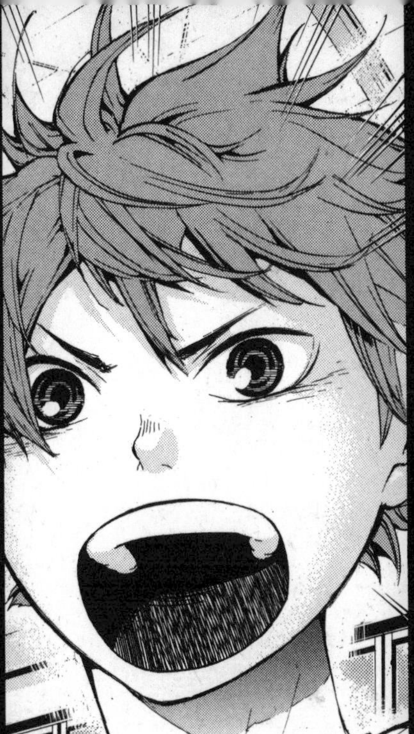

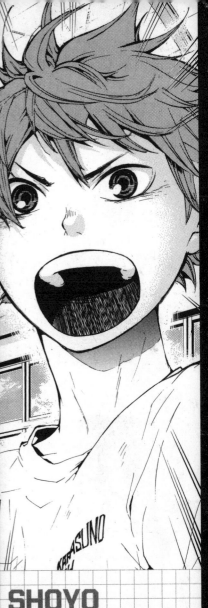

SHOYO HINATA

1ST YEAR / MIDDLE BLOCKER

Even though he doesn't have the best body type for volleyball, he is super athletic. Gets nervous easily.

TOBIO KAGEYAMA

1ST YEAR / SETTER

His instincts and athletic talent are so good that he's like a "king" who rules the court. Demanding and egocentric.

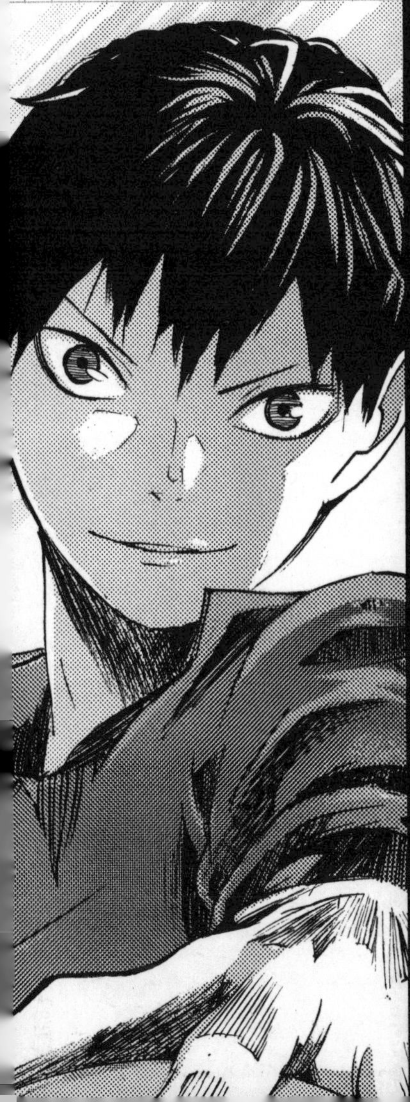

CHARACTERS

Karasuno High School Volleyball Club

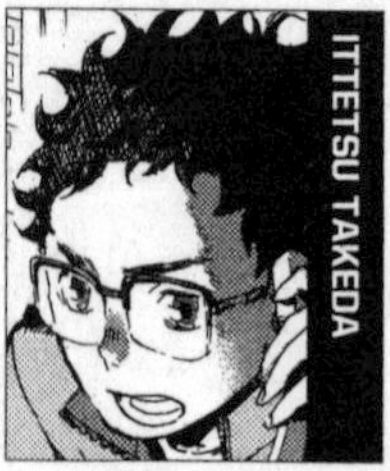
ITTETSU TAKEDA

ADVISER

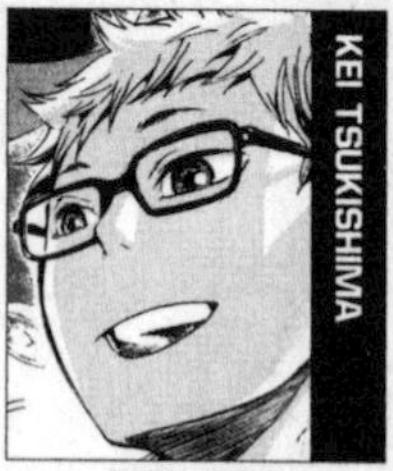
KEI TSUKISHIMA

1ST YEAR MIDDLE BLOCKER

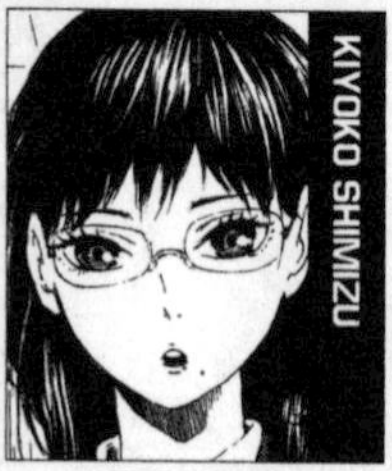
KIYOKO SHIMIZU

3RD YEAR MANAGER

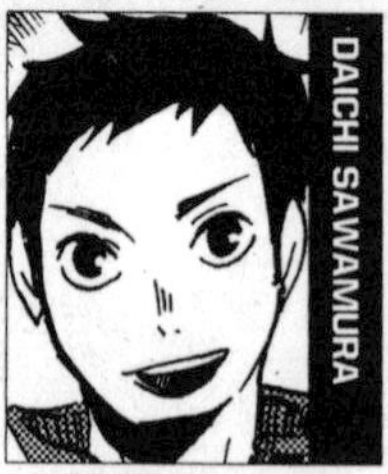
DAICHI SAWAMURA

3RD YEAR (CAPTAIN) WING SPIKER

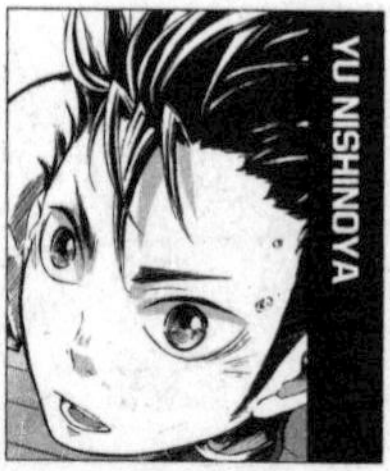
YU NISHINOYA

2ND YEAR LIBERO

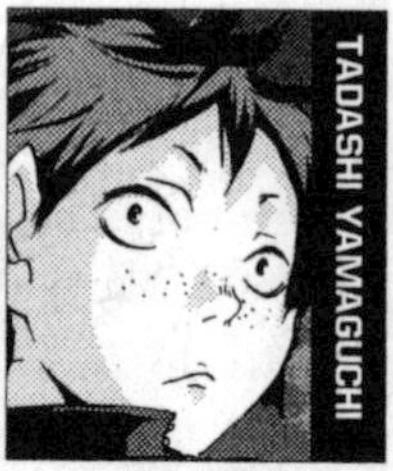
TADASHI YAMAGUCHI

1ST YEAR MIDDLE BLOCKER

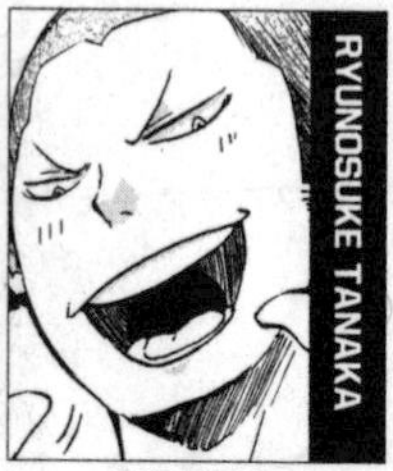
RYUNOSUKE TANAKA

2ND YEAR WING SPIKER

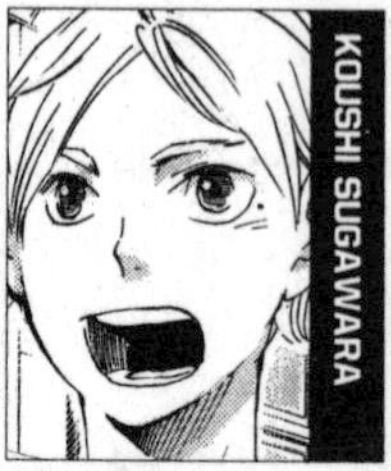
KOUSHI SUGAWARA

3RD YEAR (VICE CAPTAIN) SETTER

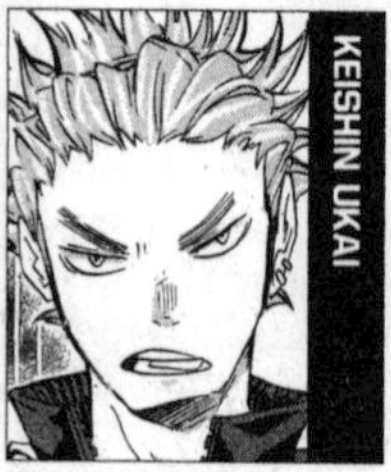
KEISHIN UKAI

COACH

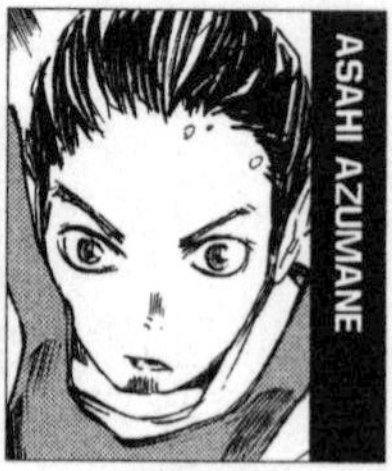
ASAHI AZUMANE

3RD YEAR WING SPIKER

Nekoma High School Volleyball Club

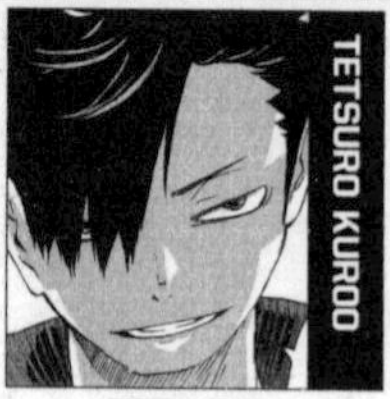
TETSURO KUROO

3RD YEAR MIDDLE BLOCKER

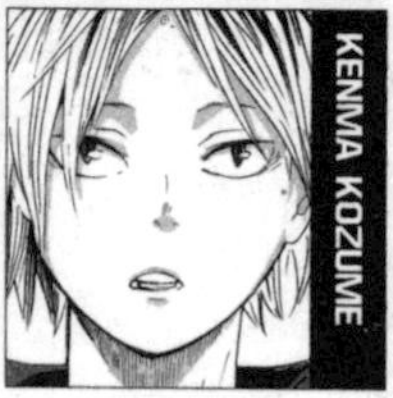
KENMA KOZUME

2ND YEAR SETTER

Ever since he saw the legendary player known as "the Little Giant" compete at the national volleyball finals, Shoyo Hinata has been aiming to be the best volleyball player ever! He decides to join the volleyball club at his middle school and gets to play in an official tournament during his third year. His team is crushed by a team led by volleyball prodigy Tobio Kageyama, also known as "the King of the Court." Swearing revenge on Kageyama, Hinata graduates middle school and enters Karasuno High School, the school where the Little Giant played. However, upon joining the club, he finds out that Kageyama is there too! The two of them bicker constantly, but they bring out the best in each other's talents and become a powerful combo! With the addition of second-year libero Nishinoya, third-year ace Azumane and coach Keishin Ukai, Karasuno's volleyball team is finally complete! Which is perfect timing because in just a few days, they will face off against their old rival Nekoma High School in their first matchup in years.

HAIKYU!!

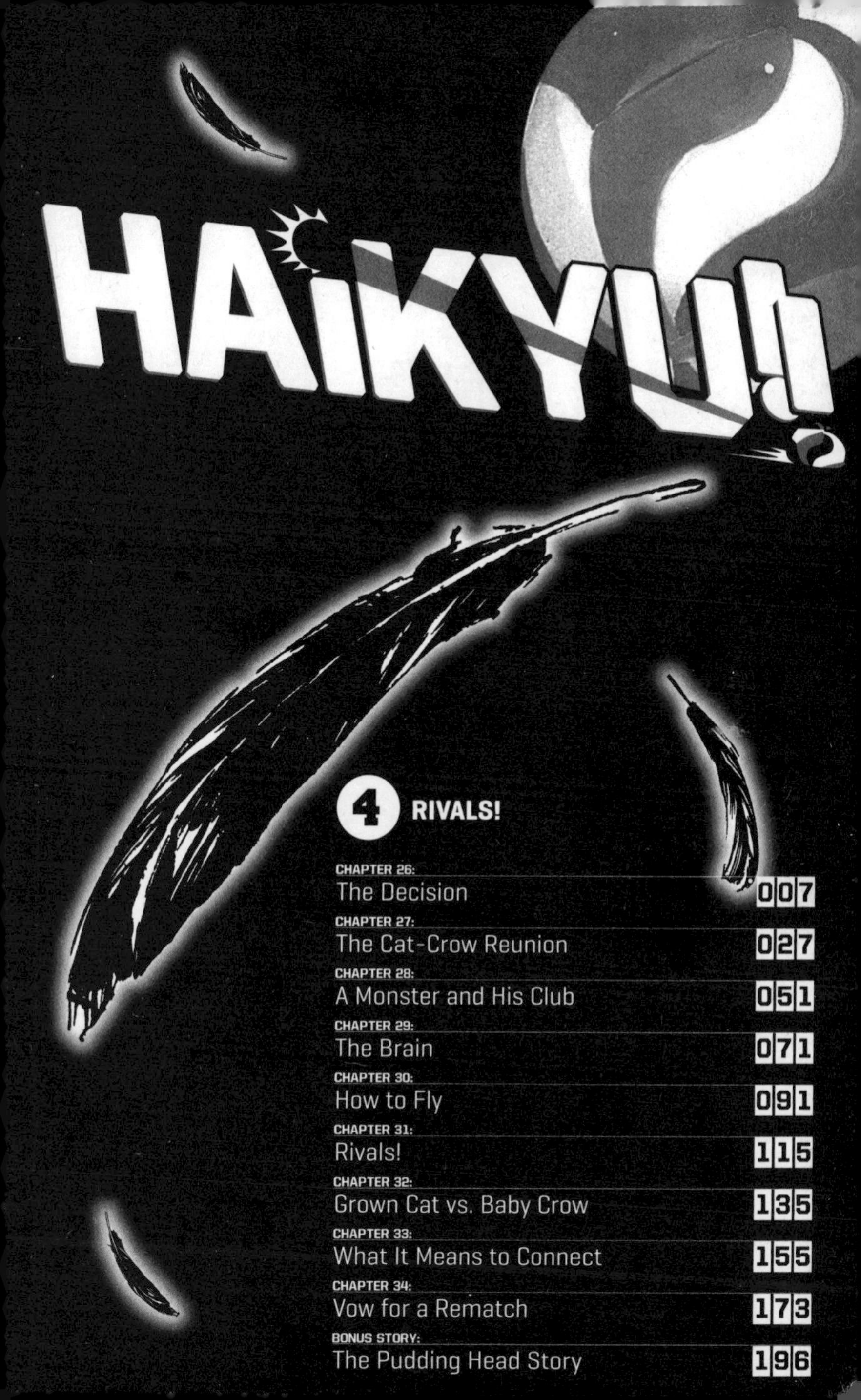

4 RIVALS!

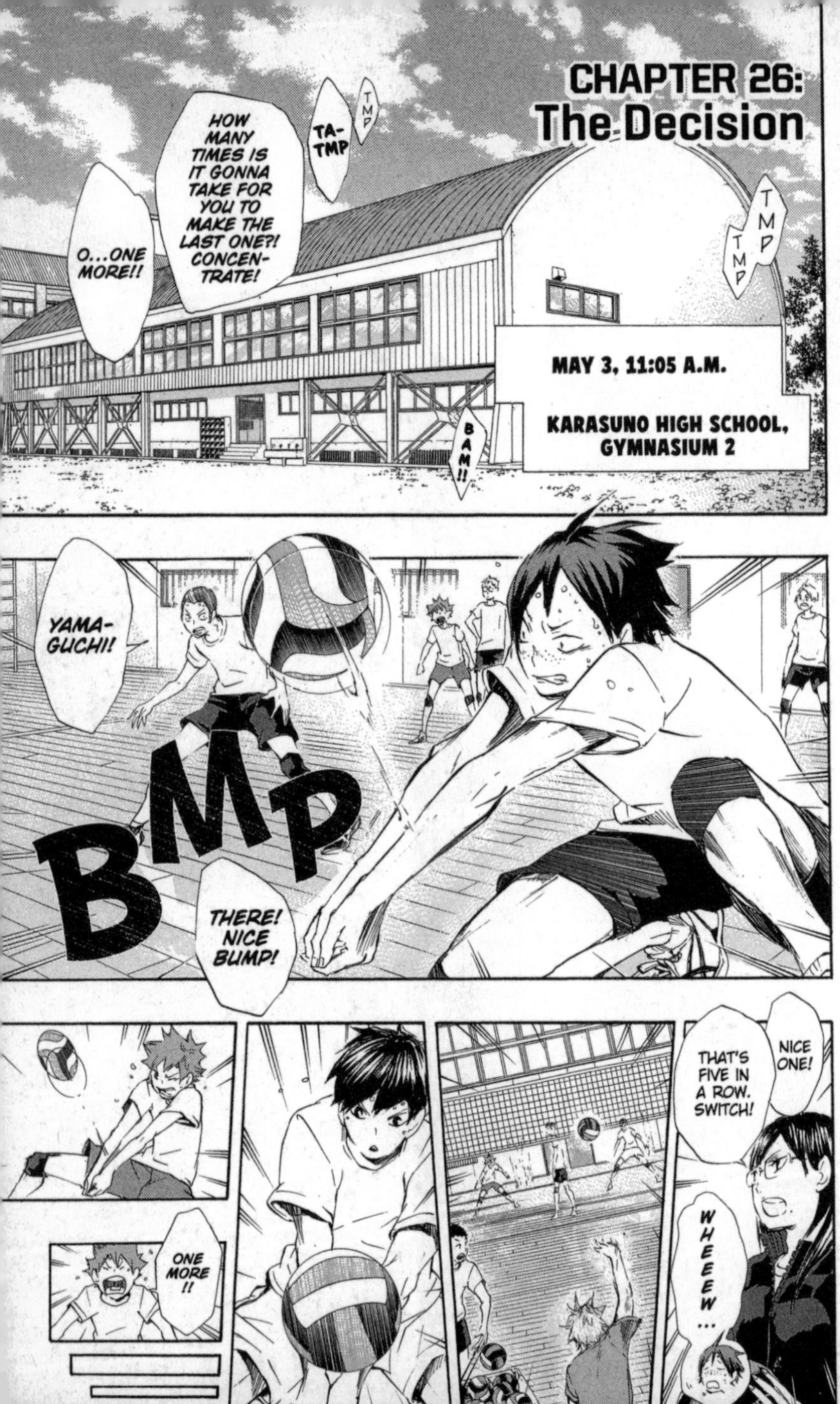
CHAPTER 26:
The Decision
TMP TMP
MAY 3, 11:05 A.M.
KARASUNO HIGH SCHOOL, GYMNASIUM 2
BAM!!
TMP
TA-TMP
HOW MANY TIMES IS IT GONNA TAKE FOR YOU TO MAKE THE LAST ONE?! CONCENTRATE!
O...ONE MORE!!
YAMAGUCHI!
BMP
THERE! NICE BUMP!
NICE ONE!
THAT'S FIVE IN A ROW. SWITCH!
WHEEEW...
ONE MORE!!

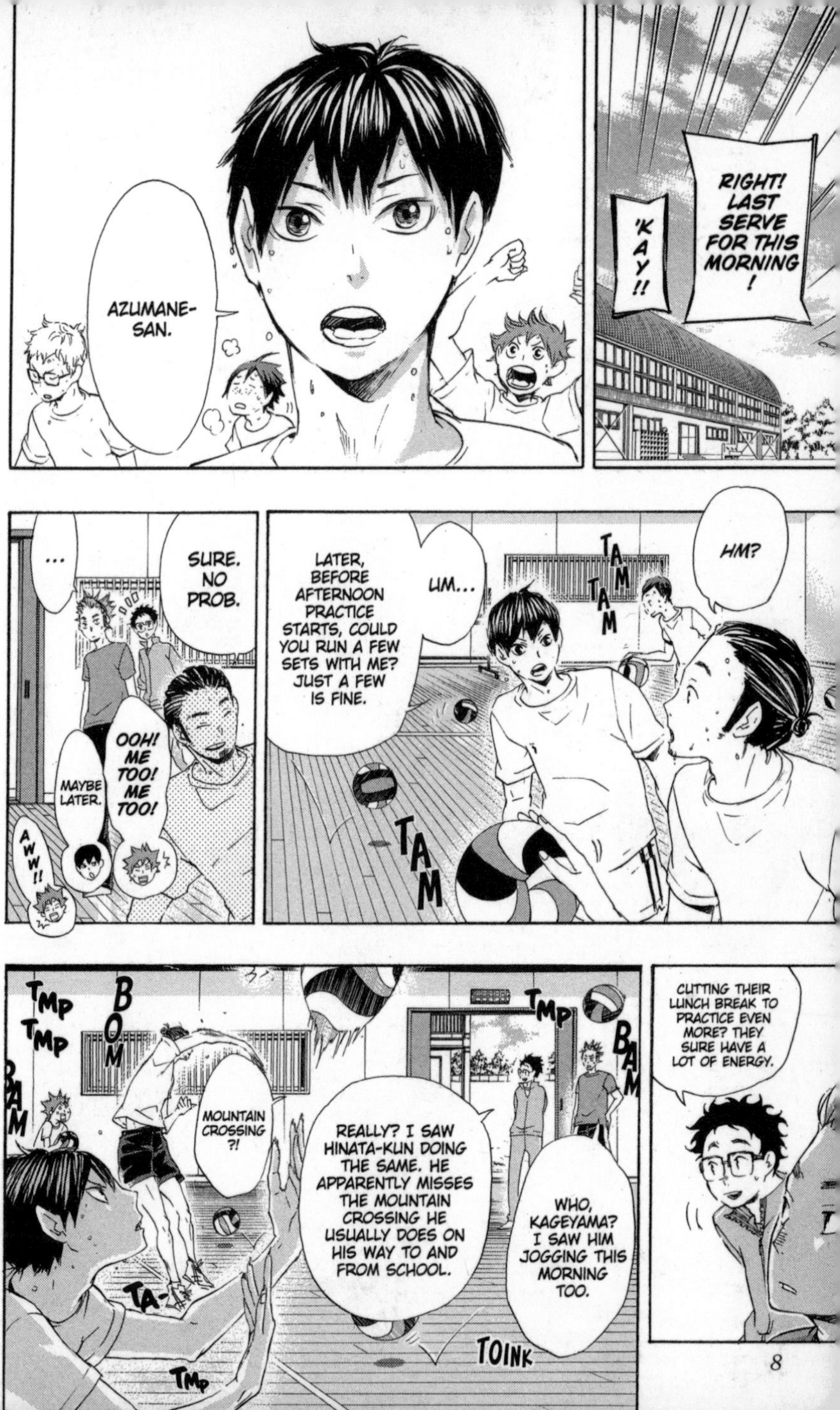
RIGHT! LAST SERVE FOR THIS MORNING!
'KAY!!
AZUMANE-SAN.
HM?
TAM TAM
UM...
LATER, BEFORE AFTERNOON PRACTICE STARTS, COULD YOU RUN A FEW SETS WITH ME? JUST A FEW IS FINE.
TAM
SURE. NO PROB.
...
OOH! ME TOO! ME TOO!
MAYBE LATER.
AWW!!
CUTTING THEIR LUNCH BREAK TO PRACTICE EVEN MORE? THEY SURE HAVE A LOT OF ENERGY.
TMP
BAM
WHO, KAGEYAMA? I SAW HIM JOGGING THIS MORNING TOO.
REALLY? I SAW HINATA-KUN DOING THE SAME. HE APPARENTLY MISSES THE MOUNTAIN CROSSING HE USUALLY DOES ON HIS WAY TO AND FROM SCHOOL.
MOUNTAIN CROSSING?!
BOM
TMP TMP
BAM
TA-
TOINK
TMP

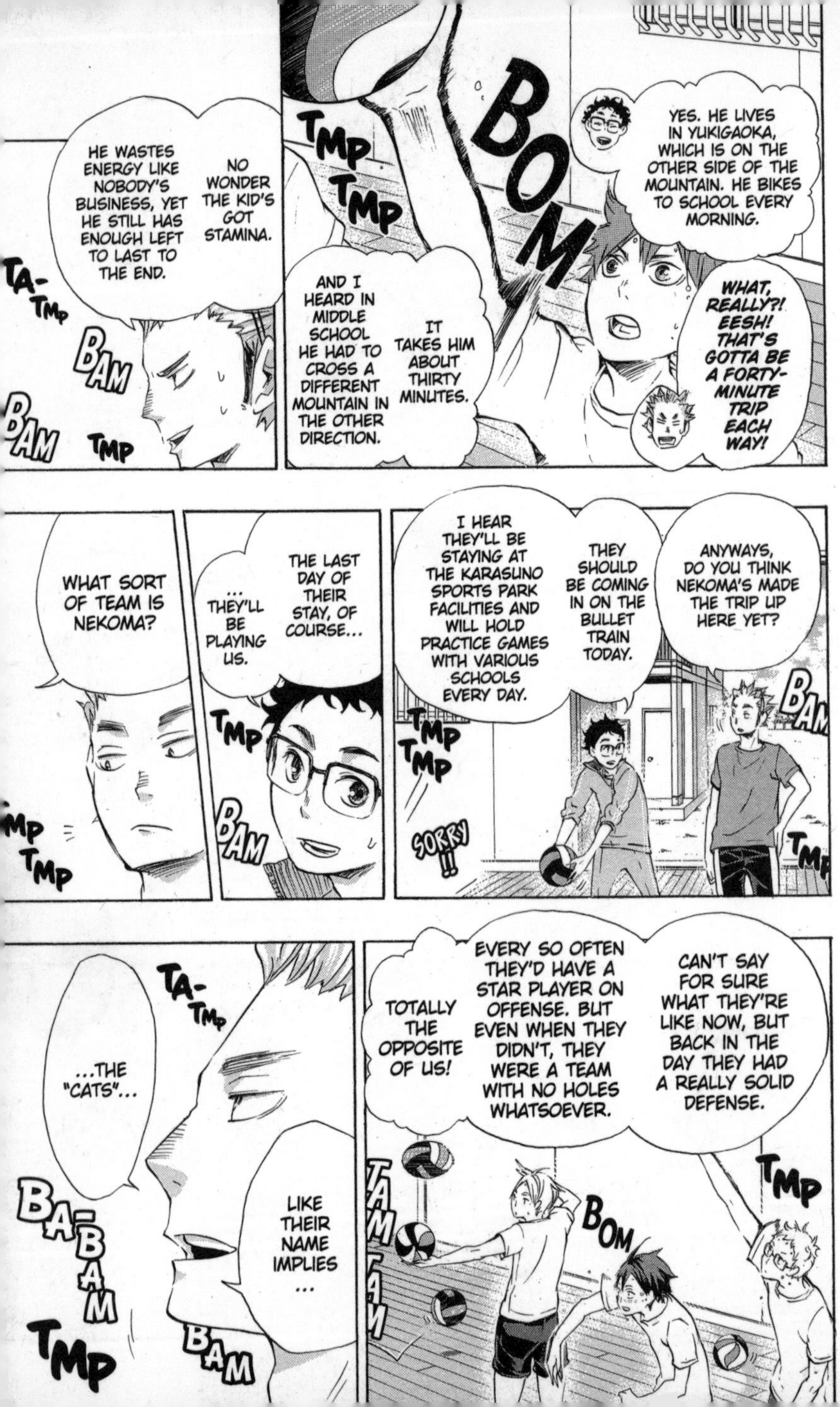
BOM
TMP TMP
YES. HE LIVES IN YUKIGAOKA, WHICH IS ON THE OTHER SIDE OF THE MOUNTAIN. HE BIKES TO SCHOOL EVERY MORNING.
WHAT, REALLY?! EESH! THAT'S GOTTA BE A FORTY-MINUTE TRIP EACH WAY!
IT TAKES HIM ABOUT THIRTY MINUTES.
AND I HEARD IN MIDDLE SCHOOL HE HAD TO CROSS A DIFFERENT MOUNTAIN IN THE OTHER DIRECTION.
NO WONDER THE KID'S GOT STAMINA.
HE WASTES ENERGY LIKE NOBODY'S BUSINESS, YET HE STILL HAS ENOUGH LEFT TO LAST TO THE END.
TA-TMP
BAM
BAM
TMP
ANYWAYS, DO YOU THINK NEKOMA'S MADE THE TRIP UP HERE YET?
BAM
THEY SHOULD BE COMING IN ON THE BULLET TRAIN TODAY.
I HEAR THEY'LL BE STAYING AT THE KARASUNO SPORTS PARK FACILITIES AND WILL HOLD PRACTICE GAMES WITH VARIOUS SCHOOLS EVERY DAY.
TMP TMP
SORRY!!
TMP
THE LAST DAY OF THEIR STAY, OF COURSE...
...THEY'LL BE PLAYING US.
TMP
BAM
WHAT SORT OF TEAM IS NEKOMA?
TMP
TMP
CAN'T SAY FOR SURE WHAT THEY'RE LIKE NOW, BUT BACK IN THE DAY THEY HAD A REALLY SOLID DEFENSE.
EVERY SO OFTEN THEY'D HAVE A STAR PLAYER ON OFFENSE. BUT EVEN WHEN THEY DIDN'T, THEY WERE A TEAM WITH NO HOLES WHATSOEVER.
TOTALLY THE OPPOSITE OF US!
TMP
BOM
TAM TAM
TA-TMP
...THE "CATS"...
LIKE THEIR NAME IMPLIES...
BA-BAM
TMP
BAM

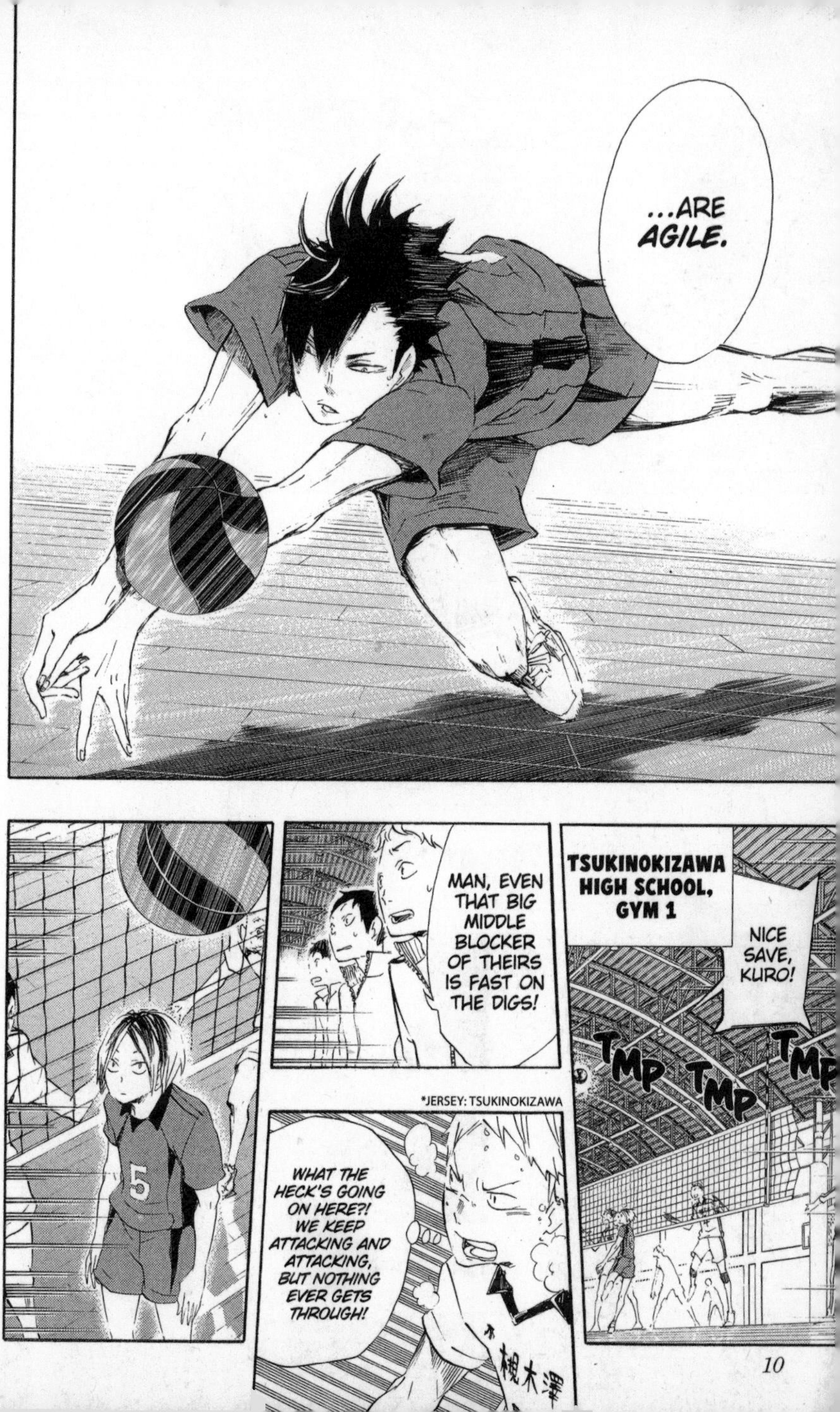
...ARE AGILE.
TSUKINOKIZAWA HIGH SCHOOL, GYM 1
NICE SAVE, KURO!
TMP TMP TMP
MAN, EVEN THAT BIG MIDDLE BLOCKER OF THEIRS IS FAST ON THE DIGS!
*JERSEY: TSUKINOKIZAWA
WHAT THE HECK'S GOING ON HERE?! WE KEEP ATTACKING AND ATTACKING, BUT NOTHING EVER GETS THROUGH!
槻木澤
5

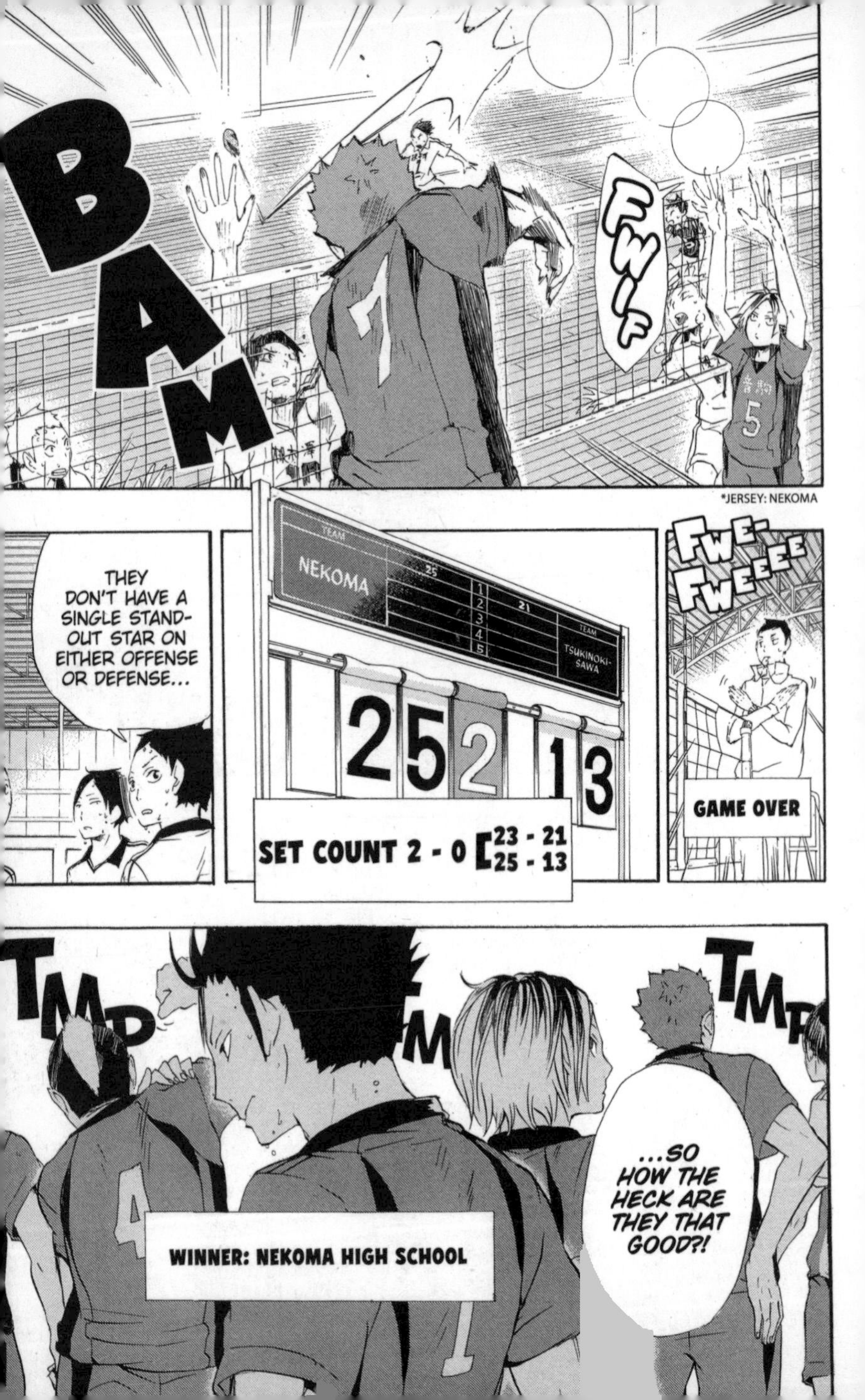
FWIF
BAM
*JERSEY: NEKOMA
FWE-FWEEEE
GAME OVER
NEKOMA
TSUKINOKI-SAWA
25 2 13
SET COUNT 2 - 0 [23 - 21 / 25 - 13
THEY DON'T HAVE A SINGLE STAND-OUT STAR ON EITHER OFFENSE OR DEFENSE...
TMP
TMP
...SO HOW THE HECK ARE THEY THAT GOOD?!
WINNER: NEKOMA HIGH SCHOOL

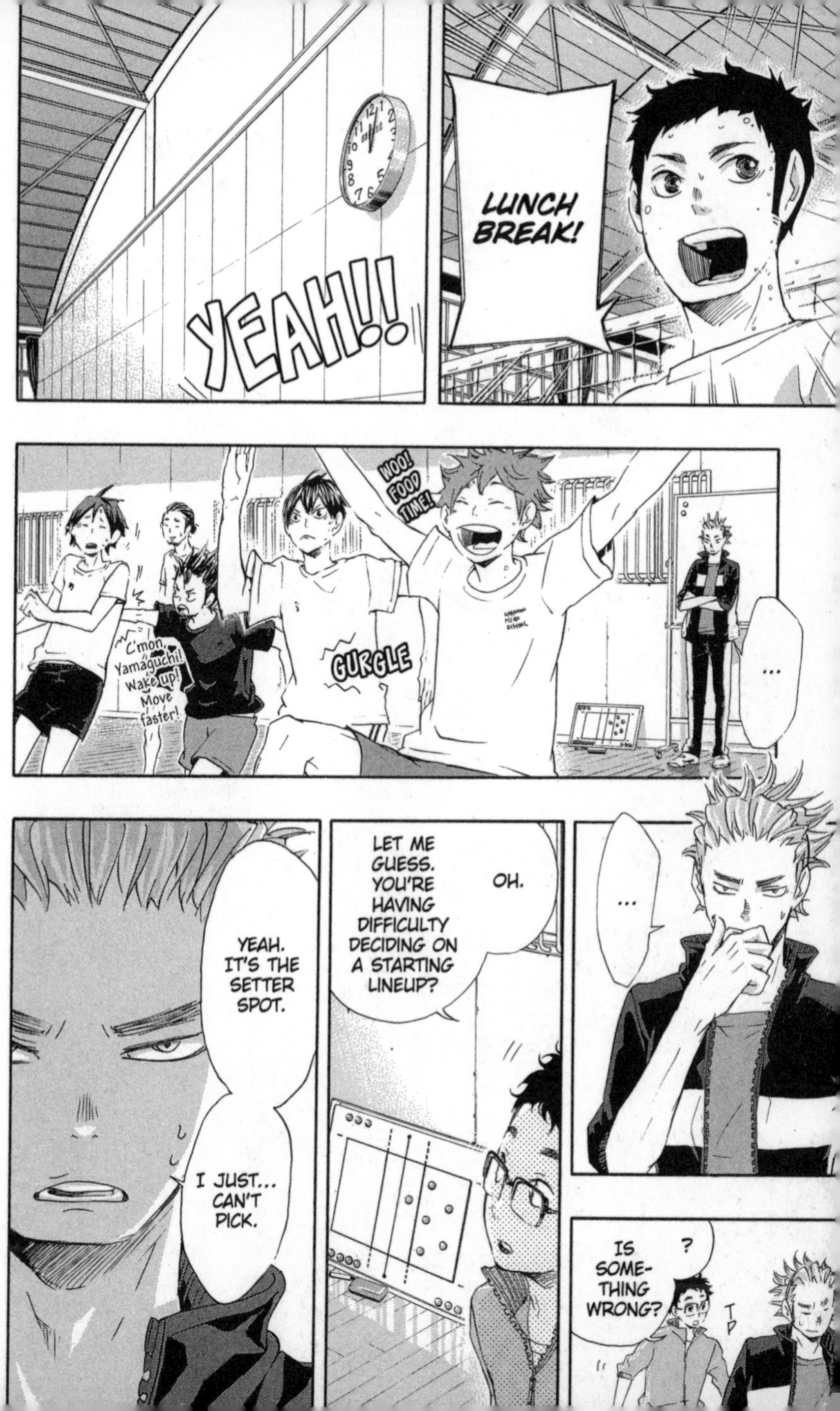
LUNCH BREAK!
YEAH!!
...
WOO! FOOD TIME!
GURGLE
C'mon, Yamaguchi! Wake up! Move faster!
...
?
IS SOME-THING WRONG?
OH.
LET ME GUESS. YOU'RE HAVING DIFFICULTY DECIDING ON A STARTING LINEUP?
YEAH. IT'S THE SETTER SPOT.
I JUST... CAN'T PICK.

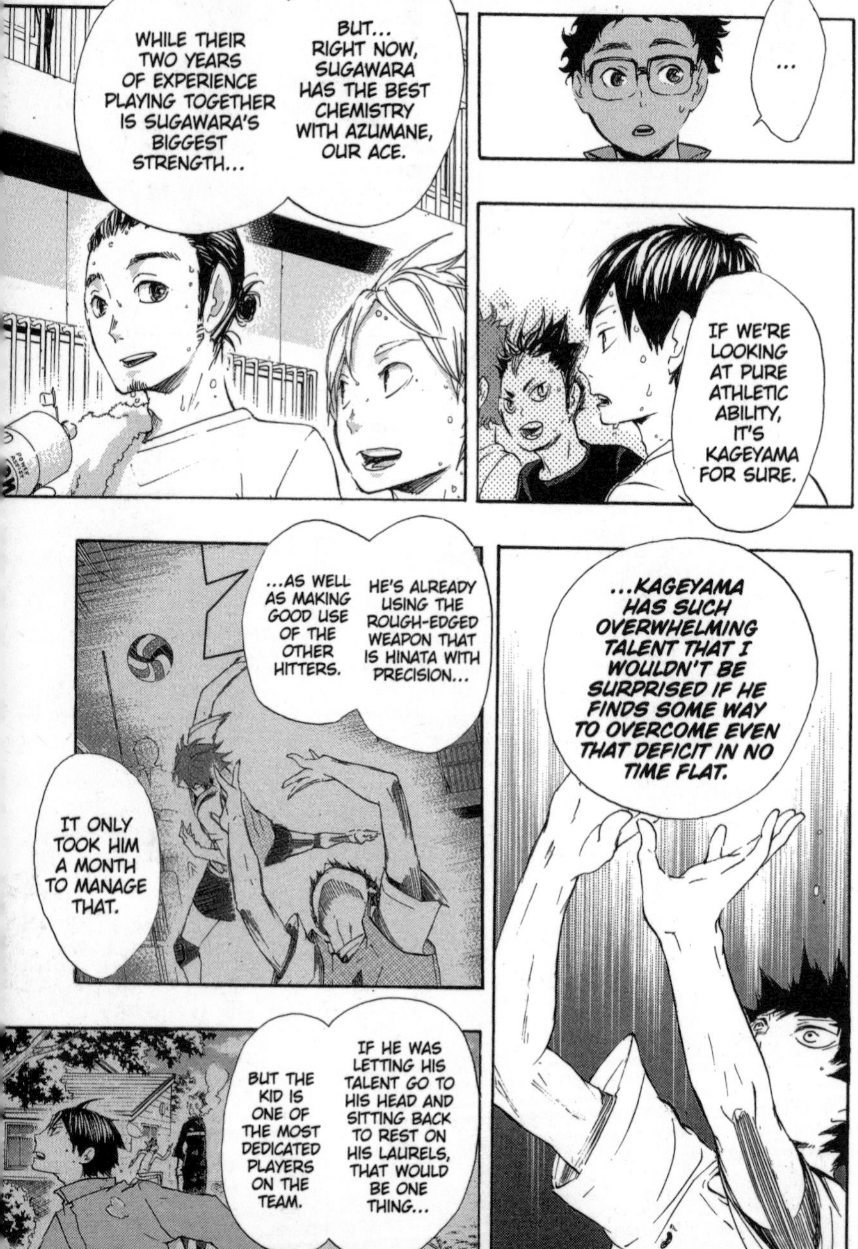

...
BUT... RIGHT NOW, SUGAWARA HAS THE BEST CHEMISTRY WITH AZUMANE, OUR ACE.
WHILE THEIR TWO YEARS OF EXPERIENCE PLAYING TOGETHER IS SUGAWARA'S BIGGEST STRENGTH...
IF WE'RE LOOKING AT PURE ATHLETIC ABILITY, IT'S KAGEYAMA FOR SURE.
...KAGEYAMA HAS SUCH OVERWHELMING TALENT THAT I WOULDN'T BE SURPRISED IF HE FINDS SOME WAY TO OVERCOME EVEN THAT DEFICIT IN NO TIME FLAT.
HE'S ALREADY USING THE ROUGH-EDGED WEAPON THAT IS HINATA WITH PRECISION...
...AS WELL AS MAKING GOOD USE OF THE OTHER HITTERS.
IT ONLY TOOK HIM A MONTH TO MANAGE THAT.
IF HE WAS LETTING HIS TALENT GO TO HIS HEAD AND SITTING BACK TO REST ON HIS LAURELS, THAT WOULD BE ONE THING...
BUT THE KID IS ONE OF THE MOST DEDICATED PLAYERS ON THE TEAM.

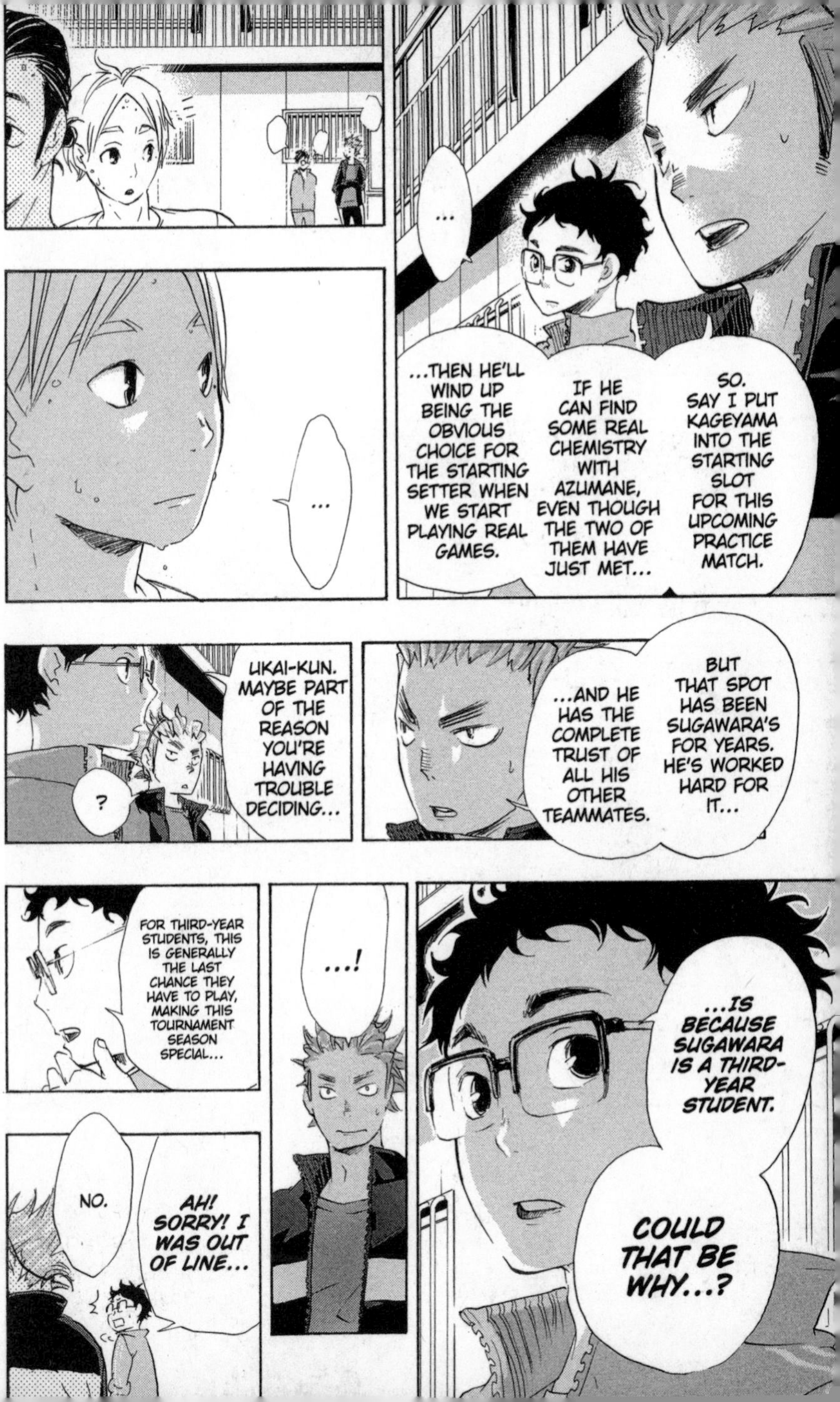
...
SO. SAY I PUT KAGEYAMA INTO THE STARTING SLOT FOR THIS UPCOMING PRACTICE MATCH.
IF HE CAN FIND SOME REAL CHEMISTRY WITH AZUMANE, EVEN THOUGH THE TWO OF THEM HAVE JUST MET...
...THEN HE'LL WIND UP BEING THE OBVIOUS CHOICE FOR THE STARTING SETTER WHEN WE START PLAYING REAL GAMES.
...
BUT THAT SPOT HAS BEEN SUGAWARA'S FOR YEARS. HE'S WORKED HARD FOR IT...
...AND HE HAS THE COMPLETE TRUST OF ALL HIS OTHER TEAMMATES.
UKAI-KUN. MAYBE PART OF THE REASON YOU'RE HAVING TROUBLE DECIDING...
?
...IS BECAUSE SUGAWARA IS A THIRD-YEAR STUDENT.
COULD THAT BE WHY...?
...!
FOR THIRD-YEAR STUDENTS, THIS IS GENERALLY THE LAST CHANCE THEY HAVE TO PLAY, MAKING THIS TOURNAMENT SEASON SPECIAL...
AH! SORRY! I WAS OUT OF LINE...
NO.

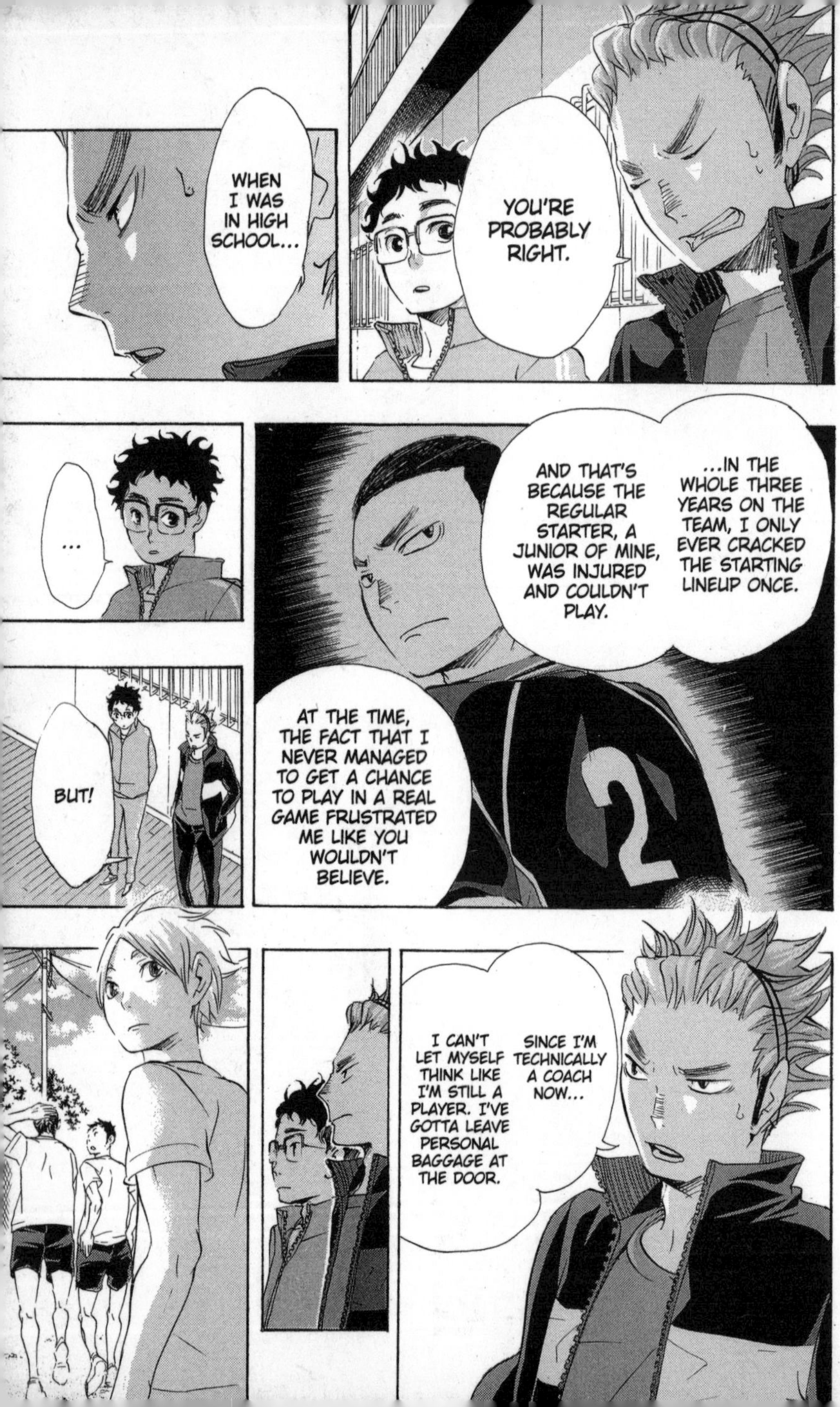
YOU'RE PROBABLY RIGHT.
WHEN I WAS IN HIGH SCHOOL...
...IN THE WHOLE THREE YEARS ON THE TEAM, I ONLY EVER CRACKED THE STARTING LINEUP ONCE.
AND THAT'S BECAUSE THE REGULAR STARTER, A JUNIOR OF MINE, WAS INJURED AND COULDN'T PLAY.
AT THE TIME, THE FACT THAT I NEVER MANAGED TO GET A CHANCE TO PLAY IN A REAL GAME FRUSTRATED ME LIKE YOU WOULDN'T BELIEVE.
...
BUT!
SINCE I'M TECHNICALLY A COACH NOW...
I CAN'T LET MYSELF THINK LIKE I'M STILL A PLAYER. I'VE GOTTA LEAVE PERSONAL BAGGAGE AT THE DOOR.

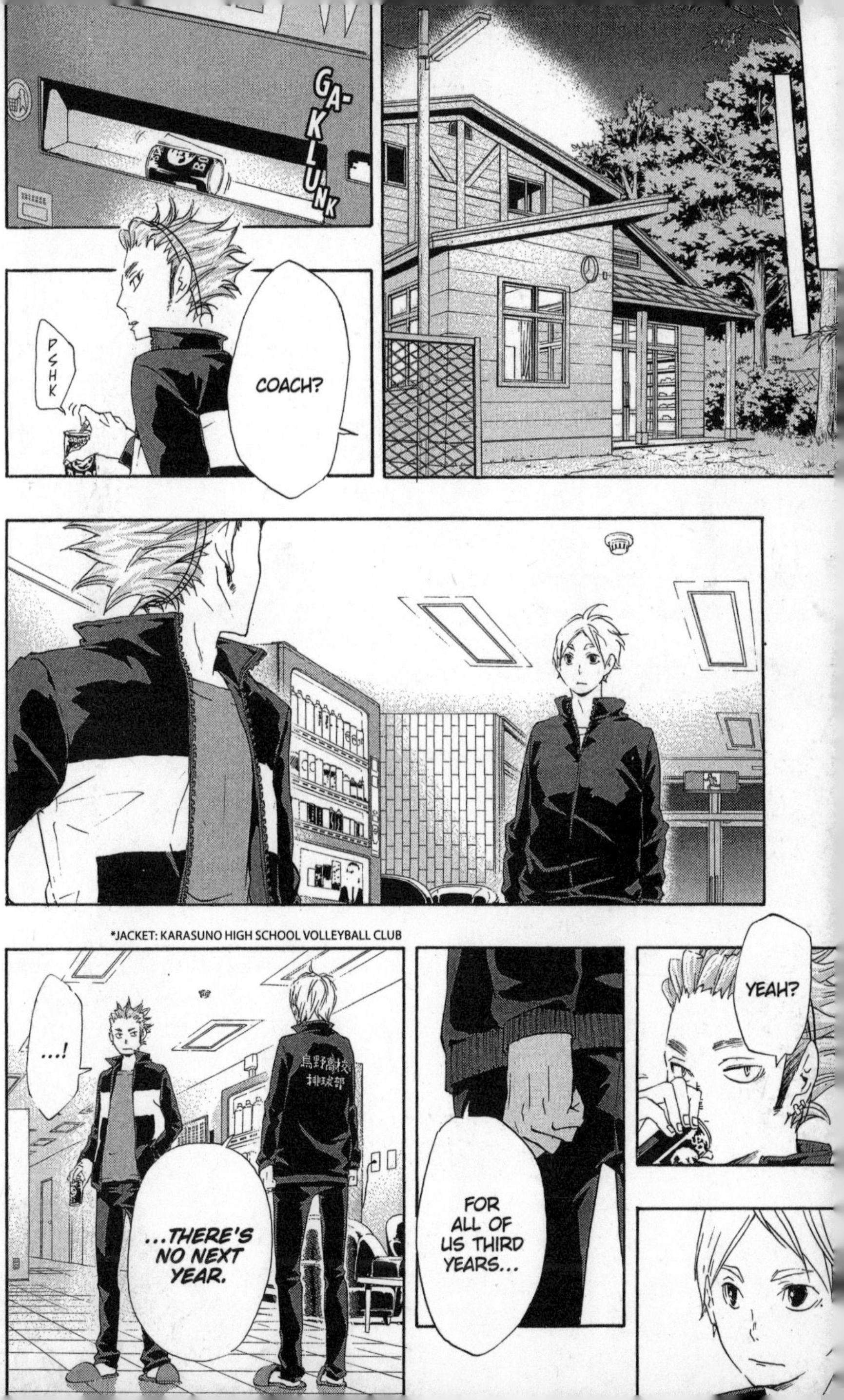
GA-KLUNK
COACH?
PSHK
YEAH?
FOR ALL OF US THIRD YEARS...
...THERE'S NO NEXT YEAR.
...!
烏野高校
排球部
*JACKET: KARASUNO HIGH SCHOOL VOLLEYBALL CLUB

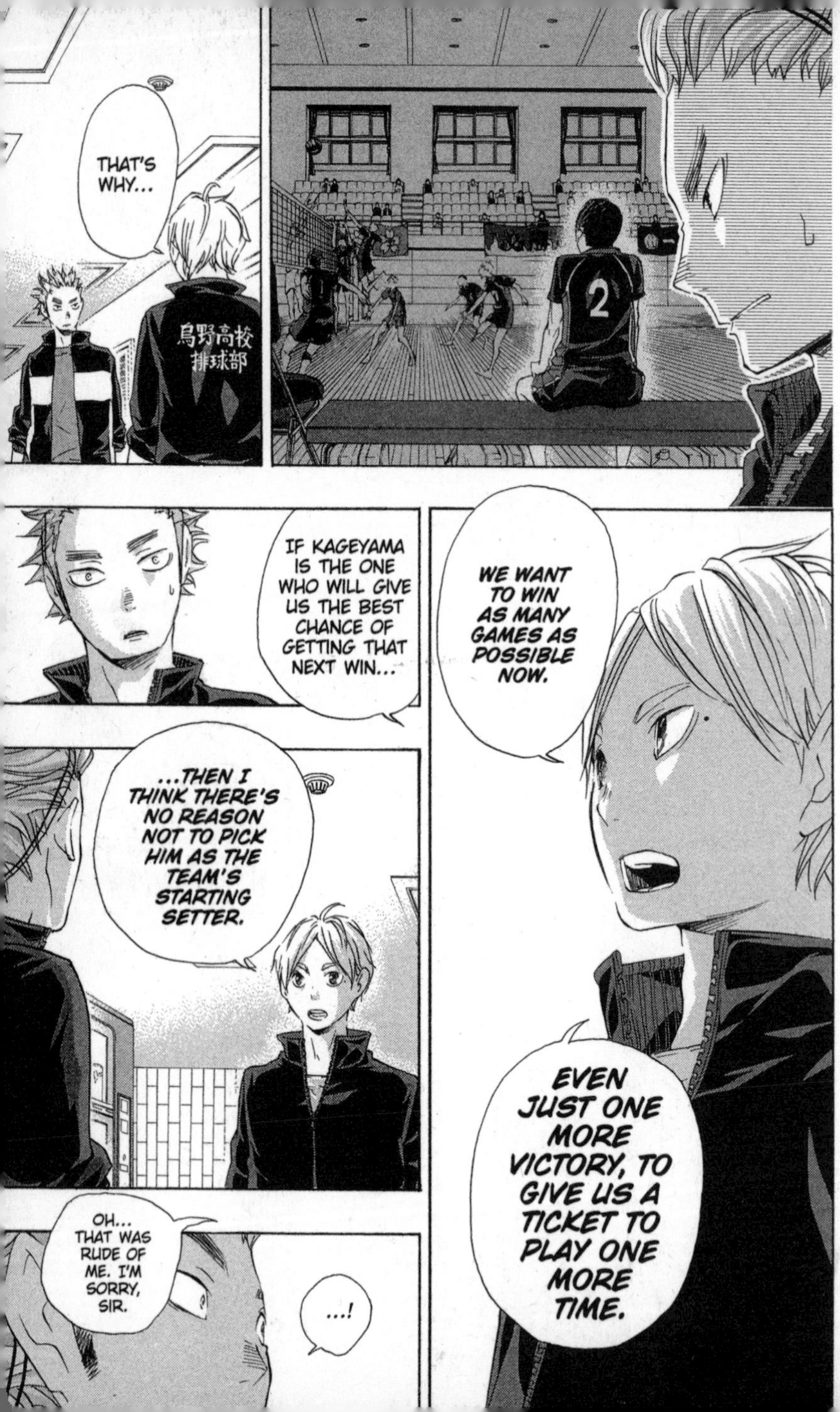
THAT'S WHY...
烏野高校
排球部
WE WANT TO WIN AS MANY GAMES AS POSSIBLE NOW.
EVEN JUST ONE MORE VICTORY, TO GIVE US A TICKET TO PLAY ONE MORE TIME.
IF KAGEYAMA IS THE ONE WHO WILL GIVE US THE BEST CHANCE OF GETTING THAT NEXT WIN...
...THEN I THINK THERE'S NO REASON NOT TO PICK HIM AS THE TEAM'S STARTING SETTER.
...!
OH... THAT WAS RUDE OF ME. I'M SORRY, SIR.

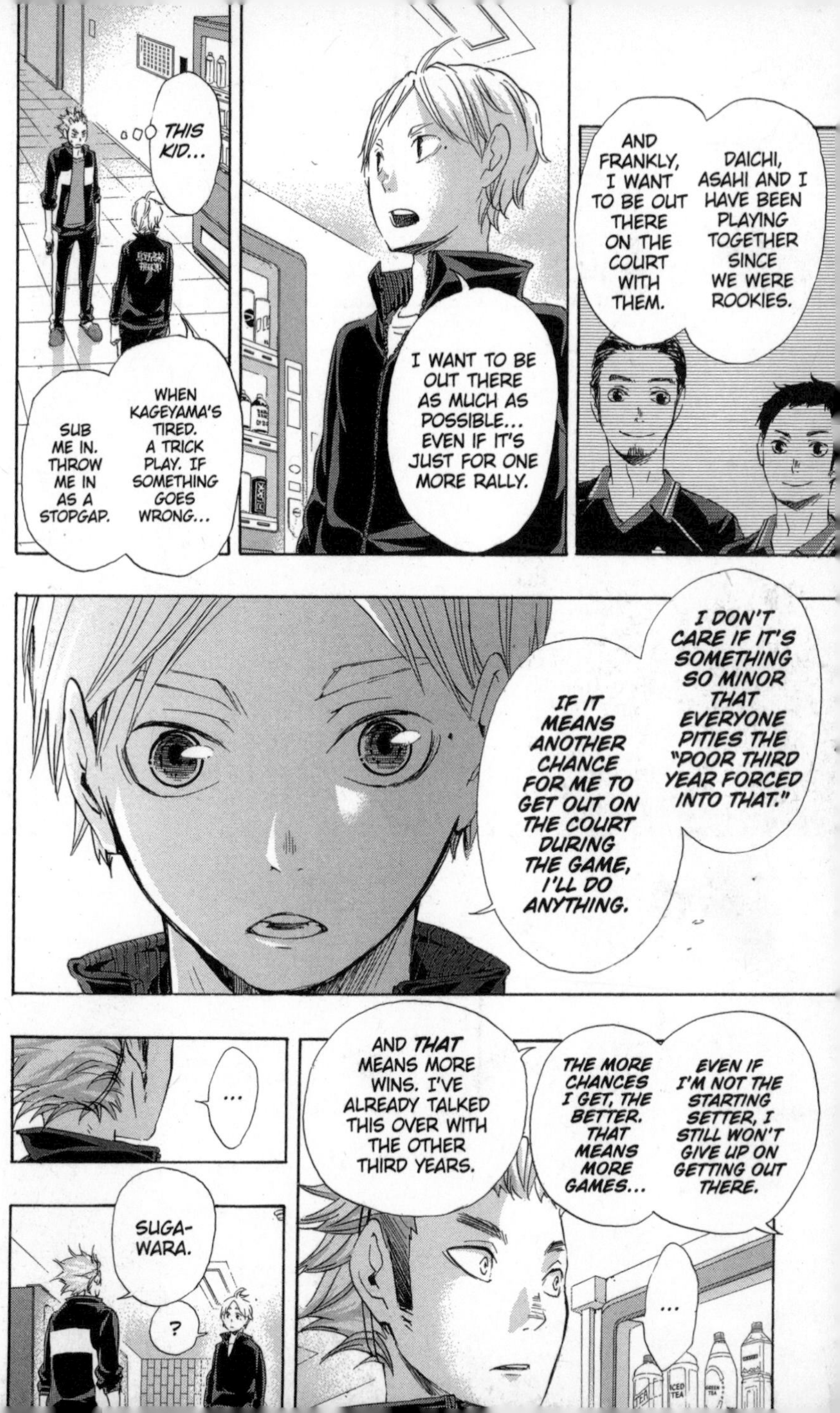
DAICHI, ASAHI AND I HAVE BEEN PLAYING TOGETHER SINCE WE WERE ROOKIES.
AND FRANKLY, I WANT TO BE OUT THERE ON THE COURT WITH THEM.
I WANT TO BE OUT THERE AS MUCH AS POSSIBLE... EVEN IF IT'S JUST FOR ONE MORE RALLY.
THIS KID...
WHEN KAGEYAMA'S TIRED. A TRICK PLAY. IF SOMETHING GOES WRONG...
SUB ME IN. THROW ME IN AS A STOPGAP.
I DON'T CARE IF IT'S SOMETHING SO MINOR THAT EVERYONE PITIES THE "POOR THIRD YEAR FORCED INTO THAT."
IF IT MEANS ANOTHER CHANCE FOR ME TO GET OUT ON THE COURT DURING THE GAME, I'LL DO ANYTHING.
EVEN IF I'M NOT THE STARTING SETTER, I STILL WON'T GIVE UP ON GETTING OUT THERE.
THE MORE CHANCES I GET, THE BETTER. THAT MEANS MORE GAMES...
AND THAT MEANS MORE WINS. I'VE ALREADY TALKED THIS OVER WITH THE OTHER THIRD YEARS.
...
...
SUGA-WARA.
?

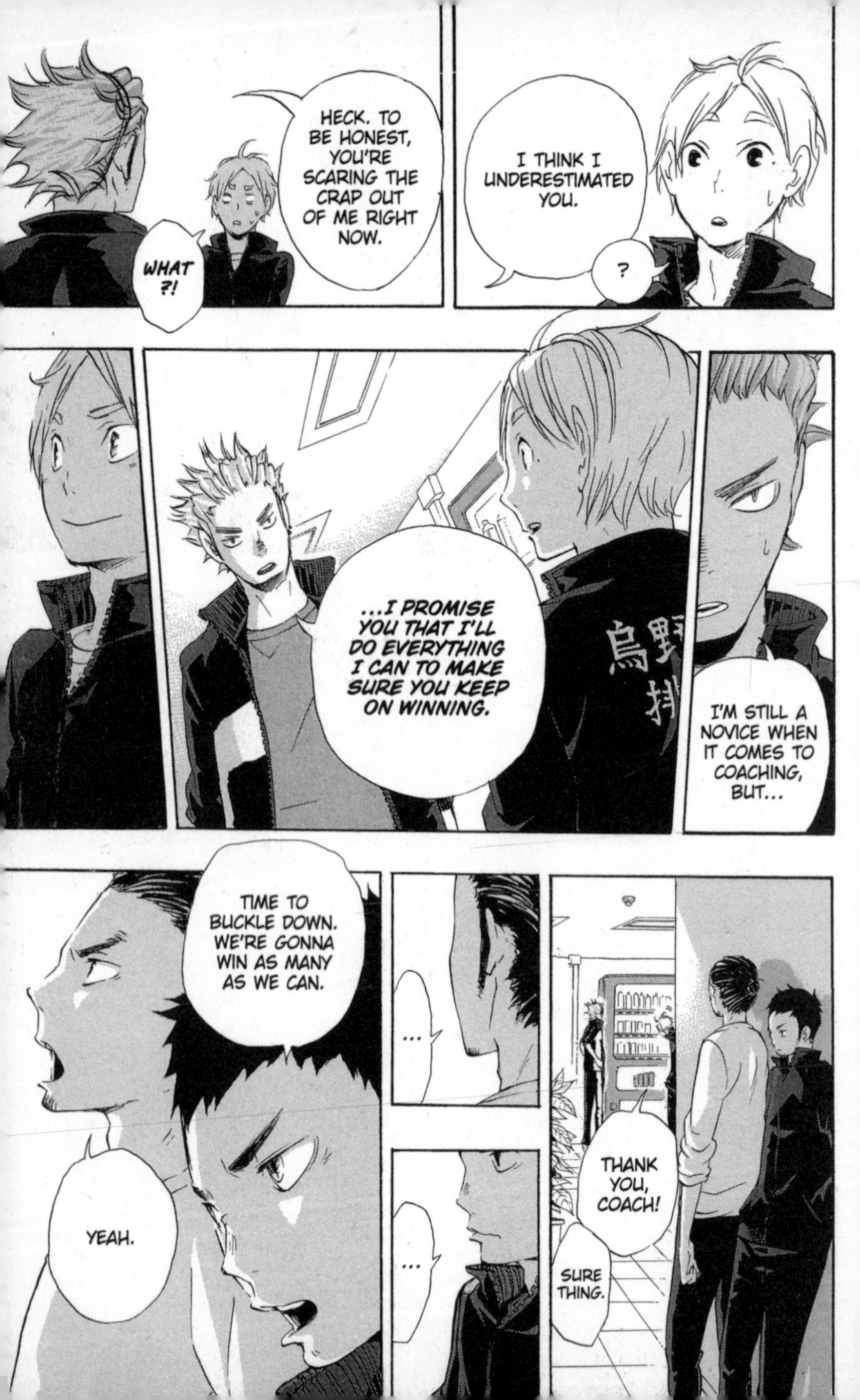
I THINK I UNDERESTIMATED YOU.
?
HECK. TO BE HONEST, YOU'RE SCARING THE CRAP OUT OF ME RIGHT NOW.
WHAT?!
I'M STILL A NOVICE WHEN IT COMES TO COACHING, BUT...
...I PROMISE YOU THAT I'LL DO EVERYTHING I CAN TO MAKE SURE YOU KEEP ON WINNING.
THANK YOU, COACH!
SURE THING.
...
...
TIME TO BUCKLE DOWN. WE'RE GONNA WIN AS MANY AS WE CAN.
YEAH.

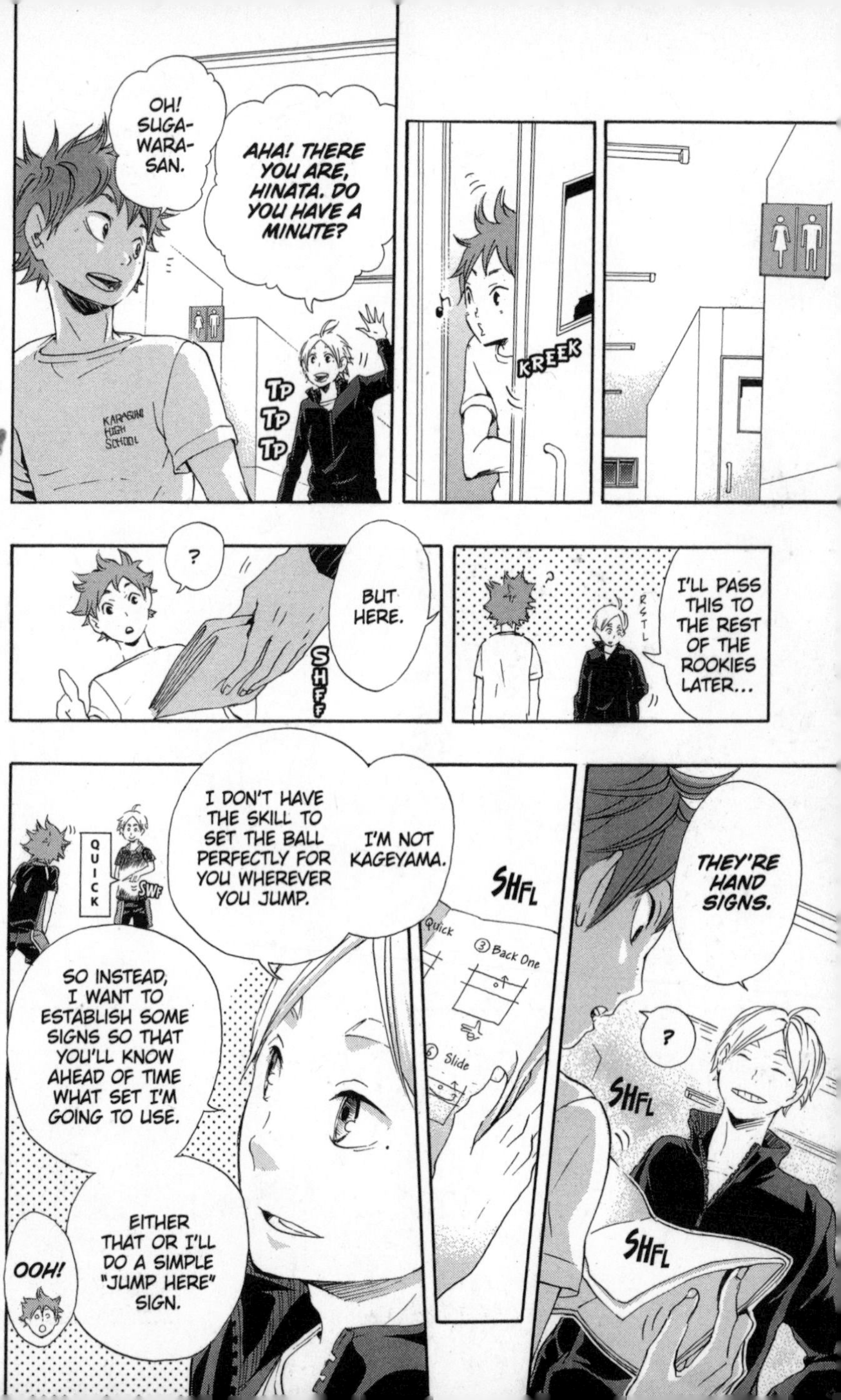
KREEK
AHA! THERE YOU ARE, HINATA. DO YOU HAVE A MINUTE?
OH! SUGA-WARA-SAN.
TP TP TP
KARASUNO HIGH SCHOOL
RSTL
I'LL PASS THIS TO THE REST OF THE ROOKIES LATER...
BUT HERE.
SHFF
?
THEY'RE HAND SIGNS.
?
SHFL
SHFL
I'M NOT KAGEYAMA.
I DON'T HAVE THE SKILL TO SET THE BALL PERFECTLY FOR YOU WHEREVER YOU JUMP.
SHFL
Quick
③ Back One
⑥ Slide
QUICK
SWF
SO INSTEAD, I WANT TO ESTABLISH SOME SIGNS SO THAT YOU'LL KNOW AHEAD OF TIME WHAT SET I'M GOING TO USE.
EITHER THAT OR I'LL DO A SIMPLE "JUMP HERE" SIGN.
OOH!

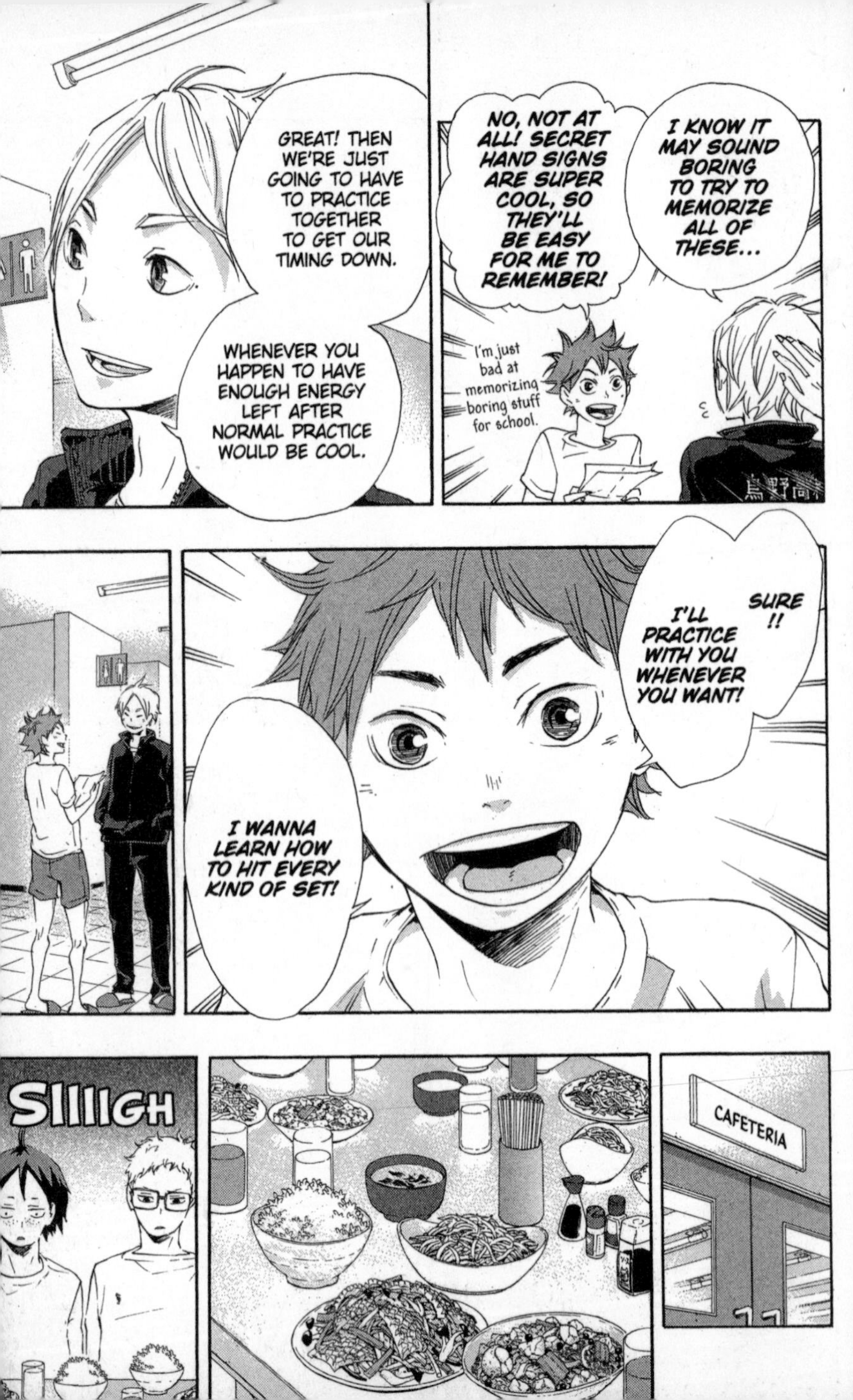
I KNOW IT MAY SOUND BORING TO TRY TO MEMORIZE ALL OF THESE...
NO, NOT AT ALL! SECRET HAND SIGNS ARE SUPER COOL, SO THEY'LL BE EASY FOR ME TO REMEMBER!
I'm just bad at memorizing boring stuff for school.
GREAT! THEN WE'RE JUST GOING TO HAVE TO PRACTICE TOGETHER TO GET OUR TIMING DOWN.
WHENEVER YOU HAPPEN TO HAVE ENOUGH ENERGY LEFT AFTER NORMAL PRACTICE WOULD BE COOL.
SURE!!
I'LL PRACTICE WITH YOU WHENEVER YOU WANT!
I WANNA LEARN HOW TO HIT EVERY KIND OF SET!
CAFETERIA
SIIIGH

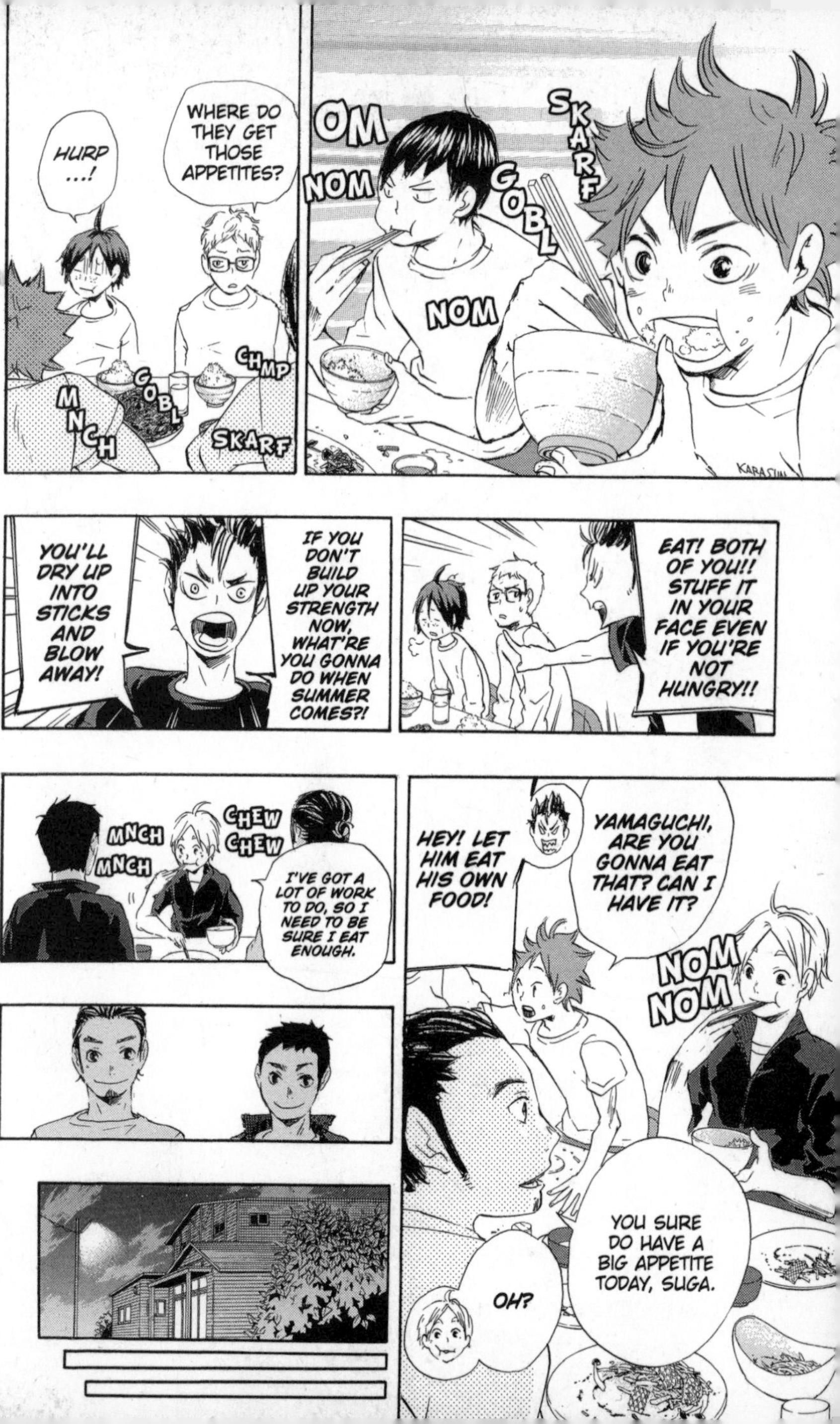
OM
NOM
NOM
GOBL
SKARF
WHERE DO THEY GET THOSE APPETITES?
HURP ...!
CHMP
GOBL
MNCH
SKARF
EAT! BOTH OF YOU!! STUFF IT IN YOUR FACE EVEN IF YOU'RE NOT HUNGRY!!
IF YOU DON'T BUILD UP YOUR STRENGTH NOW, WHAT'RE YOU GONNA DO WHEN SUMMER COMES?!
YOU'LL DRY UP INTO STICKS AND BLOW AWAY!
YAMAGUCHI, ARE YOU GONNA EAT THAT? CAN I HAVE IT?
HEY! LET HIM EAT HIS OWN FOOD!
NOM NOM
YOU SURE DO HAVE A BIG APPETITE TODAY, SUGA.
OH?
CHEW CHEW
MNCH MNCH
I'VE GOT A LOT OF WORK TO DO, SO I NEED TO BE SURE I EAT ENOUGH.

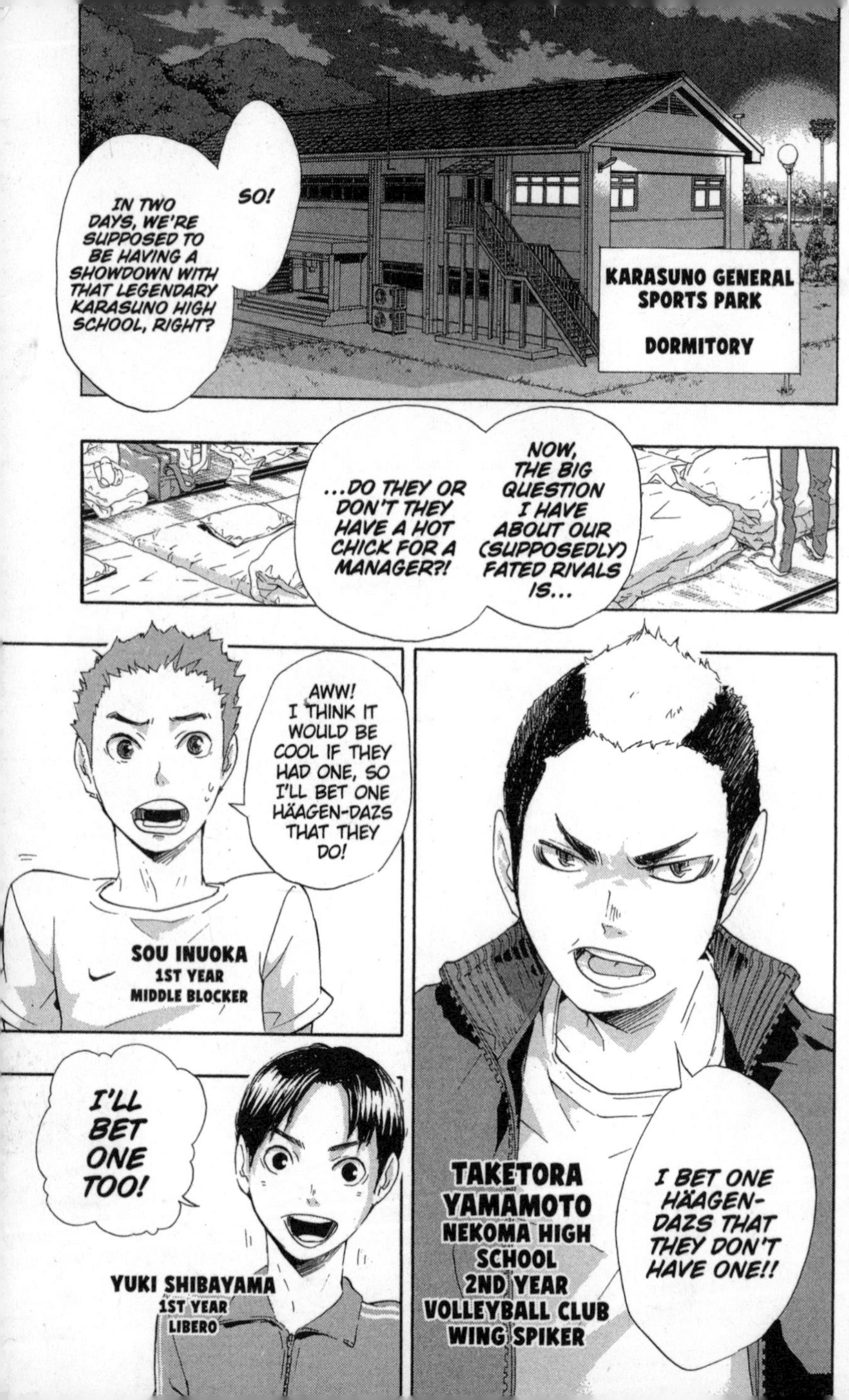
SO!
IN TWO DAYS, WE'RE SUPPOSED TO BE HAVING A SHOWDOWN WITH THAT LEGENDARY KARASUNO HIGH SCHOOL, RIGHT?
KARASUNO GENERAL SPORTS PARK
DORMITORY
NOW, THE BIG QUESTION I HAVE ABOUT OUR (SUPPOSEDLY) FATED RIVALS IS...
...DO THEY OR DON'T THEY HAVE A HOT CHICK FOR A MANAGER?!
I BET ONE HÄAGEN-DAZS THAT THEY DON'T HAVE ONE!!
TAKETORA YAMAMOTO NEKOMA HIGH SCHOOL 2ND YEAR VOLLEYBALL CLUB WING SPIKER
AWW! I THINK IT WOULD BE COOL IF THEY HAD ONE, SO I'LL BET ONE HÄAGEN-DAZS THAT THEY DO!
SOU INUOKA 1ST YEAR MIDDLE BLOCKER
I'LL BET ONE TOO!
YUKI SHIBAYAMA 1ST YEAR LIBERO

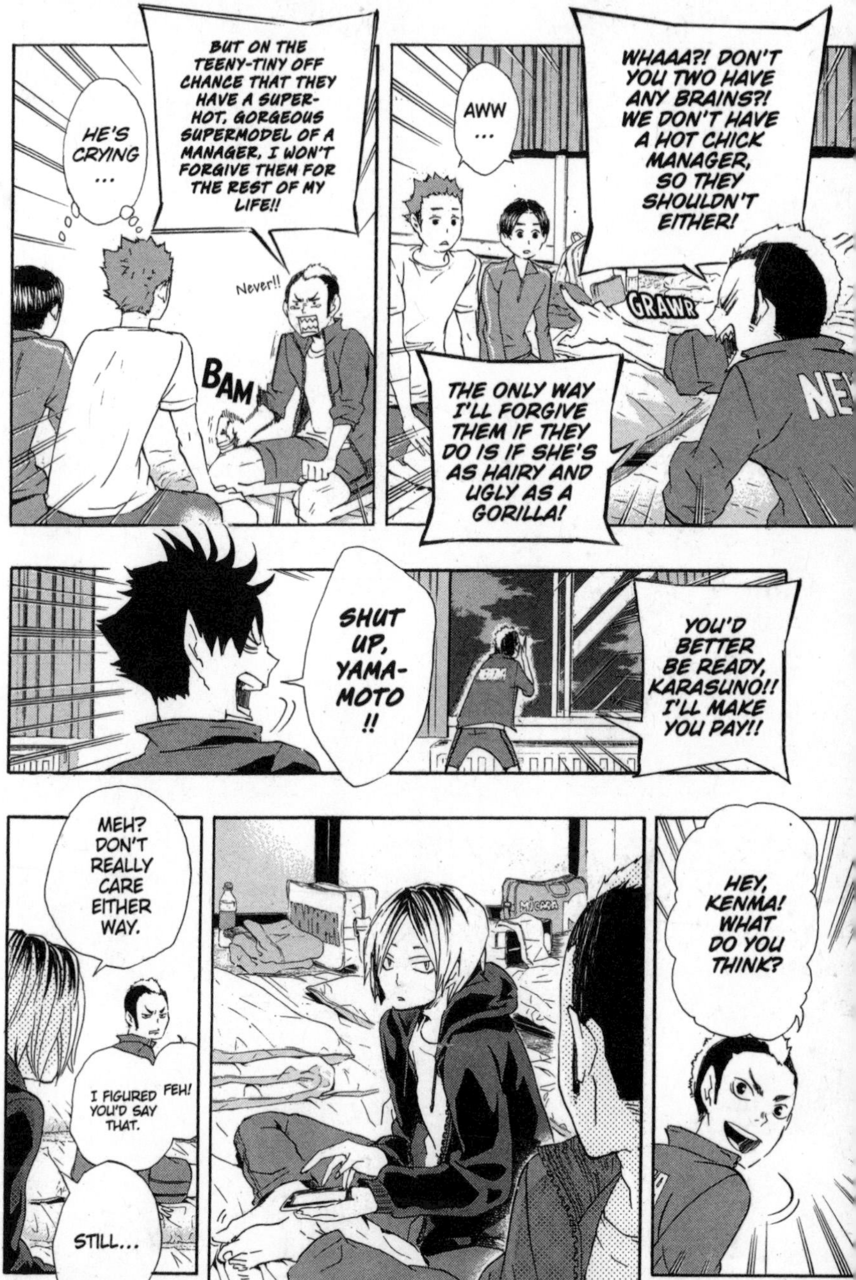
WHAAA?! DON'T YOU TWO HAVE ANY BRAINS?! WE DON'T HAVE A HOT CHICK MANAGER, SO THEY SHOULDN'T EITHER!
AWW ...
GRAWR
THE ONLY WAY I'LL FORGIVE THEM IF THEY DO IS IF SHE'S AS HAIRY AND UGLY AS A GORILLA!
BUT ON THE TEENY-TINY OFF CHANCE THAT THEY HAVE A SUPER-HOT, GORGEOUS SUPERMODEL OF A MANAGER, I WON'T FORGIVE THEM FOR THE REST OF MY LIFE!!
HE'S CRYING ...
Never!!
BAM
YOU'D BETTER BE READY, KARASUNO!! I'LL MAKE YOU PAY!!
SHUT UP, YAMA-MOTO !!
HEY, KENMA! WHAT DO YOU THINK?
MEH? DON'T REALLY CARE EITHER WAY.
FEH!
I FIGURED YOU'D SAY THAT.
STILL...

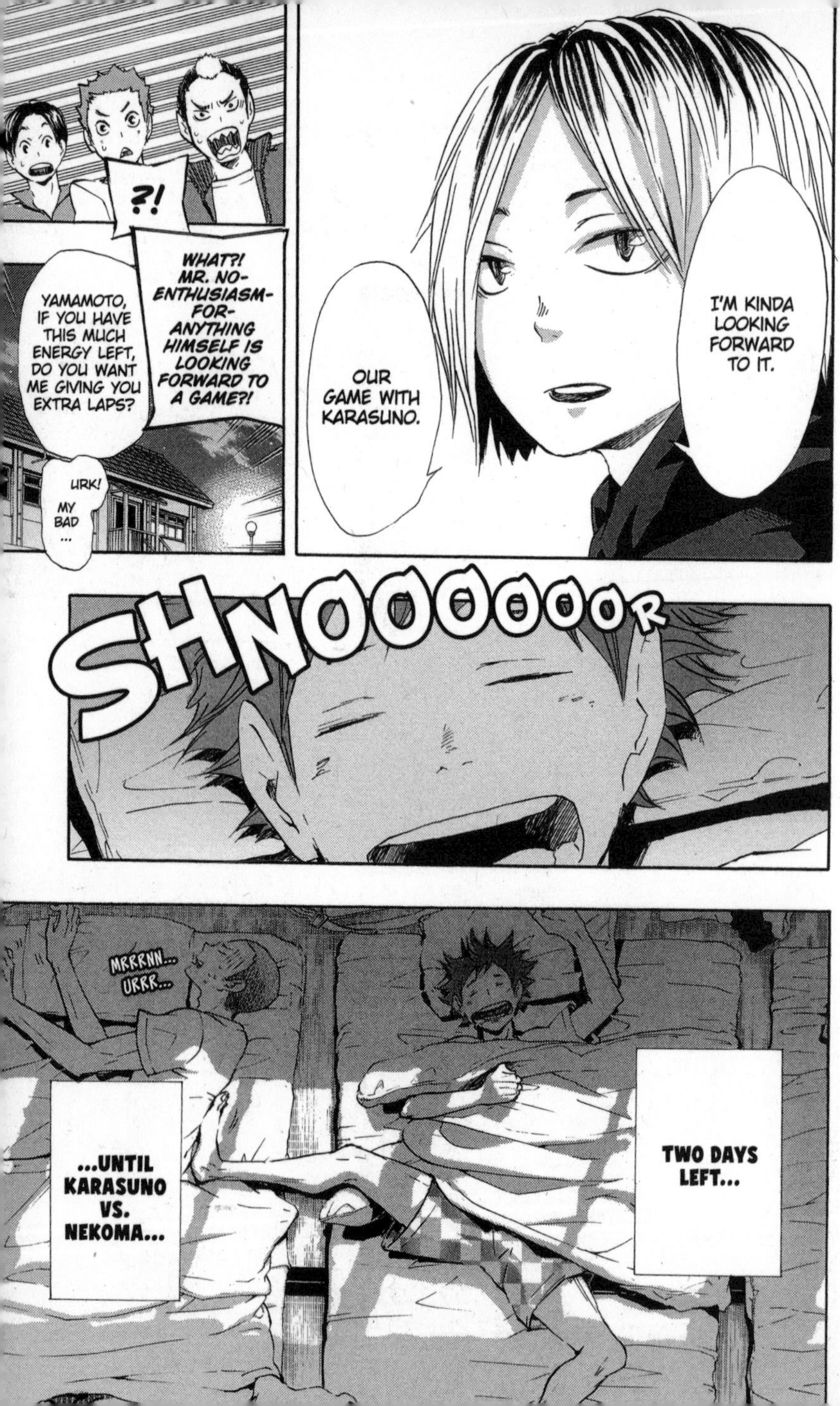
I'M KINDA LOOKING FORWARD TO IT.
OUR GAME WITH KARASUNO.
?!
WHAT?! MR. NO-ENTHUSIASM-FOR-ANYTHING HIMSELF IS LOOKING FORWARD TO A GAME?!
YAMAMOTO, IF YOU HAVE THIS MUCH ENERGY LEFT, DO YOU WANT ME GIVING YOU EXTRA LAPS?
URK! MY BAD ...
SHNOOOOOOR
MRRRNN... URRR...
TWO DAYS LEFT...
...UNTIL KARASUNO VS. NEKOMA...

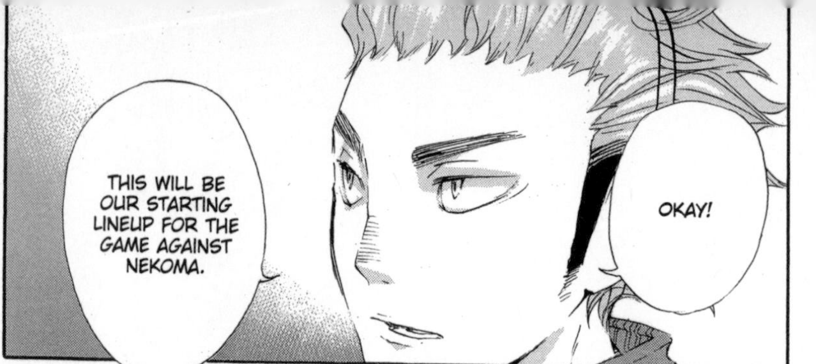
THIS WILL BE OUR STARTING LINEUP FOR THE GAME AGAINST NEKOMA.
OKAY!

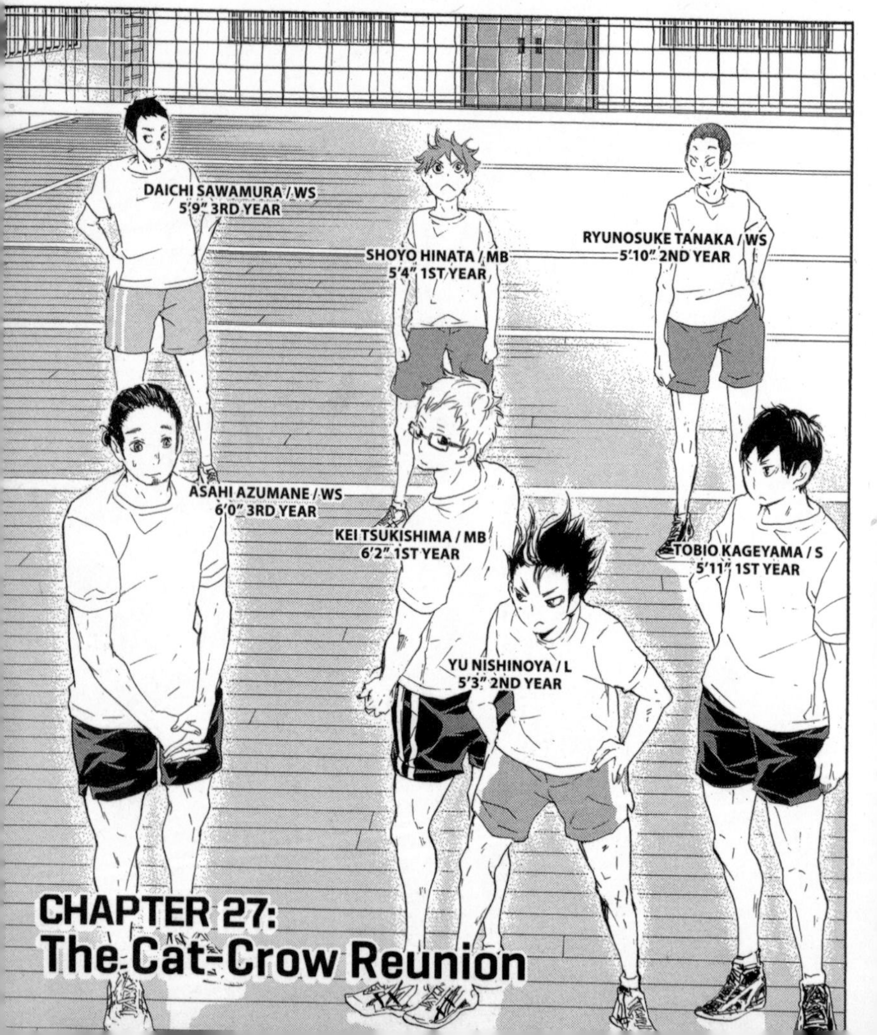
RYUNOSUKE TANAKA / WS 5'10" 2ND YEAR
SHOYO HINATA / MB 5'4" 1ST YEAR
DAICHI SAWAMURA / WS 5'9" 3RD YEAR
TOBIO KAGEYAMA / S 5'11" 1ST YEAR
KEI TSUKISHIMA / MB 6'2" 1ST YEAR
ASAHI AZUMANE / WS 6'0" 3RD YEAR
YU NISHINOYA / L 5'3" 2ND YEAR

CHAPTER 27: The Cat-Crow Reunion

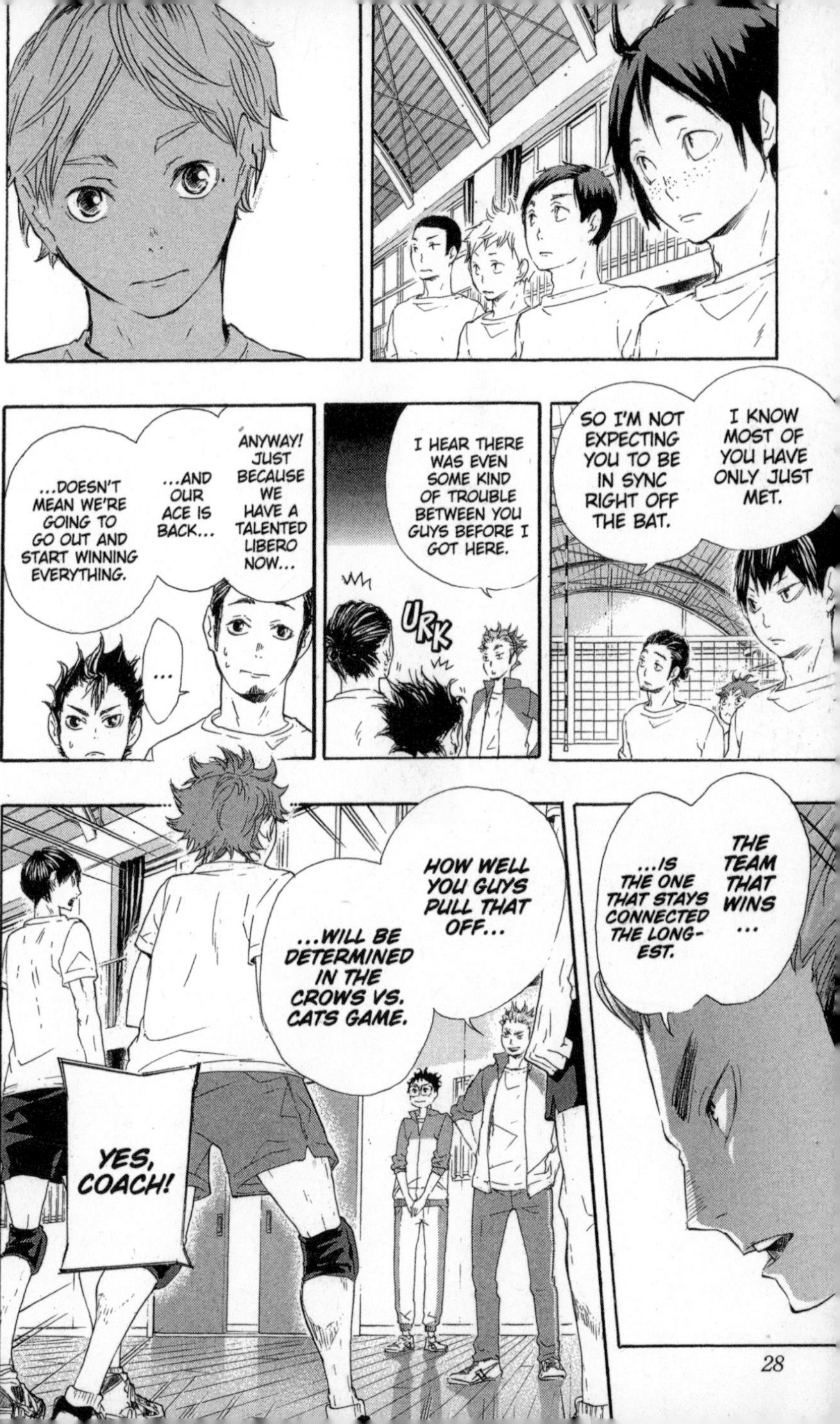
I KNOW MOST OF YOU HAVE ONLY JUST MET.
SO I'M NOT EXPECTING YOU TO BE IN SYNC RIGHT OFF THE BAT.
I HEAR THERE WAS EVEN SOME KIND OF TROUBLE BETWEEN YOU GUYS BEFORE I GOT HERE.
URK
ANYWAY! JUST BECAUSE WE HAVE A TALENTED LIBERO NOW...
...AND OUR ACE IS BACK...
...DOESN'T MEAN WE'RE GOING TO GO OUT AND START WINNING EVERYTHING.
...
THE TEAM THAT WINS...
...IS THE ONE THAT STAYS CONNECTED THE LONG-EST.
HOW WELL YOU GUYS PULL THAT OFF...
...WILL BE DETERMINED IN THE CROWS VS. CATS GAME.
YES, COACH!

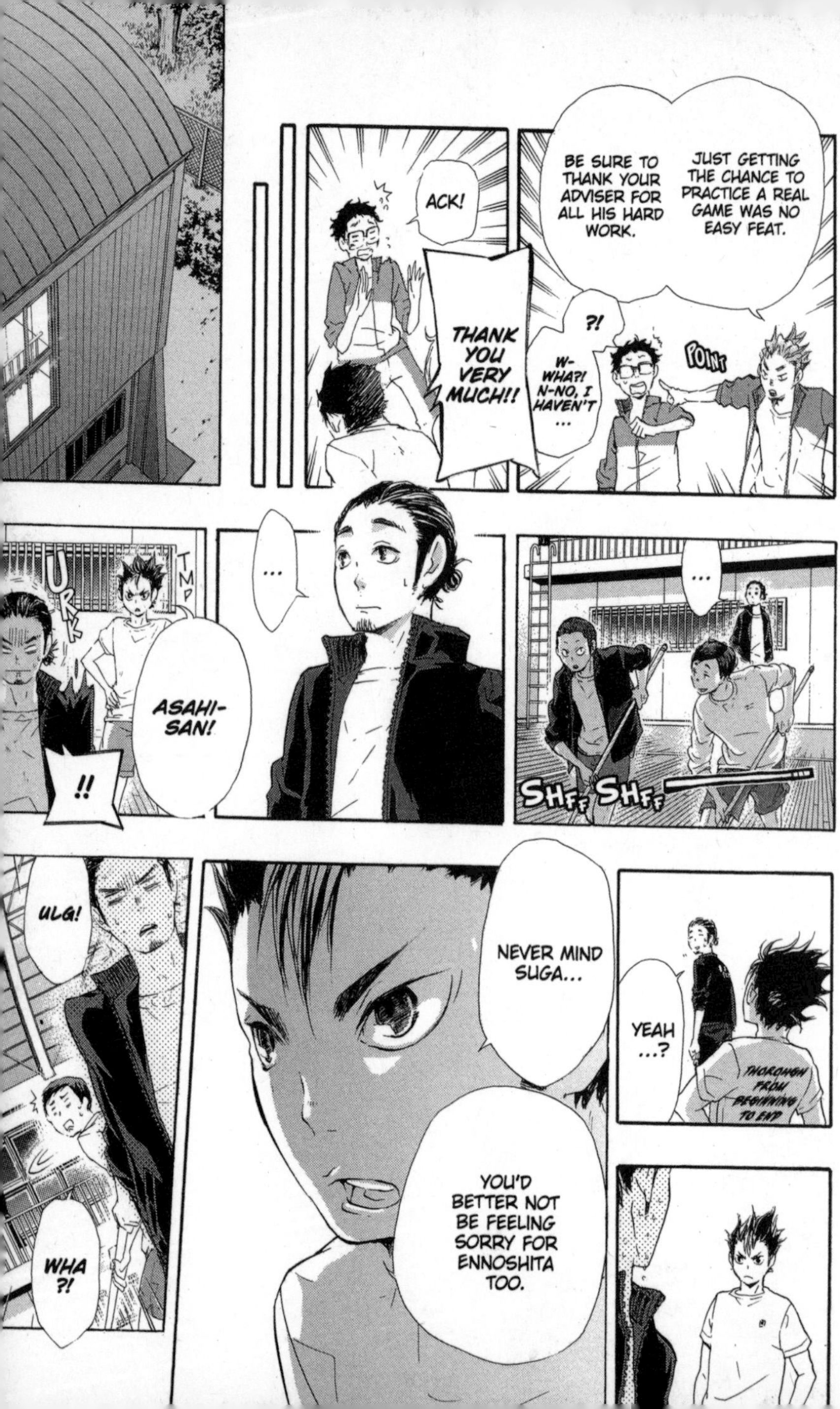
JUST GETTING THE CHANCE TO PRACTICE A REAL GAME WAS NO EASY FEAT.
BE SURE TO THANK YOUR ADVISER FOR ALL HIS HARD WORK.
POINT
?!
W-WHA?! N-NO, I HAVEN'T ...
THANK YOU VERY MUCH!!
ACK!
...
SHFF SHFF
...
TMP
ASAHI-SAN!
URK
!!
YEAH ...?
THOROUGH FROM BEGINNING TO END
NEVER MIND SUGA...
YOU'D BETTER NOT BE FEELING SORRY FOR ENNOSHITA TOO.
ULG!
WHA?!

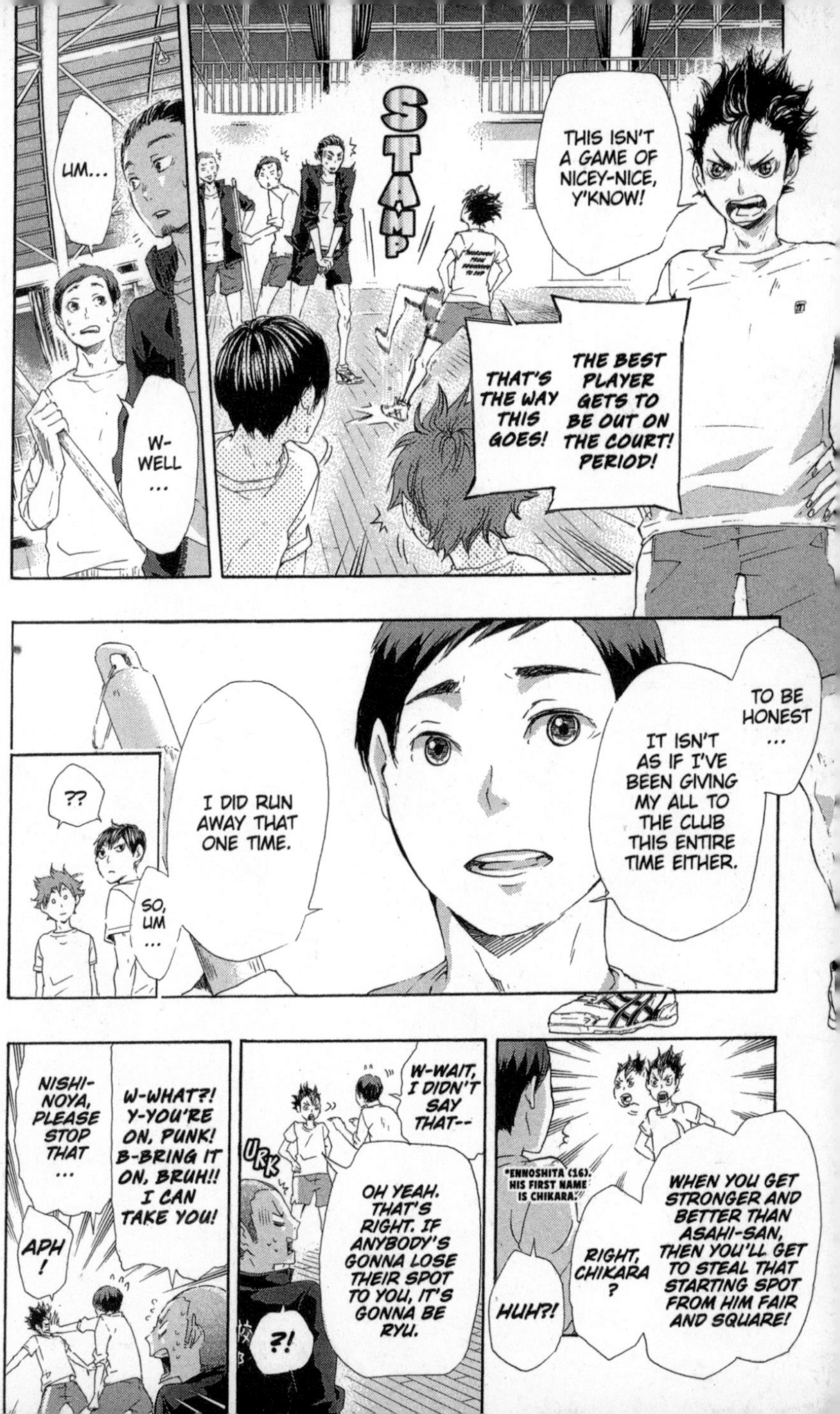
THIS ISN'T A GAME OF NICEY-NICE, Y'KNOW!
STAMP
THE BEST PLAYER GETS TO BE OUT ON THE COURT! PERIOD!
THAT'S THE WAY THIS GOES!
UM...
W-WELL ...
TO BE HONEST ...
IT ISN'T AS IF I'VE BEEN GIVING MY ALL TO THE CLUB THIS ENTIRE TIME EITHER.
I DID RUN AWAY THAT ONE TIME.
??
SO, UM ...
WHEN YOU GET STRONGER AND BETTER THAN ASAHI-SAN, THEN YOU'LL GET TO STEAL THAT STARTING SPOT FROM HIM FAIR AND SQUARE!
RIGHT, CHIKARA?
*ENNOSHITA (16). HIS FIRST NAME IS CHIKARA.
HUH?!
W-WAIT, I DIDN'T SAY THAT--
OH YEAH. THAT'S RIGHT. IF ANYBODY'S GONNA LOSE THEIR SPOT TO YOU, IT'S GONNA BE RYU.
URK
?!
W-WHAT?! Y-YOU'RE ON, PUNK! B-BRING IT ON, BRUH!! I CAN TAKE YOU!
NISHI-NOYA, PLEASE STOP THAT ...
APH !

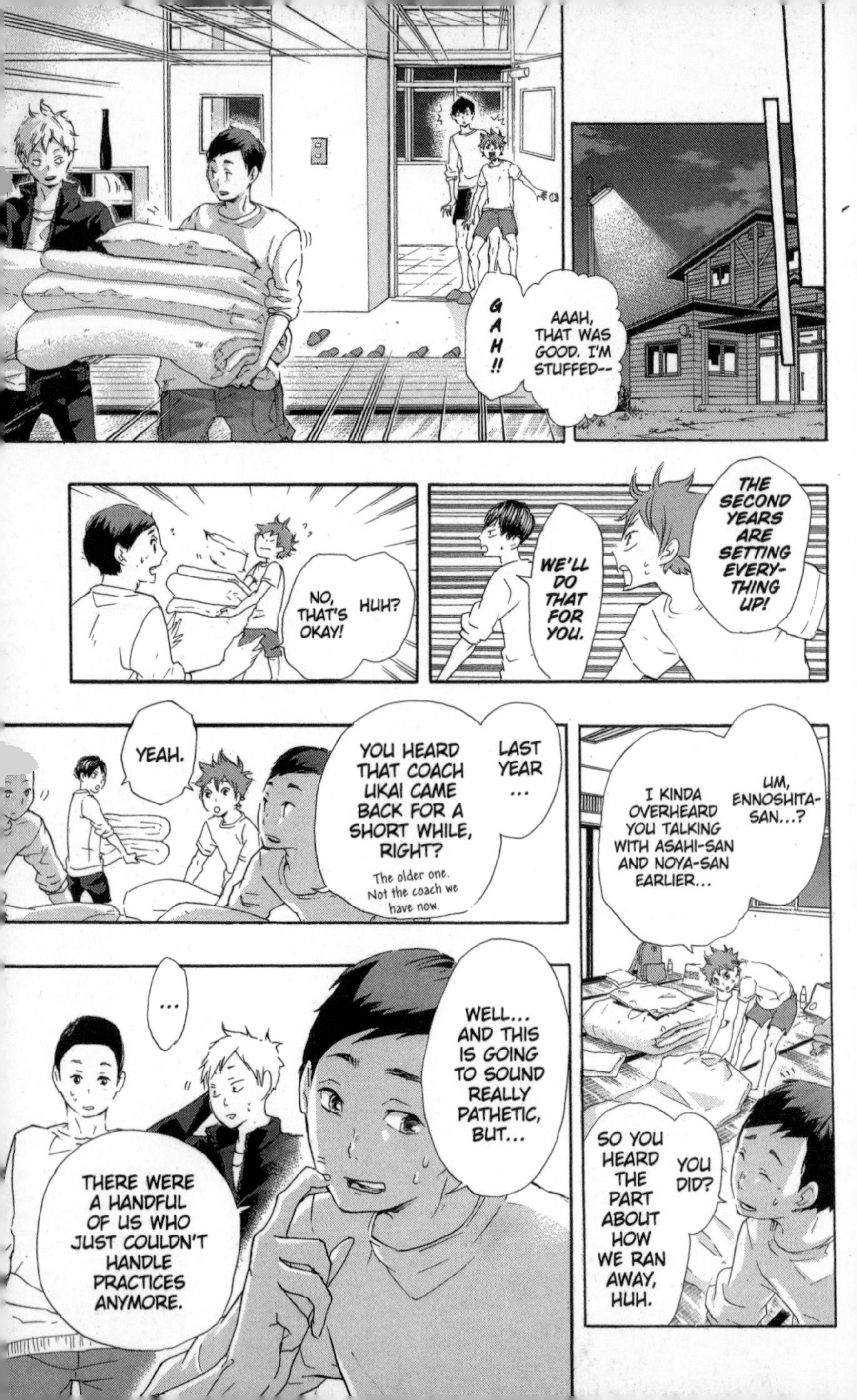
AAAH, THAT WAS GOOD. I'M STUFFED--
GAH!!
THE SECOND YEARS ARE SETTING EVERYTHING UP!
WE'LL DO THAT FOR YOU.
HUH?
NO, THAT'S OKAY!
UM, ENNOSHITA-SAN...?
I KINDA OVERHEARD YOU TALKING WITH ASAHI-SAN AND NOYA-SAN EARLIER...
YOU DID?
SO YOU HEARD THE PART ABOUT HOW WE RAN AWAY, HUH.
LAST YEAR...
YOU HEARD THAT COACH UKAI CAME BACK FOR A SHORT WHILE, RIGHT?
The older one. Not the coach we have now.
YEAH.
WELL... AND THIS IS GOING TO SOUND REALLY PATHETIC, BUT...
...
THERE WERE A HANDFUL OF US WHO JUST COULDN'T HANDLE PRACTICES ANYMORE.

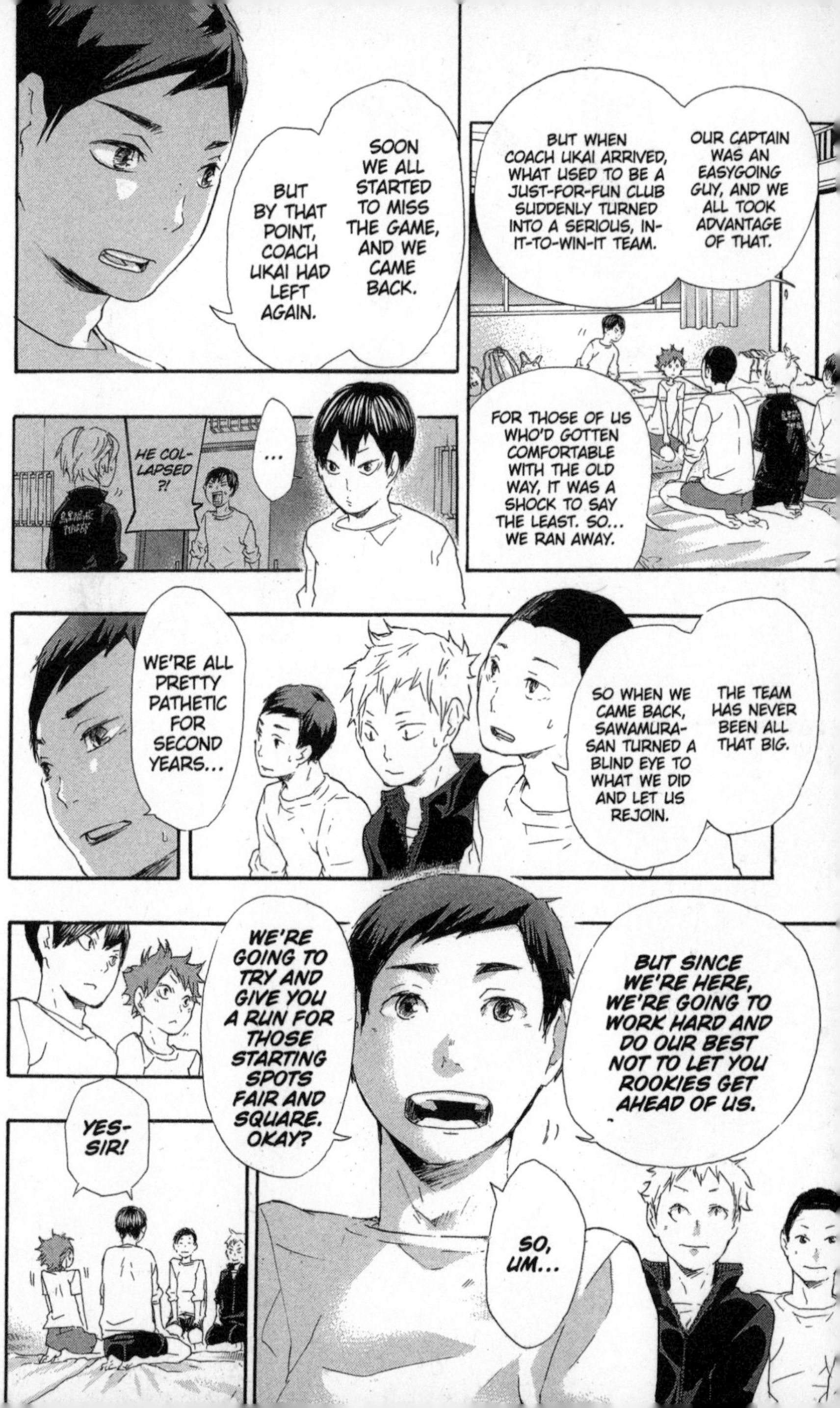
OUR CAPTAIN WAS AN EASYGOING GUY, AND WE ALL TOOK ADVANTAGE OF THAT.
BUT WHEN COACH UKAI ARRIVED, WHAT USED TO BE A JUST-FOR-FUN CLUB SUDDENLY TURNED INTO A SERIOUS, IN-IT-TO-WIN-IT TEAM.
FOR THOSE OF US WHO'D GOTTEN COMFORTABLE WITH THE OLD WAY, IT WAS A SHOCK TO SAY THE LEAST. SO... WE RAN AWAY.
SOON WE ALL STARTED TO MISS THE GAME, AND WE CAME BACK.
BUT BY THAT POINT, COACH UKAI HAD LEFT AGAIN.
...
HE COL-LAPSED ?!
THE TEAM HAS NEVER BEEN ALL THAT BIG.
SO WHEN WE CAME BACK, SAWAMURA-SAN TURNED A BLIND EYE TO WHAT WE DID AND LET US REJOIN.
WE'RE ALL PRETTY PATHETIC FOR SECOND YEARS...
BUT SINCE WE'RE HERE, WE'RE GOING TO WORK HARD AND DO OUR BEST NOT TO LET YOU ROOKIES GET AHEAD OF US.
WE'RE GOING TO TRY AND GIVE YOU A RUN FOR THOSE STARTING SPOTS FAIR AND SQUARE. OKAY?
SO, UM...
YES-SIR!

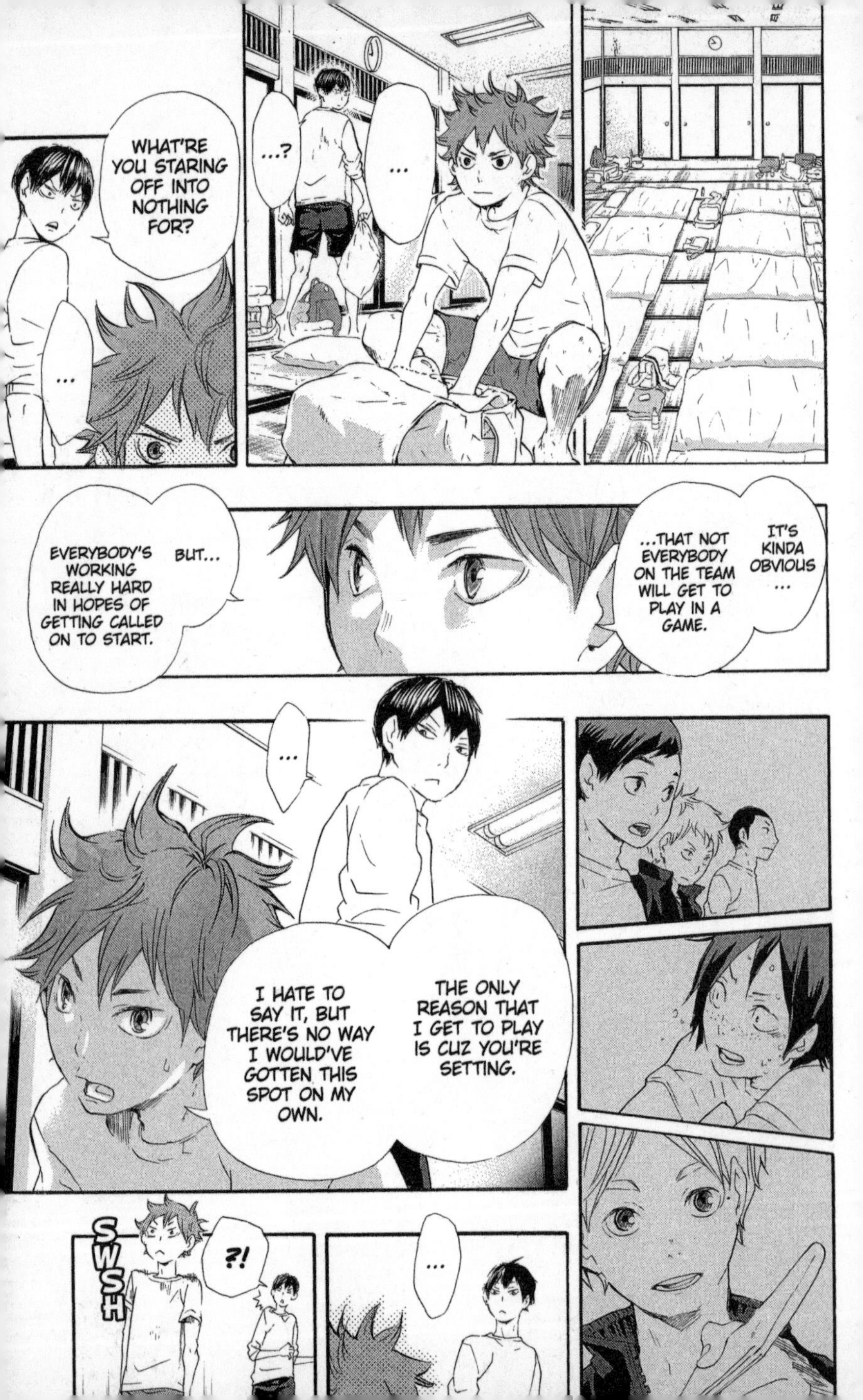
...
...?
WHAT'RE YOU STARING OFF INTO NOTHING FOR?
...
IT'S KINDA OBVIOUS ...
...THAT NOT EVERYBODY ON THE TEAM WILL GET TO PLAY IN A GAME.
BUT...
EVERYBODY'S WORKING REALLY HARD IN HOPES OF GETTING CALLED ON TO START.
...
THE ONLY REASON THAT I GET TO PLAY IS CUZ YOU'RE SETTING.
I HATE TO SAY IT, BUT THERE'S NO WAY I WOULD'VE GOTTEN THIS SPOT ON MY OWN.
...
?!
SWSH

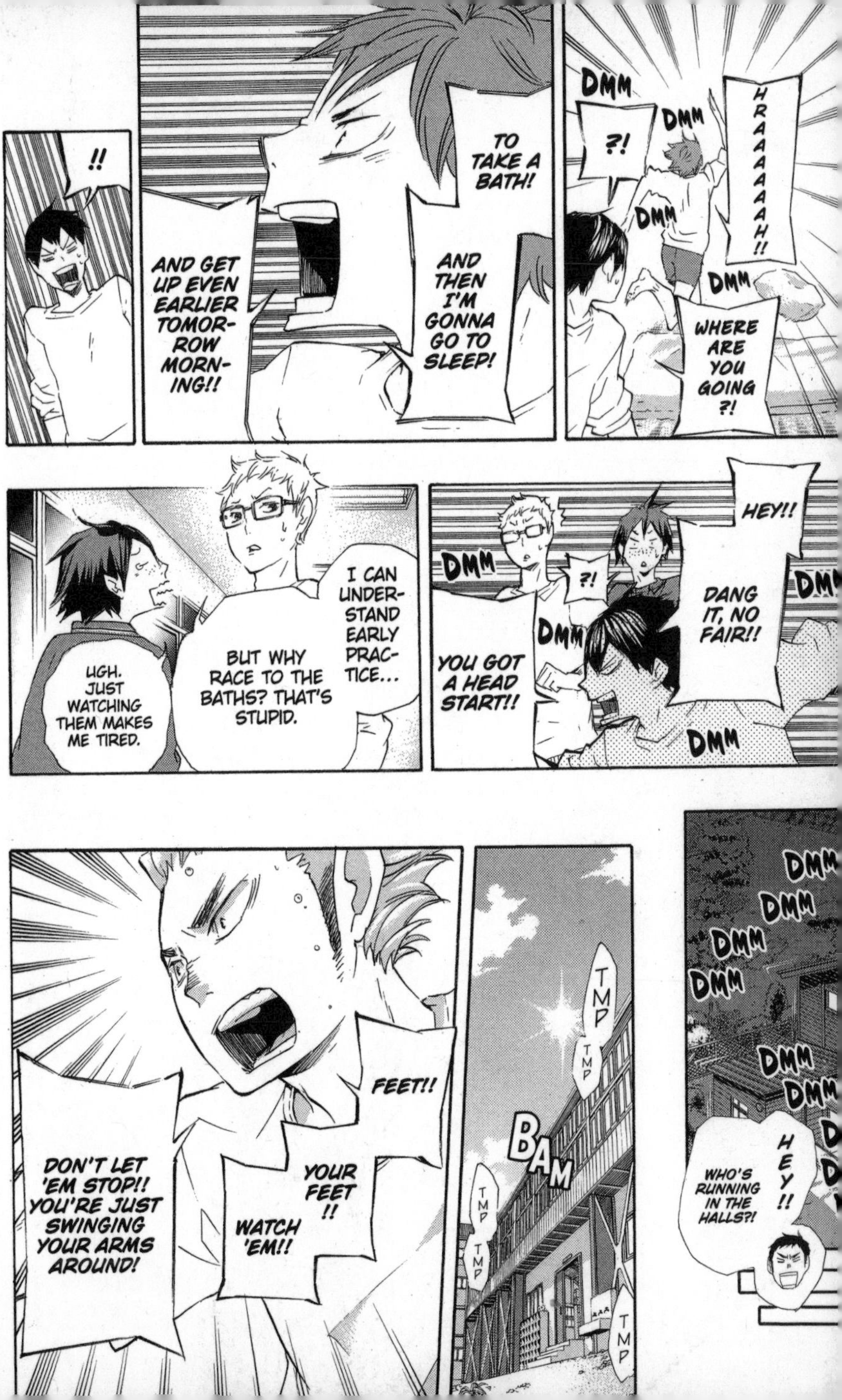
HRAAAAAAH!!
DMM
DMM
?!
DMM
DMM
WHERE ARE YOU GOING?!
TO TAKE A BATH!
AND THEN I'M GONNA GO TO SLEEP!
AND GET UP EVEN EARLIER TOMORROW MORNING!!
!!
HEY!!
DANG IT, NO FAIR!!
DMM
DMM
?!
DMM
YOU GOT A HEAD START!!
DMM
I CAN UNDER-STAND EARLY PRAC-TICE...
BUT WHY RACE TO THE BATHS? THAT'S STUPID.
UGH. JUST WATCHING THEM MAKES ME TIRED.
DMM
DMM
DMM
DMM
DMM
DMM
HEY!!
WHO'S RUNNING IN THE HALLS?!
TMP
TMP
BAM
TMP
TMP
TMP
TMP
FEET!!
YOUR FEET!!
WATCH 'EM!!
DON'T LET 'EM STOP!! YOU'RE JUST SWINGING YOUR ARMS AROUND!

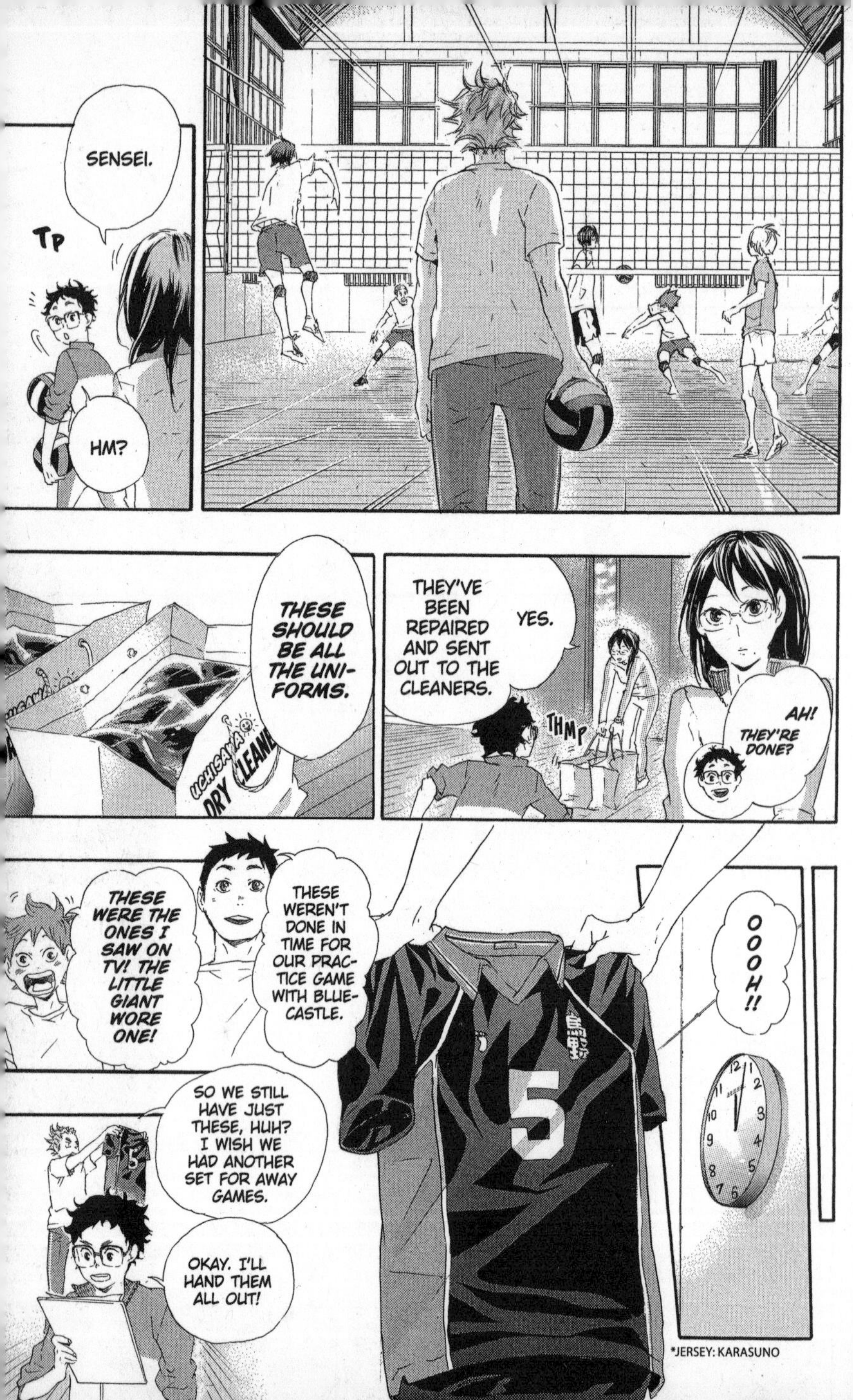
SENSEI.
Tp
HM?
YES.
THEY'VE BEEN REPAIRED AND SENT OUT TO THE CLEANERS.
THMP
AH! THEY'RE DONE?
THESE SHOULD BE ALL THE UNI-FORMS.
UCHISAWA DRY CLEANE
OOOOH!!
烏野
5
THESE WEREN'T DONE IN TIME FOR OUR PRAC-TICE GAME WITH BLUE-CASTLE.
THESE WERE THE ONES I SAW ON TV! THE LITTLE GIANT WORE ONE!
SO WE STILL HAVE JUST THESE, HUH? I WISH WE HAD ANOTHER SET FOR AWAY GAMES.
OKAY. I'LL HAND THEM ALL OUT!
*JERSEY: KARASUNO

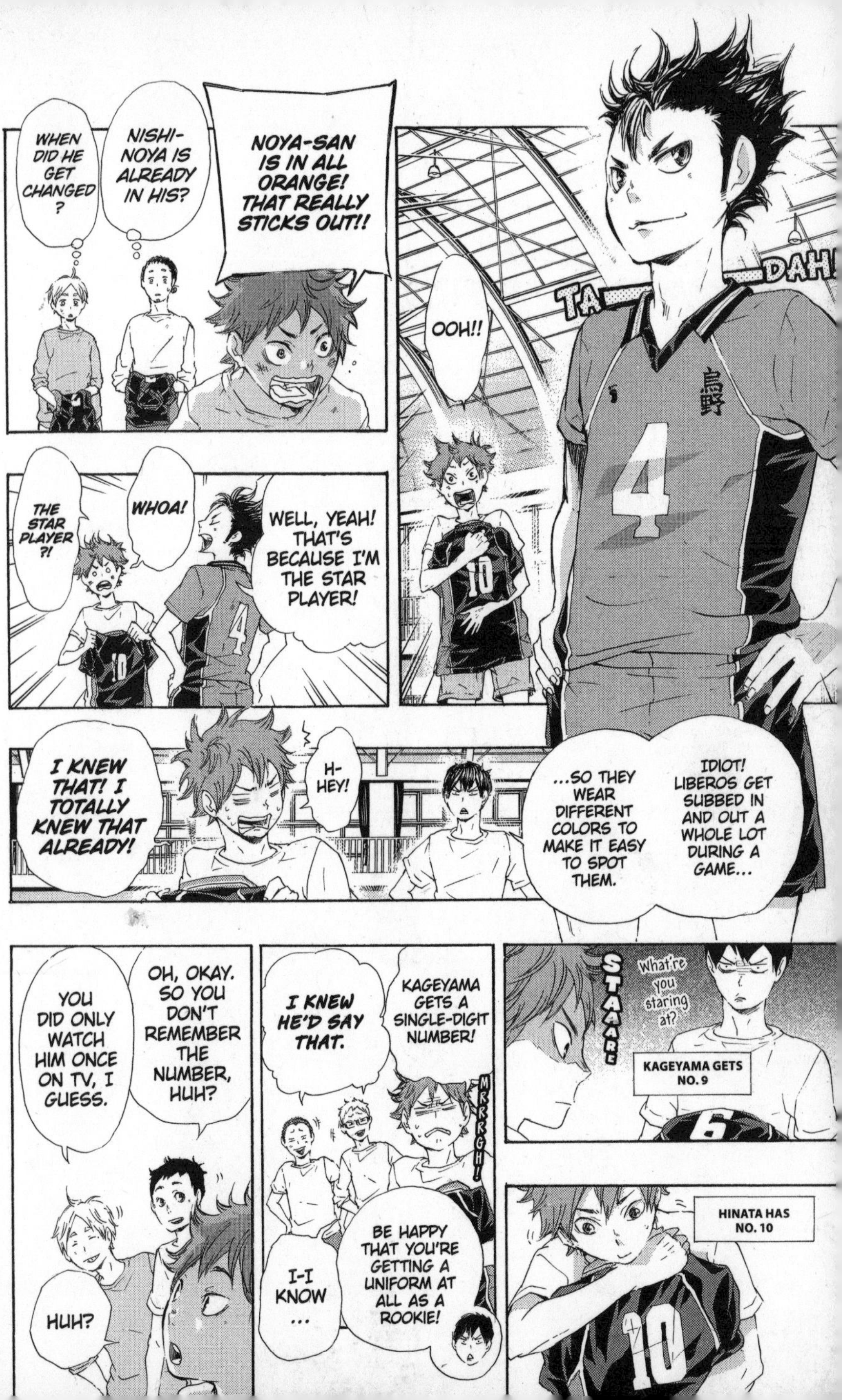
TA-DAH!
OOH!!
NOYA-SAN IS IN ALL ORANGE! THAT REALLY STICKS OUT!!
NISHI-NOYA IS ALREADY IN HIS?
WHEN DID HE GET CHANGED?
WELL, YEAH! THAT'S BECAUSE I'M THE STAR PLAYER!
WHOA!
THE STAR PLAYER?!
IDIOT! LIBEROS GET SUBBED IN AND OUT A WHOLE LOT DURING A GAME...
...SO THEY WEAR DIFFERENT COLORS TO MAKE IT EASY TO SPOT THEM.
H-HEY!
I KNEW THAT! I TOTALLY KNEW THAT ALREADY!
STAAARE
What're you staring at?
KAGEYAMA GETS NO. 9
HINATA HAS NO. 10
KAGEYAMA GETS A SINGLE-DIGIT NUMBER!
I KNEW HE'D SAY THAT.
MRRRGH!
BE HAPPY THAT YOU'RE GETTING A UNIFORM AT ALL AS A ROOKIE!
I-I KNOW...
OH, OKAY. SO YOU DON'T REMEMBER THE NUMBER, HUH?
YOU DID ONLY WATCH HIM ONCE ON TV, I GUESS.
HUH?

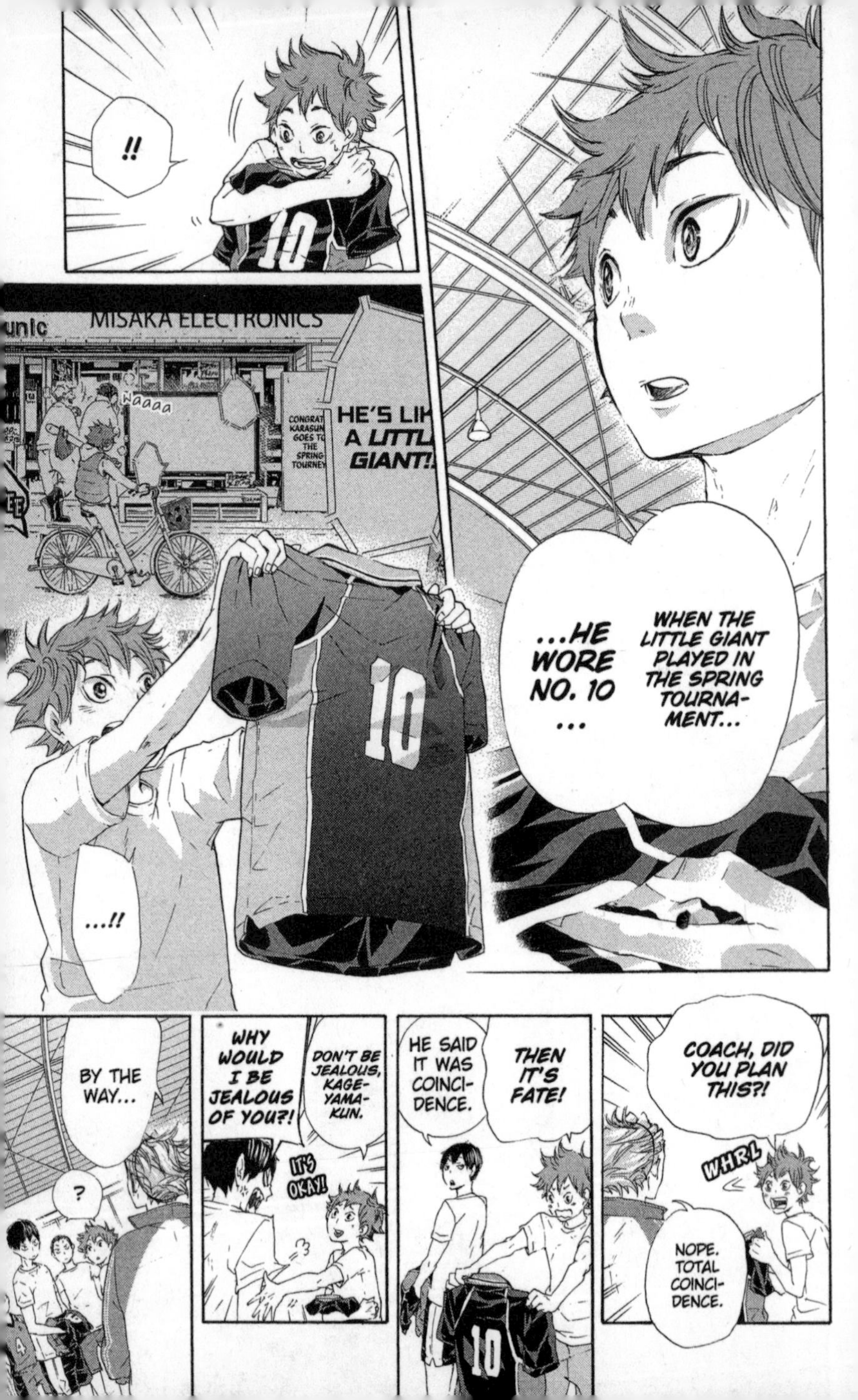
WHEN THE LITTLE GIANT PLAYED IN THE SPRING TOURNA-MENT...
...HE WORE NO. 10 ...
!!
MISAKA ELECTRONICS
unic
Naaaa
CONGRAT KARASUN GOES TO THE SPRING TOURNEY
HE'S LIK A LITTL GIANT!
...!!
COACH, DID YOU PLAN THIS?!
WHRL
NOPE. TOTAL COINCI-DENCE.
THEN IT'S FATE!
HE SAID IT WAS COINCI-DENCE.
DON'T BE JEALOUS, KAGE-YAMA-KUN.
WHY WOULD I BE JEALOUS OF YOU?!
IT'S OKAY!
BY THE WAY...
?

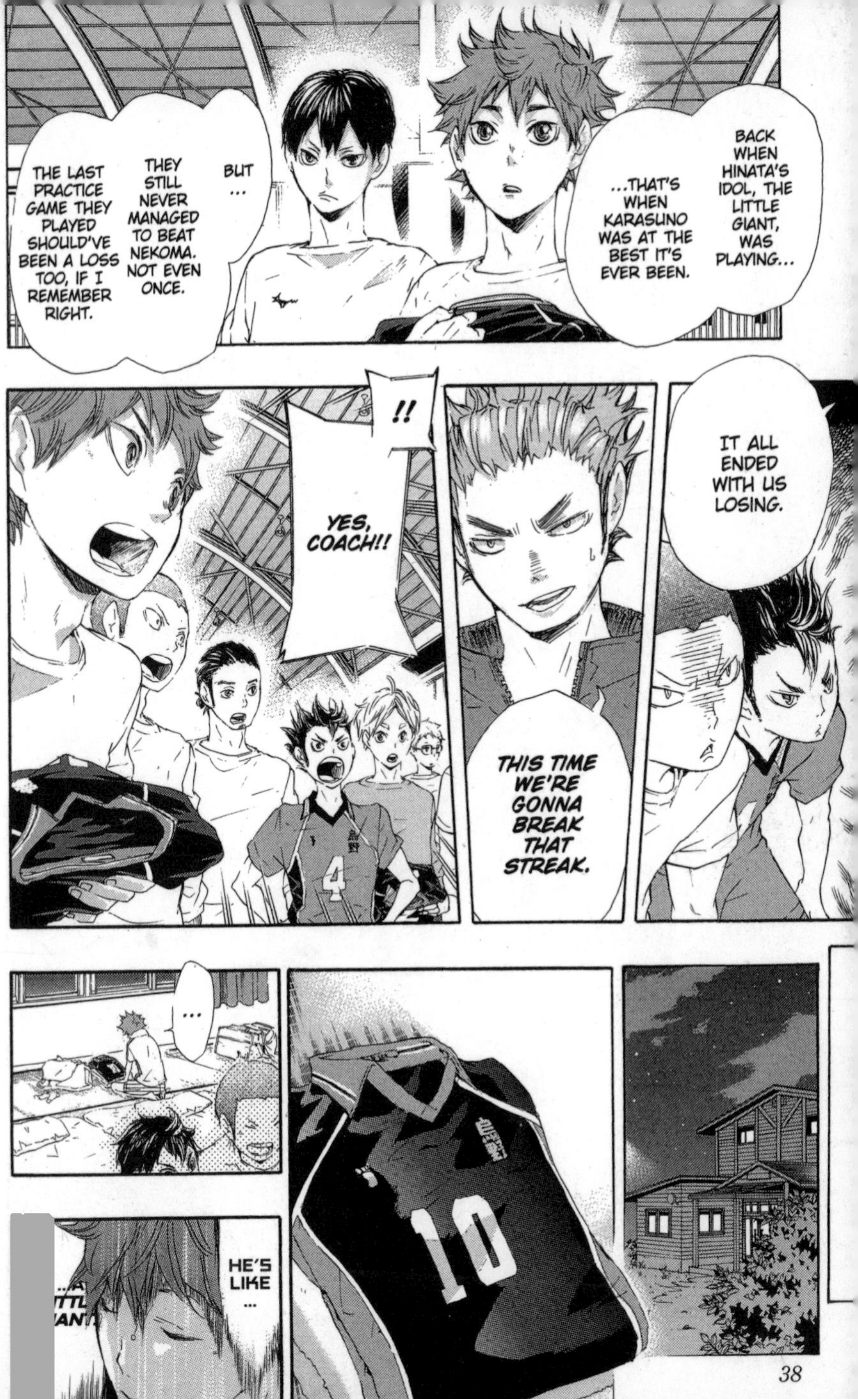
BACK WHEN HINATA'S IDOL, THE LITTLE GIANT, WAS PLAYING...
...THAT'S WHEN KARASUNO WAS AT THE BEST IT'S EVER BEEN.
BUT ...
THEY STILL NEVER MANAGED TO BEAT NEKOMA. NOT EVEN ONCE.
THE LAST PRACTICE GAME THEY PLAYED SHOULD'VE BEEN A LOSS TOO, IF I REMEMBER RIGHT.
IT ALL ENDED WITH US LOSING.
THIS TIME WE'RE GONNA BREAK THAT STREAK.
!!
YES, COACH!!
...
HE'S LIKE ...

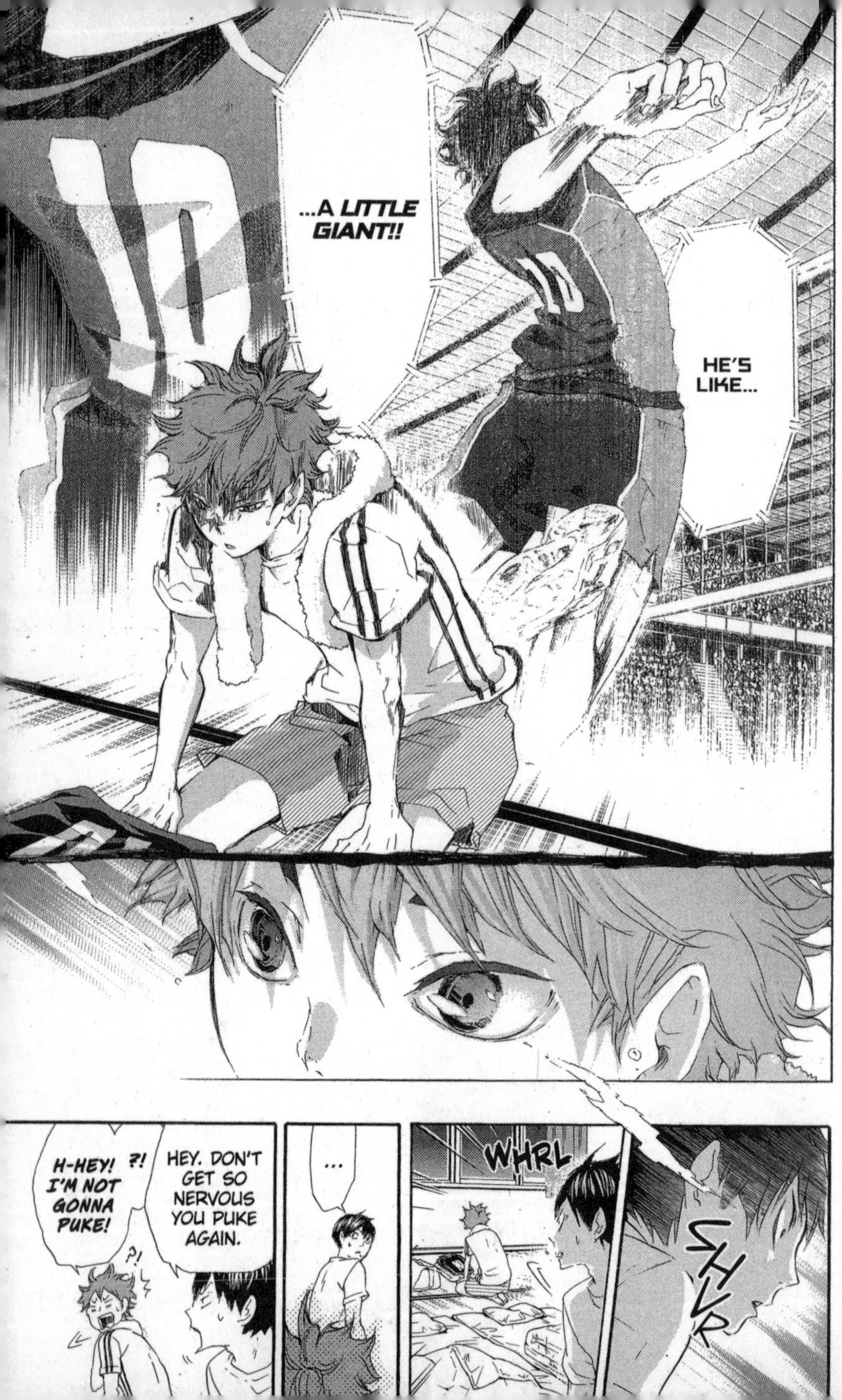
HE'S LIKE...
...A LITTLE GIANT!!
SHVR
WHRL
...
HEY. DON'T GET SO NERVOUS YOU PUKE AGAIN.
?!
H-HEY! I'M NOT GONNA PUKE!
?!

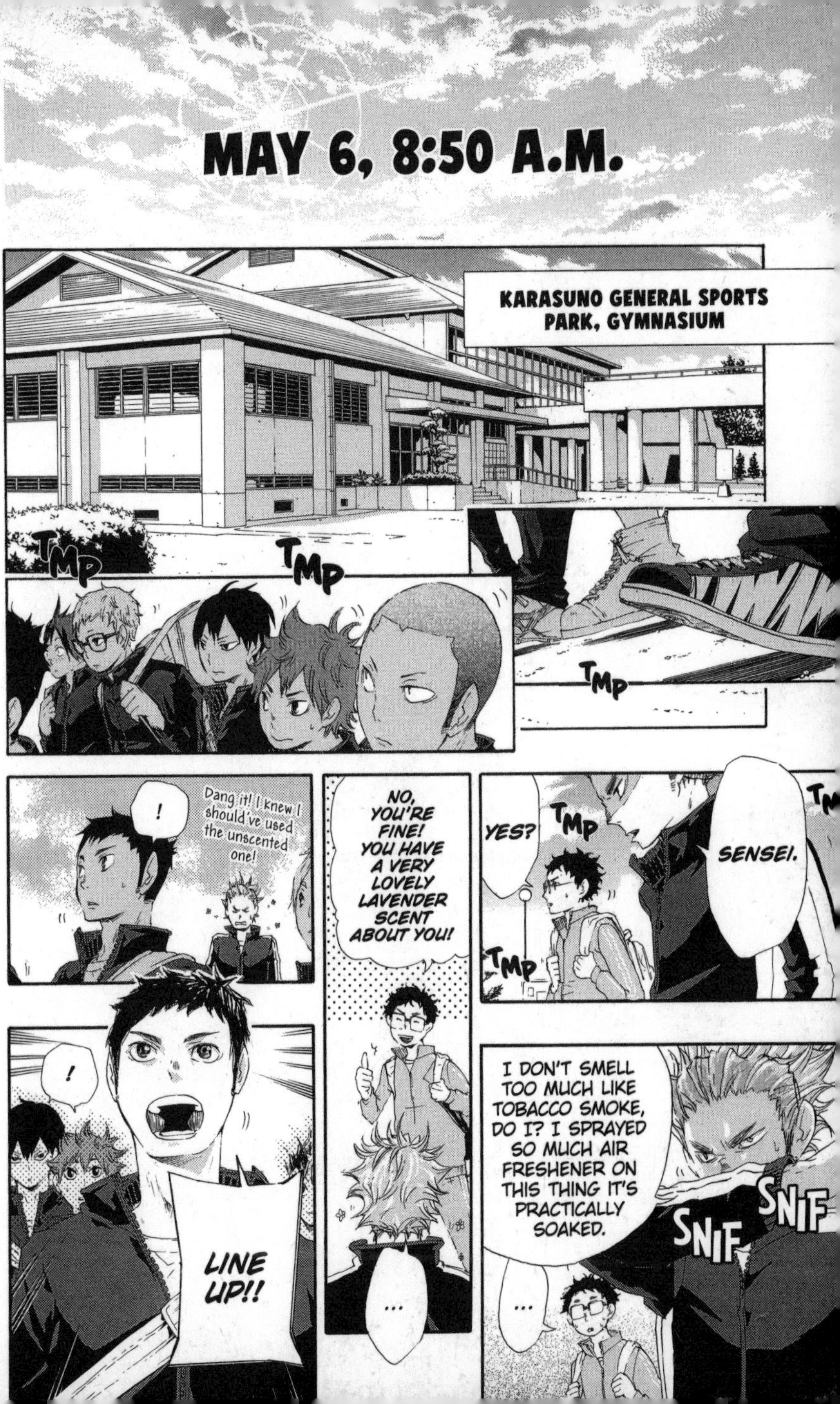
MAY 6, 8:50 A.M.
KARASUNO GENERAL SPORTS PARK, GYMNASIUM
TMP
TMP
TMP
TMP
SENSEI.
YES?
TMP
TMP
I DON'T SMELL TOO MUCH LIKE TOBACCO SMOKE, DO I? I SPRAYED SO MUCH AIR FRESHENER ON THIS THING IT'S PRACTICALLY SOAKED.
SNIF
SNIF
...
NO, YOU'RE FINE! YOU HAVE A VERY LOVELY LAVENDER SCENT ABOUT YOU!
...
!
Dang it! I knew I should've used the unscented one!
!
LINE UP!!

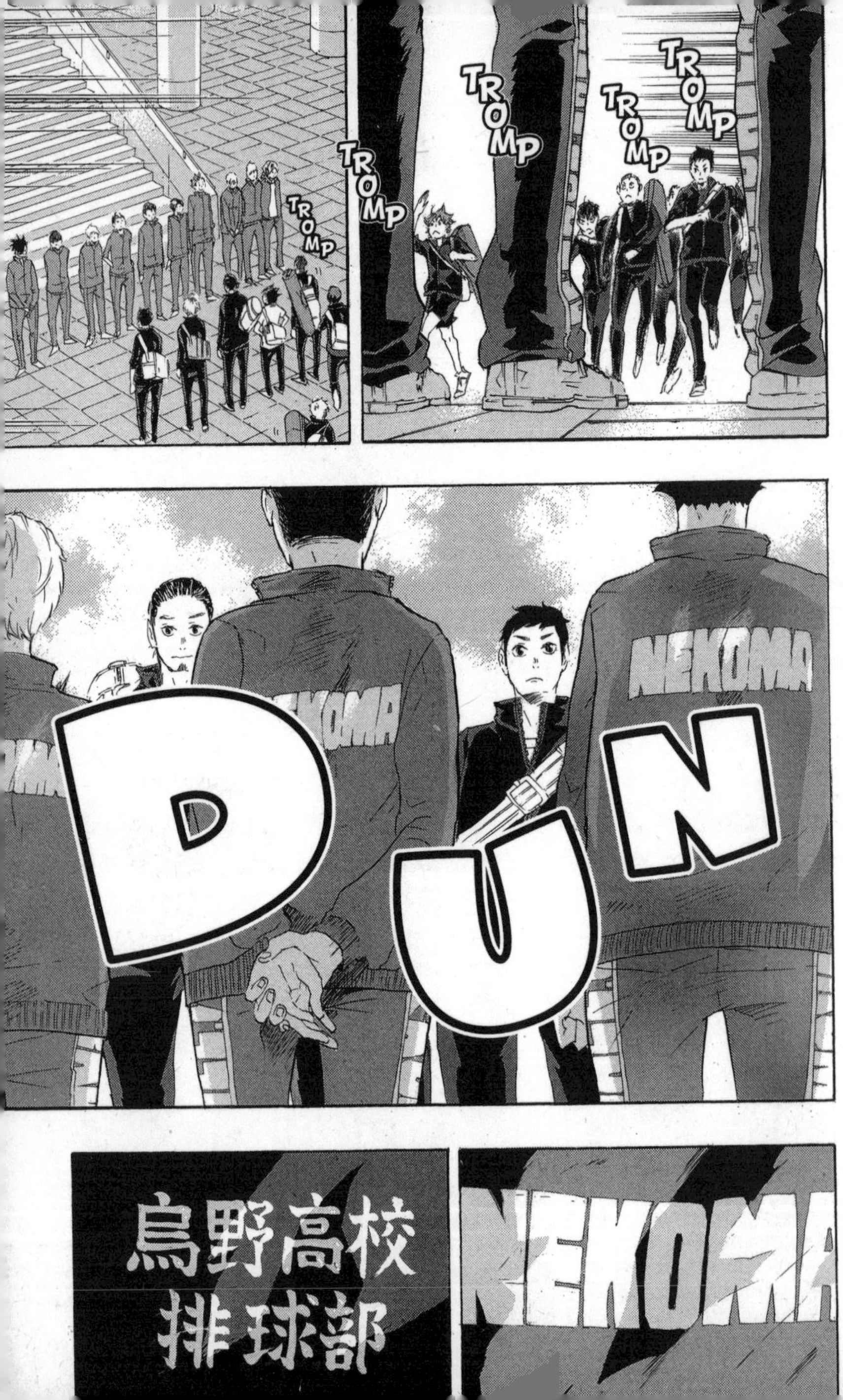
TROMP
TROMP
TROMP
TROMP
TROMP
NEKOMA
DUN
NEKOMA
NEKOMA
烏野高校
排球部

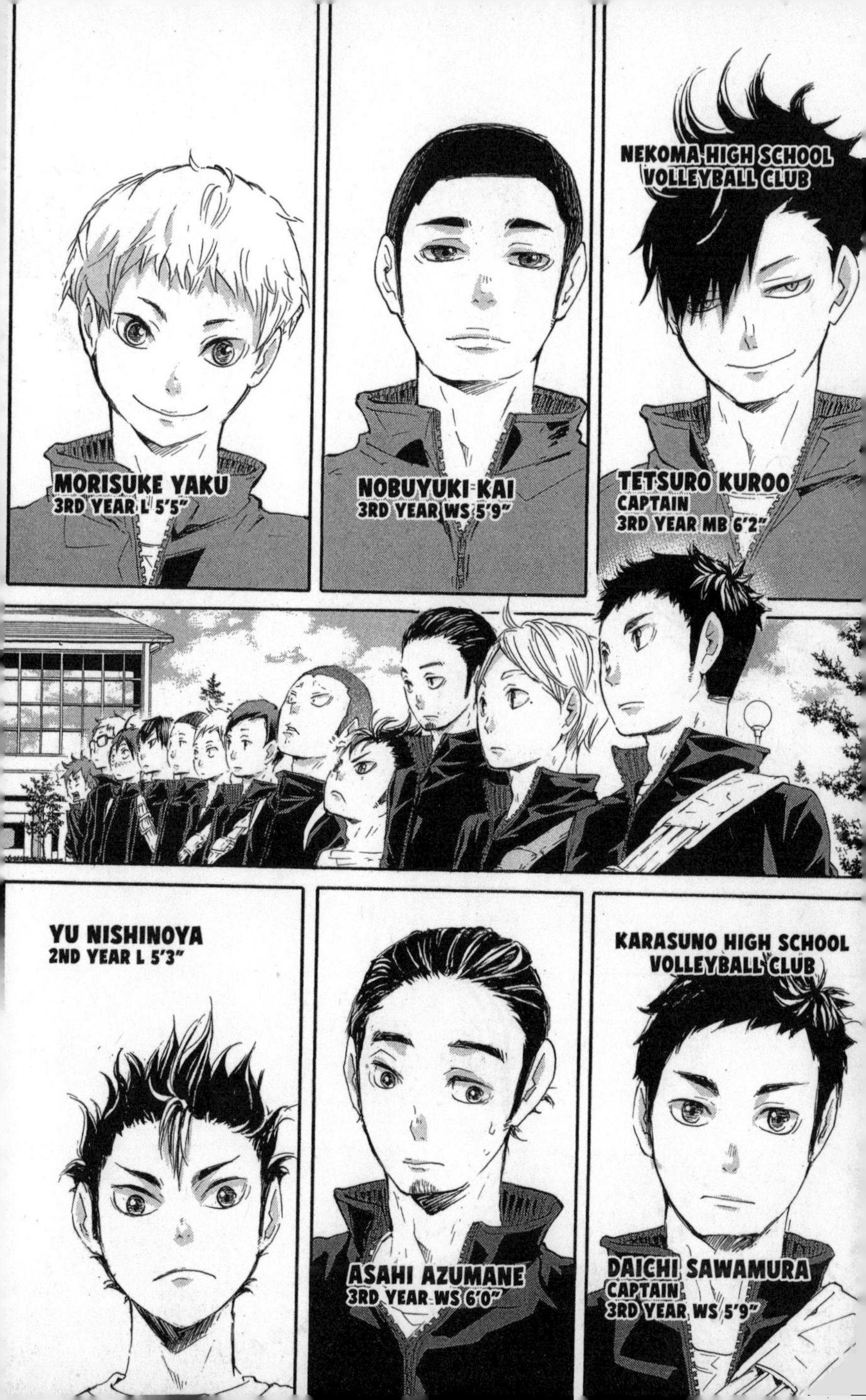
NEKOMA HIGH SCHOOL VOLLEYBALL CLUB
TETSURO KUROO
CAPTAIN
3RD YEAR MB 6'2"
NOBUYUKI KAI
3RD YEAR WS 5'9"
MORISUKE YAKU
3RD YEAR L 5'5"
KARASUNO HIGH SCHOOL VOLLEYBALL CLUB
DAICHI SAWAMURA
CAPTAIN
3RD YEAR WS 5'9"
ASAHI AZUMANE
3RD YEAR WS 6'0"
YU NISHINOYA
2ND YEAR L 5'3"

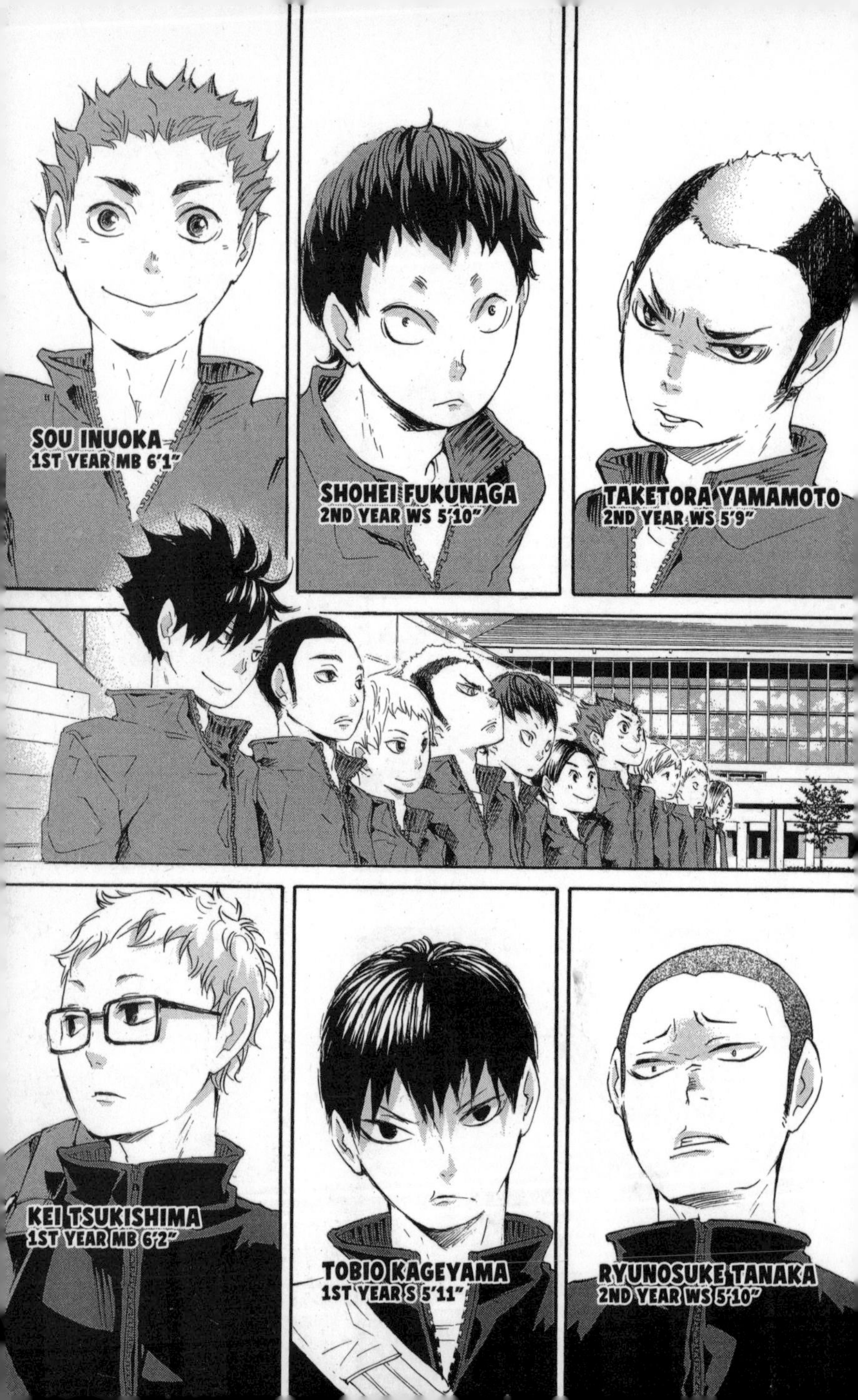
TAKETORA YAMAMOTO
2ND YEAR WS 5'9"
SHOHEI FUKUNAGA
2ND YEAR WS 5'10"
SOU INUOKA
1ST YEAR MB 6'1"
RYUNOSUKE TANAKA
2ND YEAR WS 5'10"
TOBIO KAGEYAMA
1ST YEAR S 5'11"
KEI TSUKISHIMA
1ST YEAR MB 6'2"

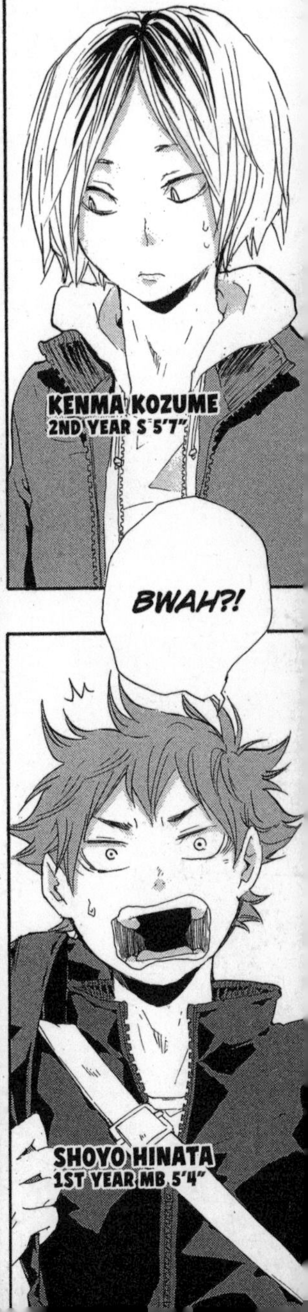
KENMA KOZUME
2ND YEAR S 5'7"
BWAH?!
SHOYO HINATA
1ST YEAR MB 5'4"

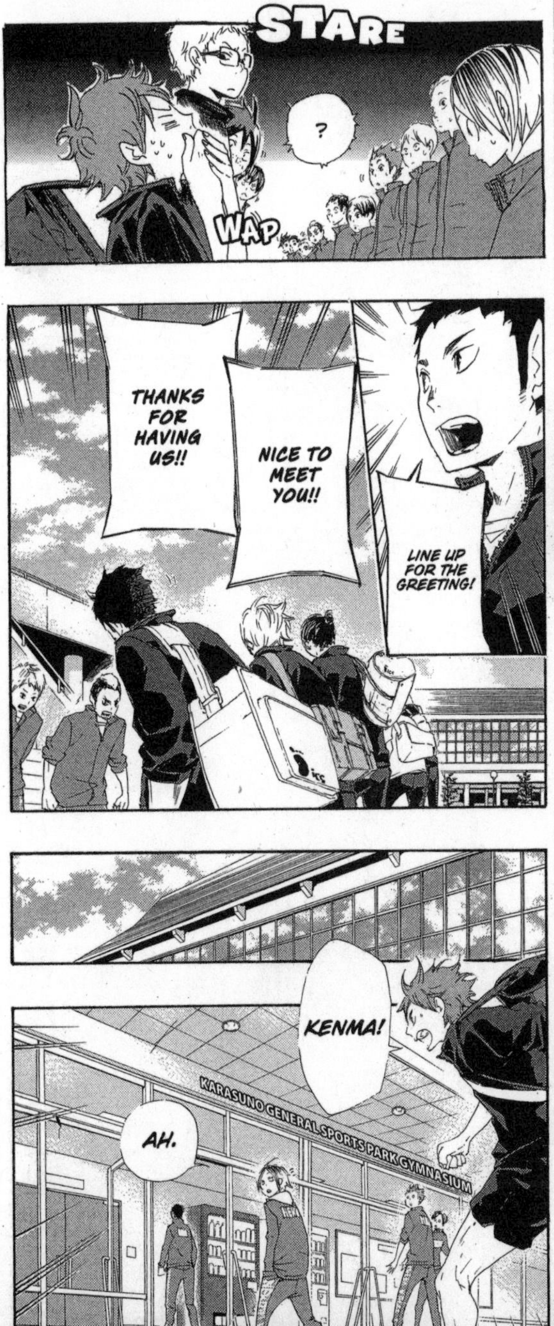
STARE
?
WAP
LINE UP FOR THE GREETING!
NICE TO MEET YOU!!
THANKS FOR HAVING US!!
KENMA!
KARASUNO GENERAL SPORTS PARK GYMNASIUM
AH.

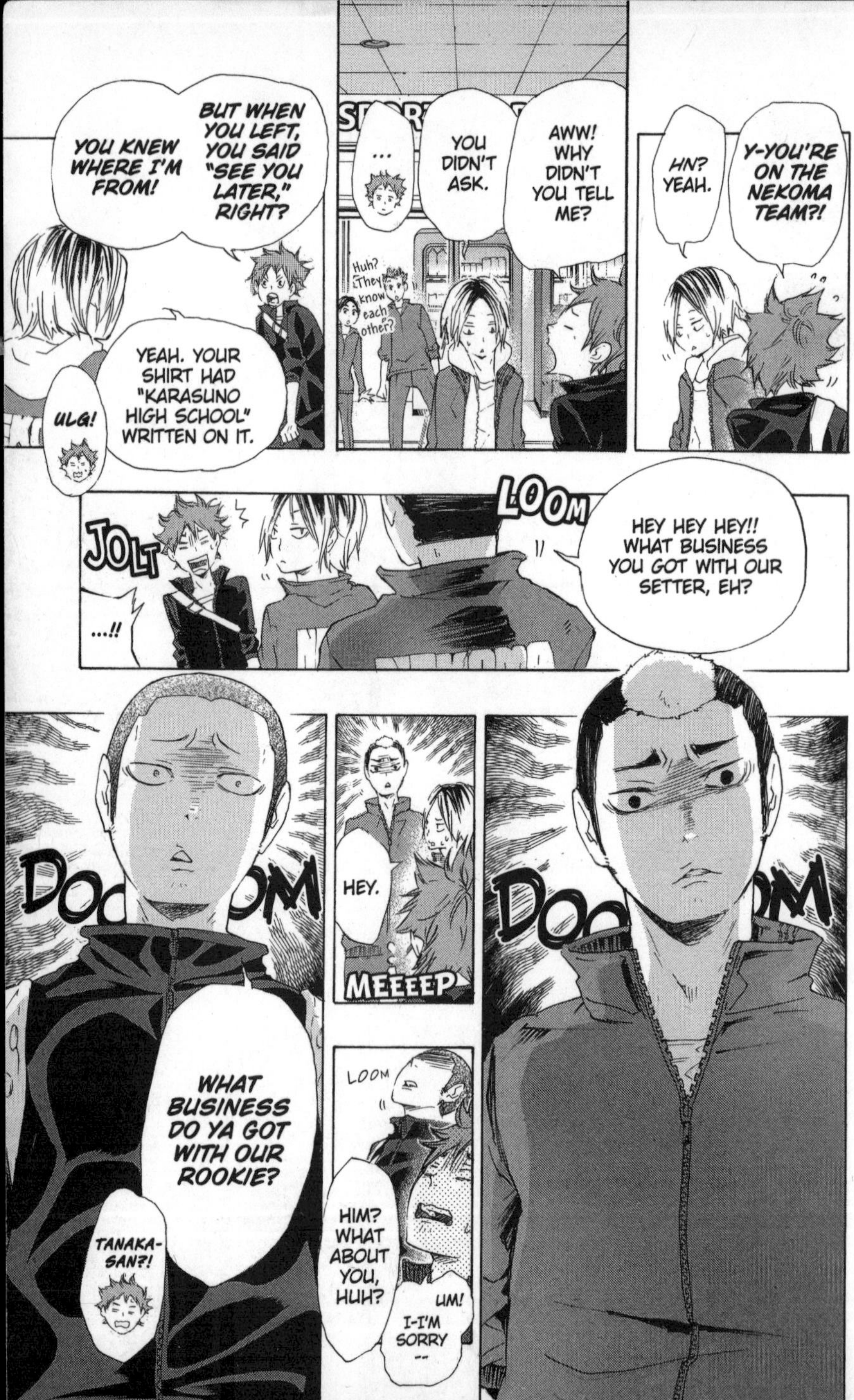

Y-YOU'RE ON THE NEKOMA TEAM?!
HN? YEAH.
AWW! WHY DIDN'T YOU TELL ME?
YOU DIDN'T ASK.
...
Huh? They know each other?
BUT WHEN YOU LEFT, YOU SAID "SEE YOU LATER," RIGHT?
YOU KNEW WHERE I'M FROM!
YEAH. YOUR SHIRT HAD "KARASUNO HIGH SCHOOL" WRITTEN ON IT.
ULG!
LOOM
HEY HEY HEY!! WHAT BUSINESS YOU GOT WITH OUR SETTER, EH?
JOLT
...!!
DOO OM
HEY.
MEEEEP
LOOM
HIM? WHAT ABOUT YOU, HUH?
UM! I-I'M SORRY--
DOO OM
WHAT BUSINESS DO YA GOT WITH OUR ROOKIE?
TANAKA-SAN?!

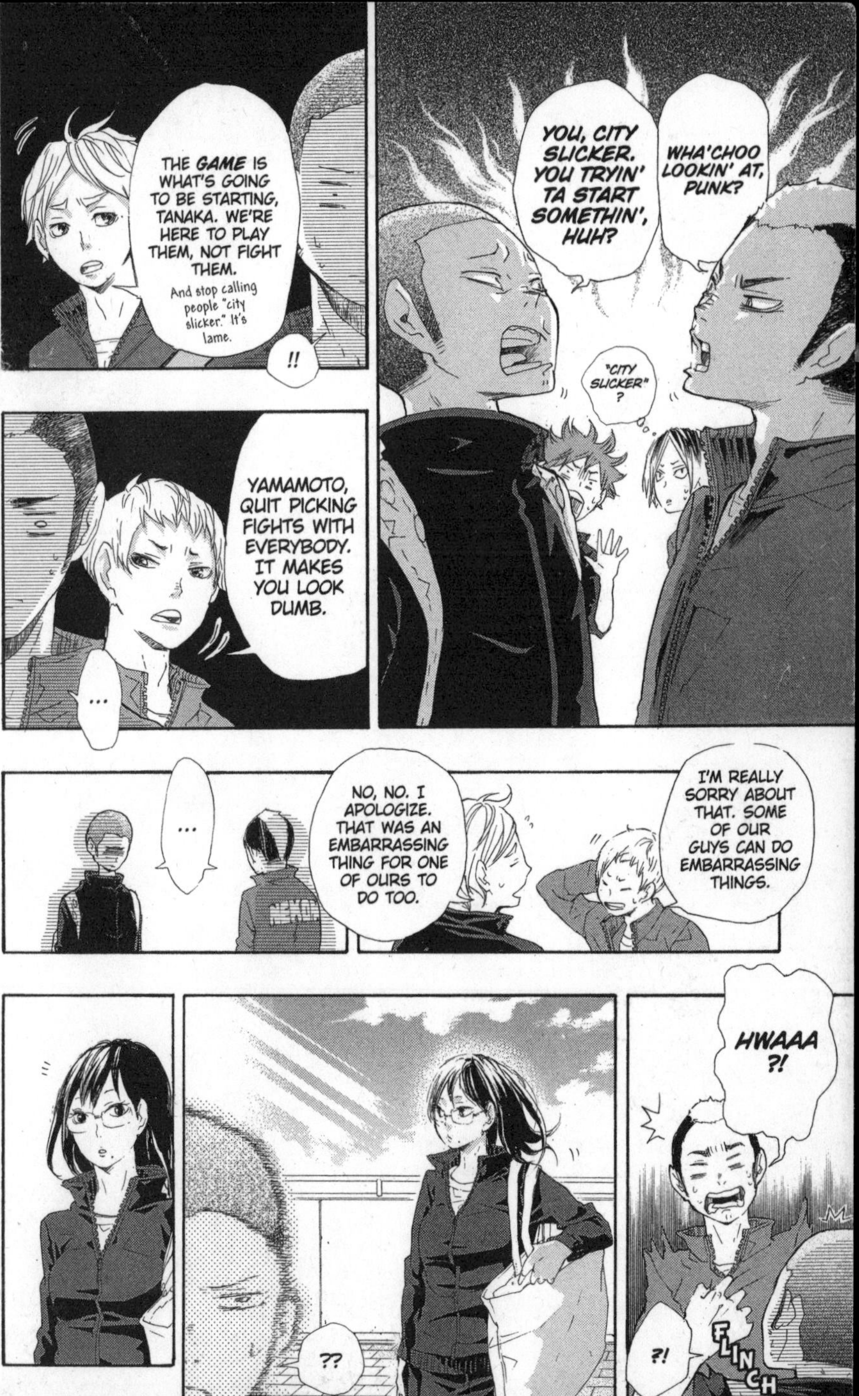
WHA'CHOO LOOKIN' AT, PUNK?
YOU, CITY SLICKER. YOU TRYIN' TA START SOMETHIN', HUH?
"CITY SLICKER"?
THE *GAME* IS WHAT'S GOING TO BE STARTING, TANAKA. WE'RE HERE TO PLAY THEM, NOT FIGHT THEM.
And stop calling people "city slicker." It's lame.
!!
YAMAMOTO, QUIT PICKING FIGHTS WITH EVERYBODY. IT MAKES YOU LOOK DUMB.
...
I'M REALLY SORRY ABOUT THAT. SOME OF OUR GUYS CAN DO EMBARRASSING THINGS.
NO, NO. I APOLOGIZE. THAT WAS AN EMBARRASSING THING FOR ONE OF OURS TO DO TOO.
...
HWAAA?!
?!
FLINCH
??

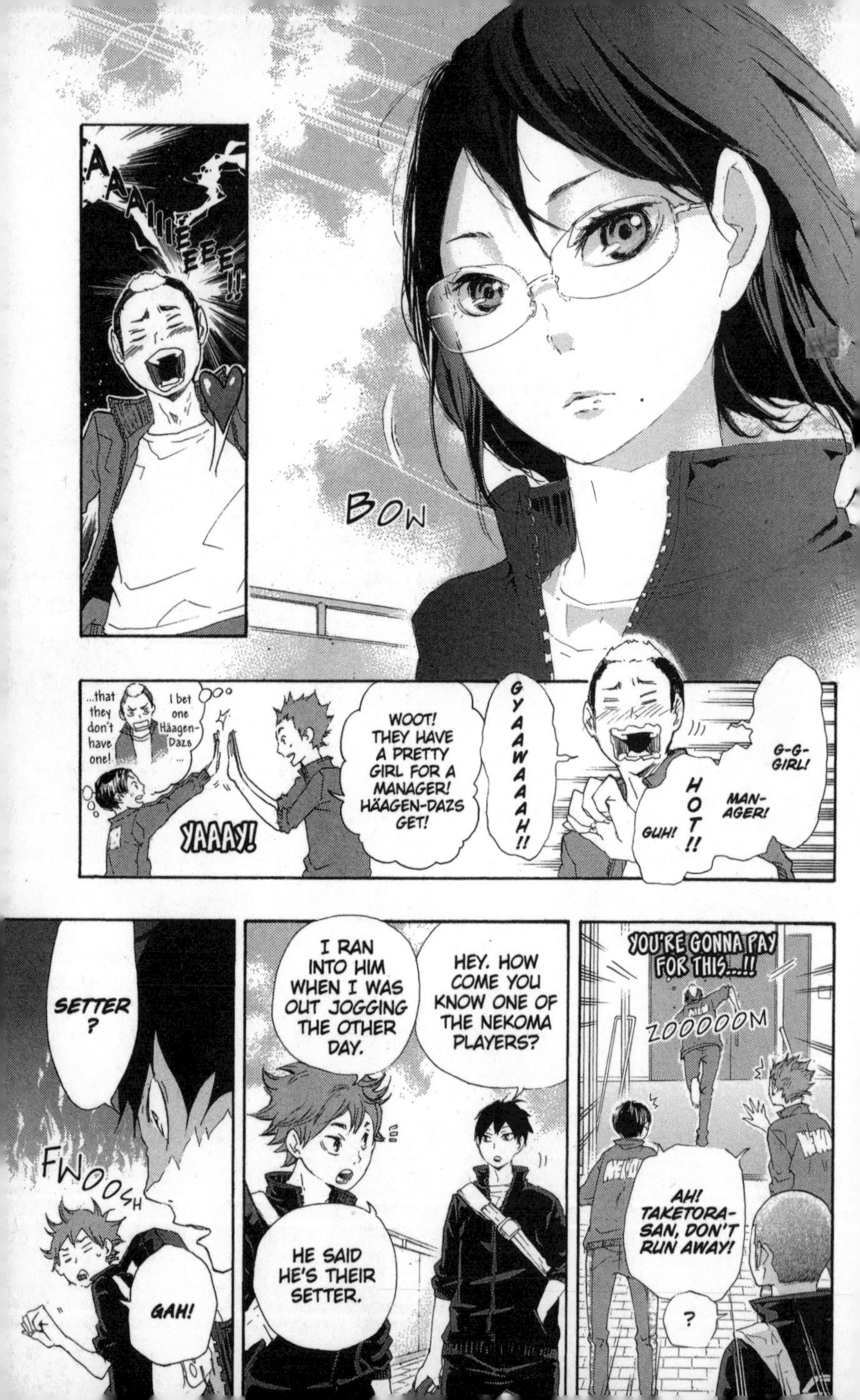
BOW
AAAIIIEEEE!!
G-G-GIRL!
MANAGER!
HOT!!
GUH!
GYAAAWAAAAH!!
WOOT! THEY HAVE A PRETTY GIRL FOR A MANAGER! HÄAGEN-DAZS GET!
YAAAY!
I bet one Häagen-Dazs ...
...that they don't have one!
YOU'RE GONNA PAY FOR THIS...!!
ZOOOOOM
AH! TAKETORA-SAN, DON'T RUN AWAY!
?
HEY. HOW COME YOU KNOW ONE OF THE NEKOMA PLAYERS?
I RAN INTO HIM WHEN I WAS OUT JOGGING THE OTHER DAY.
HE SAID HE'S THEIR SETTER.
SETTER?
FWOOSH
GAH!

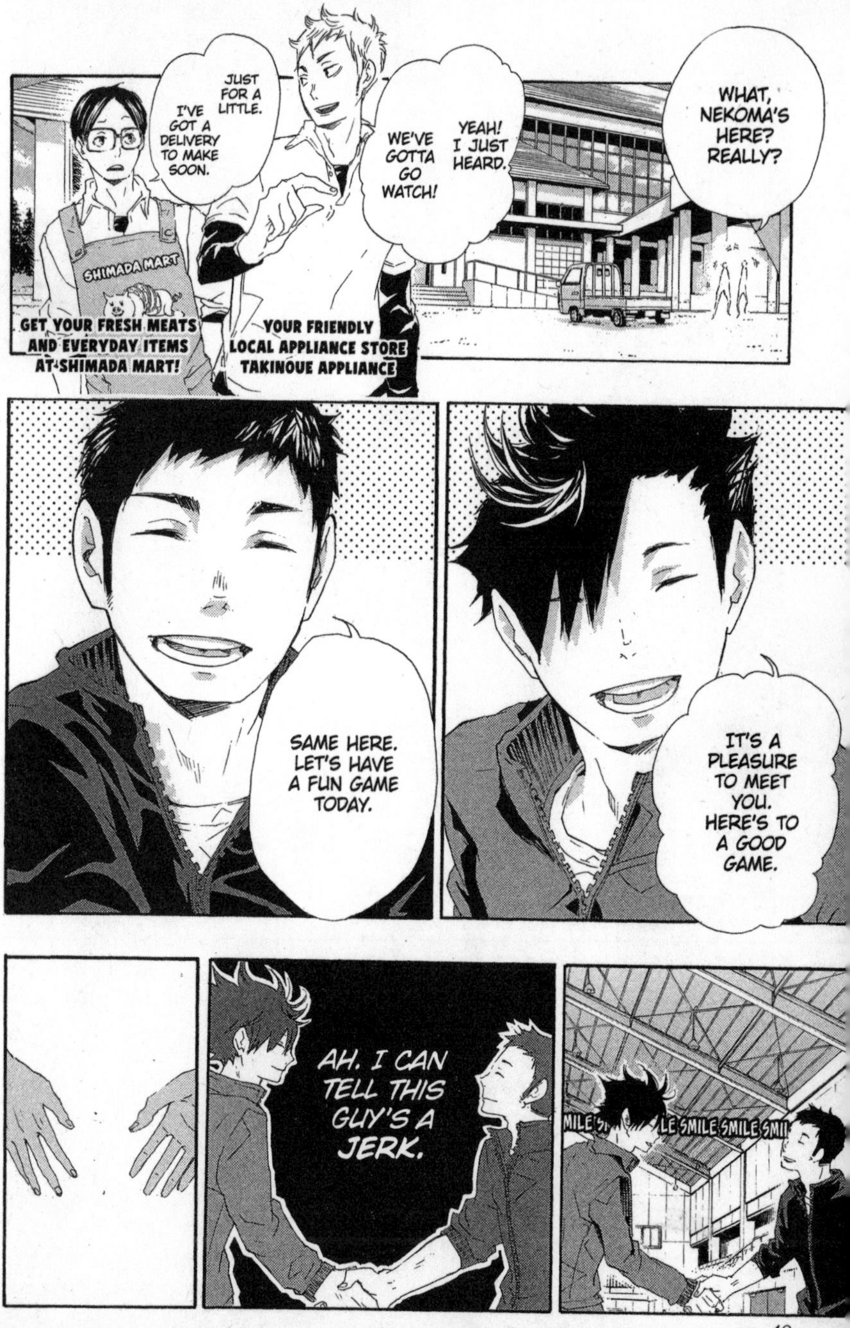
WHAT, NEKOMA'S HERE? REALLY?
YEAH! I JUST HEARD.
WE'VE GOTTA GO WATCH!
JUST FOR A LITTLE.
I'VE GOT A DELIVERY TO MAKE SOON.
SHIMADA MART
YOUR FRIENDLY LOCAL APPLIANCE STORE TAKINOUE APPLIANCE
GET YOUR FRESH MEATS AND EVERYDAY ITEMS AT SHIMADA MART!
IT'S A PLEASURE TO MEET YOU. HERE'S TO A GOOD GAME.
SAME HERE. LET'S HAVE A FUN GAME TODAY.
MILE S
LE SMILE SMILE SMI
AH. I CAN TELL THIS GUY'S A JERK.

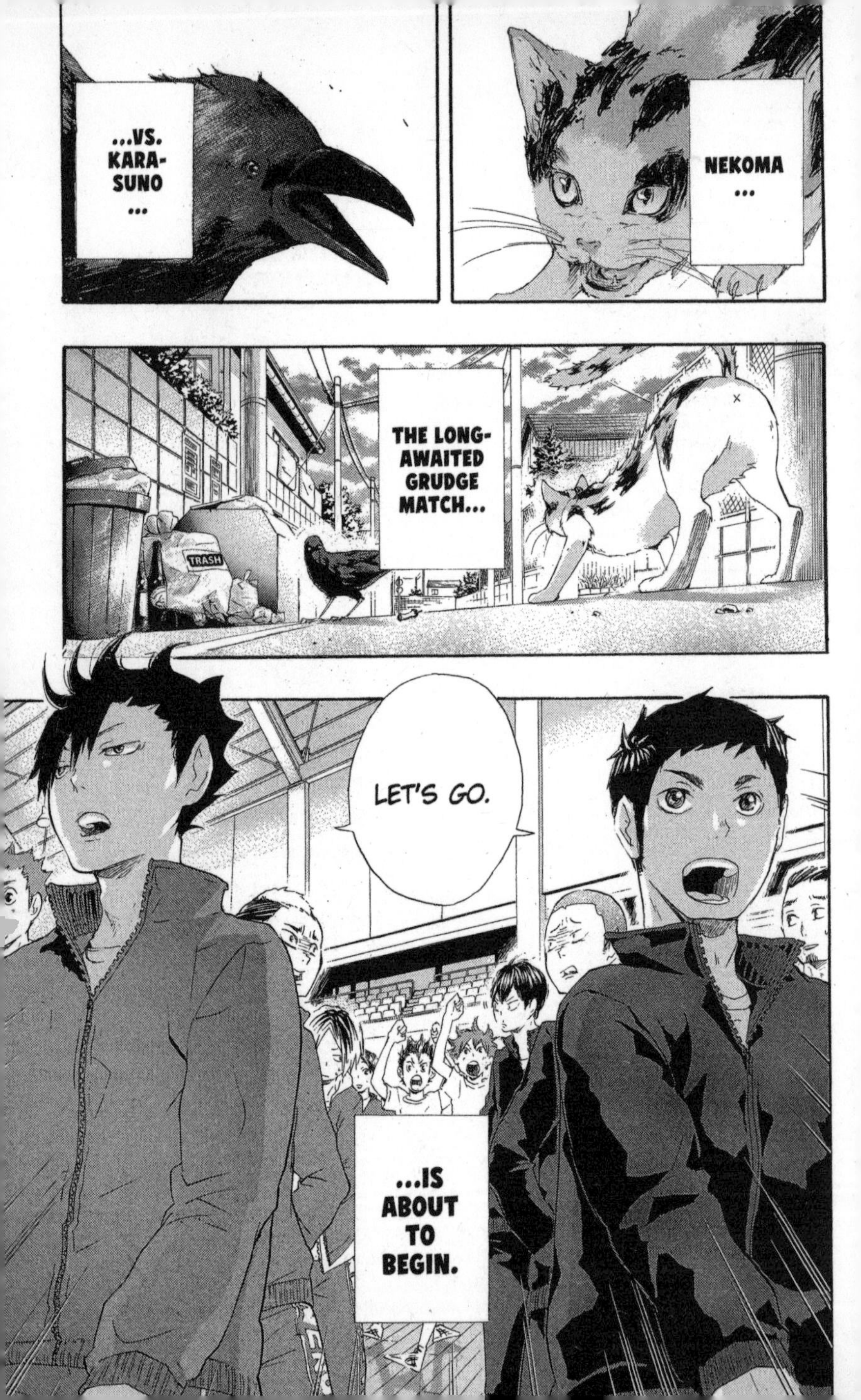
NEKOMA ...
...VS. KARA-SUNO ...
THE LONG-AWAITED GRUDGE MATCH...
LET'S GO.
...IS ABOUT TO BEGIN.

HISASHI KINOSHITA

KARASUNO HIGH SCHOOL
CLASS 2-2

POSITION:
WING SPIKER

HEIGHT: 5'9"

WEIGHT: 144 LBS.
(AS OF APRIL, 2ND YEAR
OF HIGH SCHOOL)

BIRTHDAY: FEBRUARY 15

FAVORITE FOOD:
PICKLED GINGER

ABILITY PARAMETERS
(5-POINT SCALE)

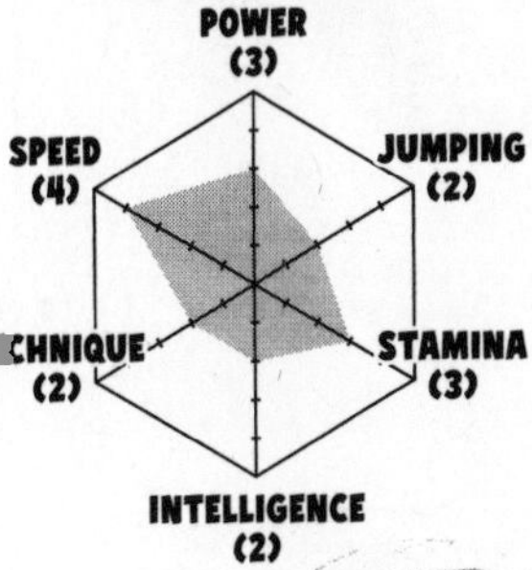
POWER (3)
JUMPING (2)
STAMINA (3)
INTELLIGENCE (2)
CHNIQUE (2)
SPEED (4)

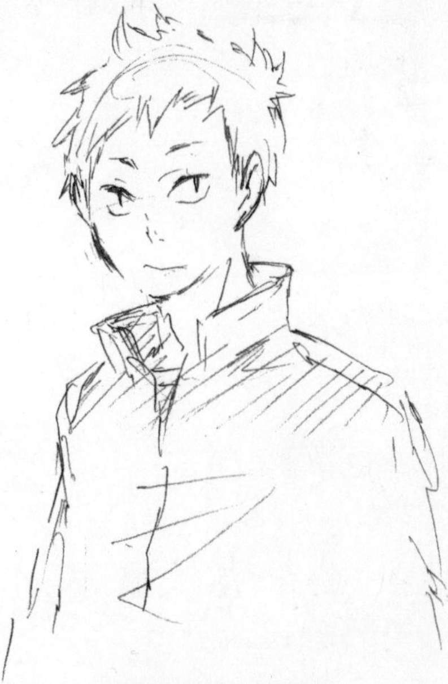

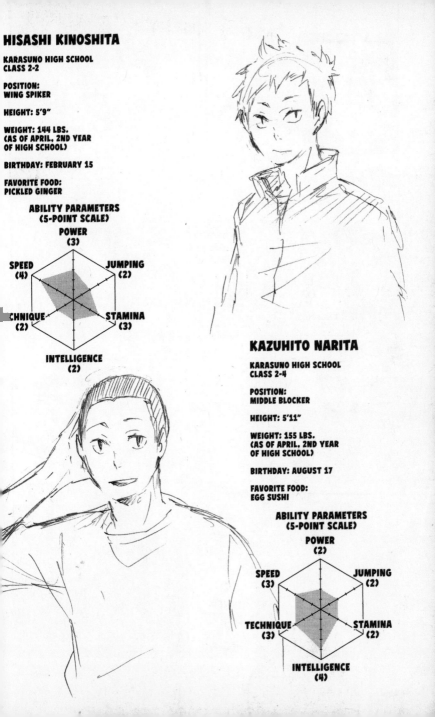

KAZUHITO NARITA

KARASUNO HIGH SCHOOL
CLASS 2-4

POSITION:
MIDDLE BLOCKER

HEIGHT: 5'11"

WEIGHT: 155 LBS.
(AS OF APRIL, 2ND YEAR
OF HIGH SCHOOL)

BIRTHDAY: AUGUST 17

FAVORITE FOOD:
EGG SUSHI

ABILITY PARAMETERS
(5-POINT SCALE)

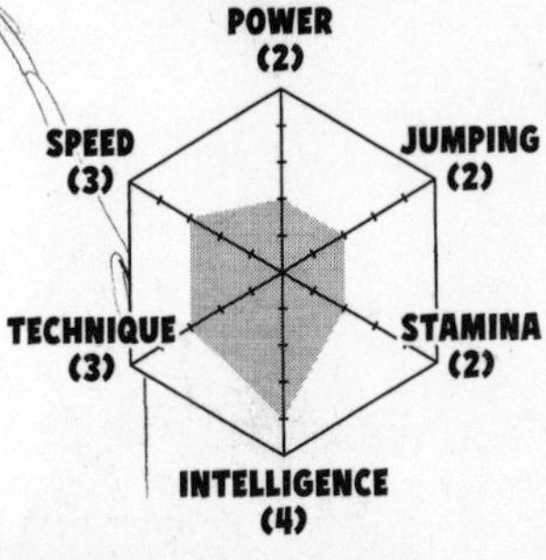
POWER (2)
JUMPING (2)
STAMINA (2)
INTELLIGENCE (4)
TECHNIQUE (3)
SPEED (3)

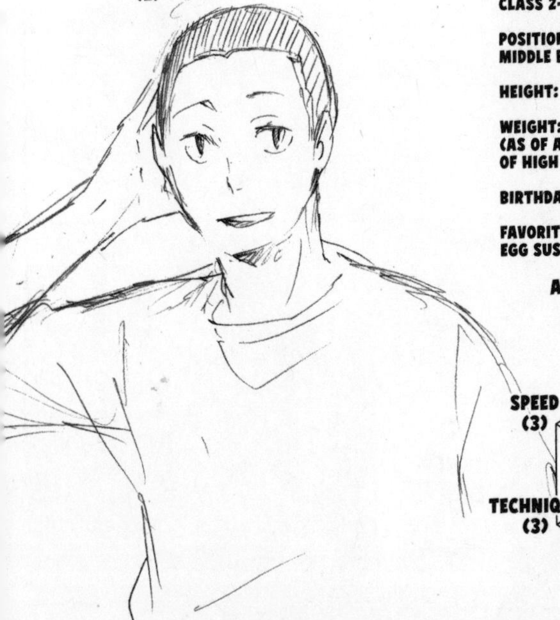

CHAPTER 28: A Monster and His Club

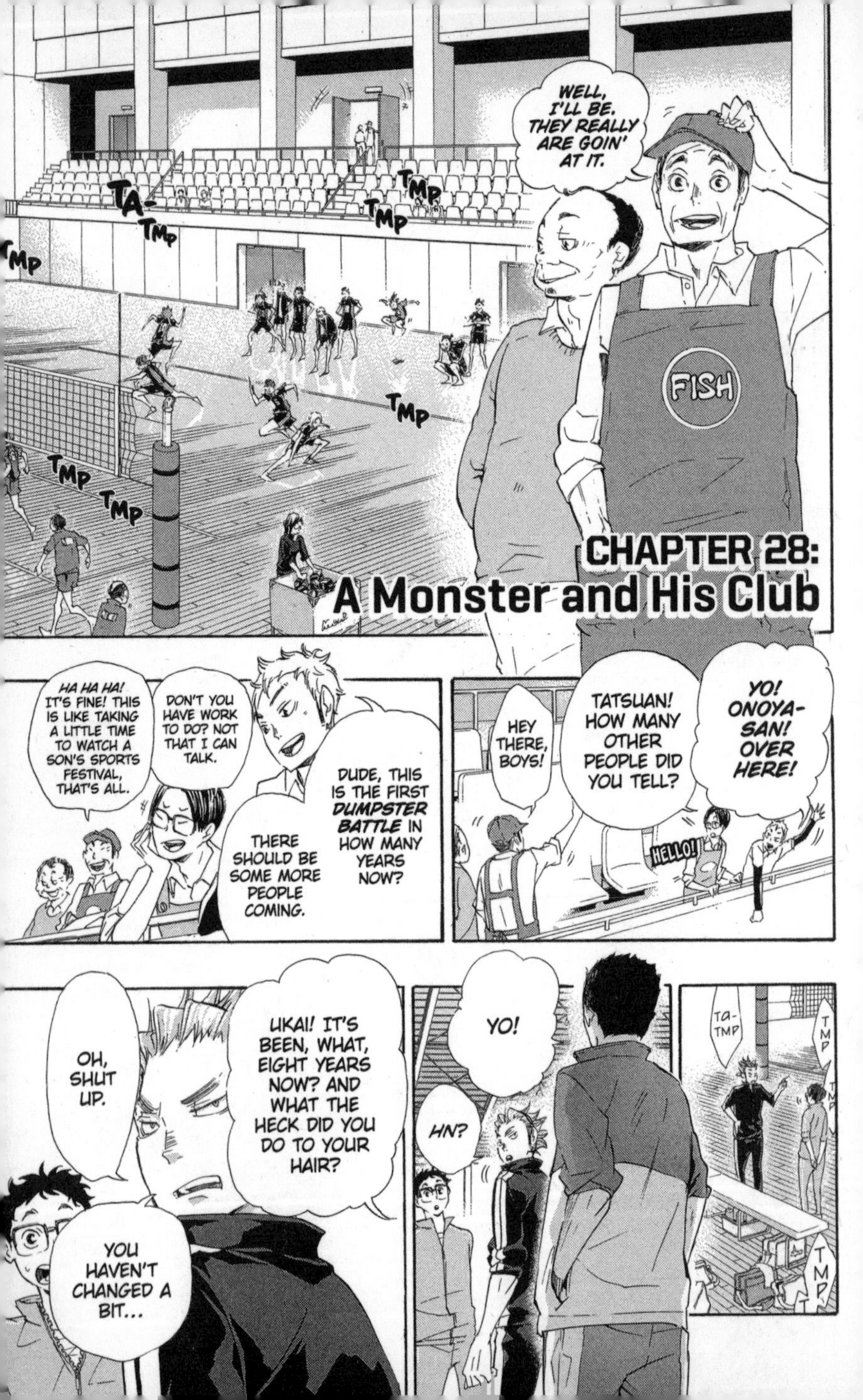

WELL, I'LL BE. THEY REALLY ARE GOIN' AT IT.
TMP
TMP
TA-TMP
TMP
TMP
TMP
TMP
YO! ONOYA-SAN! OVER HERE!
TATSUAN! HOW MANY OTHER PEOPLE DID YOU TELL?
HEY THERE, BOYS!
HELLO!
DUDE, THIS IS THE FIRST DUMPSTER BATTLE IN HOW MANY YEARS NOW?
THERE SHOULD BE SOME MORE PEOPLE COMING.
DON'T YOU HAVE WORK TO DO? NOT THAT I CAN TALK.
HA HA HA! IT'S FINE! THIS IS LIKE TAKING A LITTLE TIME TO WATCH A SON'S SPORTS FESTIVAL, THAT'S ALL.
TA-TMP
TMP
TMP
TMP
YO!
HN?
UKAI! IT'S BEEN, WHAT, EIGHT YEARS NOW? AND WHAT THE HECK DID YOU DO TO YOUR HAIR?
OH, SHUT UP.
YOU HAVEN'T CHANGED A BIT...

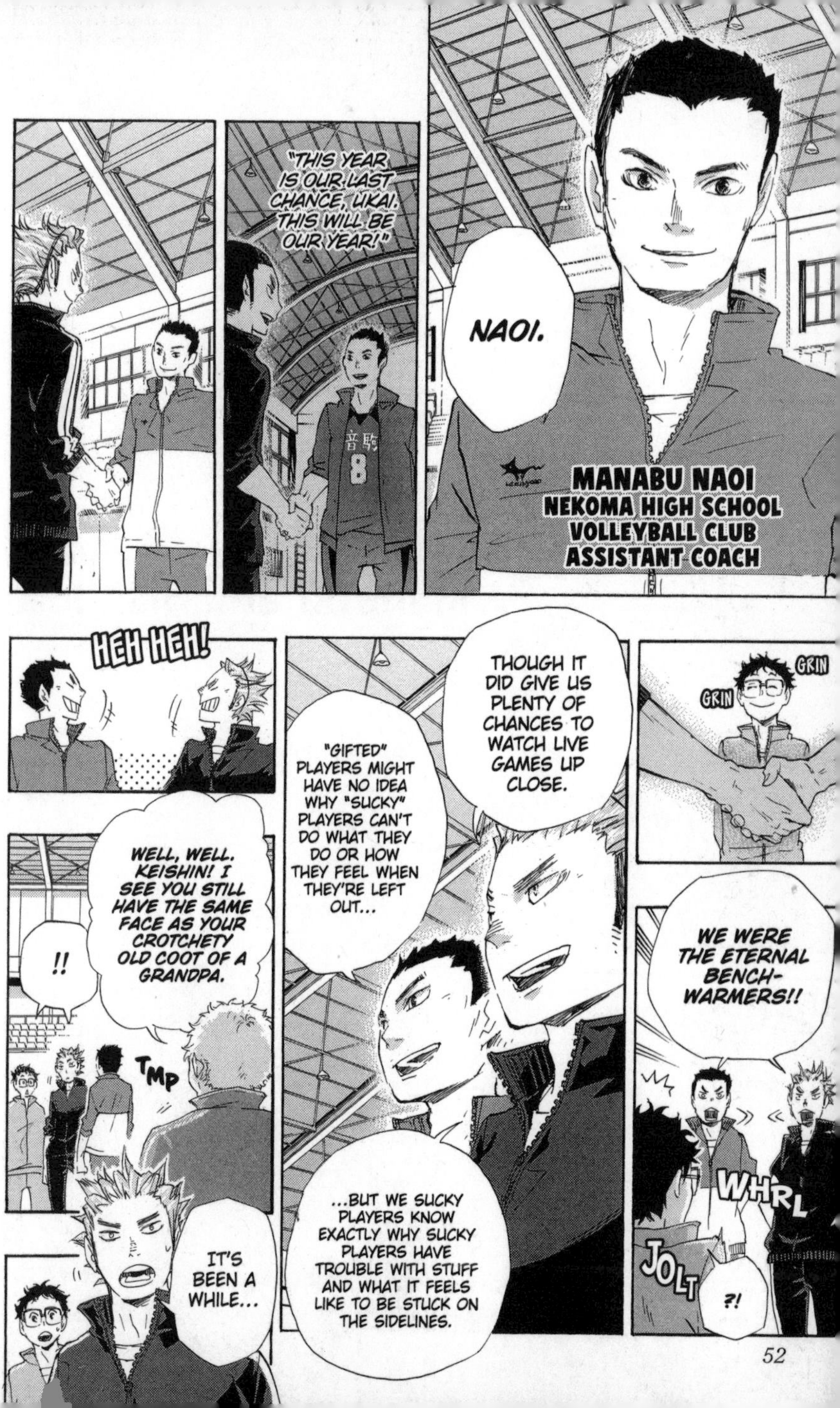
NAOI.
MANABU NAOI
NEKOMA HIGH SCHOOL
VOLLEYBALL CLUB
ASSISTANT COACH
"THIS YEAR IS OUR LAST CHANCE, UKAI. THIS WILL BE OUR YEAR!"
GRIN
GRIN
WE WERE THE ETERNAL BENCH-WARMERS!!
WHRL
JOLT
?!
THOUGH IT DID GIVE US PLENTY OF CHANCES TO WATCH LIVE GAMES UP CLOSE.
"GIFTED" PLAYERS MIGHT HAVE NO IDEA WHY "SUCKY" PLAYERS CAN'T DO WHAT THEY DO OR HOW THEY FEEL WHEN THEY'RE LEFT OUT...
...BUT WE SUCKY PLAYERS KNOW EXACTLY WHY SUCKY PLAYERS HAVE TROUBLE WITH STUFF AND WHAT IT FEELS LIKE TO BE STUCK ON THE SIDELINES.
HEH HEH!
WELL, WELL. KEISHIN! I SEE YOU STILL HAVE THE SAME FACE AS YOUR CROTCHETY OLD COOT OF A GRANDPA.
!!
TMP
IT'S BEEN A WHILE...

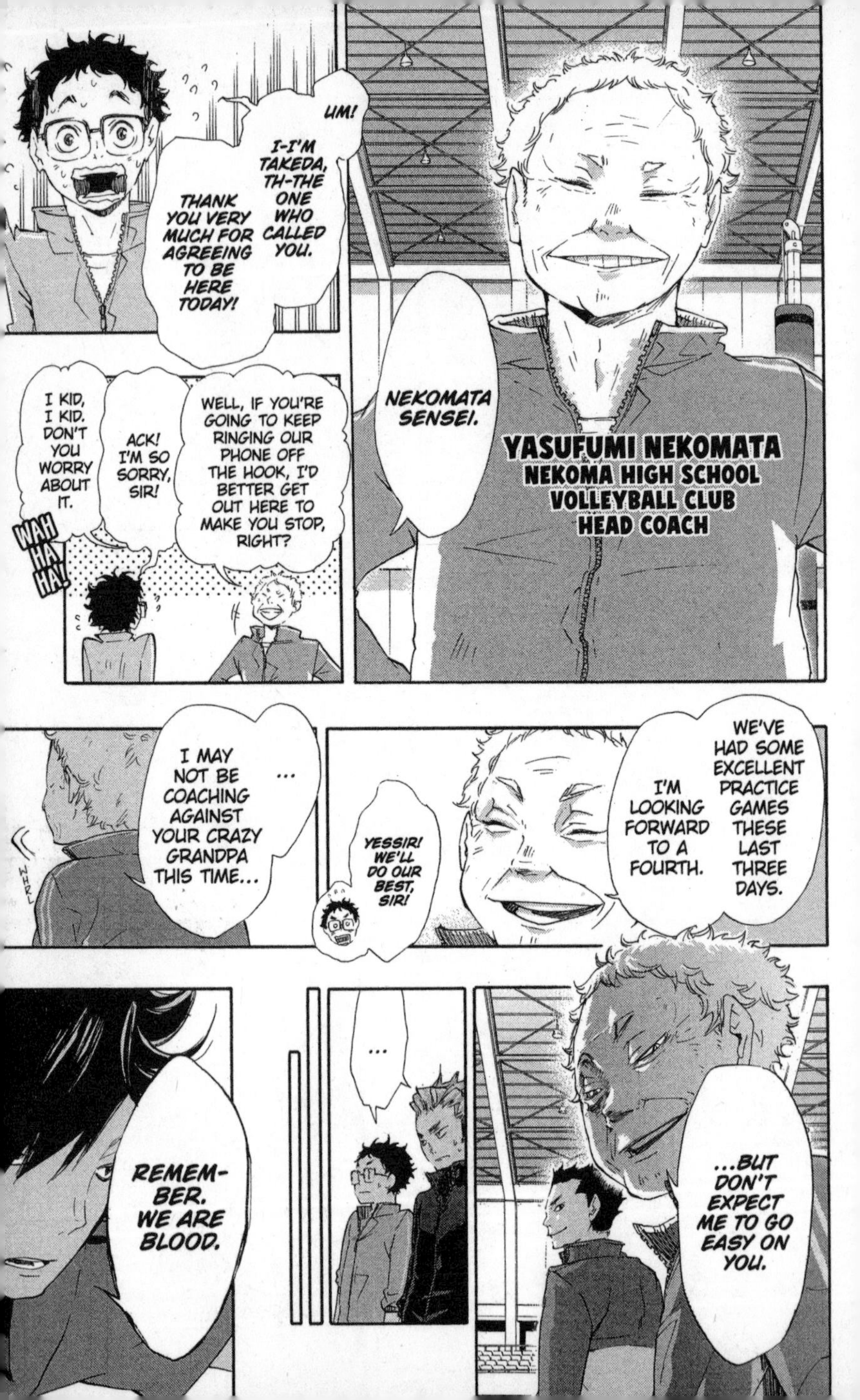
NEKOMATA SENSEI.
YASUFUMI NEKOMATA NEKOMA HIGH SCHOOL VOLLEYBALL CLUB HEAD COACH
UM!
I-I'M TAKEDA, TH-THE ONE WHO CALLED YOU.
THANK YOU VERY MUCH FOR AGREEING TO BE HERE TODAY!
WELL, IF YOU'RE GOING TO KEEP RINGING OUR PHONE OFF THE HOOK, I'D BETTER GET OUT HERE TO MAKE YOU STOP, RIGHT?
ACK! I'M SO SORRY, SIR!
I KID, I KID. DON'T YOU WORRY ABOUT IT.
WAH HA HA!
WE'VE HAD SOME EXCELLENT PRACTICE GAMES THESE LAST THREE DAYS.
I'M LOOKING FORWARD TO A FOURTH.
YESSIR! WE'LL DO OUR BEST, SIR!
...
I MAY NOT BE COACHING AGAINST YOUR CRAZY GRANDPA THIS TIME...
WHRL
...BUT DON'T EXPECT ME TO GO EASY ON YOU.
...
REMEM-BER. WE ARE BLOOD.

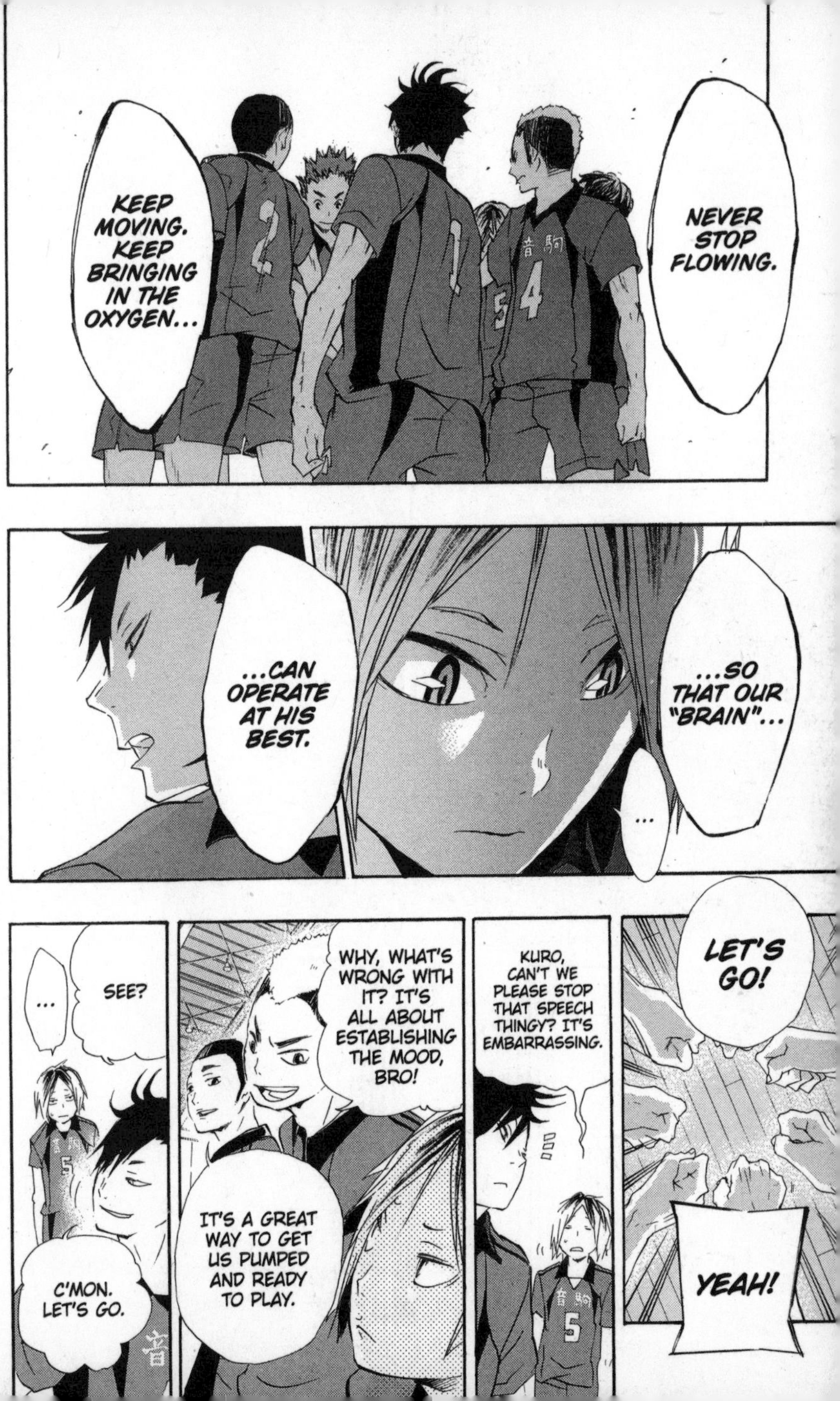
NEVER STOP FLOWING.
KEEP MOVING. KEEP BRINGING IN THE OXYGEN...
...SO THAT OUR "BRAIN"...
...
...CAN OPERATE AT HIS BEST.
LET'S GO!
YEAH!
KURO, CAN'T WE PLEASE STOP THAT SPEECH THINGY? IT'S EMBARRASSING.
WHY, WHAT'S WRONG WITH IT? IT'S ALL ABOUT ESTABLISHING THE MOOD, BRO!
IT'S A GREAT WAY TO GET US PUMPED AND READY TO PLAY.
SEE?
...
C'MON. LET'S GO.

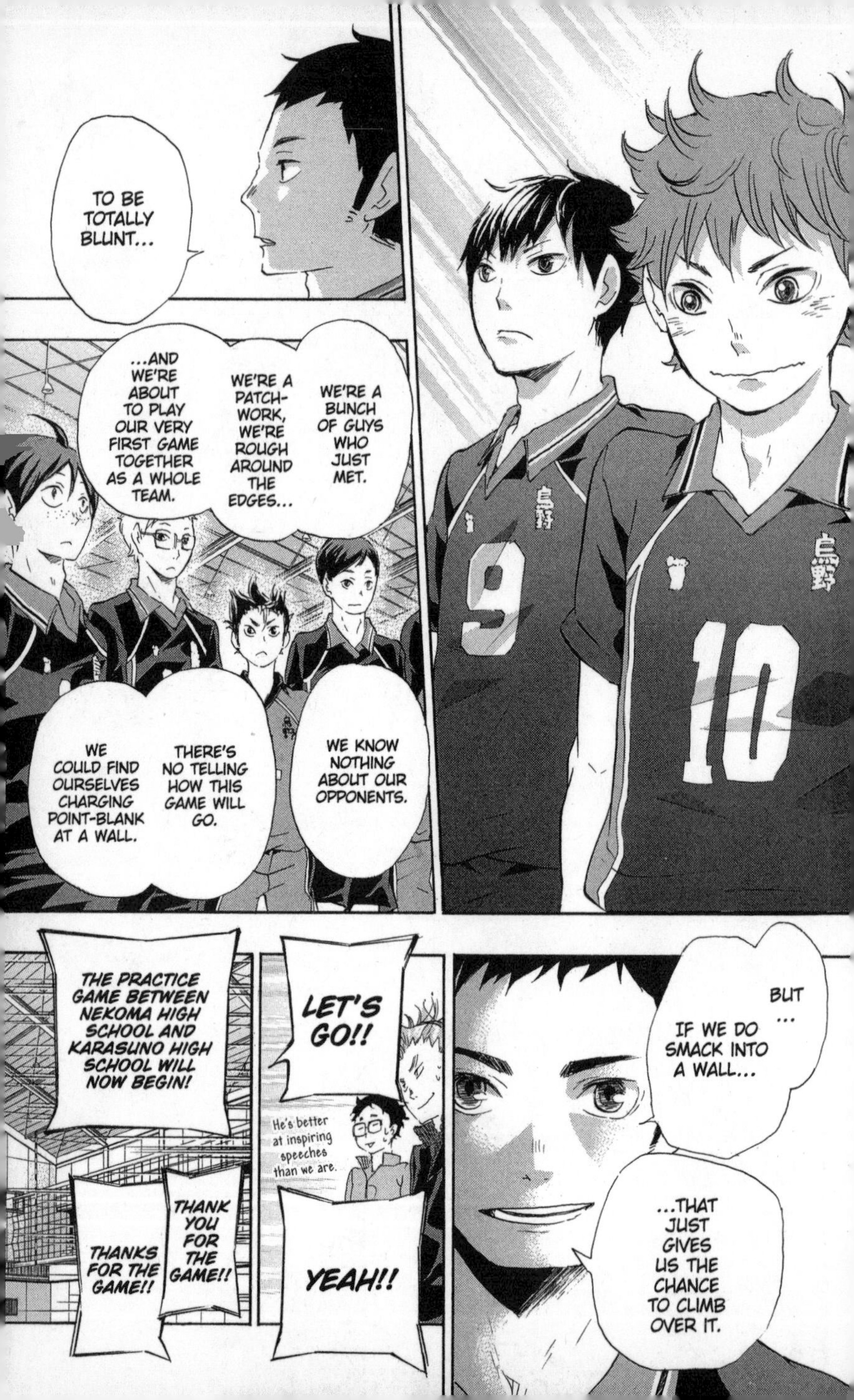
TO BE TOTALLY BLUNT...
WE'RE A BUNCH OF GUYS WHO JUST MET.
WE'RE A PATCHWORK, WE'RE ROUGH AROUND THE EDGES...
...AND WE'RE ABOUT TO PLAY OUR VERY FIRST GAME TOGETHER AS A WHOLE TEAM.
WE KNOW NOTHING ABOUT OUR OPPONENTS.
THERE'S NO TELLING HOW THIS GAME WILL GO.
WE COULD FIND OURSELVES CHARGING POINT-BLANK AT A WALL.
BUT...
IF WE DO SMACK INTO A WALL...
...THAT JUST GIVES US THE CHANCE TO CLIMB OVER IT.
LET'S GO!!
He's better at inspiring speeches than we are.
YEAH!!
THE PRACTICE GAME BETWEEN NEKOMA HIGH SCHOOL AND KARASUNO HIGH SCHOOL WILL NOW BEGIN!
THANK YOU FOR THE GAME!!
THANKS FOR THE GAME!!

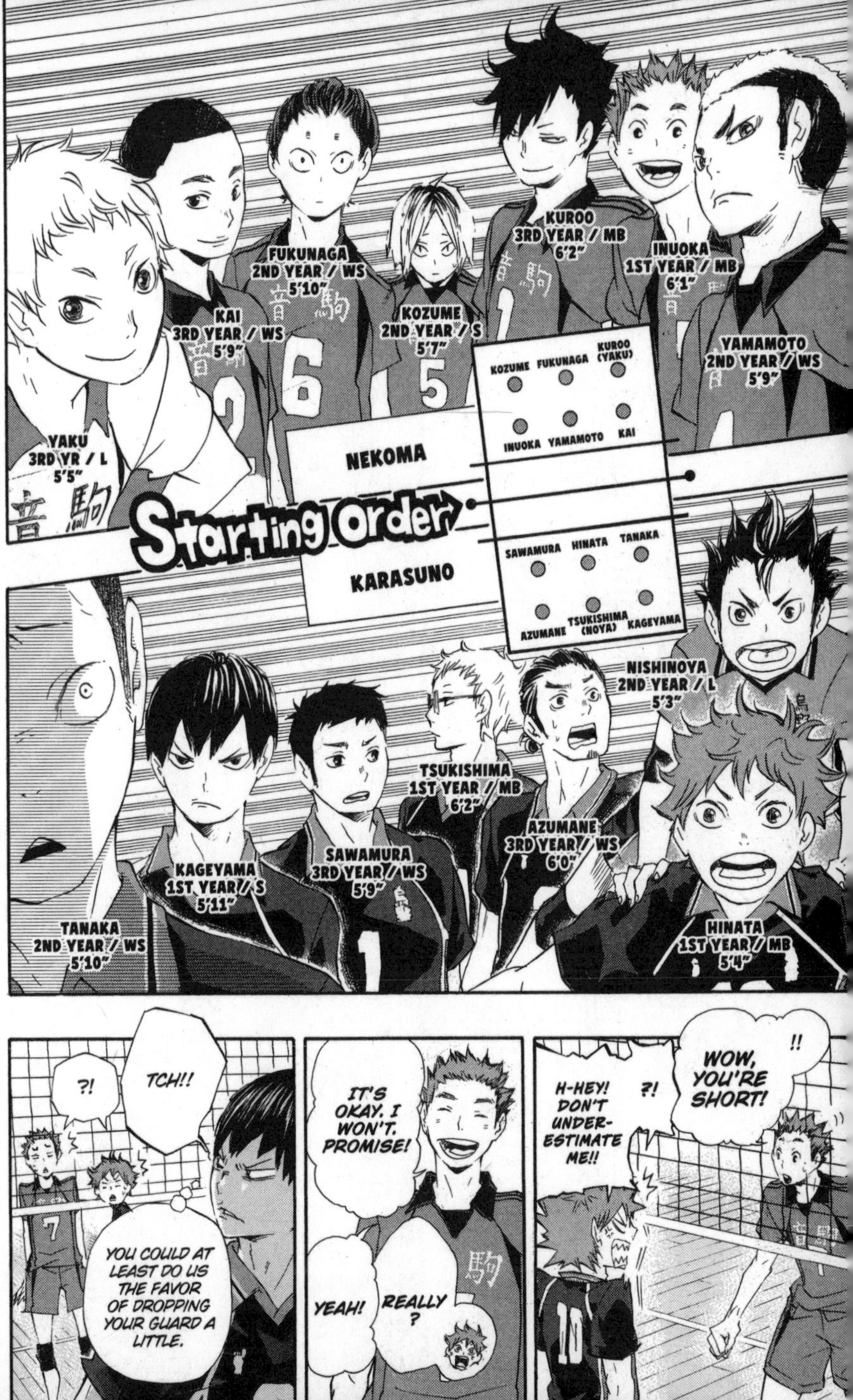
YAMAMOTO
2ND YEAR / WS
5'9"
INUOKA
1ST YEAR / MB
6'1"
KUROO
3RD YEAR / MB
6'2"
KOZUME
2ND YEAR / S
5'7"
FUKUNAGA
2ND YEAR / WS
5'10"
KAI
3RD YEAR / WS
5'9"
YAKU
3RD YR / L
5'5"
Starting Order
NEKOMA
KOZUME FUKUNAGA KUROO (YAKU)
INUOKA YAMAMOTO KAI
KARASUNO
SAWAMURA HINATA TANAKA
AZUMANE TSUKISHIMA (NOYA) KAGEYAMA
NISHINOYA
2ND YEAR / L
5'3"
TSUKISHIMA
1ST YEAR / MB
6'2"
AZUMANE
3RD YEAR / WS
6'0"
HINATA
1ST YEAR / MB
5'4"
SAWAMURA
3RD YEAR / WS
5'9"
KAGEYAMA
1ST YEAR / S
5'11"
TANAKA
2ND YEAR / WS
5'10"
!!
WOW, YOU'RE SHORT!
?!
H-HEY! DON'T UNDER-ESTIMATE ME!!
IT'S OKAY. I WON'T. PROMISE!
REALLY?
YEAH!
TCH!!
?!
YOU COULD AT LEAST DO US THE FAVOR OF DROPPING YOUR GUARD A LITTLE.

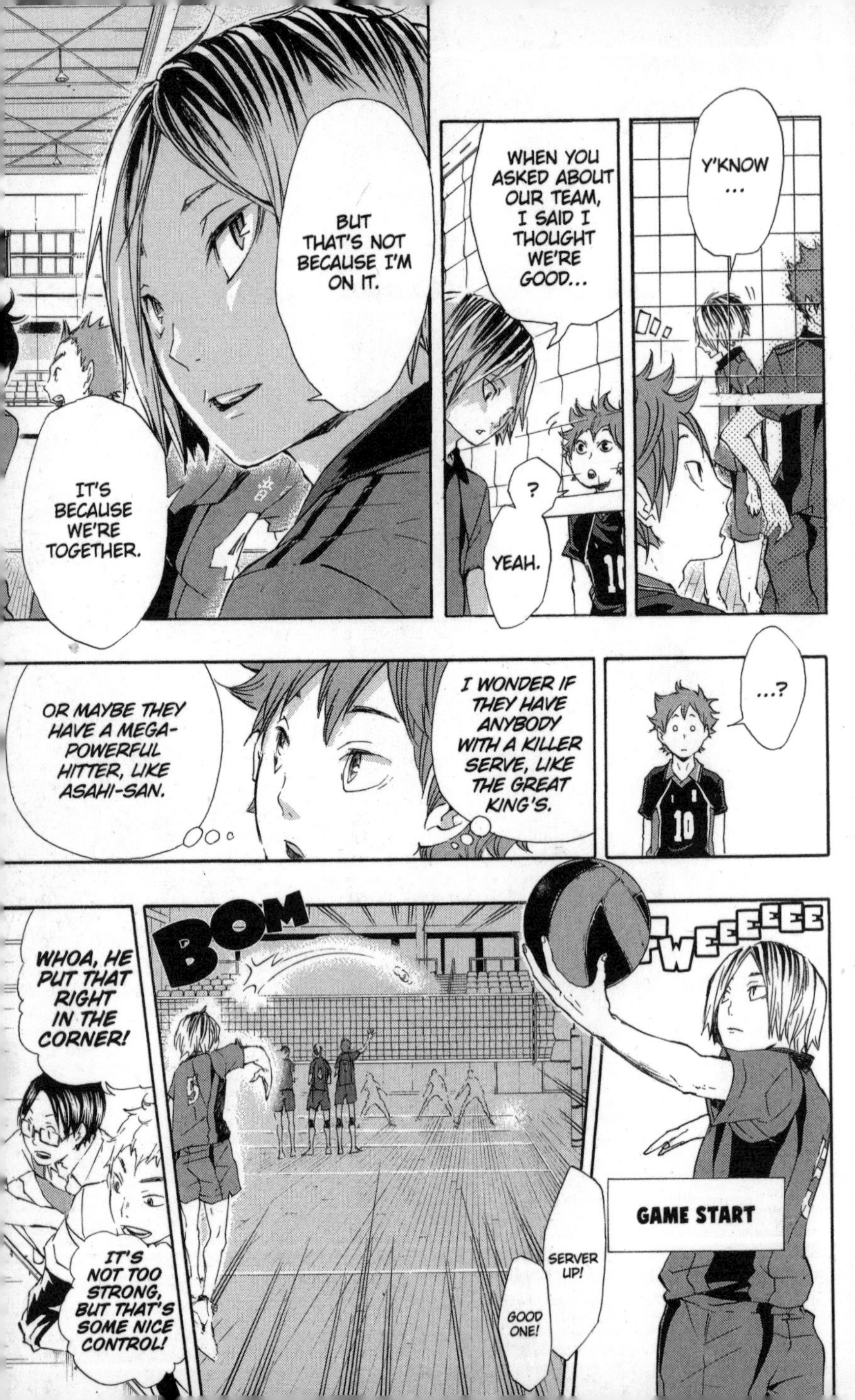
Y'KNOW ...
WHEN YOU ASKED ABOUT OUR TEAM, I SAID I THOUGHT WE'RE GOOD...
?
YEAH.
BUT THAT'S NOT BECAUSE I'M ON IT.
IT'S BECAUSE WE'RE TOGETHER.
...?
I WONDER IF THEY HAVE ANYBODY WITH A KILLER SERVE, LIKE THE GREAT KING'S.
OR MAYBE THEY HAVE A MEGA-POWERFUL HITTER, LIKE ASAHI-SAN.
TWEEEEEE
GAME START
SERVER UP!
GOOD ONE!
BOM
WHOA, HE PUT THAT RIGHT IN THE CORNER!
IT'S NOT TOO STRONG, BUT THAT'S SOME NICE CONTROL!

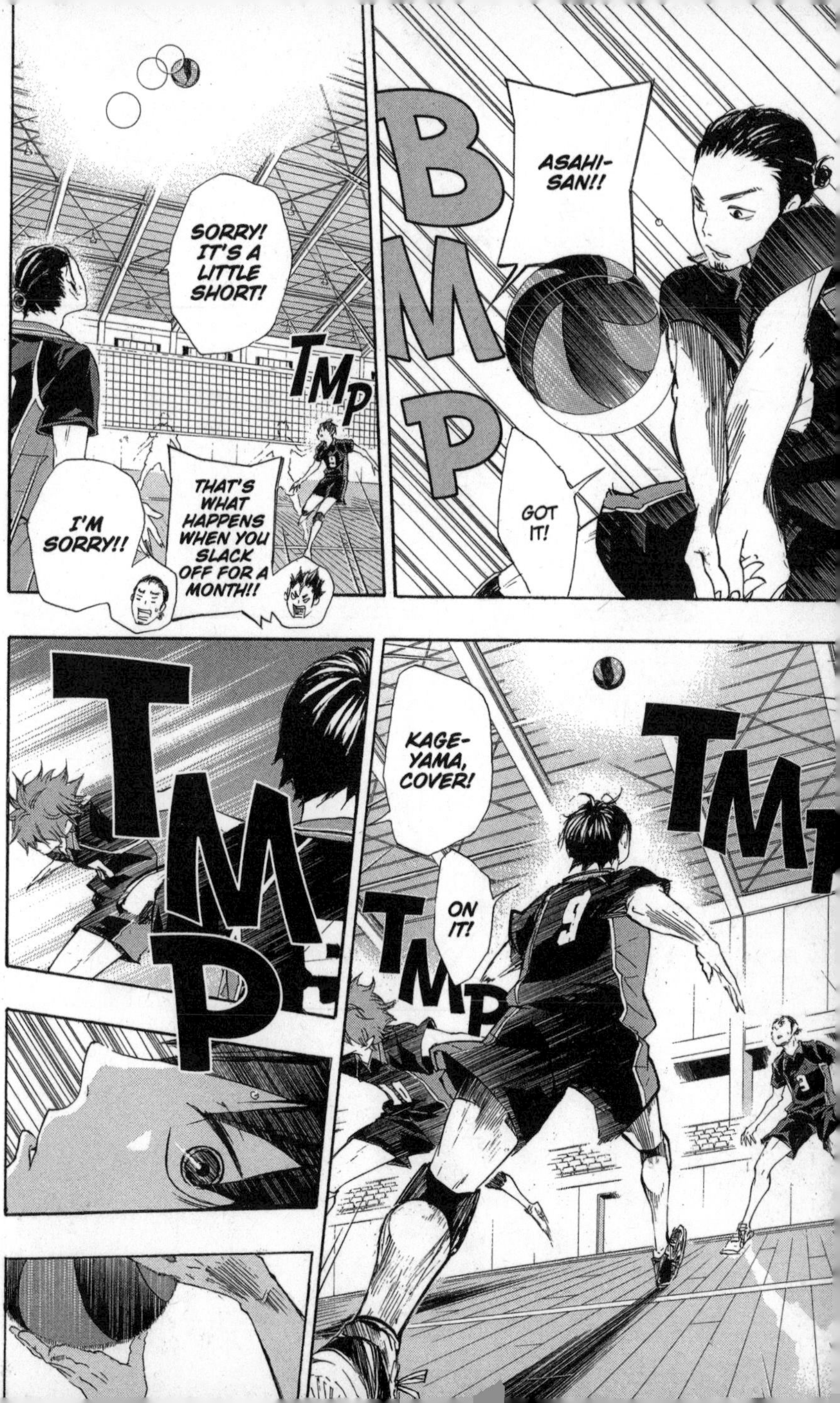
ASAHI-SAN!!
BMP
GOT IT!
SORRY! IT'S A LITTLE SHORT!
TMP
THAT'S WHAT HAPPENS WHEN YOU SLACK OFF FOR A MONTH!!
I'M SORRY!!
TM
KAGE-YAMA, COVER!
ON IT!
TMP
TMP

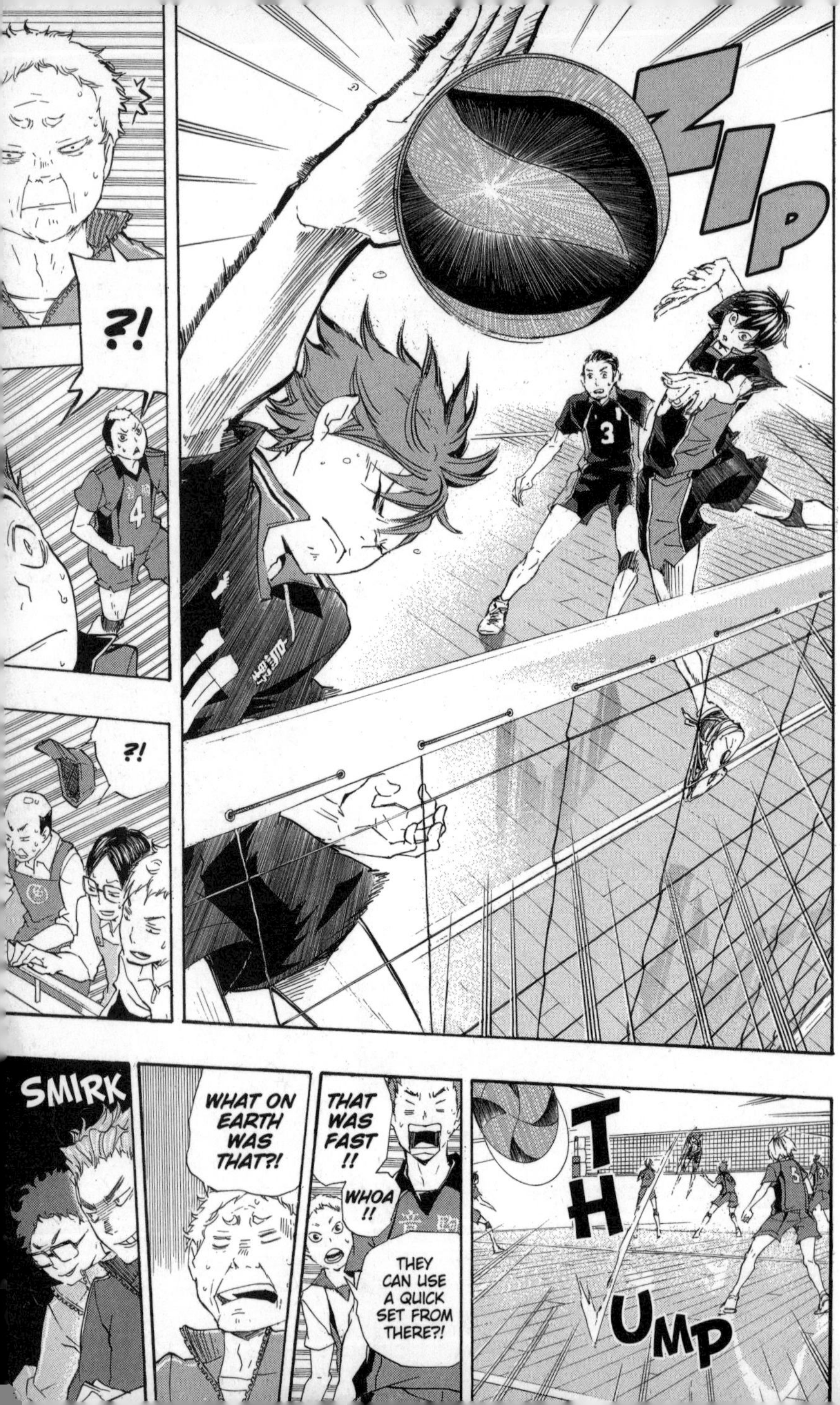
ZIP
?!
?!
THUMP
THAT WAS FAST!!
WHOA!!
THEY CAN USE A QUICK SET FROM THERE?!
WHAT ON EARTH WAS THAT?!
SMIRK

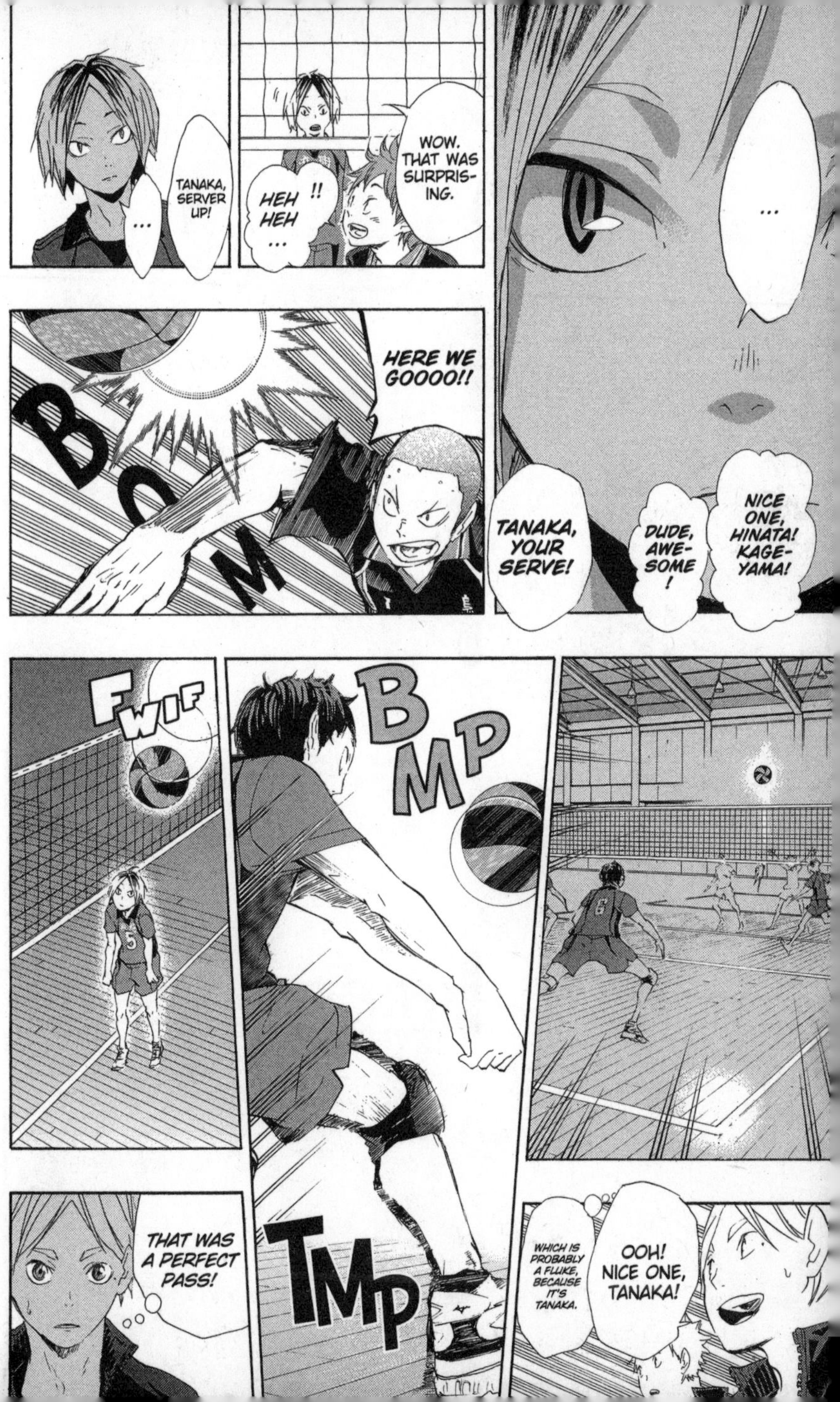
...
NICE ONE, HINATA! KAGEYAMA!
DUDE, AWESOME!
TANAKA, YOUR SERVE!
WOW. THAT WAS SURPRISING.
HEH HEH... !!
TANAKA, SERVER UP!
...
HERE WE GOOOO!!
BOOM
BMP
FWIF
OOH! NICE ONE, TANAKA!
WHICH IS PROBABLY A FLUKE, BECAUSE IT'S TANAKA.
TMP
THAT WAS A PERFECT PASS!

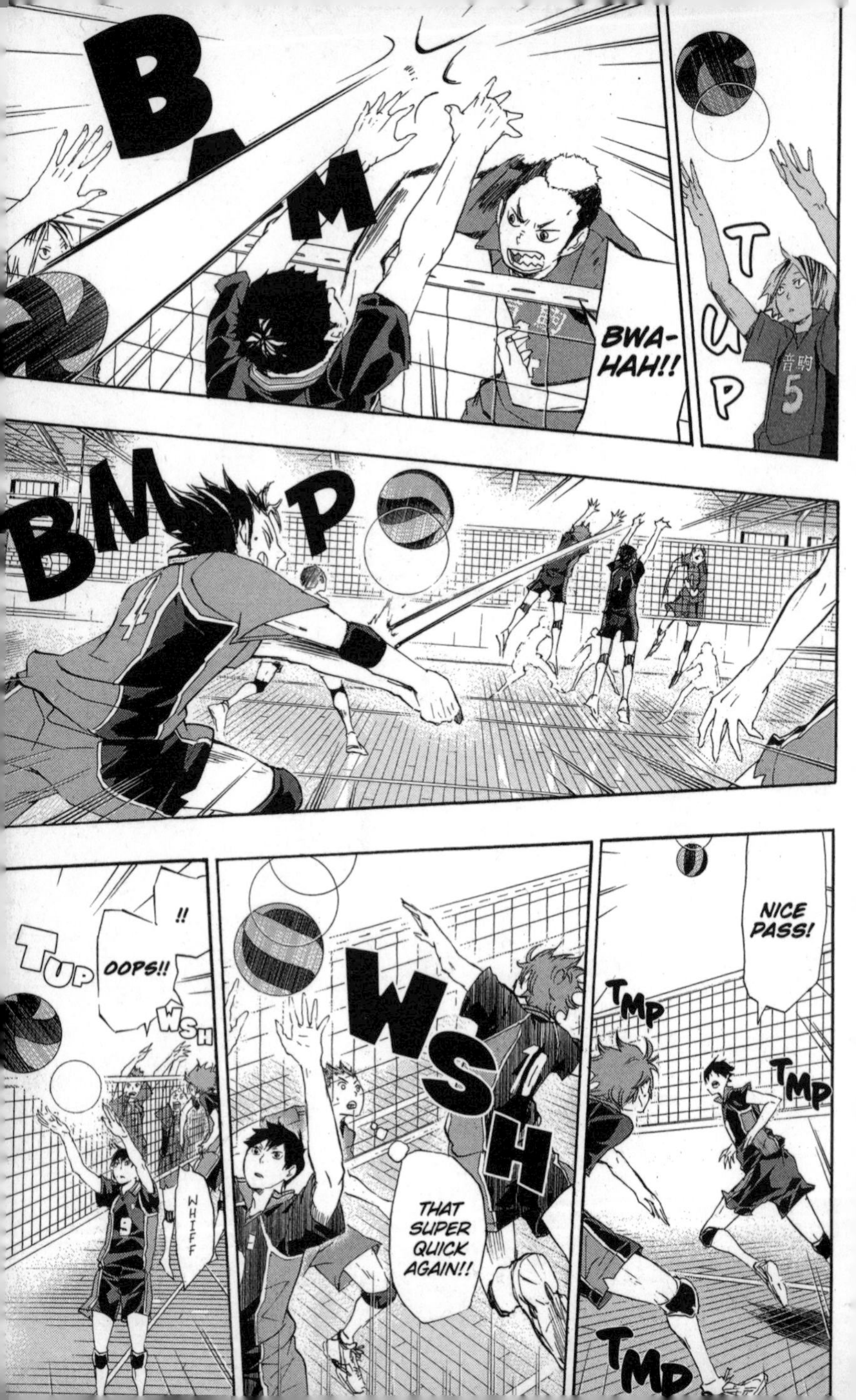
TUP
BWA-HAH!!
BAM
BMP
NICE PASS!
TMP
TMP
TMP
WSH
THAT SUPER QUICK AGAIN!!
!!
OOPS!!
TUP
WSH
WHIFF

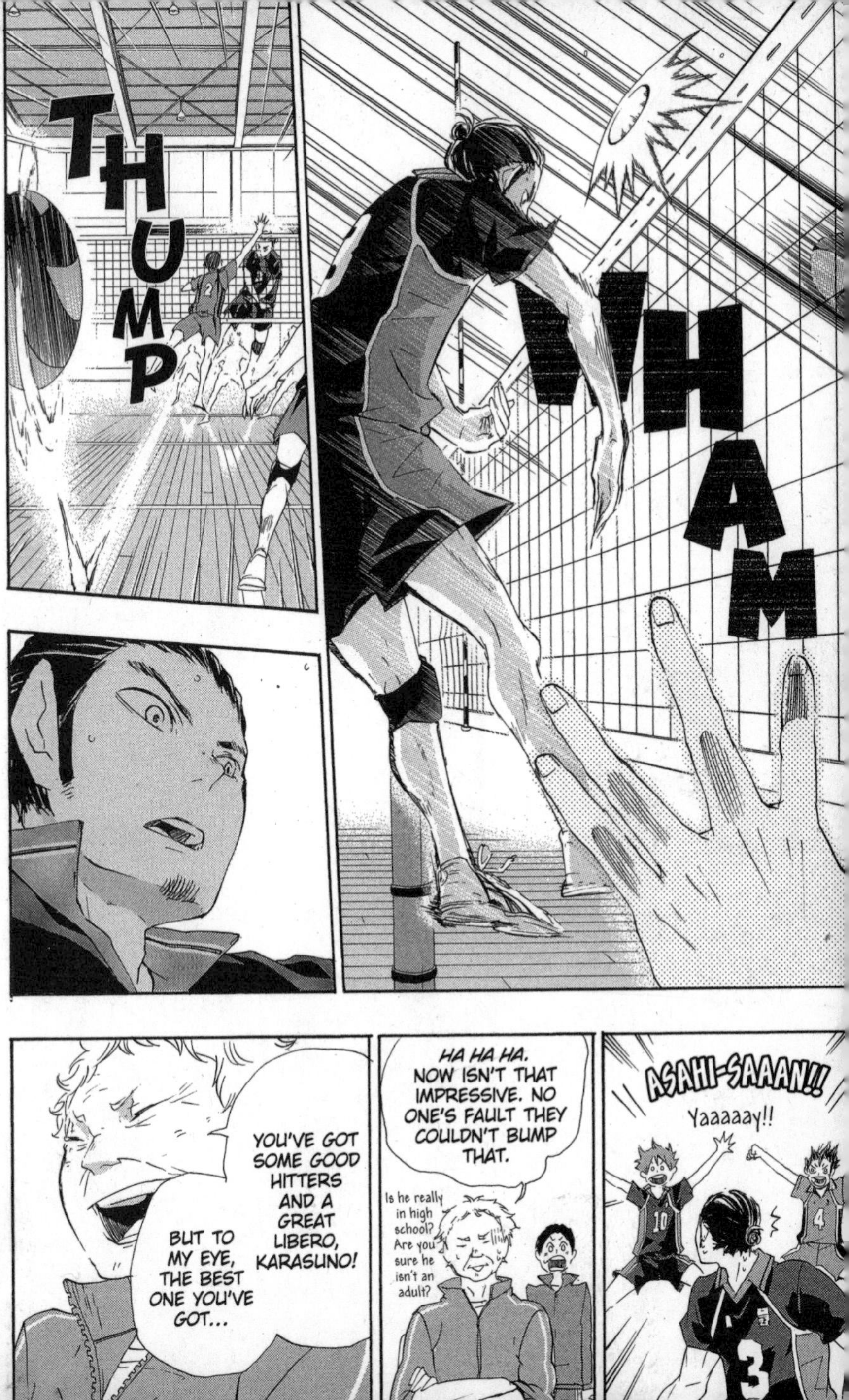
WHAM
THUMP
ASAHI-SAAAN!!
Yaaaaay!!
HA HA HA. NOW ISN'T THAT IMPRESSIVE. NO ONE'S FAULT THEY COULDN'T BUMP THAT.
Is he really in high school? Are you sure he isn't an adult?
YOU'VE GOT SOME GOOD HITTERS AND A GREAT LIBERO, KARASUNO!
BUT TO MY EYE, THE BEST ONE YOU'VE GOT...

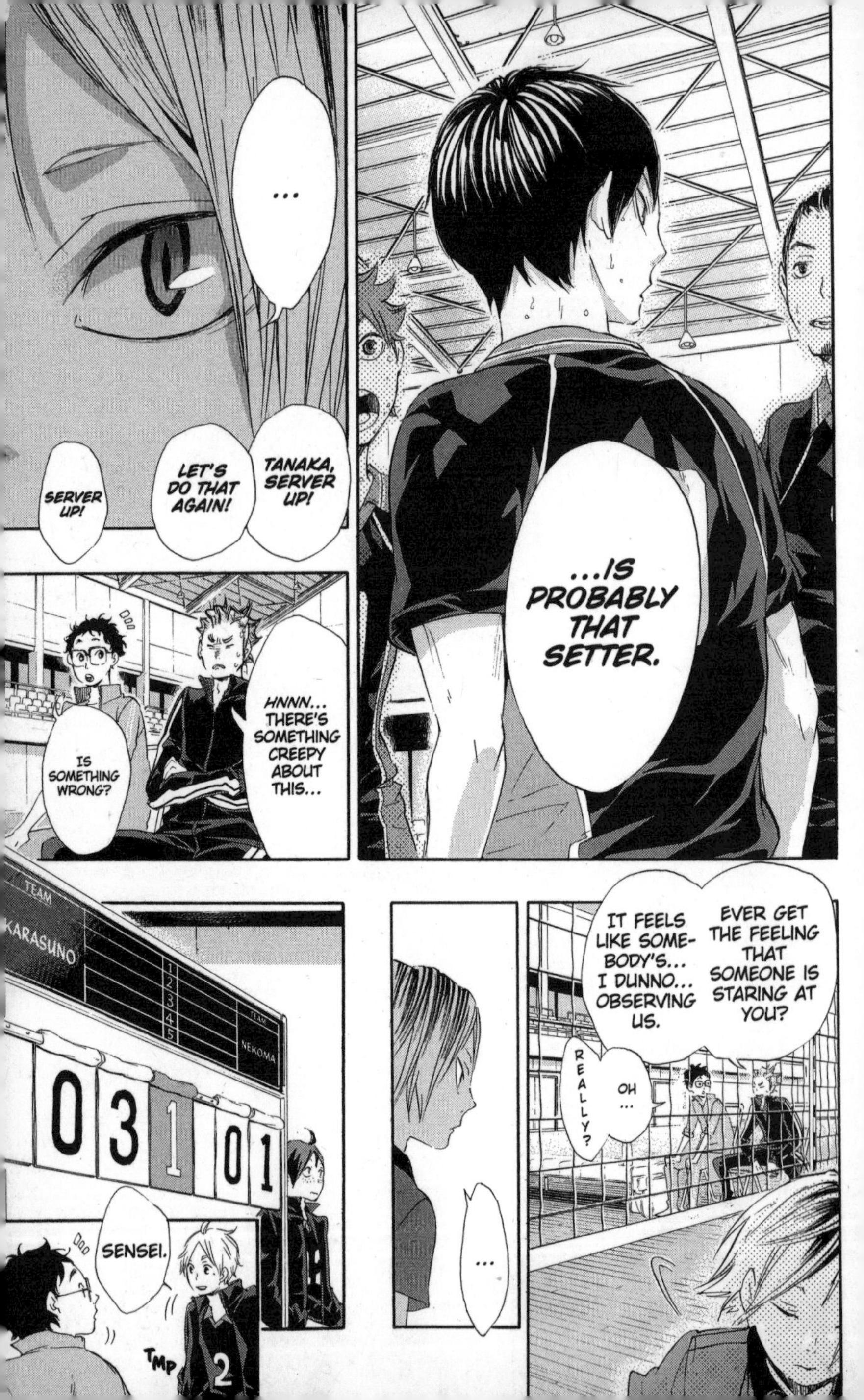
...IS PROBABLY THAT SETTER.
...
TANAKA, SERVER UP!
LET'S DO THAT AGAIN!
SERVER UP!
HNNN... THERE'S SOMETHING CREEPY ABOUT THIS...
IS SOMETHING WRONG?
EVER GET THE FEELING THAT SOMEONE IS STARING AT YOU?
IT FEELS LIKE SOME-BODY'S... I DUNNO... OBSERVING US.
OH...
REALLY?
...
TEAM
KARASUNO
1
2
3
4
5
TEAM
NEKOMA
03
1
01
SENSEI.
TMP
2

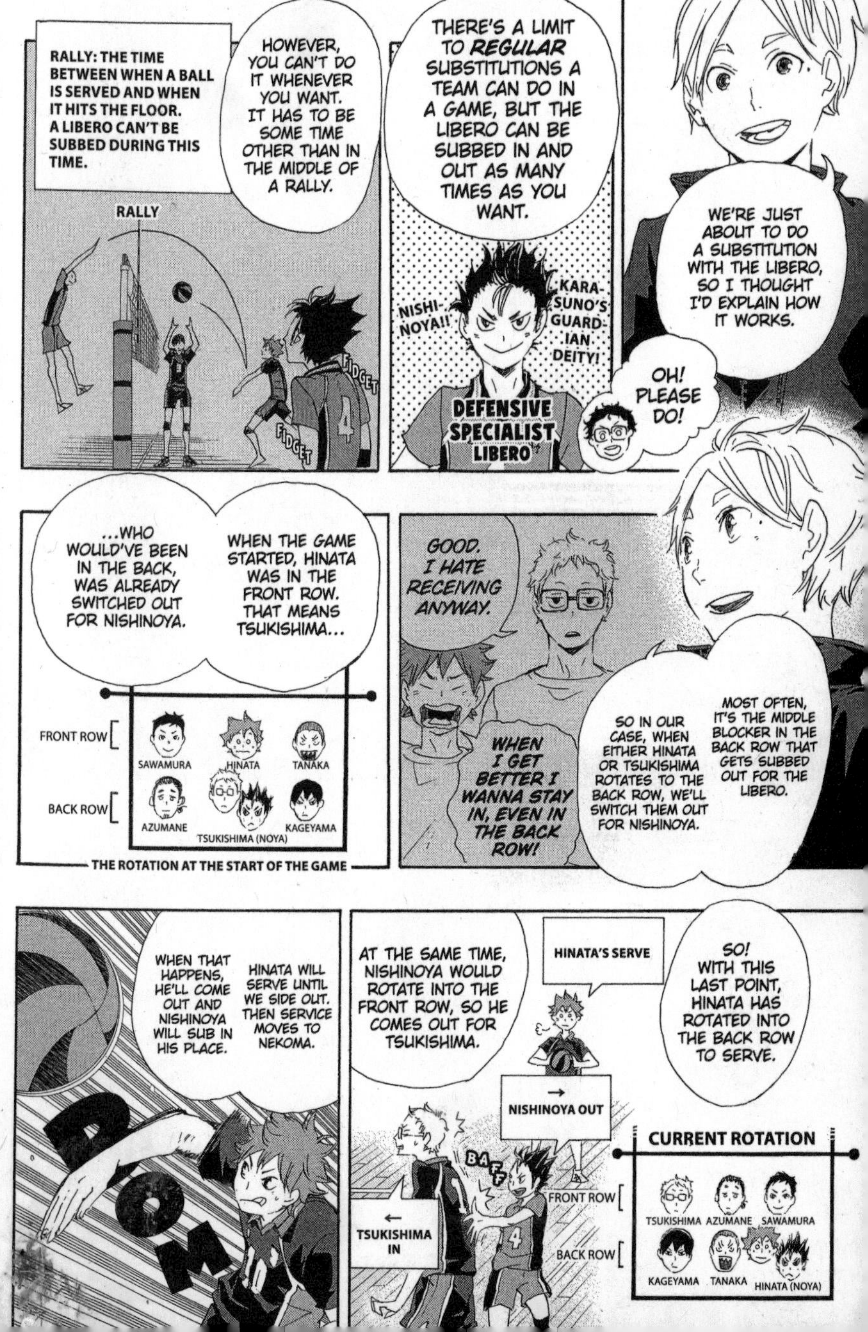
WE'RE JUST ABOUT TO DO A SUBSTITUTION WITH THE LIBERO, SO I THOUGHT I'D EXPLAIN HOW IT WORKS.
OH! PLEASE DO!
THERE'S A LIMIT TO REGULAR SUBSTITUTIONS A TEAM CAN DO IN A GAME, BUT THE LIBERO CAN BE SUBBED IN AND OUT AS MANY TIMES AS YOU WANT.
KARASUNO'S GUARDIAN DEITY!
NISHINOYA!!
DEFENSIVE SPECIALIST
LIBERO
HOWEVER, YOU CAN'T DO IT WHENEVER YOU WANT. IT HAS TO BE SOME TIME OTHER THAN IN THE MIDDLE OF A RALLY.
RALLY: THE TIME BETWEEN WHEN A BALL IS SERVED AND WHEN IT HITS THE FLOOR. A LIBERO CAN'T BE SUBBED DURING THIS TIME.
RALLY
FIDGET
FIDGET
MOST OFTEN, IT'S THE MIDDLE BLOCKER IN THE BACK ROW THAT GETS SUBBED OUT FOR THE LIBERO.
SO IN OUR CASE, WHEN EITHER HINATA OR TSUKISHIMA ROTATES TO THE BACK ROW, WE'LL SWITCH THEM OUT FOR NISHINOYA.
GOOD. I HATE RECEIVING ANYWAY.
WHEN I GET BETTER I WANNA STAY IN, EVEN IN THE BACK ROW!
WHEN THE GAME STARTED, HINATA WAS IN THE FRONT ROW. THAT MEANS TSUKISHIMA...
...WHO WOULD'VE BEEN IN THE BACK, WAS ALREADY SWITCHED OUT FOR NISHINOYA.
FRONT ROW
SAWAMURA
HINATA
TANAKA
BACK ROW
AZUMANE
TSUKISHIMA (NOYA)
KAGEYAMA
THE ROTATION AT THE START OF THE GAME
SO! WITH THIS LAST POINT, HINATA HAS ROTATED INTO THE BACK ROW TO SERVE.
CURRENT ROTATION
FRONT ROW
TSUKISHIMA
AZUMANE
SAWAMURA
BACK ROW
KAGEYAMA
TANAKA
HINATA (NOYA)
HINATA'S SERVE
AT THE SAME TIME, NISHINOYA WOULD ROTATE INTO THE FRONT ROW, SO HE COMES OUT FOR TSUKISHIMA.
→ NISHINOYA OUT
BAFF
← TSUKISHIMA IN
HINATA WILL SERVE UNTIL WE SIDE OUT. THEN SERVICE MOVES TO NEKOMA.
WHEN THAT HAPPENS, HE'LL COME OUT AND NISHINOYA WILL SUB IN HIS PLACE.

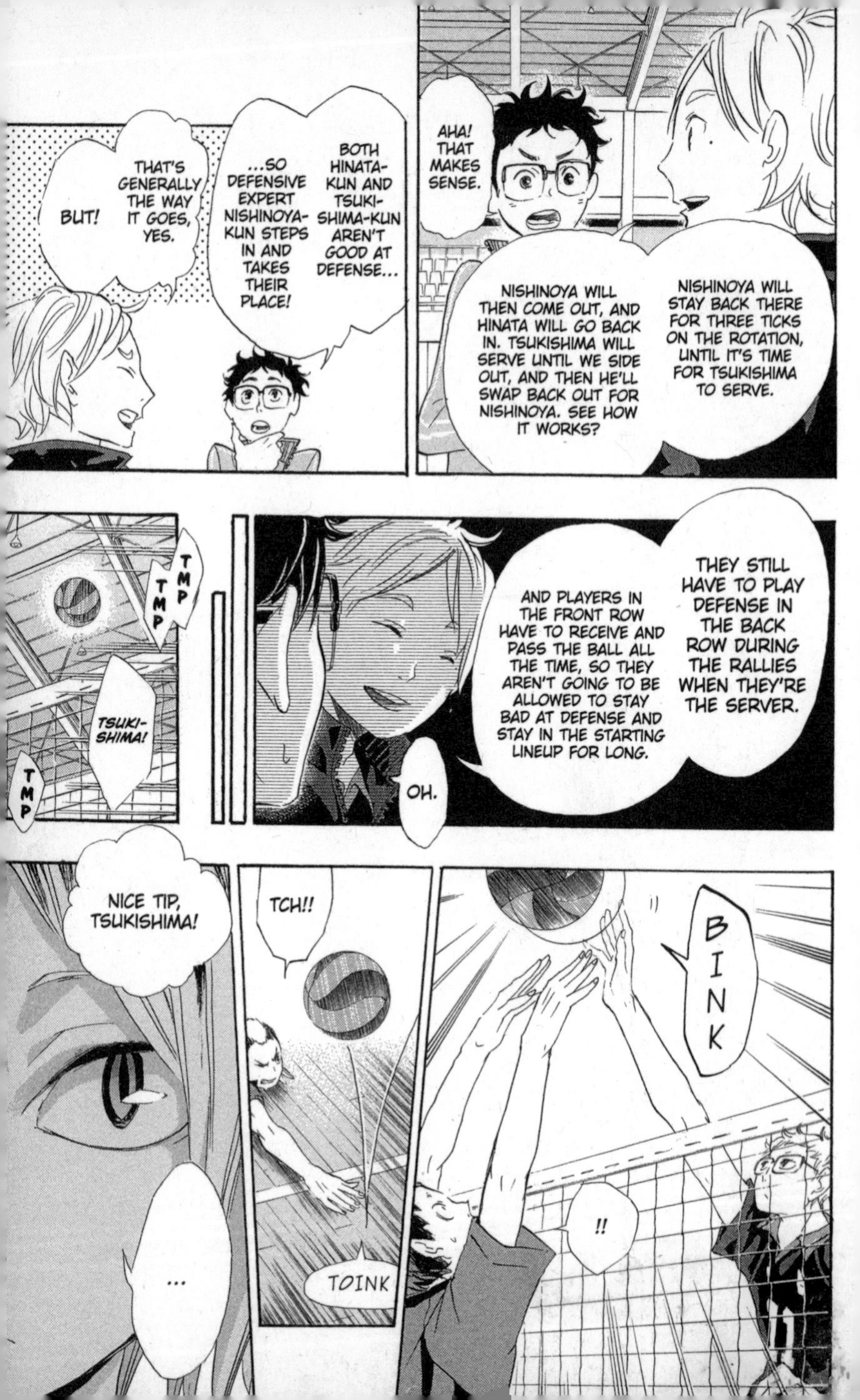
NISHINOYA WILL STAY BACK THERE FOR THREE TICKS ON THE ROTATION, UNTIL IT'S TIME FOR TSUKISHIMA TO SERVE.
NISHINOYA WILL THEN COME OUT, AND HINATA WILL GO BACK IN. TSUKISHIMA WILL SERVE UNTIL WE SIDE OUT, AND THEN HE'LL SWAP BACK OUT FOR NISHINOYA. SEE HOW IT WORKS?
AHA! THAT MAKES SENSE.
BOTH HINATA-KUN AND TSUKI-SHIMA-KUN AREN'T GOOD AT DEFENSE...
...SO DEFENSIVE EXPERT NISHINOYA-KUN STEPS IN AND TAKES THEIR PLACE!
THAT'S GENERALLY THE WAY IT GOES, YES.
BUT!
THEY STILL HAVE TO PLAY DEFENSE IN THE BACK ROW DURING THE RALLIES WHEN THEY'RE THE SERVER.
AND PLAYERS IN THE FRONT ROW HAVE TO RECEIVE AND PASS THE BALL ALL THE TIME, SO THEY AREN'T GOING TO BE ALLOWED TO STAY BAD AT DEFENSE AND STAY IN THE STARTING LINEUP FOR LONG.
OH.
TMP
TMP
TSUKI-SHIMA!
TMP
BINK
!!
TCH!!
TOINK
NICE TIP, TSUKISHIMA!
...

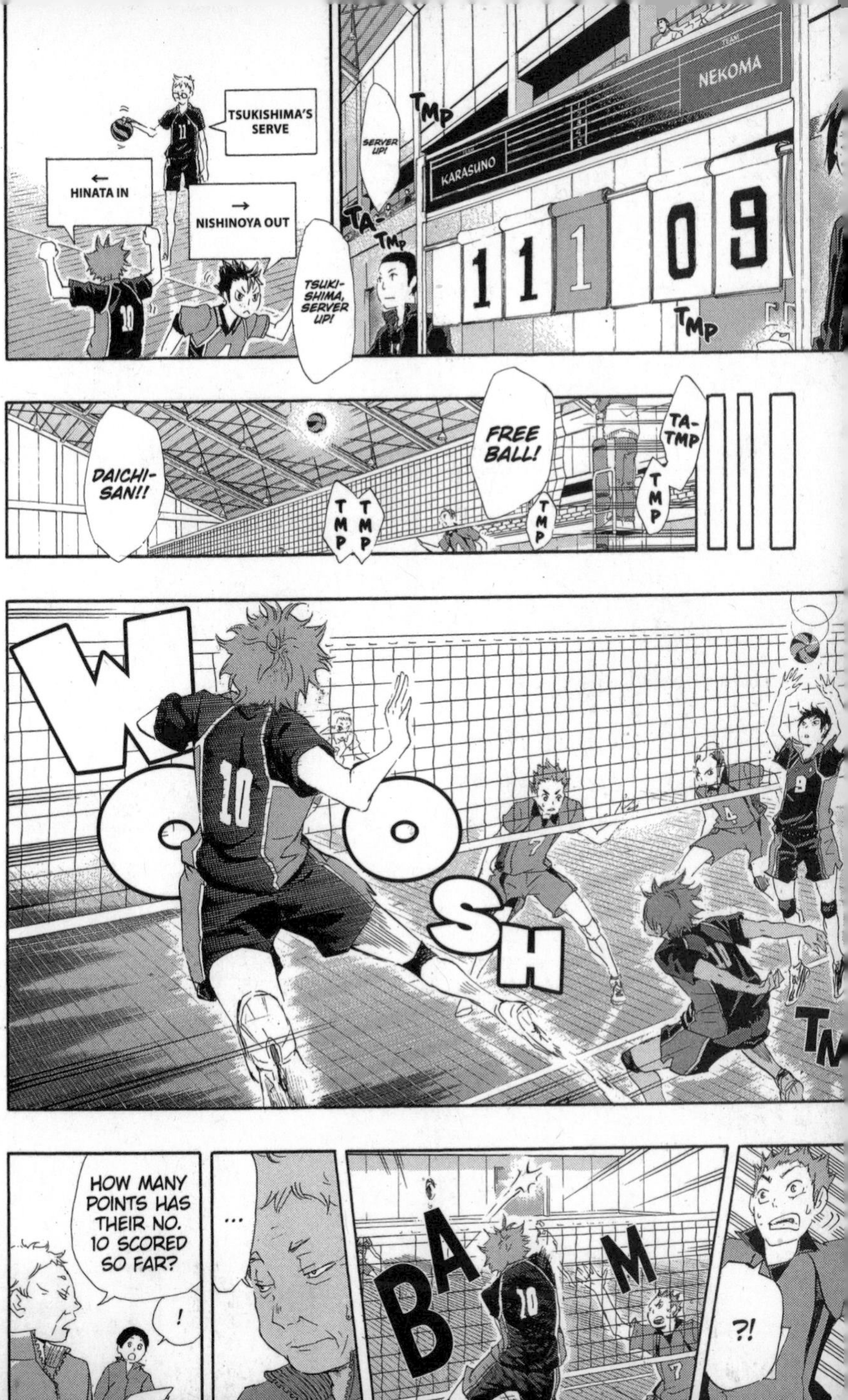
TMP
NEKOMA
KARASUNO
11
1
0
9
SERVER UP!
TA-TMP
TSUKISHIMA, SERVER UP!
TMP
TSUKISHIMA'S SERVE
→ NISHINOYA OUT
← HINATA IN
TA-TMP
TMP
FREE BALL!
TMP
TMP TMP
DAICHI-SAN!!
WOOSH
?!
BAM
...
HOW MANY POINTS HAS THEIR NO. 10 SCORED SO FAR?
!

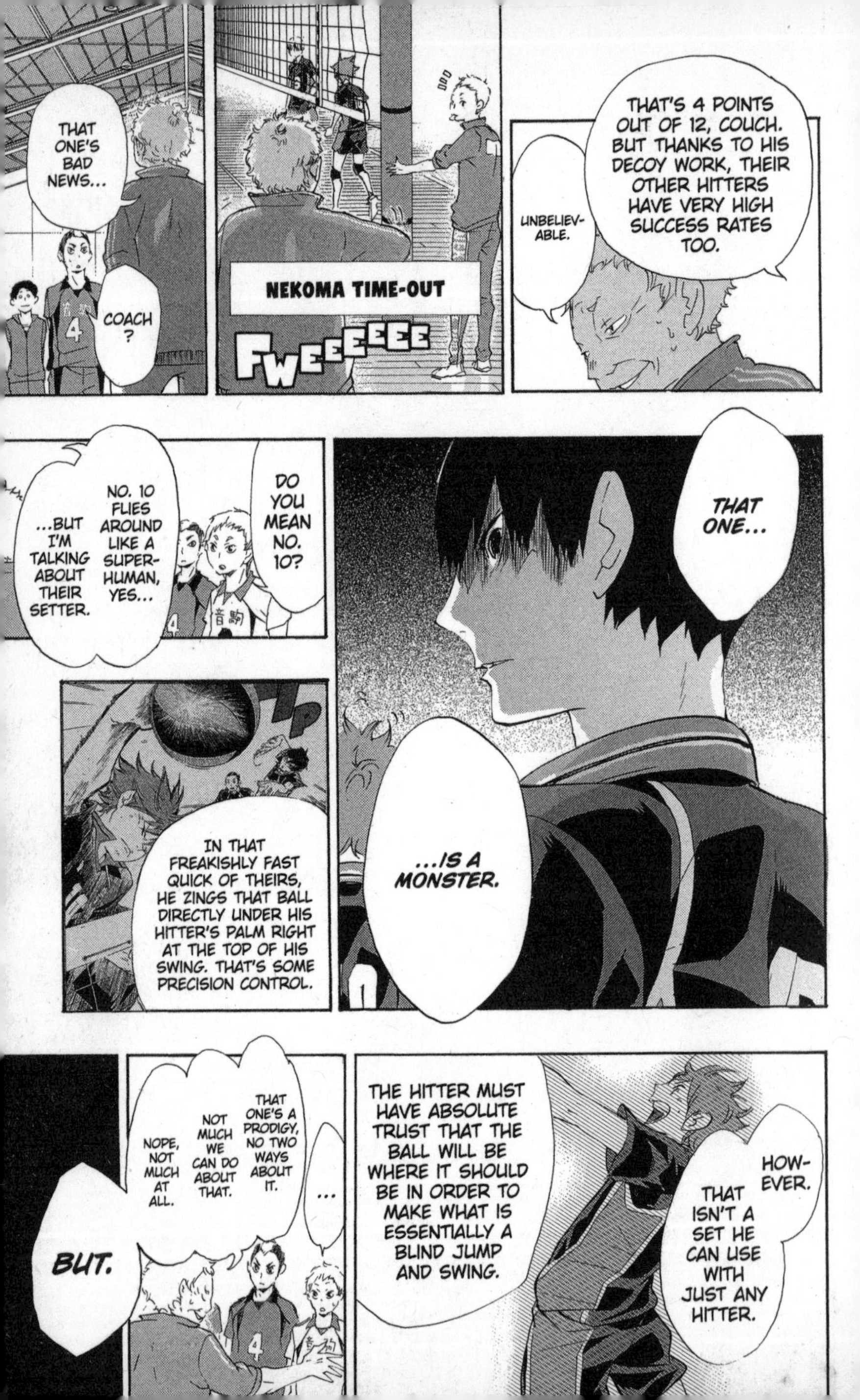
THAT'S 4 POINTS OUT OF 12, COUCH. BUT THANKS TO HIS DECOY WORK, THEIR OTHER HITTERS HAVE VERY HIGH SUCCESS RATES TOO.
UNBELIEV-ABLE.
NEKOMA TIME-OUT
FWEEEEEE
THAT ONE'S BAD NEWS...
COACH?
THAT ONE...
...IS A MONSTER.
DO YOU MEAN NO. 10?
NO. 10 FLIES AROUND LIKE A SUPER-HUMAN, YES...
...BUT I'M TALKING ABOUT THEIR SETTER.
IN THAT FREAKISHLY FAST QUICK OF THEIRS, HE ZINGS THAT BALL DIRECTLY UNDER HIS HITTER'S PALM RIGHT AT THE TOP OF HIS SWING. THAT'S SOME PRECISION CONTROL.
HOW-EVER.
THAT ISN'T A SET HE CAN USE WITH JUST ANY HITTER.
THE HITTER MUST HAVE ABSOLUTE TRUST THAT THE BALL WILL BE WHERE IT SHOULD BE IN ORDER TO MAKE WHAT IS ESSENTIALLY A BLIND JUMP AND SWING.
...
THAT ONE'S A PRODIGY, NO TWO WAYS ABOUT IT.
NOT MUCH WE CAN DO ABOUT THAT.
NOPE, NOT MUCH AT ALL.
BUT.

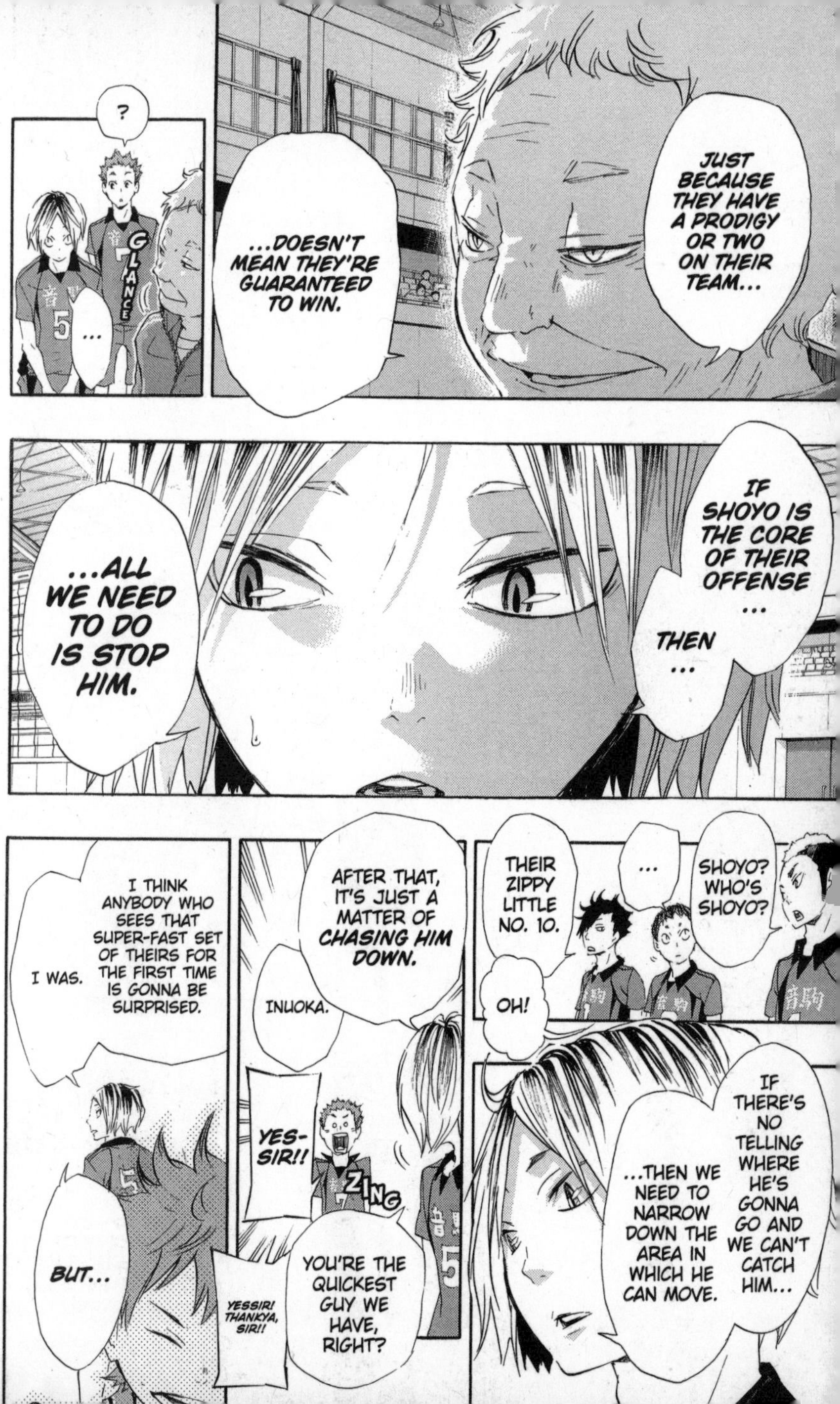
JUST BECAUSE THEY HAVE A PRODIGY OR TWO ON THEIR TEAM...
...DOESN'T MEAN THEY'RE GUARANTEED TO WIN.
?
GLANCE
...
IF SHOYO IS THE CORE OF THEIR OFFENSE...
THEN...
...ALL WE NEED TO DO IS STOP HIM.
SHOYO? WHO'S SHOYO?
...
THEIR ZIPPY LITTLE NO. 10.
OH!
IF THERE'S NO TELLING WHERE HE'S GONNA GO AND WE CAN'T CATCH HIM...
...THEN WE NEED TO NARROW DOWN THE AREA IN WHICH HE CAN MOVE.
AFTER THAT, IT'S JUST A MATTER OF CHASING HIM DOWN.
INUOKA.
YES-SIR!!
ZING
YOU'RE THE QUICKEST GUY WE HAVE, RIGHT?
YESSIR! THANKYA, SIR!!
I THINK ANYBODY WHO SEES THAT SUPER-FAST SET OF THEIRS FOR THE FIRST TIME IS GONNA BE SURPRISED.
I WAS.
BUT...

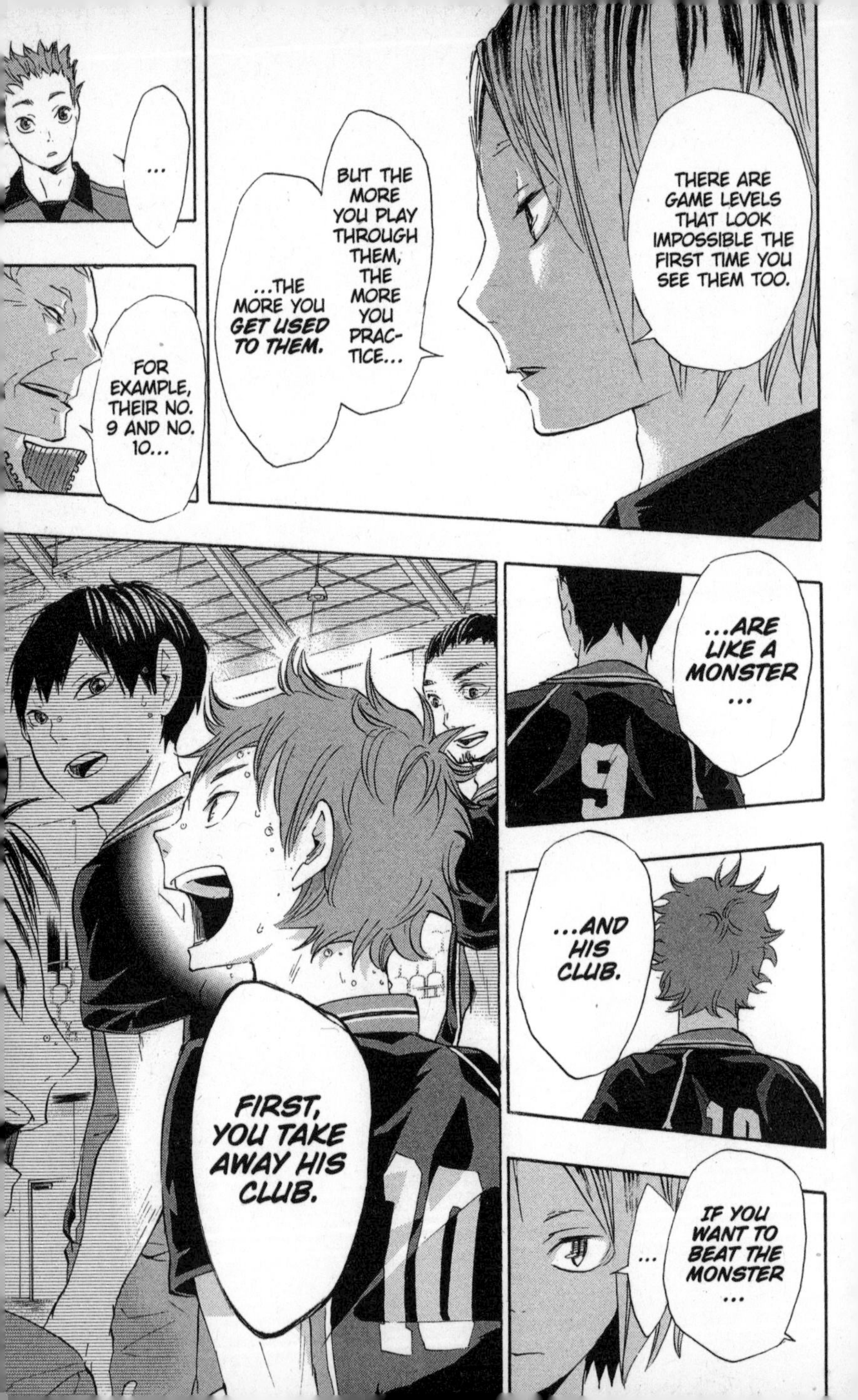
THERE ARE GAME LEVELS THAT LOOK IMPOSSIBLE THE FIRST TIME YOU SEE THEM TOO.
BUT THE MORE YOU PLAY THROUGH THEM, THE MORE YOU PRAC-TICE...
...THE MORE YOU GET USED TO THEM.
...
FOR EXAMPLE, THEIR NO. 9 AND NO. 10...
...ARE LIKE A MONSTER ...
...AND HIS CLUB.
IF YOU WANT TO BEAT THE MONSTER ...
...
FIRST, YOU TAKE AWAY HIS CLUB.

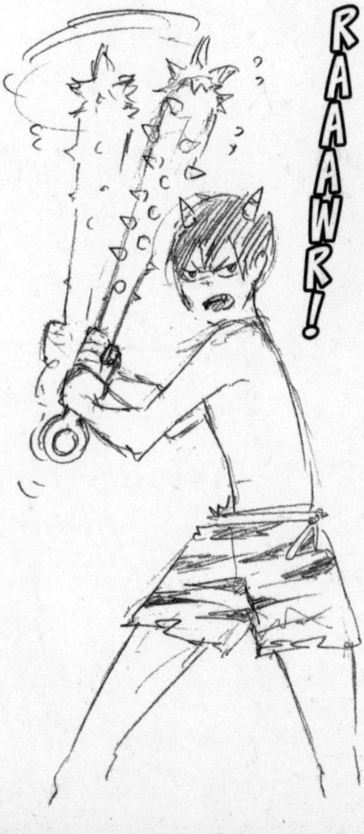
RAAAAWR!

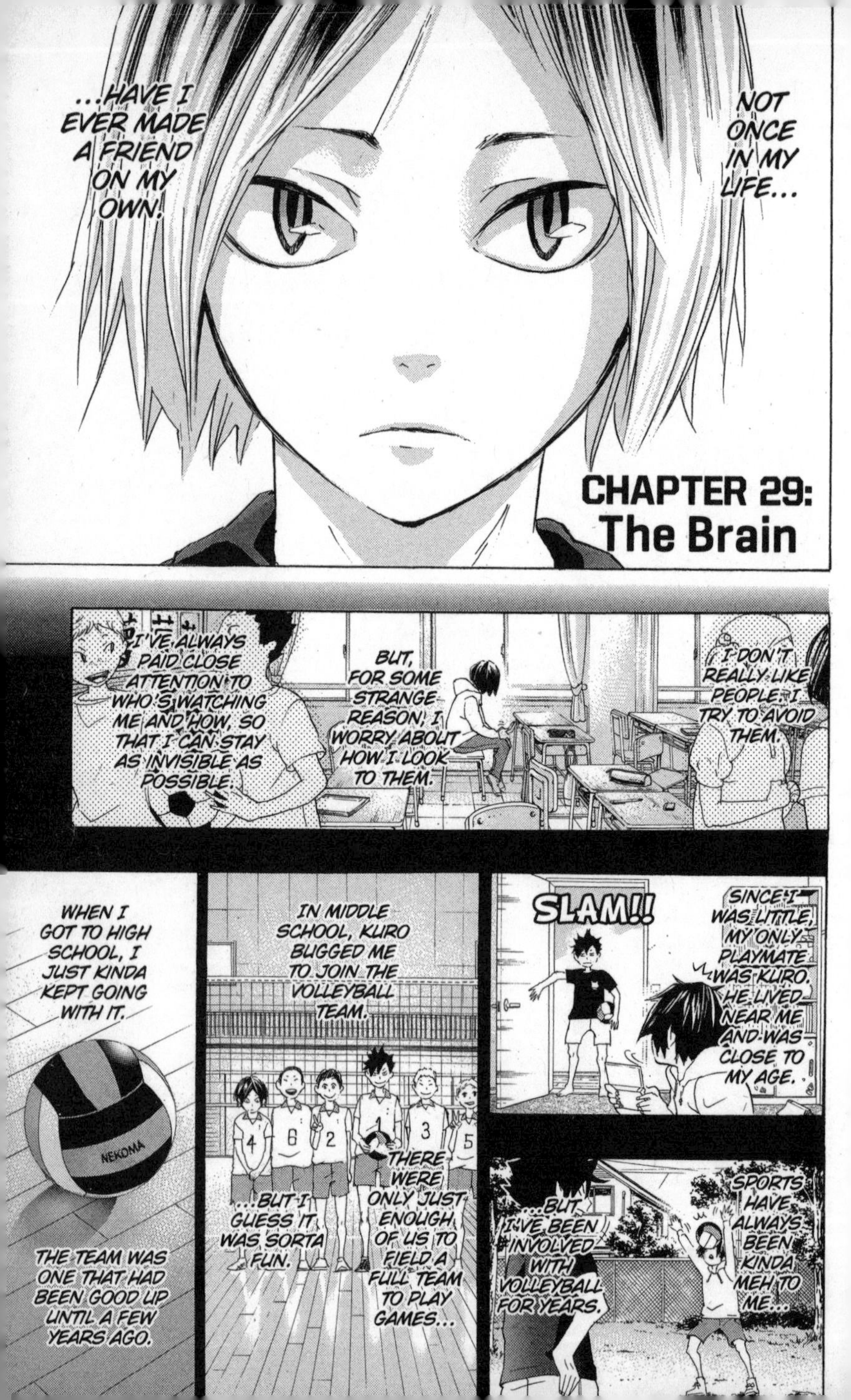
NOT ONCE IN MY LIFE...
...HAVE I EVER MADE A FRIEND ON MY OWN!
CHAPTER 29: The Brain
I DON'T REALLY LIKE PEOPLE. I TRY TO AVOID THEM.
BUT, FOR SOME STRANGE REASON, I WORRY ABOUT HOW I LOOK TO THEM.
I'VE ALWAYS PAID CLOSE ATTENTION TO WHO'S WATCHING ME AND HOW, SO THAT I CAN STAY AS INVISIBLE AS POSSIBLE.
SINCE I WAS LITTLE, MY ONLY PLAYMATE WAS KURO. HE LIVED NEAR ME AND WAS CLOSE TO MY AGE.
SLAM!!
SPORTS HAVE ALWAYS BEEN KINDA MEH TO ME...
...BUT I'VE BEEN INVOLVED WITH VOLLEYBALL FOR YEARS.
IN MIDDLE SCHOOL, KURO BUGGED ME TO JOIN THE VOLLEYBALL TEAM.
THERE WERE ONLY JUST ENOUGH OF US TO FIELD A FULL TEAM TO PLAY GAMES...
...BUT I GUESS IT WAS SORTA FUN.
WHEN I GOT TO HIGH SCHOOL, I JUST KINDA KEPT GOING WITH IT.
NEKOMA
THE TEAM WAS ONE THAT HAD BEEN GOOD UP UNTIL A FEW YEARS AGO.

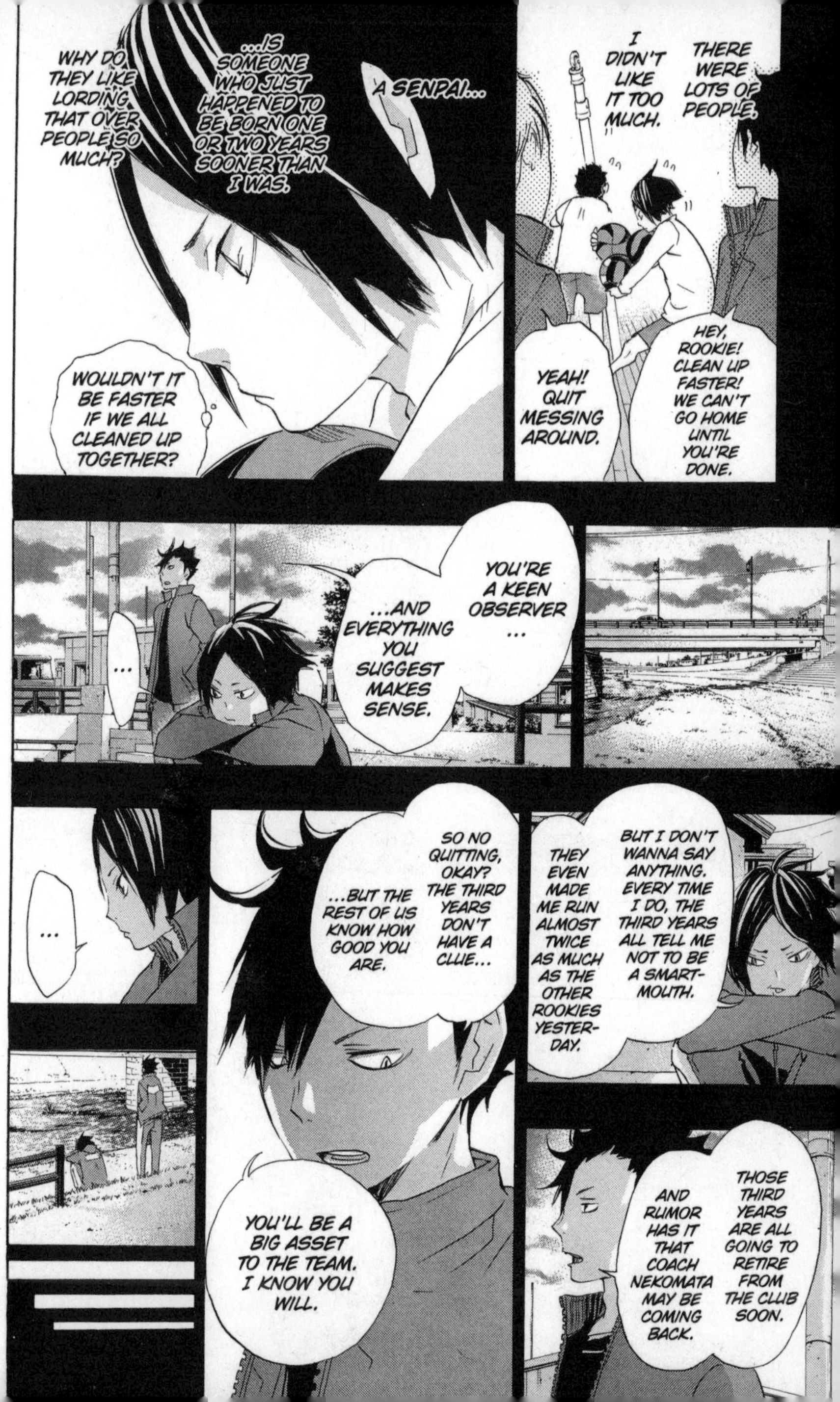
THERE WERE LOTS OF PEOPLE.
I DIDN'T LIKE IT TOO MUCH.
HEY, ROOKIE! CLEAN UP FASTER! WE CAN'T GO HOME UNTIL YOU'RE DONE.
YEAH! QUIT MESSING AROUND.
A SENPAI...
...IS SOMEONE WHO JUST HAPPENED TO BE BORN ONE OR TWO YEARS SOONER THAN I WAS.
WHY DO THEY LIKE LORDING THAT OVER PEOPLE SO MUCH?
WOULDN'T IT BE FASTER IF WE ALL CLEANED UP TOGETHER?
YOU'RE A KEEN OBSERVER...
...AND EVERYTHING YOU SUGGEST MAKES SENSE.
...
BUT I DON'T WANNA SAY ANYTHING. EVERY TIME I DO, THE THIRD YEARS ALL TELL ME NOT TO BE A SMART-MOUTH.
THEY EVEN MADE ME RUN ALMOST TWICE AS MUCH AS THE OTHER ROOKIES YESTERDAY.
THOSE THIRD YEARS ARE ALL GOING TO RETIRE FROM THE CLUB SOON.
AND RUMOR HAS IT THAT COACH NEKOMATA MAY BE COMING BACK.
SO NO QUITTING, OKAY? THE THIRD YEARS DON'T HAVE A CLUE...
...BUT THE REST OF US KNOW HOW GOOD YOU ARE.
YOU'LL BE A BIG ASSET TO THE TEAM. I KNOW YOU WILL.
...

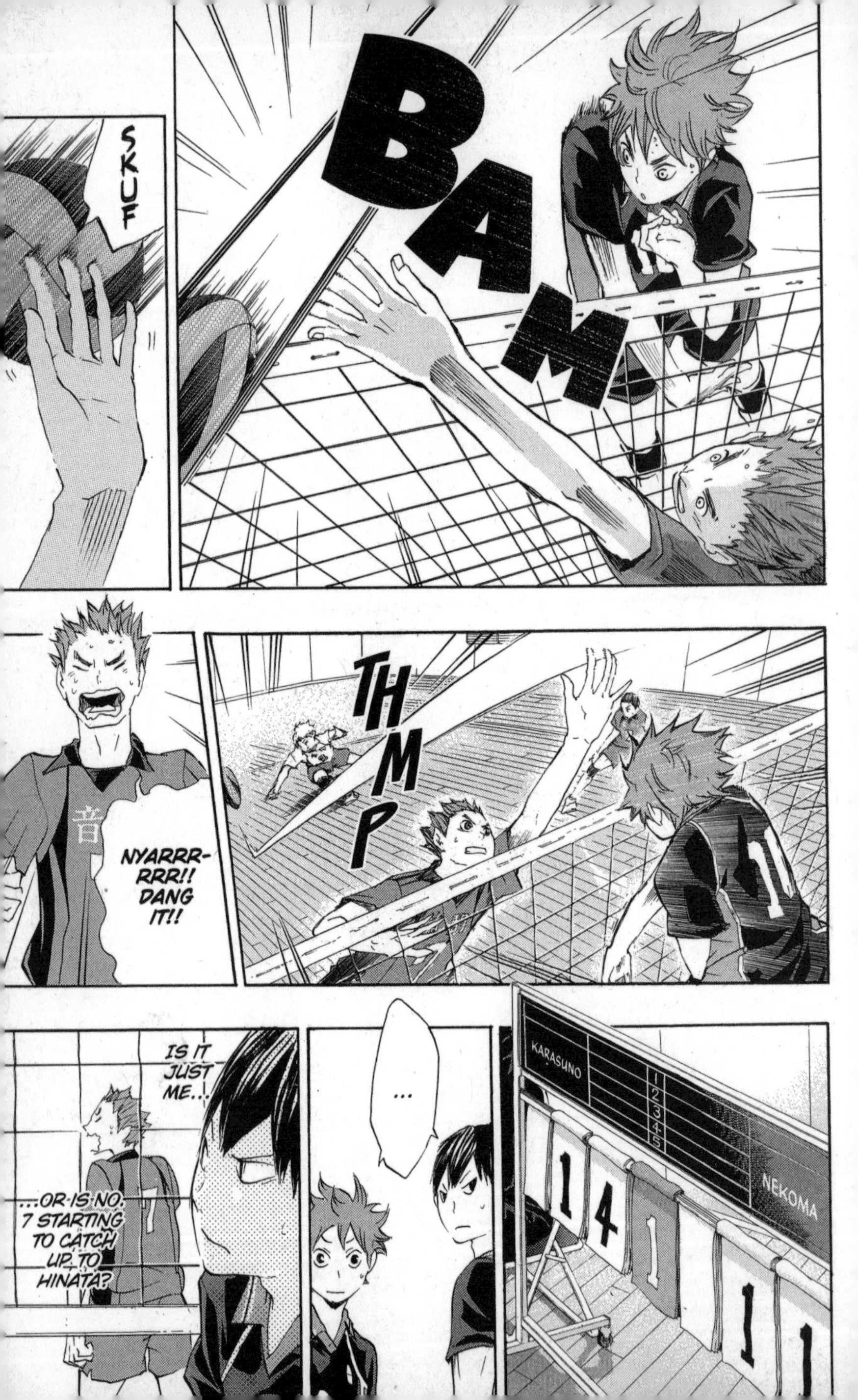
BAM
SKUF
THMP
NYARRR-RRR!! DANG IT!!
KARASUNO
1 2 3 4 5
NEKOMA
14
...
IS IT JUST ME...
...OR IS NO. 7 STARTING TO CATCH UP TO HINATA?

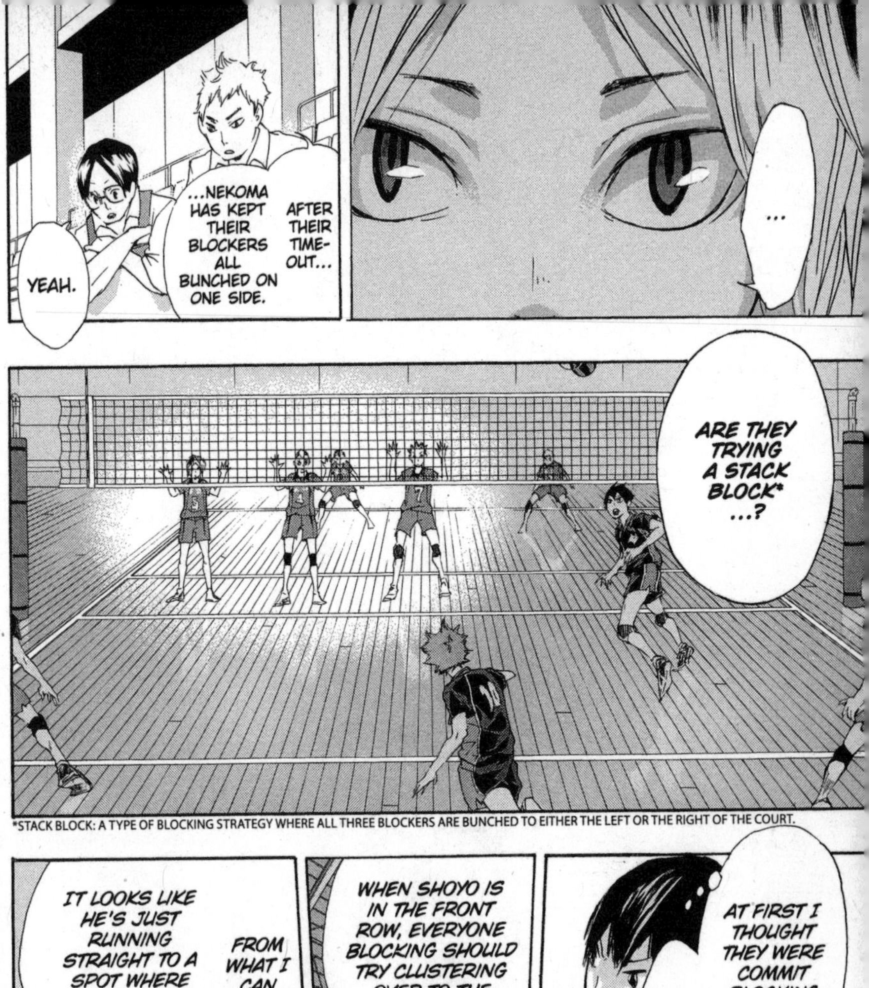
...
AFTER THEIR TIME-OUT...
...NEKOMA HAS KEPT THEIR BLOCKERS ALL BUNCHED ON ONE SIDE.
YEAH.
ARE THEY TRYING A STACK BLOCK* ...?

*STACK BLOCK: A TYPE OF BLOCKING STRATEGY WHERE ALL THREE BLOCKERS ARE BUNCHED TO EITHER THE LEFT OR THE RIGHT OF THE COURT.

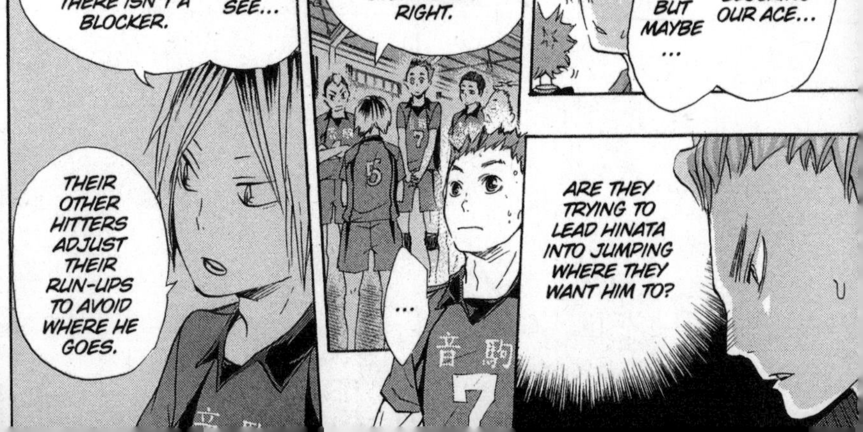
AT FIRST I THOUGHT THEY WERE COMMIT BLOCKING OUR ACE...
BUT MAYBE...
ARE THEY TRYING TO LEAD HINATA INTO JUMPING WHERE THEY WANT HIM TO?
WHEN SHOYO IS IN THE FRONT ROW, EVERYONE BLOCKING SHOULD TRY CLUSTERING OVER TO THE RIGHT.
...
FROM WHAT I CAN SEE...
IT LOOKS LIKE HE'S JUST RUNNING STRAIGHT TO A SPOT WHERE THERE ISN'T A BLOCKER.
THEIR OTHER HITTERS ADJUST THEIR RUN-UPS TO AVOID WHERE HE GOES.

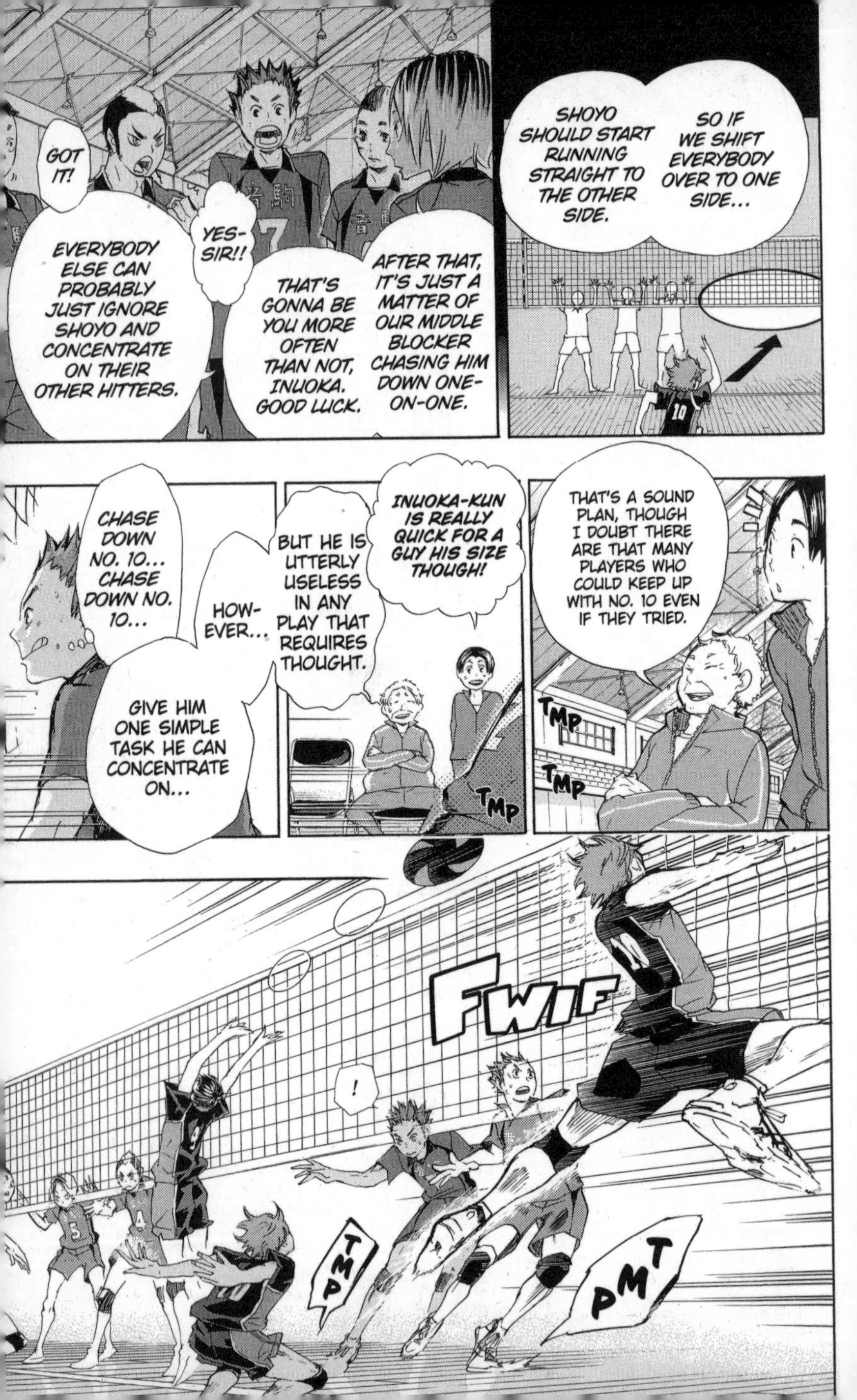
SO IF WE SHIFT EVERYBODY OVER TO ONE SIDE...
SHOYO SHOULD START RUNNING STRAIGHT TO THE OTHER SIDE.
AFTER THAT, IT'S JUST A MATTER OF OUR MIDDLE BLOCKER CHASING HIM DOWN ONE-ON-ONE.
THAT'S GONNA BE YOU MORE OFTEN THAN NOT, INUOKA. GOOD LUCK.
YES-SIR!!
EVERYBODY ELSE CAN PROBABLY JUST IGNORE SHOYO AND CONCENTRATE ON THEIR OTHER HITTERS.
GOT IT!
THAT'S A SOUND PLAN, THOUGH I DOUBT THERE ARE THAT MANY PLAYERS WHO COULD KEEP UP WITH NO. 10 EVEN IF THEY TRIED.
TMP
TMP
INUOKA-KUN IS REALLY QUICK FOR A GUY HIS SIZE THOUGH!
BUT HE IS UTTERLY USELESS IN ANY PLAY THAT REQUIRES THOUGHT.
TMP
HOW-EVER...
GIVE HIM ONE SIMPLE TASK HE CAN CONCENTRATE ON...
CHASE DOWN NO. 10... CHASE DOWN NO. 10...
FWIF
!
PMT
TMP

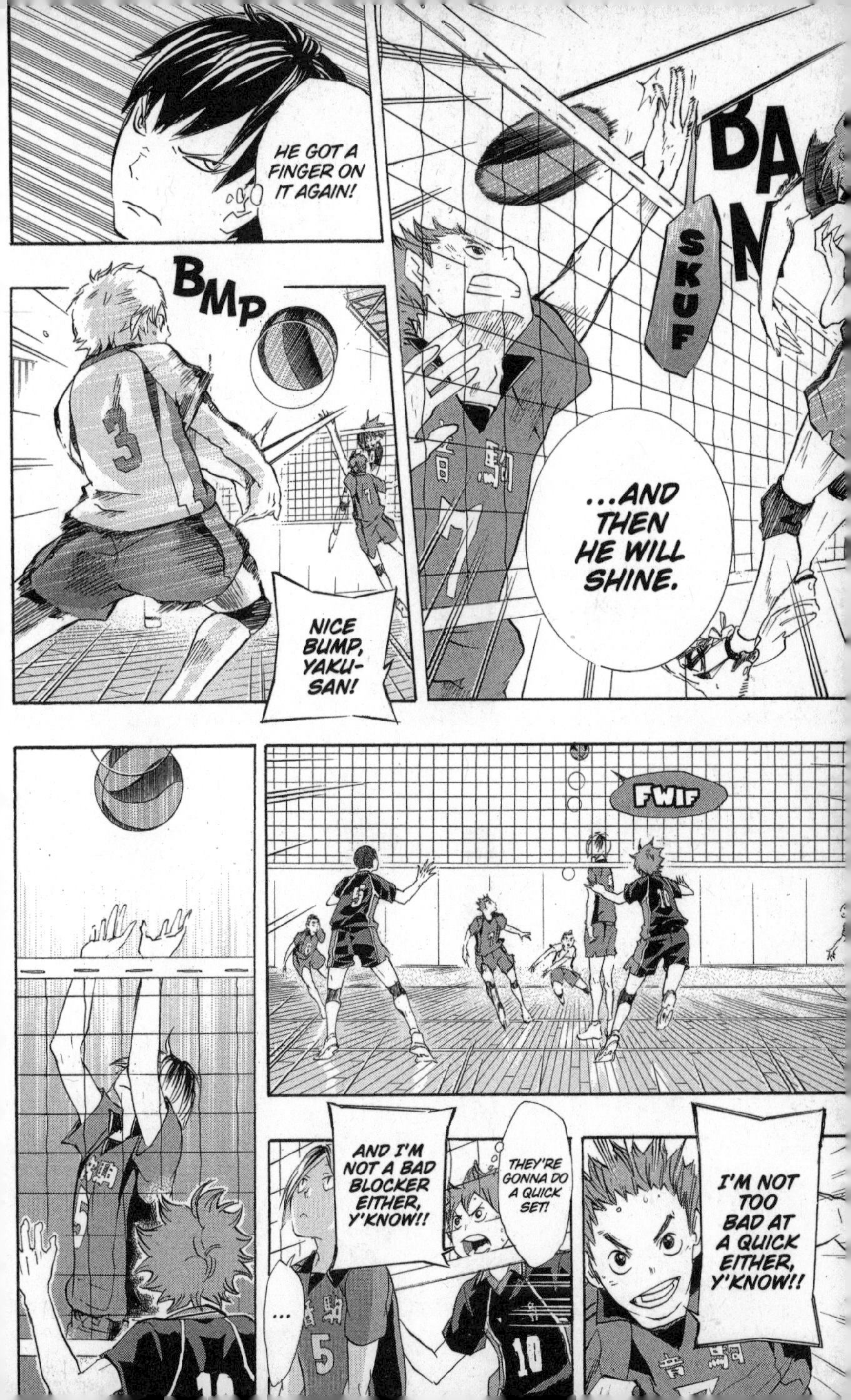
BAM
SKUF
...AND THEN HE WILL SHINE.
HE GOT A FINGER ON IT AGAIN!
BMP
NICE BUMP, YAKU-SAN!
FWIF
I'M NOT TOO BAD AT A QUICK EITHER, Y'KNOW!!
THEY'RE GONNA DO A QUICK SET!
AND I'M NOT A BAD BLOCKER EITHER, Y'KNOW!!
...

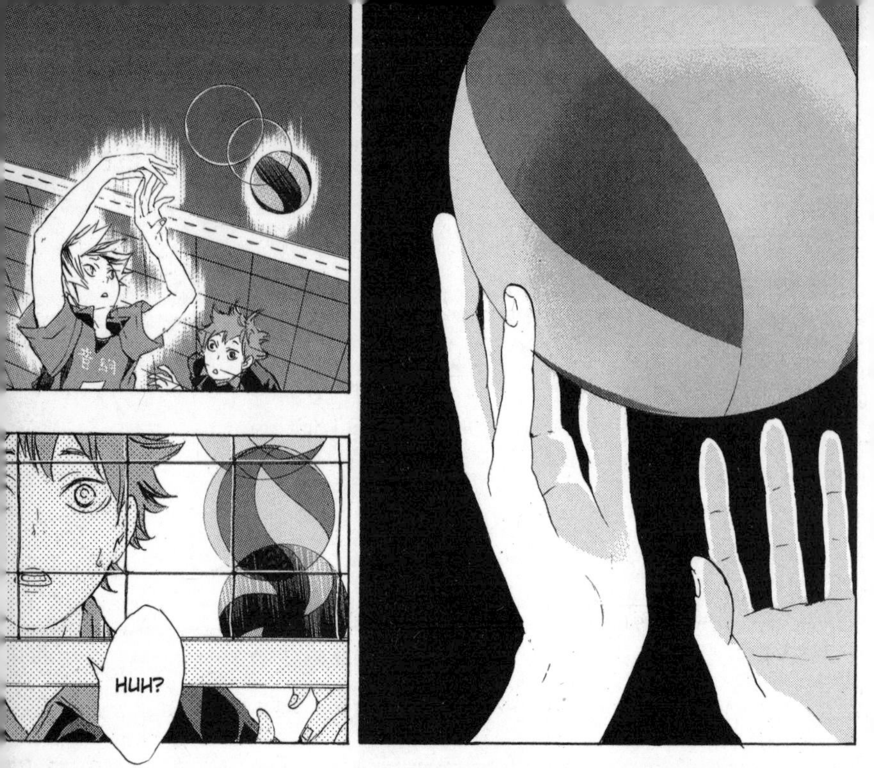
HUH?
TUMP
AAAAARGH!!
STAMP STAMP
...
OOH! THAT WAS A SETTER DUMP,* RIGHT? I WAS COMPLETELY CONVINCED HE WOULD PUT THE BALL UP FOR SOMEONE ELSE.
...

*SETTER DUMP: THE SETTER FAKES SETTING THE BALL AND INSTEAD TIPS IT OVER THE NET IN AN OFFENSIVE ATTACK.

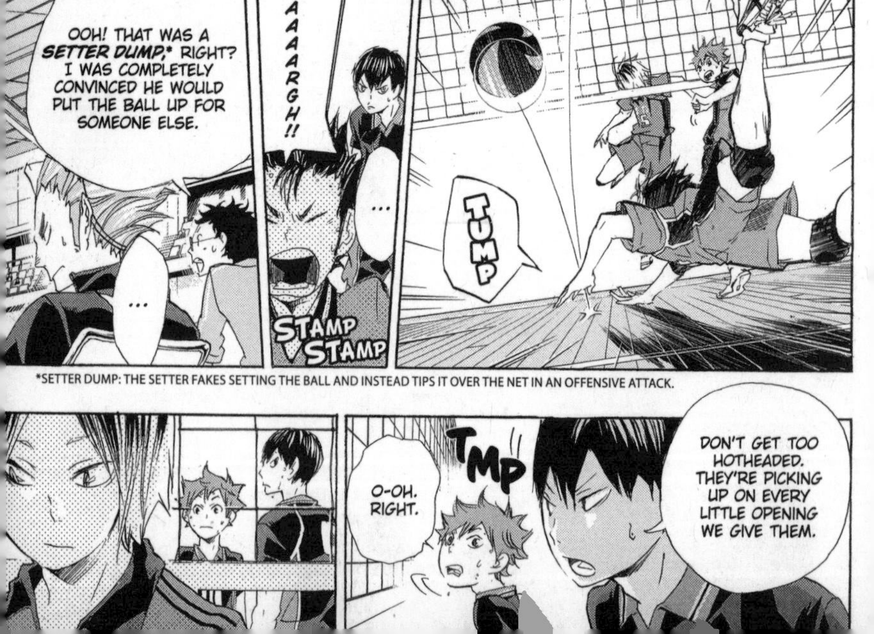
DON'T GET TOO HOTHEADED. THEY'RE PICKING UP ON EVERY LITTLE OPENING WE GIVE THEM.
TMP
O-OH. RIGHT.

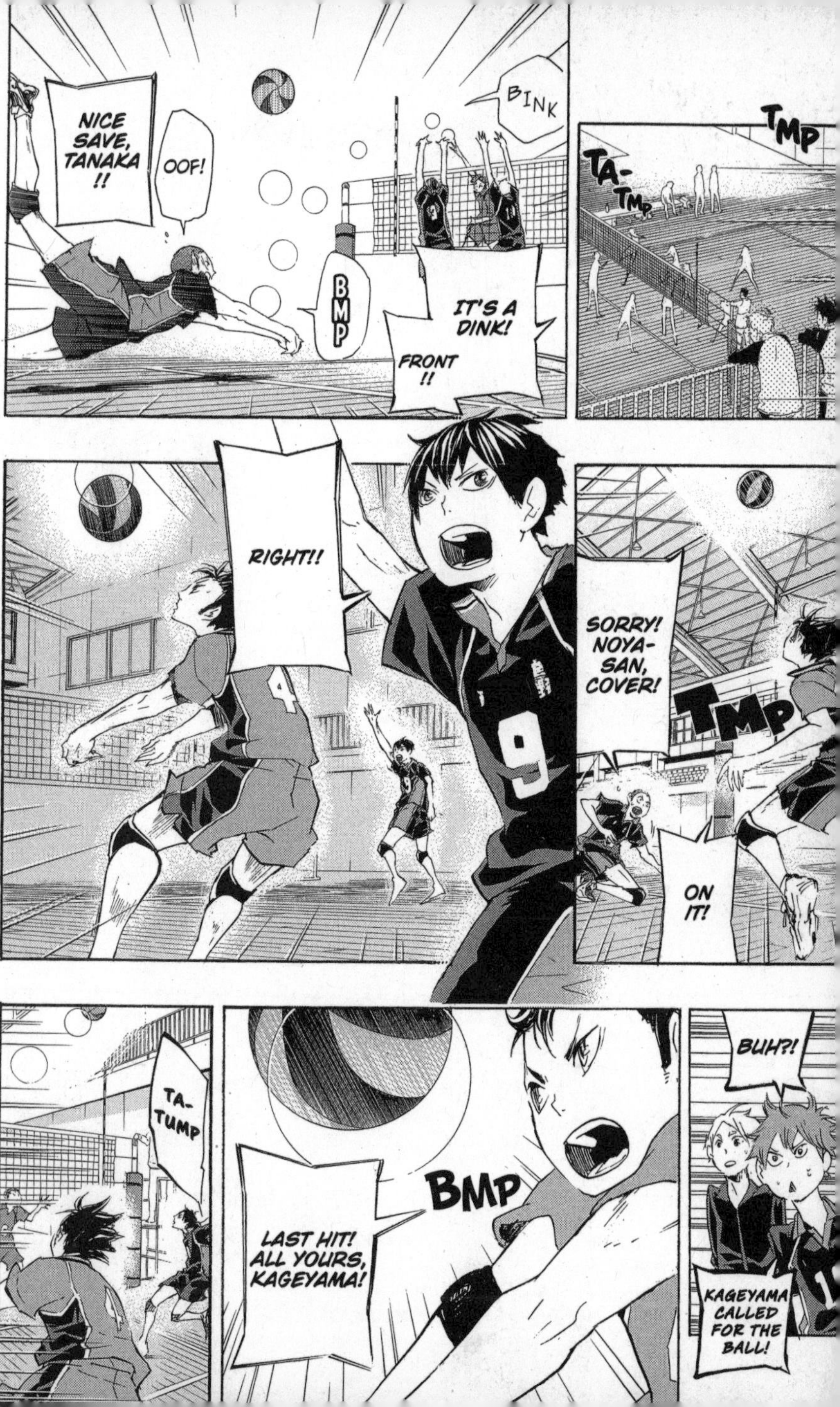
TMP
TA-TMP
BINK
IT'S A DINK!
FRONT!!
BMP
OOF!
NICE SAVE, TANAKA!!
SORRY! NOYA-SAN, COVER!
TMP
ON IT!
RIGHT!!
BUH?!
KAGEYAMA CALLED FOR THE BALL!
BMP
LAST HIT! ALL YOURS, KAGEYAMA!
TA-TUMP

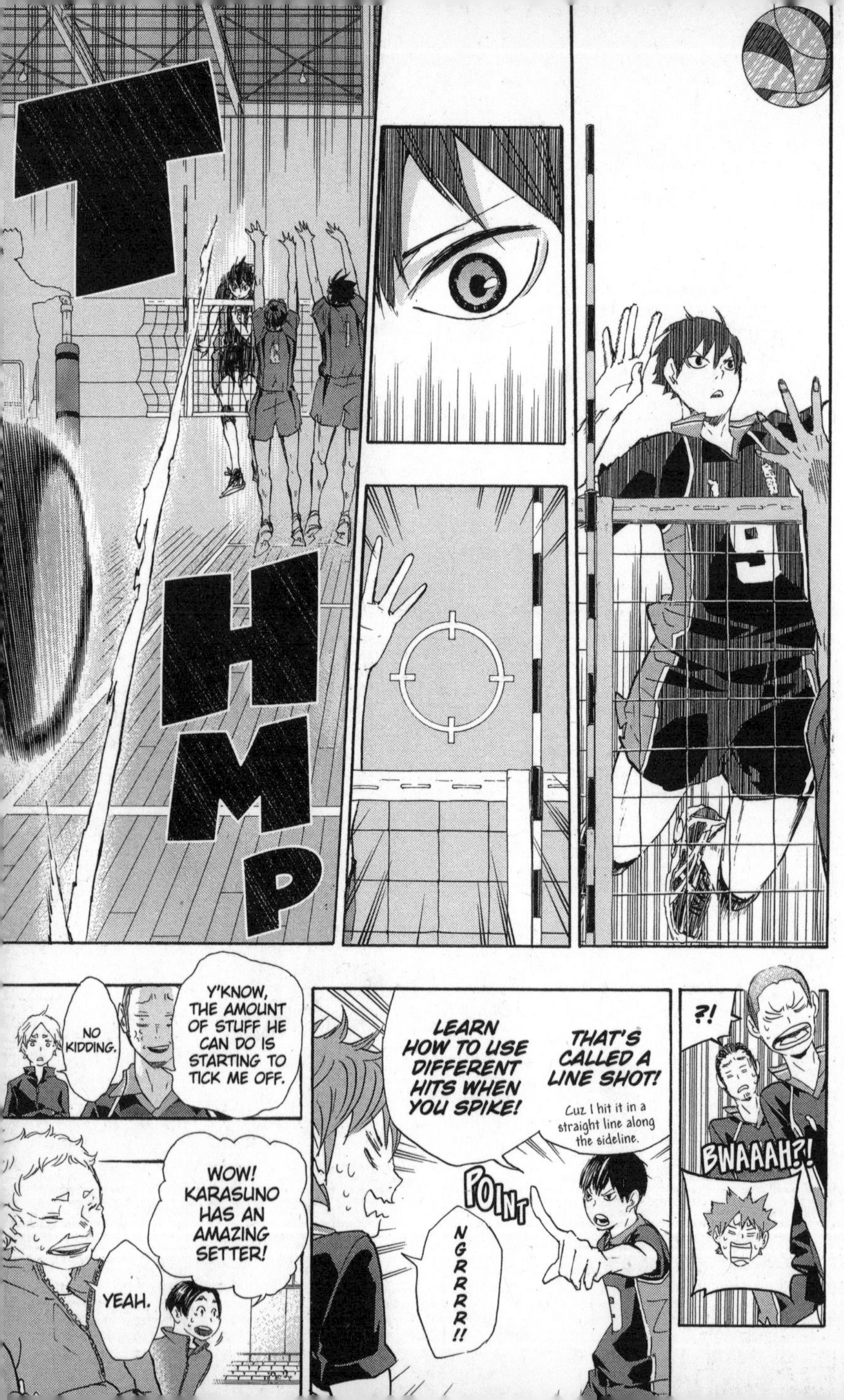
THMP
?!
BWAAAH?!
THAT'S CALLED A LINE SHOT!
Cuz I hit it in a straight line along the sideline.
LEARN HOW TO USE DIFFERENT HITS WHEN YOU SPIKE!
POINT
NGRRRR!!
Y'KNOW, THE AMOUNT OF STUFF HE CAN DO IS STARTING TO TICK ME OFF.
NO KIDDING.
WOW! KARASUNO HAS AN AMAZING SETTER!
YEAH.

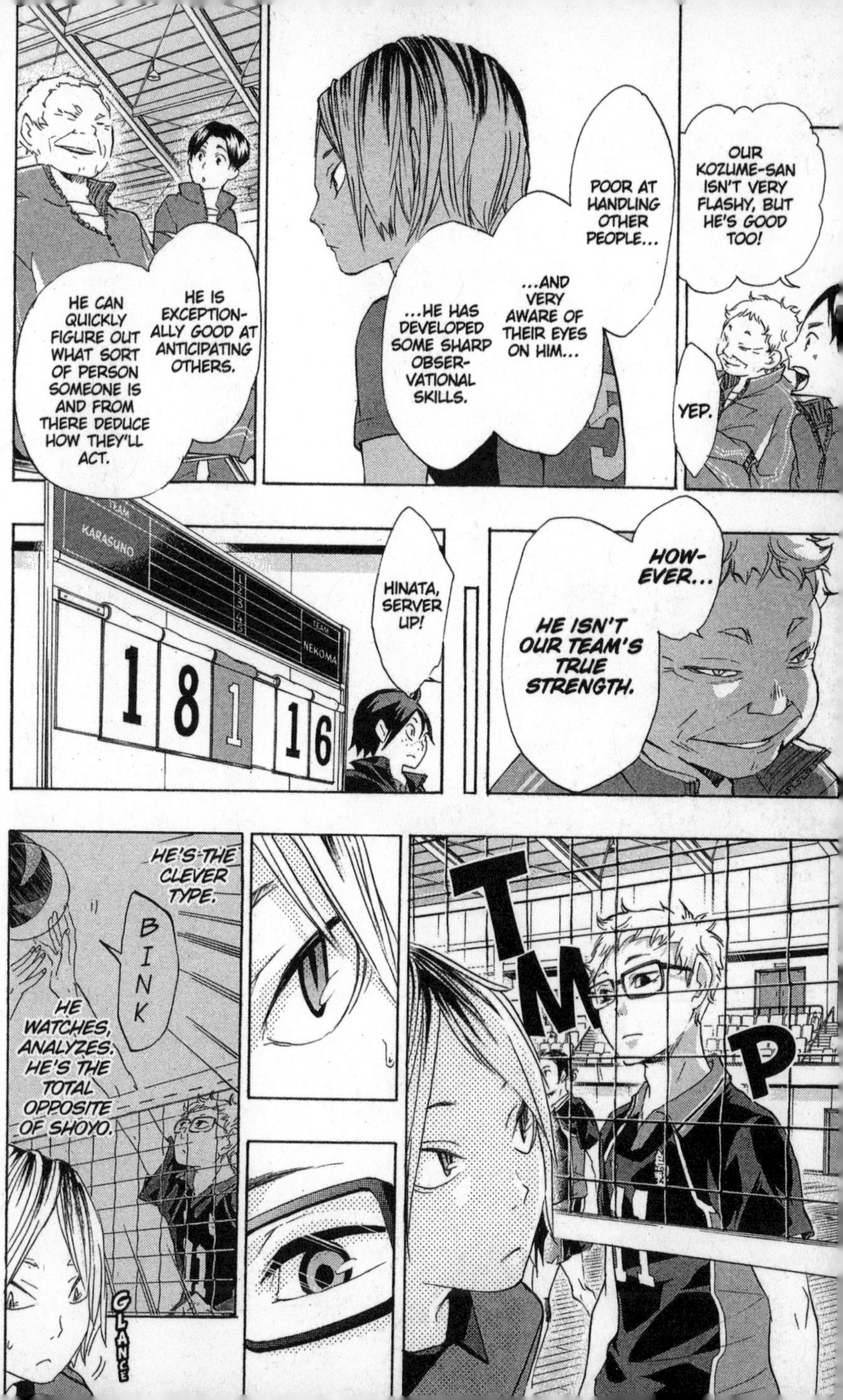
OUR KOZUME-SAN ISN'T VERY FLASHY, BUT HE'S GOOD TOO!
YEP.
POOR AT HANDLING OTHER PEOPLE...
...AND VERY AWARE OF THEIR EYES ON HIM...
...HE HAS DEVELOPED SOME SHARP OBSERVATIONAL SKILLS.
HE IS EXCEPTIONALLY GOOD AT ANTICIPATING OTHERS.
HE CAN QUICKLY FIGURE OUT WHAT SORT OF PERSON SOMEONE IS AND FROM THERE DEDUCE HOW THEY'LL ACT.
HOWEVER...
HE ISN'T OUR TEAM'S TRUE STRENGTH.
HINATA, SERVER UP!
TEAM
KARASUNO
TEAM
NEKOMA
18
1
16
TMP
HE'S THE CLEVER TYPE.
BINK
HE WATCHES, ANALYZES. HE'S THE TOTAL OPPOSITE OF SHOYO.
GLANCE

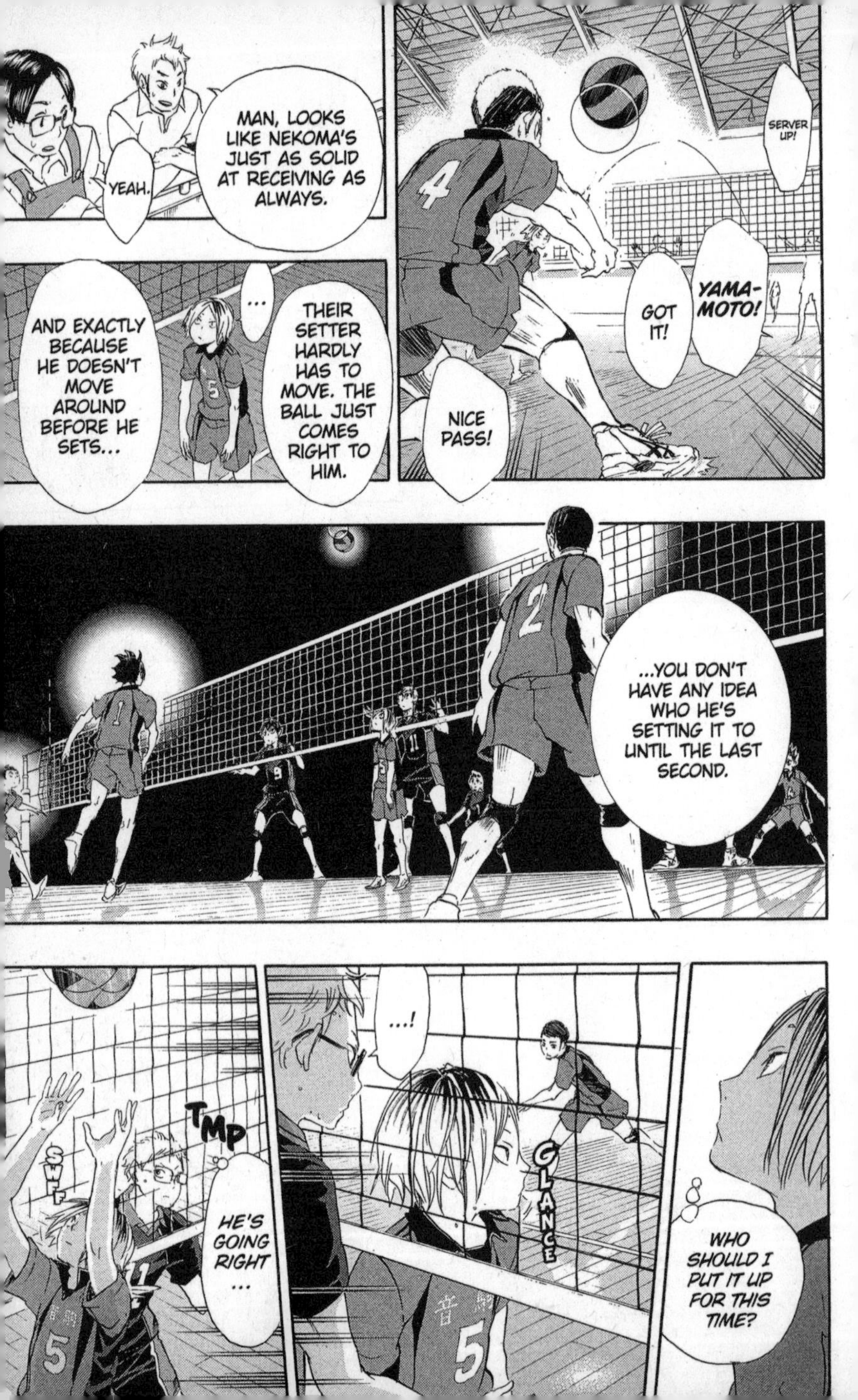
SERVER UP!
YAMAMOTO!
GOT IT!
NICE PASS!
MAN, LOOKS LIKE NEKOMA'S JUST AS SOLID AT RECEIVING AS ALWAYS.
YEAH.
THEIR SETTER HARDLY HAS TO MOVE. THE BALL JUST COMES RIGHT TO HIM.
...
AND EXACTLY BECAUSE HE DOESN'T MOVE AROUND BEFORE HE SETS...
...YOU DON'T HAVE ANY IDEA WHO HE'S SETTING IT TO UNTIL THE LAST SECOND.
WHO SHOULD I PUT IT UP FOR THIS TIME?
...!
GLANCE
TMP
HE'S GOING RIGHT ...
SWFF

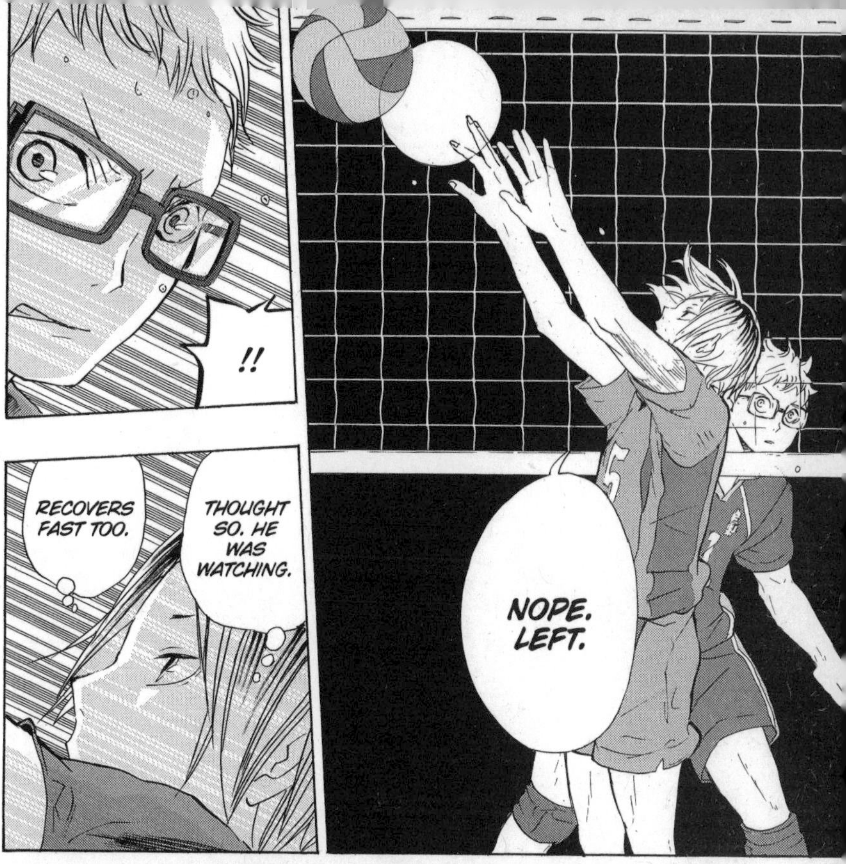
NOPE. LEFT.
!!
THOUGHT SO. HE WAS WATCHING.
RECOVERS FAST TOO.

*LOOK OFF: A MOVE USED BY SETTERS WHERE THEY WILL LOOK AT ONE HITTER AND SET TO ANOTHER.

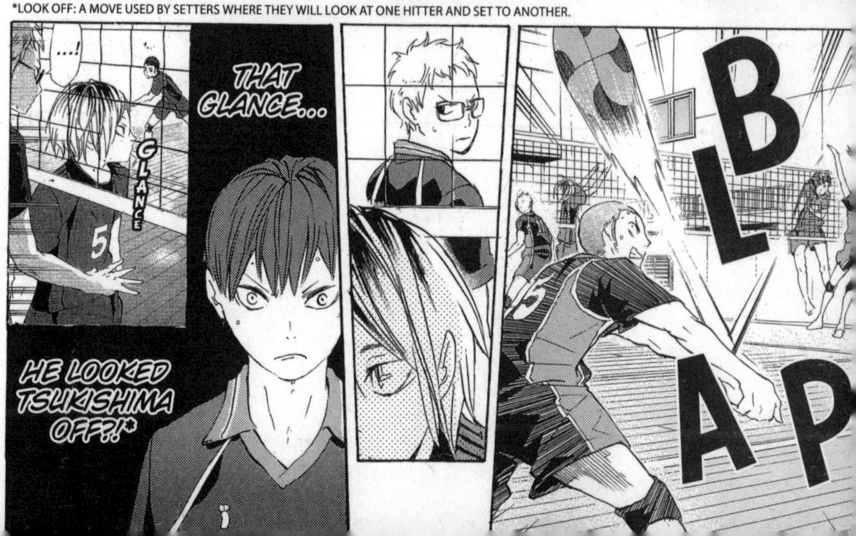
BLAP
THAT GLANCE...
...!
GLANCE
HE LOOKED TSUKISHIMA OFF?!*

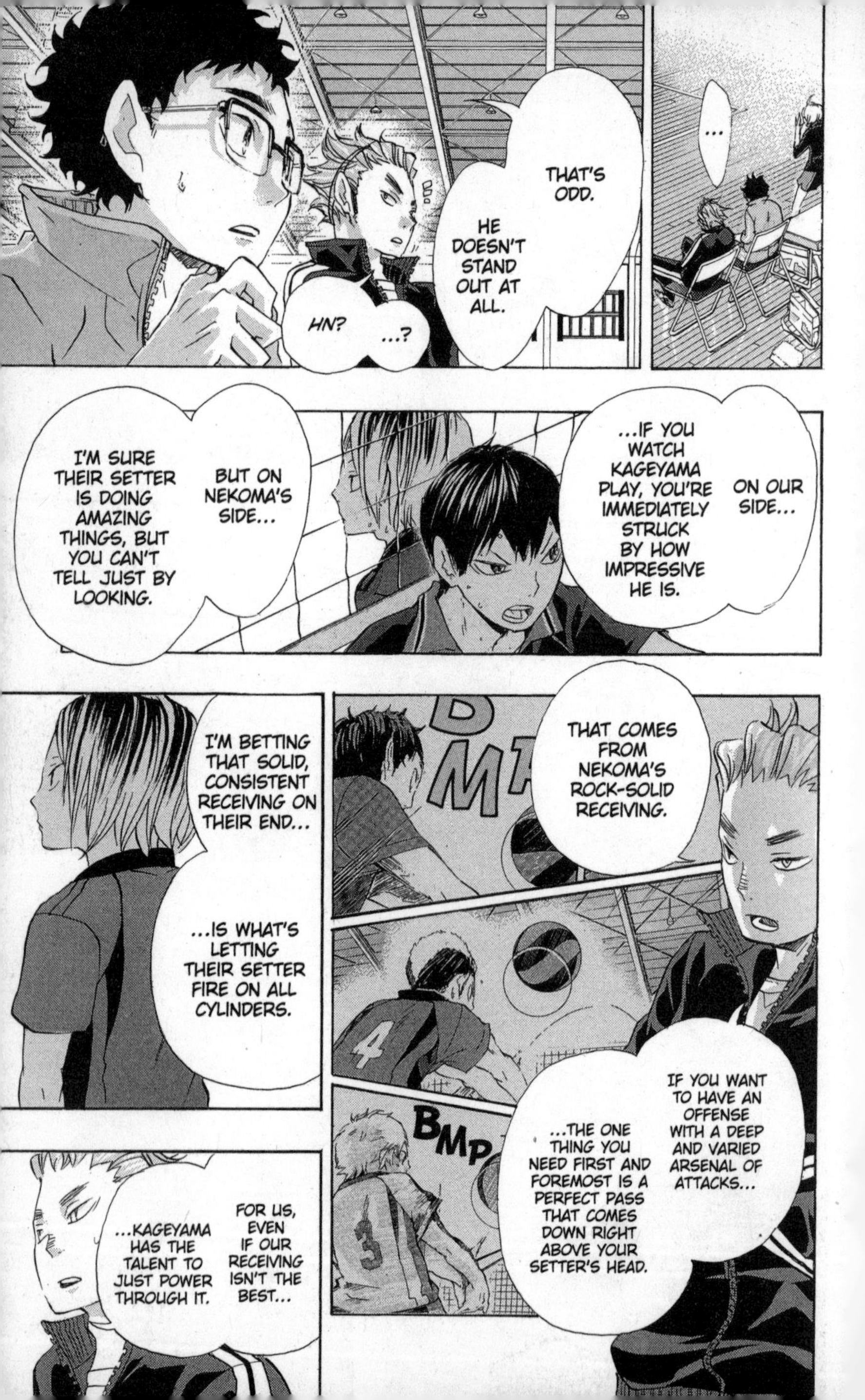
...
THAT'S ODD.
HE DOESN'T STAND OUT AT ALL.
...?
HN?
ON OUR SIDE...
...IF YOU WATCH KAGEYAMA PLAY, YOU'RE IMMEDIATELY STRUCK BY HOW IMPRESSIVE HE IS.
BUT ON NEKOMA'S SIDE...
I'M SURE THEIR SETTER IS DOING AMAZING THINGS, BUT YOU CAN'T TELL JUST BY LOOKING.
THAT COMES FROM NEKOMA'S ROCK-SOLID RECEIVING.
BMP
IF YOU WANT TO HAVE AN OFFENSE WITH A DEEP AND VARIED ARSENAL OF ATTACKS...
...THE ONE THING YOU NEED FIRST AND FOREMOST IS A PERFECT PASS THAT COMES DOWN RIGHT ABOVE YOUR SETTER'S HEAD.
BMP
I'M BETTING THAT SOLID, CONSISTENT RECEIVING ON THEIR END...
...IS WHAT'S LETTING THEIR SETTER FIRE ON ALL CYLINDERS.
FOR US, EVEN IF OUR RECEIVING ISN'T THE BEST...
...KAGEYAMA HAS THE TALENT TO JUST POWER THROUGH IT.

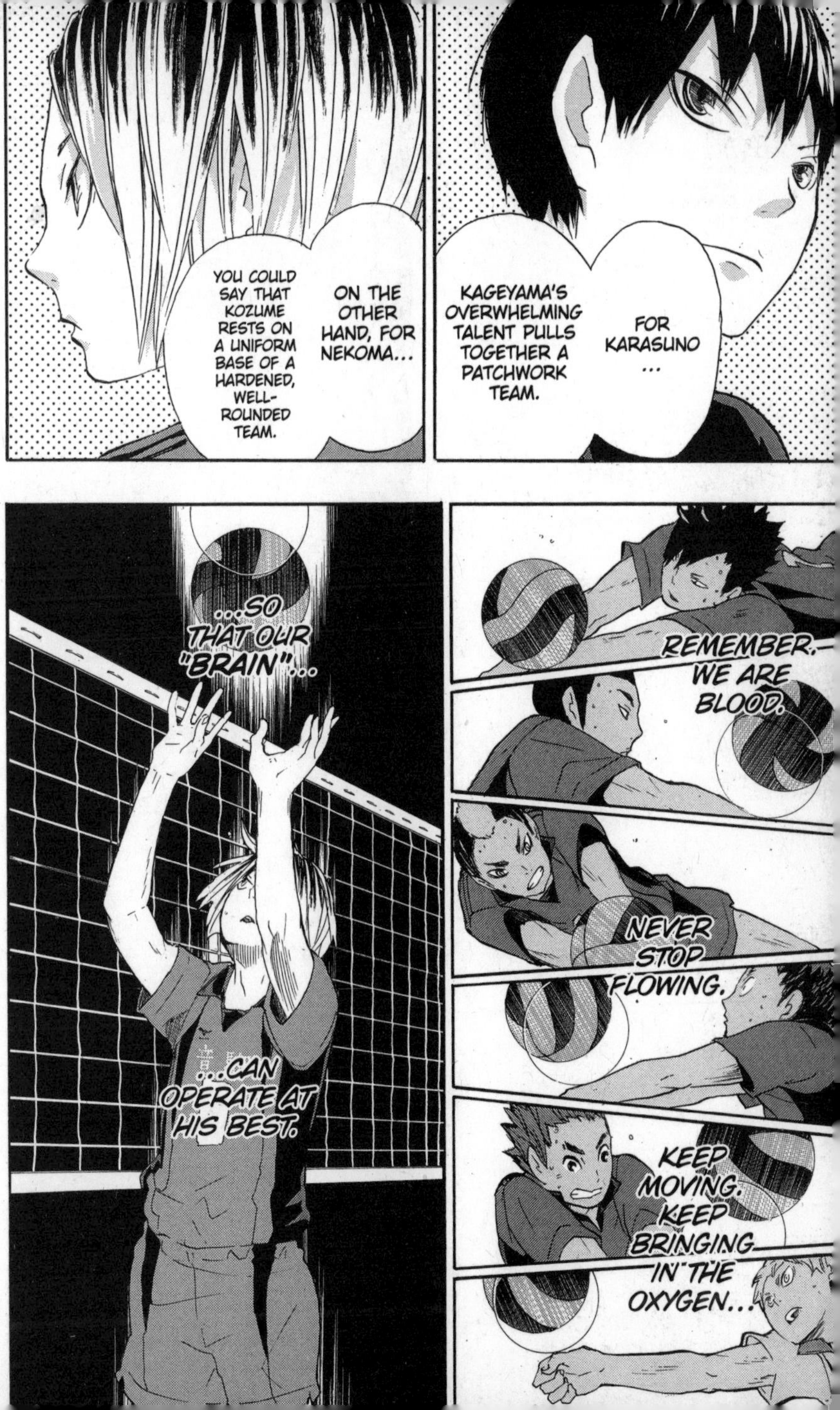
FOR KARASUNO ...
KAGEYAMA'S OVERWHELMING TALENT PULLS TOGETHER A PATCHWORK TEAM.
ON THE OTHER HAND, FOR NEKOMA...
YOU COULD SAY THAT KOZUME RESTS ON A UNIFORM BASE OF A HARDENED, WELL-ROUNDED TEAM.
REMEMBER. WE ARE BLOOD.
NEVER STOP FLOWING.
KEEP MOVING. KEEP BRINGING IN THE OXYGEN...
...SO THAT OUR "BRAIN"...
...CAN OPERATE AT HIS BEST.

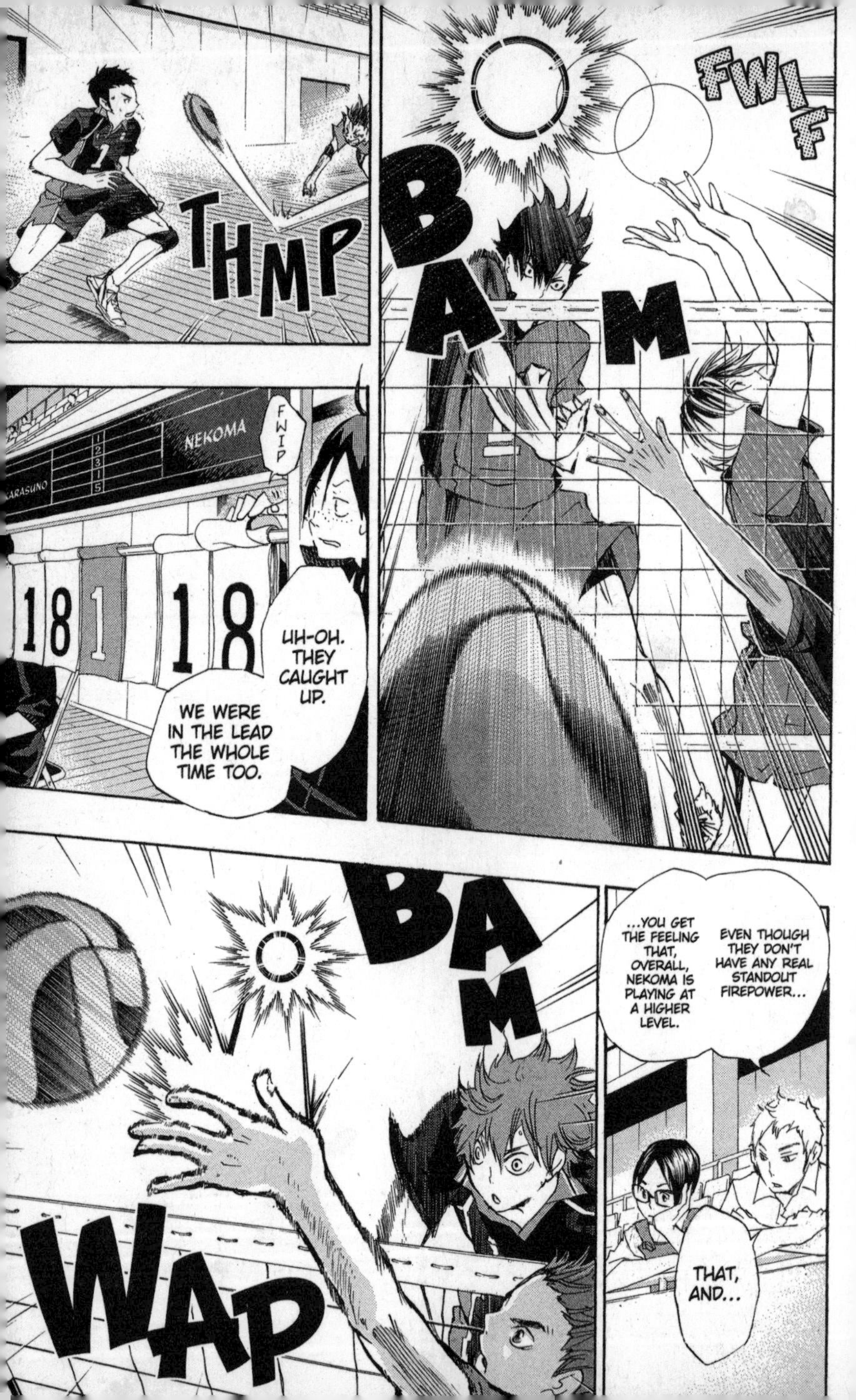
FWIF
BAM
THMP
NEKOMA
FWIP
18
18
UH-OH. THEY CAUGHT UP.
WE WERE IN THE LEAD THE WHOLE TIME TOO.
EVEN THOUGH THEY DON'T HAVE ANY REAL STANDOUT FIREPOWER...
...YOU GET THE FEELING THAT, OVERALL, NEKOMA IS PLAYING AT A HIGHER LEVEL.
THAT, AND...
BAM
WAP

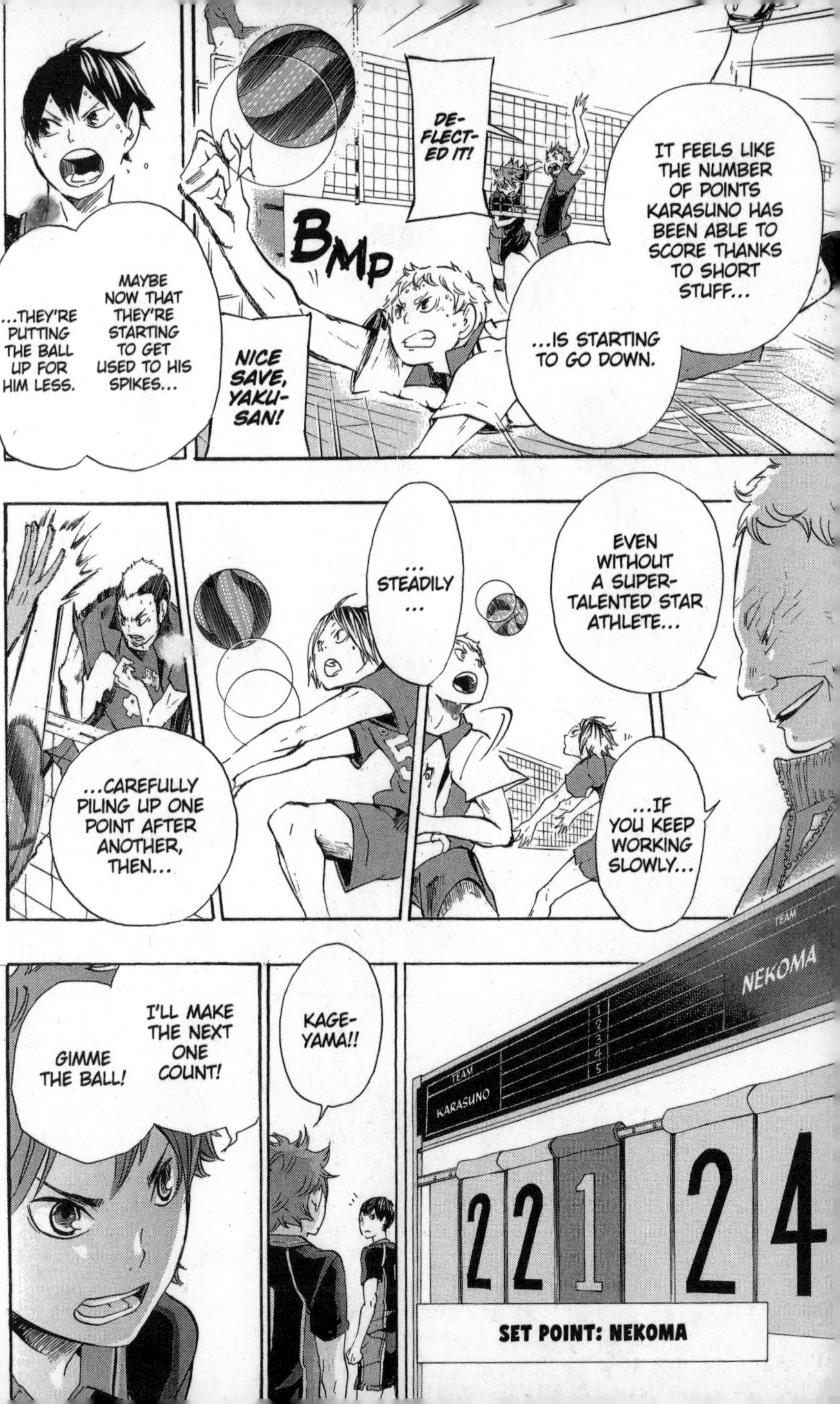
DE-FLECTED IT!
IT FEELS LIKE THE NUMBER OF POINTS KARASUNO HAS BEEN ABLE TO SCORE THANKS TO SHORT STUFF...
BMP
...IS STARTING TO GO DOWN.
NICE SAVE, YAKU-SAN!
MAYBE NOW THAT THEY'RE STARTING TO GET USED TO HIS SPIKES...
...THEY'RE PUTTING THE BALL UP FOR HIM LESS.
EVEN WITHOUT A SUPER-TALENTED STAR ATHLETE...
...IF YOU KEEP WORKING SLOWLY...
...STEADILY...
...CAREFULLY PILING UP ONE POINT AFTER ANOTHER, THEN...
TEAM
NEKOMA
1
2
3
4
5
TEAM
KARASUNO
22
1
24
SET POINT: NEKOMA
KAGE-YAMA!!
I'LL MAKE THE NEXT ONE COUNT!
GIMME THE BALL!

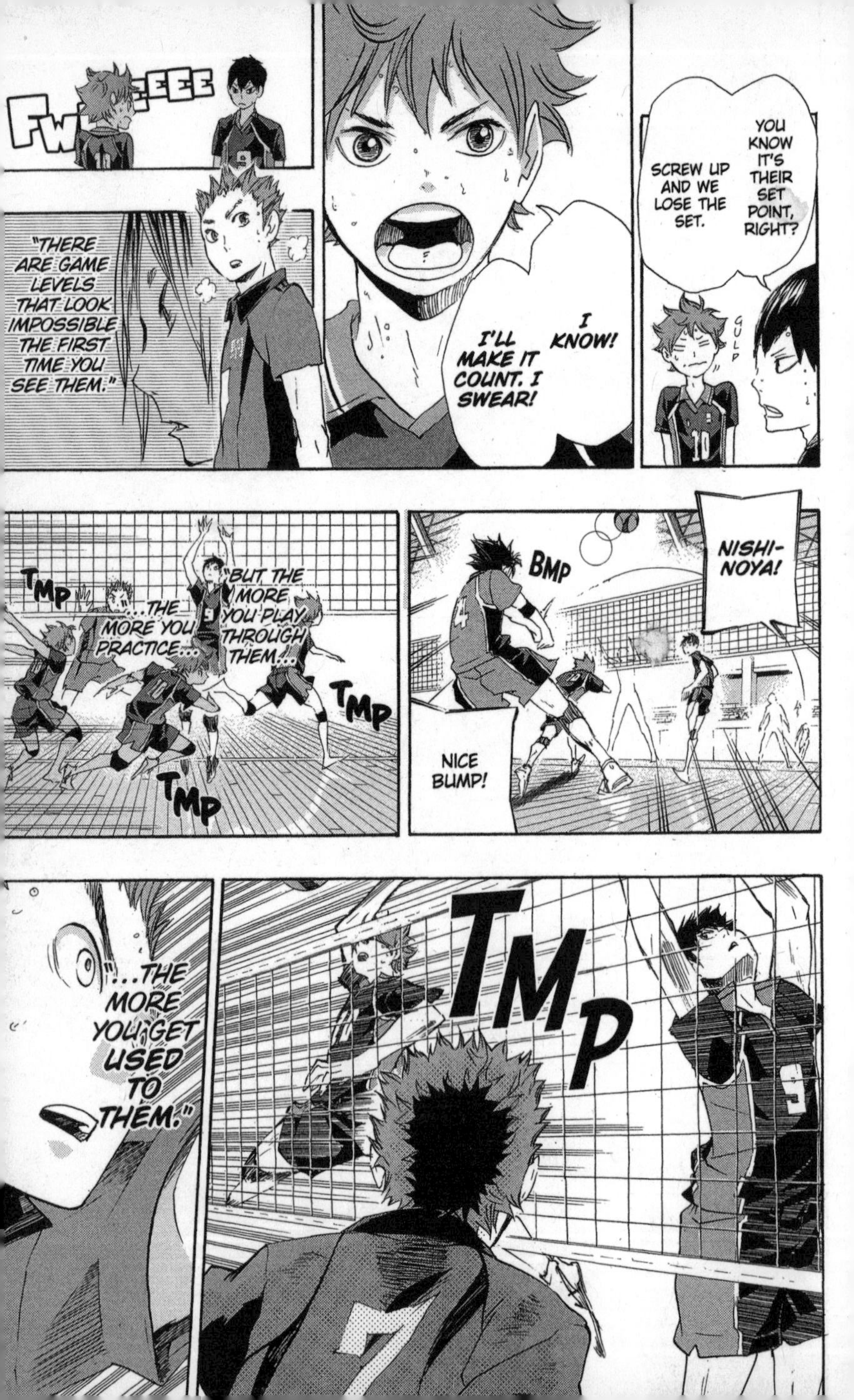
YOU KNOW IT'S THEIR SET POINT, RIGHT?
SCREW UP AND WE LOSE THE SET.
GULP
I KNOW!
I'LL MAKE IT COUNT. I SWEAR!
FWEEEE
"THERE ARE GAME LEVELS THAT LOOK IMPOSSIBLE THE FIRST TIME YOU SEE THEM."
NISHI-NOYA!
BMP
NICE BUMP!
"BUT THE MORE YOU PLAY THROUGH THEM...
TMP
...THE MORE YOU PRACTICE...
TMP
TMP
TMP
"...THE MORE YOU GET USED TO THEM."

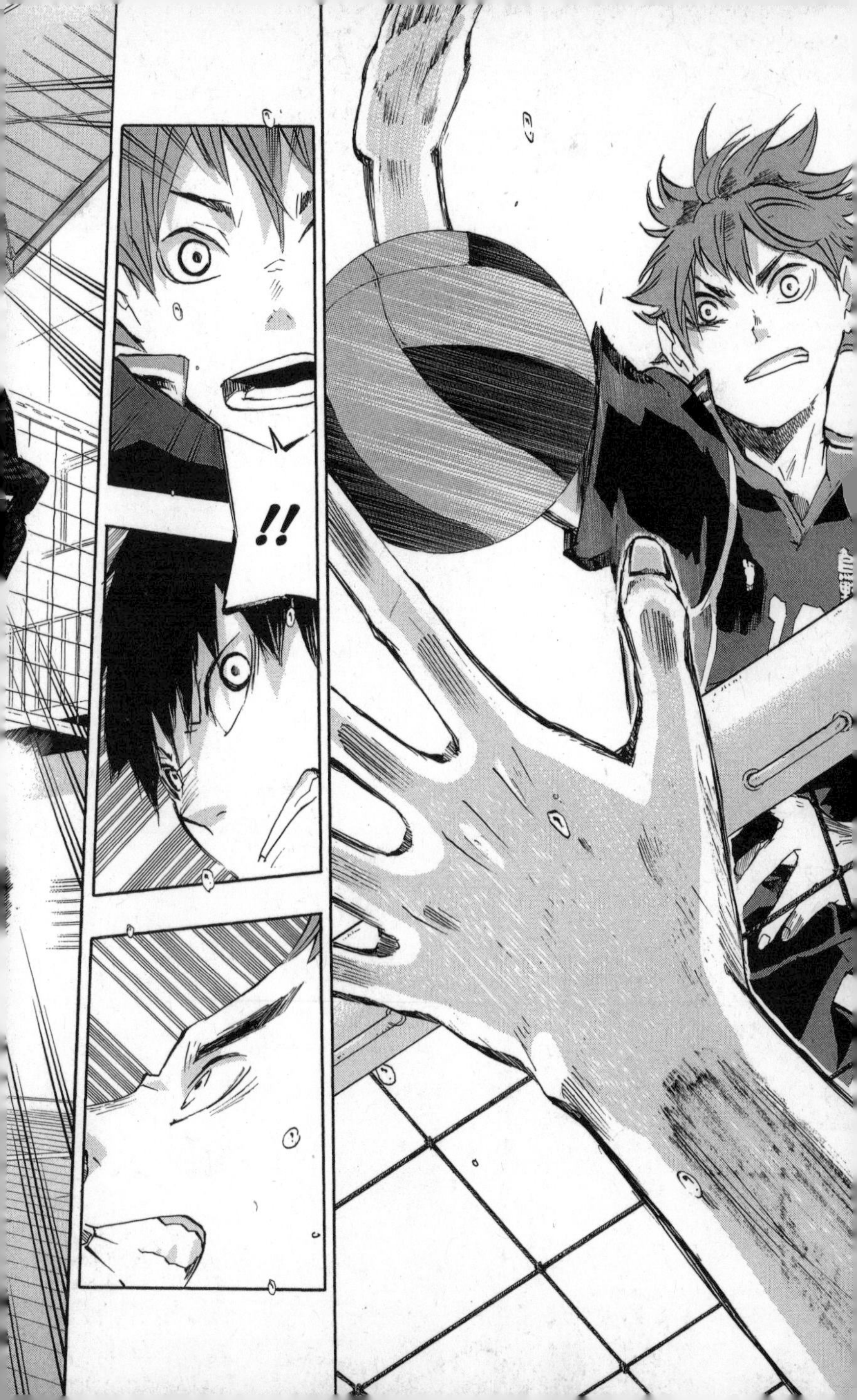
!!

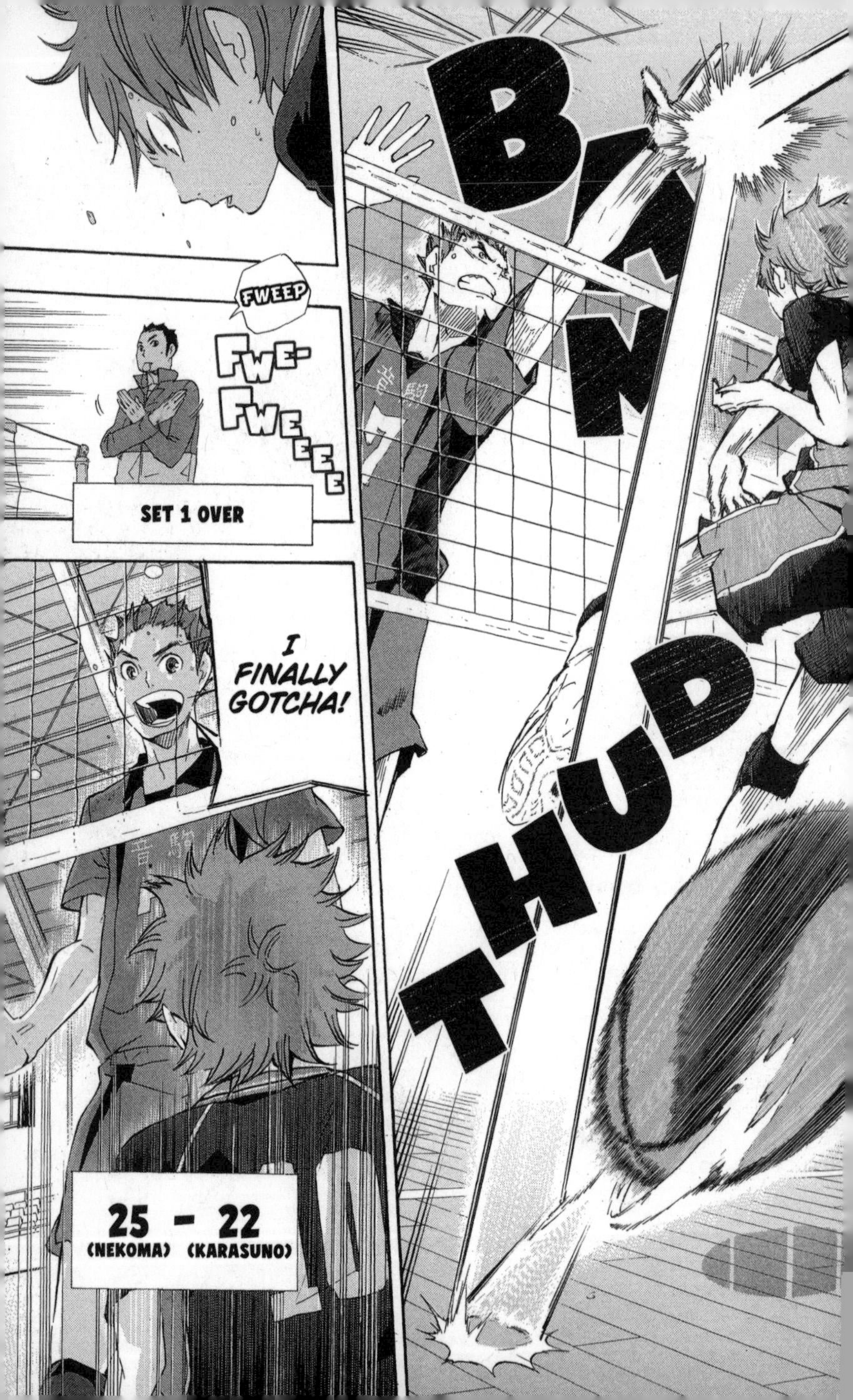
BAM
THUD
FWEEP
FWE-FWEEEEE
SET 1 OVER
I FINALLY GOTCHA!
25 - 22
(NEKOMA) (KARASUNO)

KENMA KOZUME

**NEKOMA HIGH SCHOOL
CLASS 2-3**

POSITION: SETTER

HEIGHT: 5'7"

**WEIGHT: 129 LBS.
(AS OF APRIL, 2ND YEAR
OF HIGH SCHOOL)**

BIRTHDAY: OCTOBER 16

**FAVORITE FOOD:
APPLE PIE**

**CURRENT WORRY:
SUMMER IS TOO HOT.
WINTER IS TOO COLD.**

**ABILITY PARAMETERS
(5-POINT SCALE)**

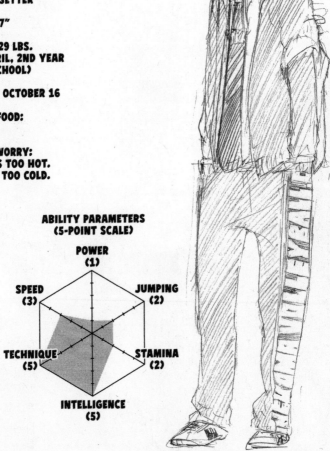

POWER
(1)

JUMPING
(2)

SPEED
(3)

STAMINA
(2)

TECHNIQUE
(5)

INTELLIGENCE
(5)

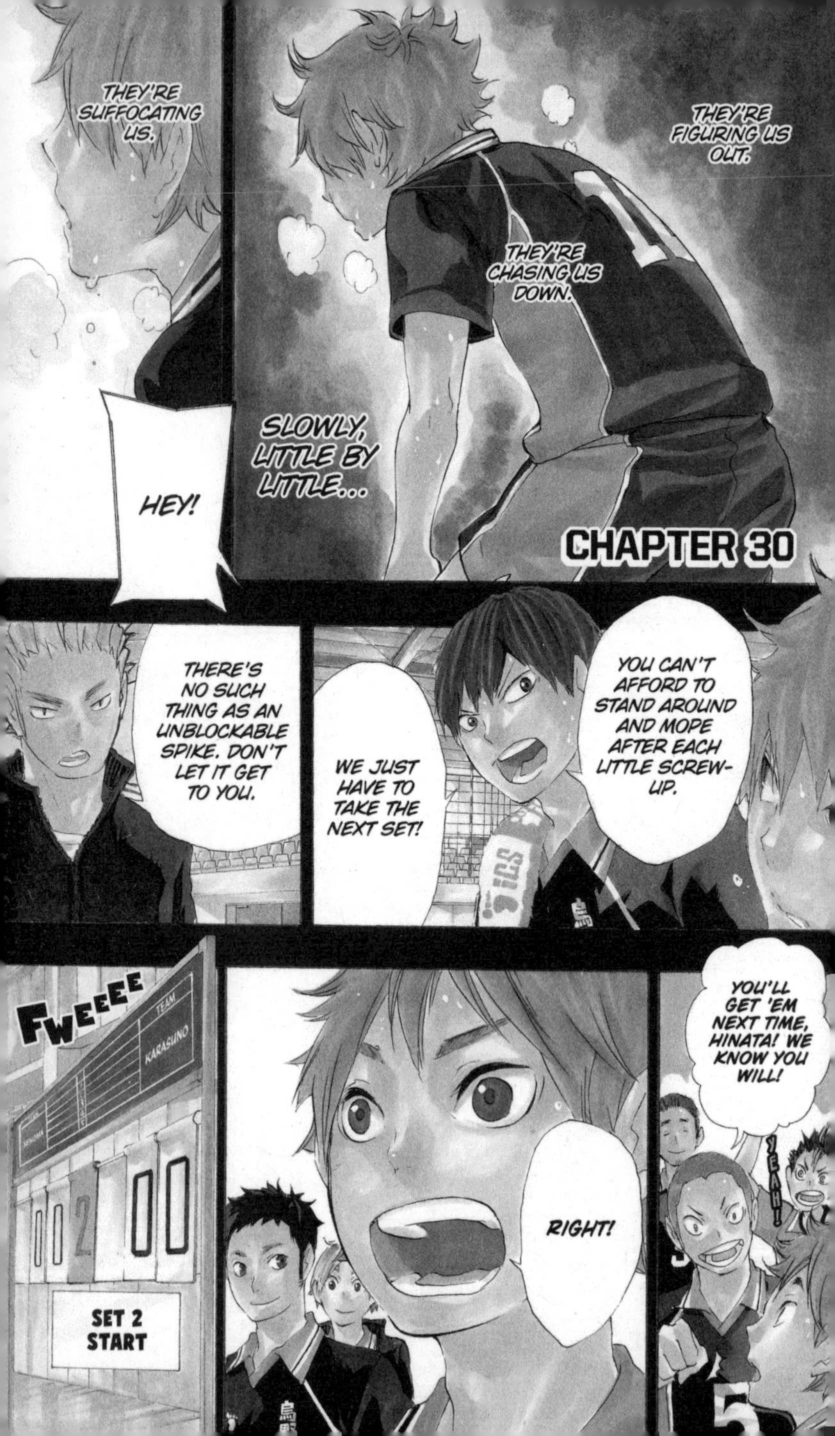
THEY'RE FIGURING US OUT.
THEY'RE CHASING US DOWN.
SLOWLY, LITTLE BY LITTLE...
CHAPTER 30
THEY'RE SUFFOCATING US.
HEY!
YOU CAN'T AFFORD TO STAND AROUND AND MOPE AFTER EACH LITTLE SCREW-UP.
WE JUST HAVE TO TAKE THE NEXT SET!
THERE'S NO SUCH THING AS AN UNBLOCKABLE SPIKE. DON'T LET IT GET TO YOU.
YOU'LL GET 'EM NEXT TIME, HINATA! WE KNOW YOU WILL!
YEAH!
RIGHT!
FWEEEE
TEAM
KARASUNO
SET 2 START

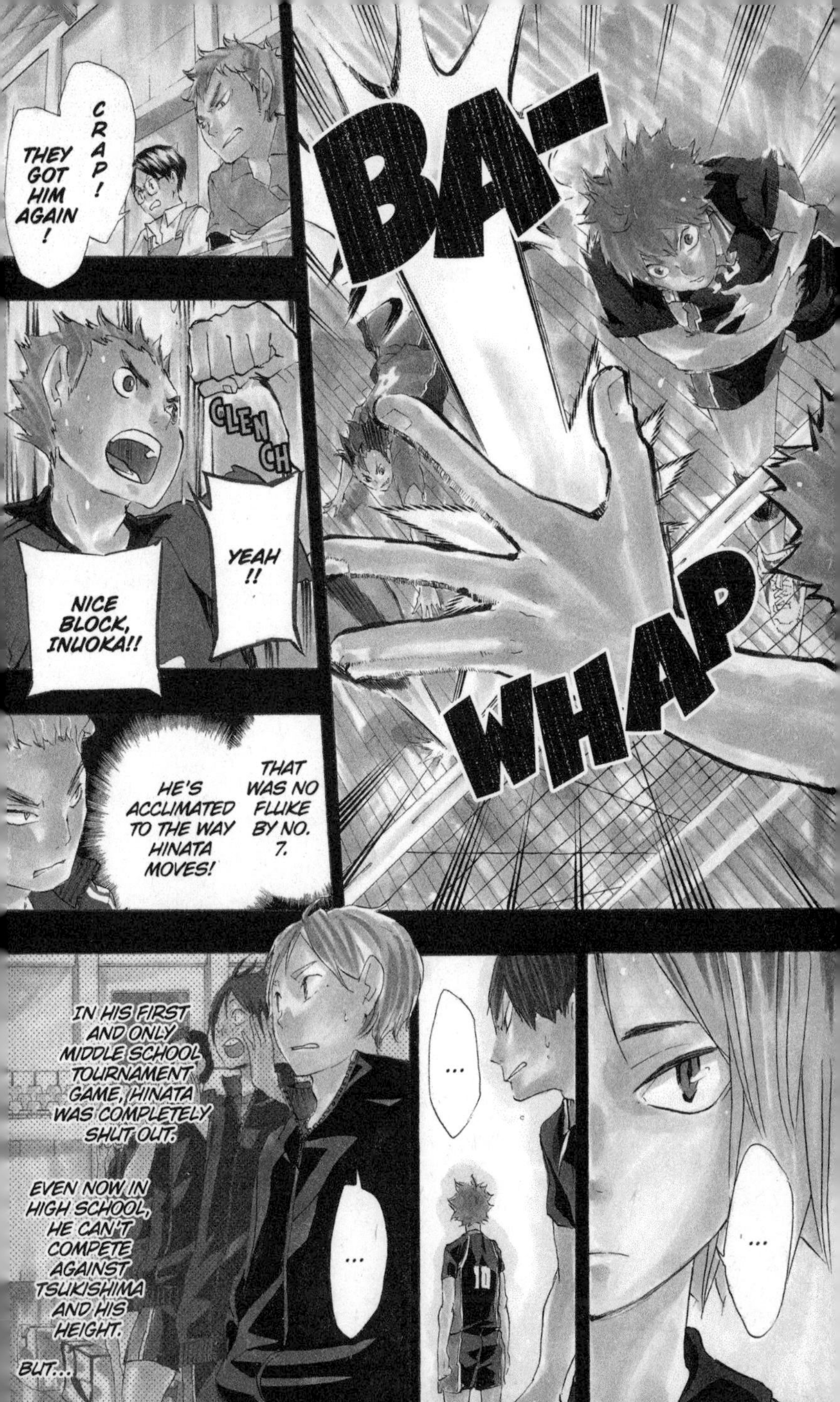
BA-
WHAP
CRAP!
THEY GOT HIM AGAIN!
CLENCH
YEAH!!
NICE BLOCK, INUOKA!!
THAT WAS NO FLUKE BY NO. 7.
HE'S ACCLIMATED TO THE WAY HINATA MOVES!
...
...
IN HIS FIRST AND ONLY MIDDLE SCHOOL TOURNAMENT GAME, HINATA WAS COMPLETELY SHUT OUT.
EVEN NOW IN HIGH SCHOOL, HE CAN'T COMPETE AGAINST TSUKISHIMA AND HIS HEIGHT.
BUT...
...

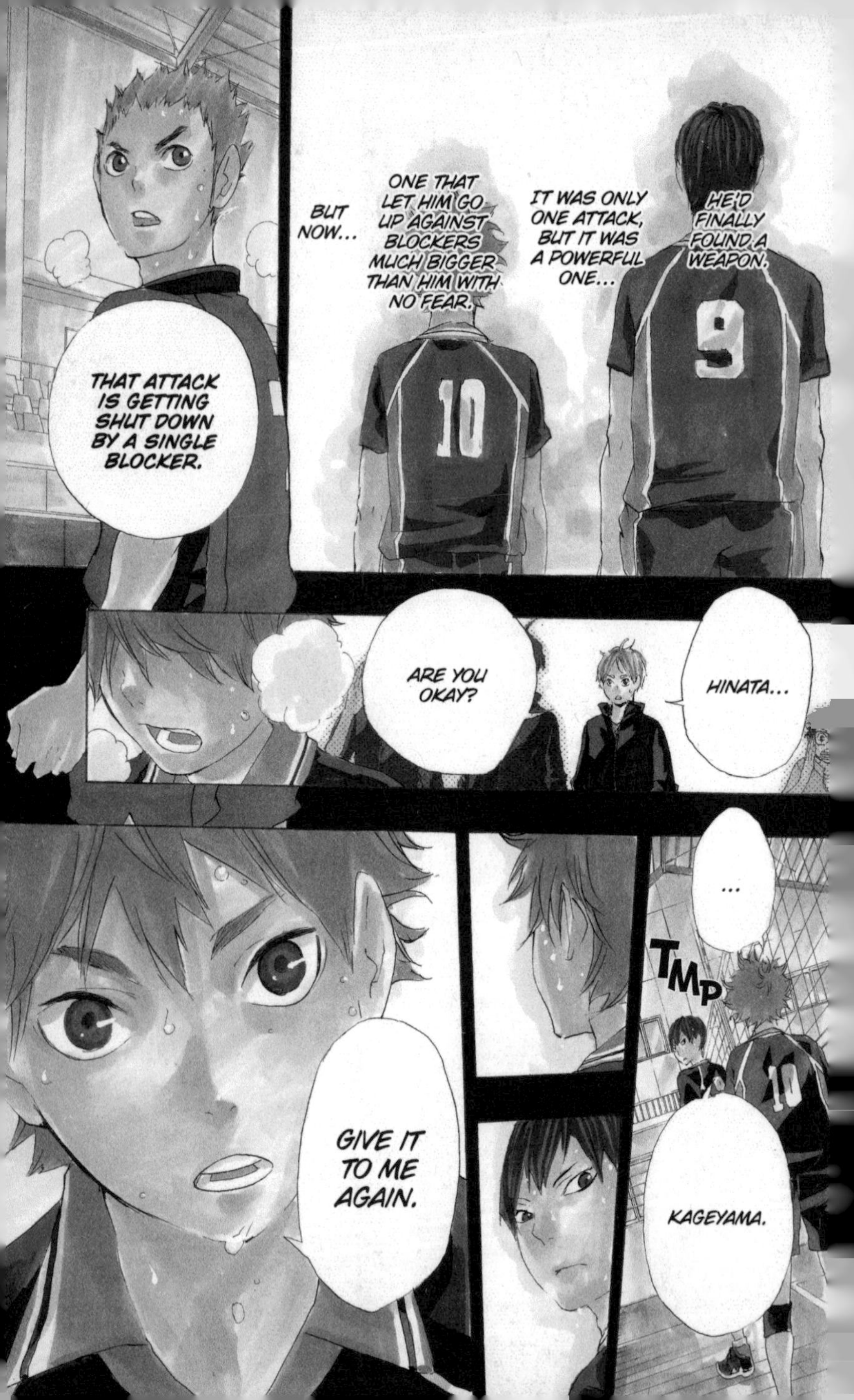
HE'D FINALLY FOUND A WEAPON.
IT WAS ONLY ONE ATTACK, BUT IT WAS A POWERFUL ONE...
ONE THAT LET HIM GO UP AGAINST BLOCKERS MUCH BIGGER THAN HIM WITH NO FEAR.
BUT NOW...
THAT ATTACK IS GETTING SHUT DOWN BY A SINGLE BLOCKER.
HINATA...
ARE YOU OKAY?
...
TMP
KAGEYAMA.
GIVE IT TO ME AGAIN.

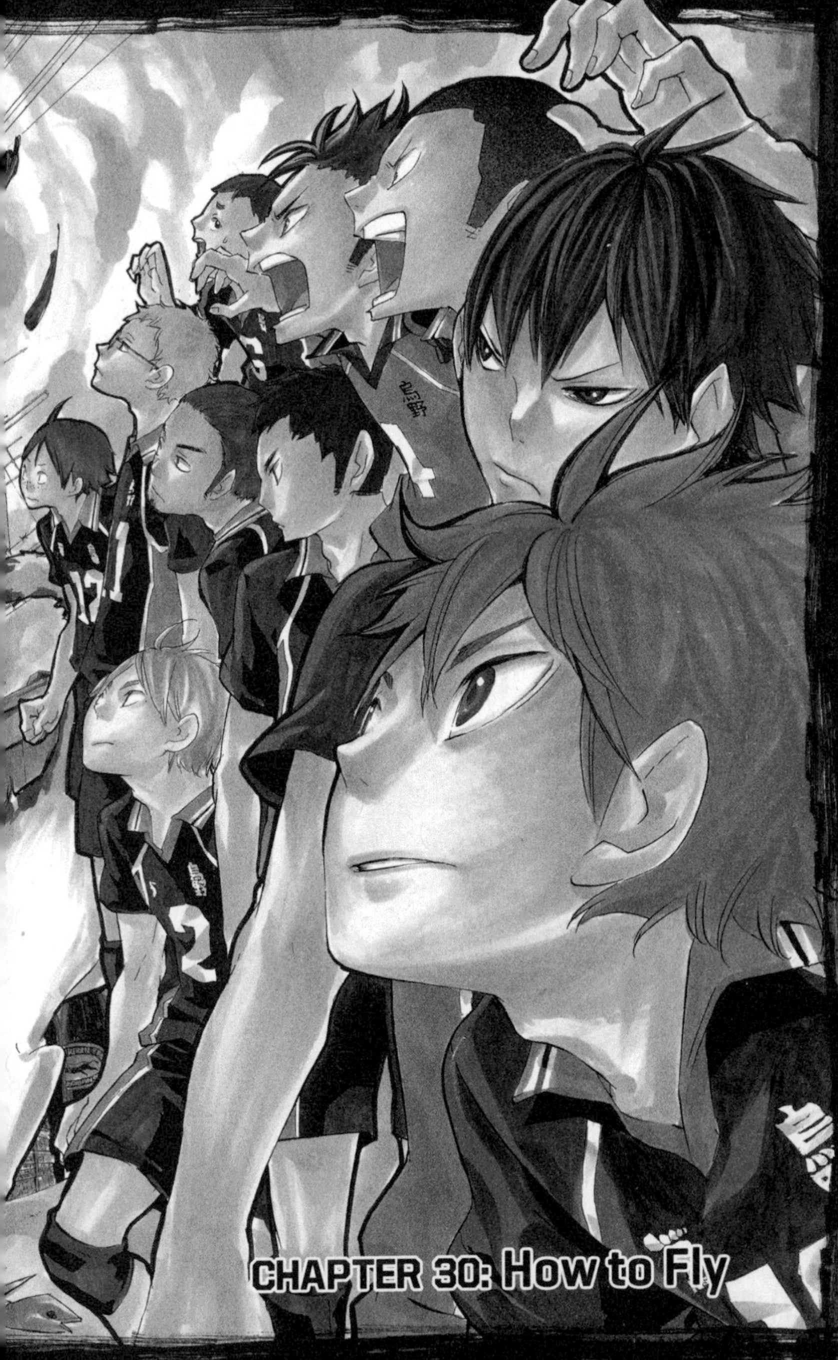

CHAPTER 30: How to Fly

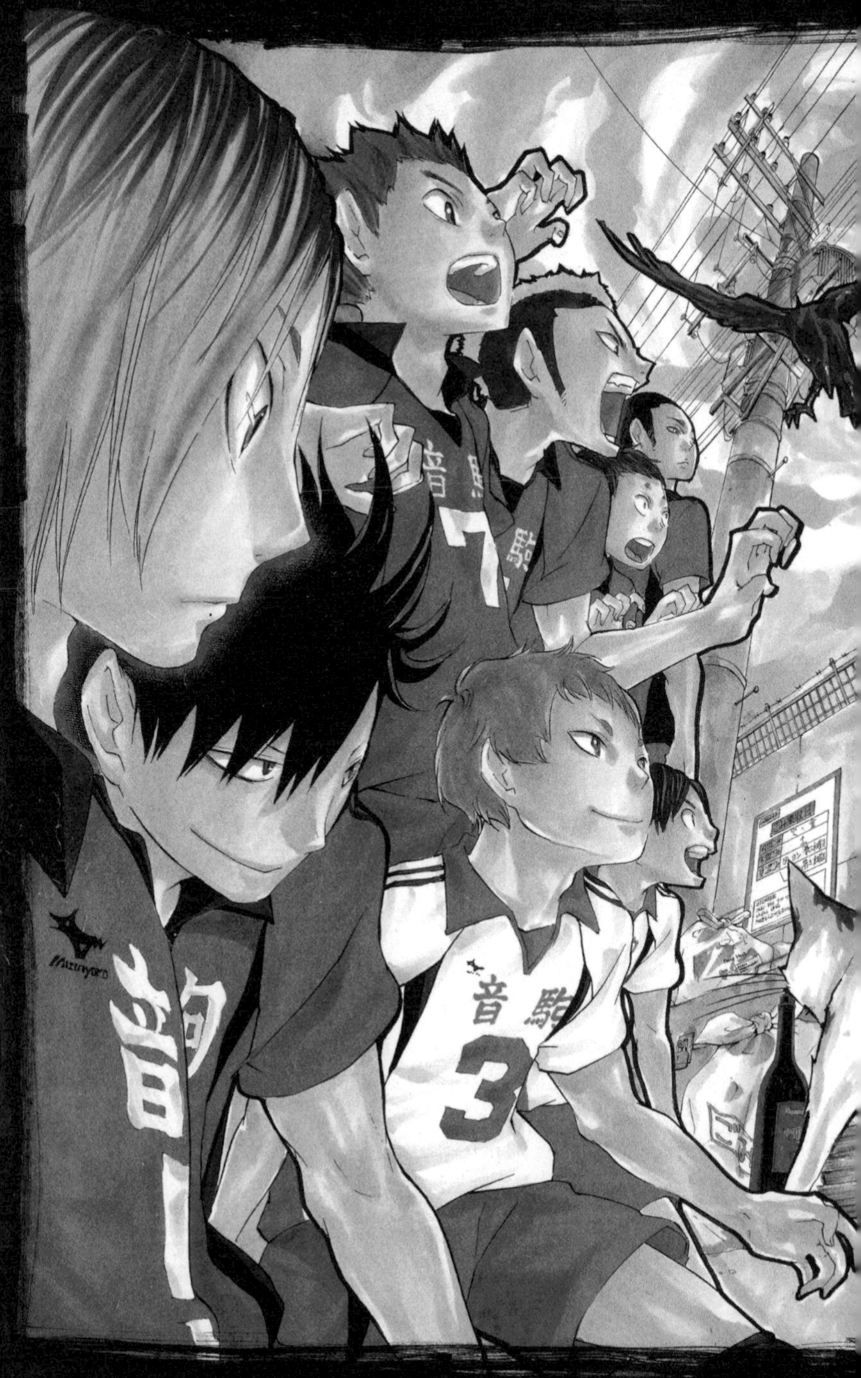
音駒
3

HAIKYU!!

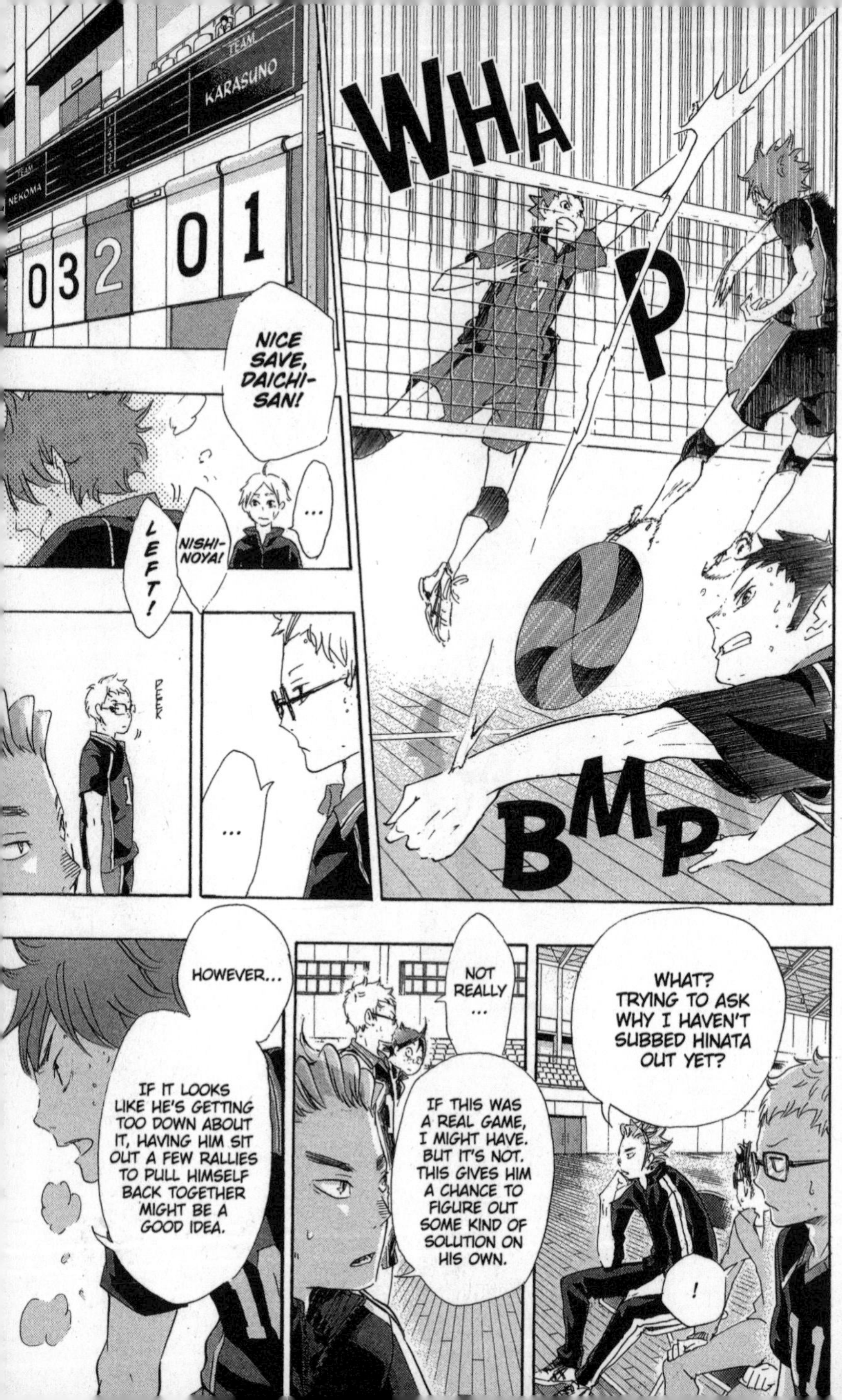
WHAP
BMP
TEAM
KARASUNO
TEAM
NEKOMA
03
2
0
1
NICE SAVE, DAICHI-SAN!
...
NISHINOYA!
LEFT!
...
PEEK
WHAT? TRYING TO ASK WHY I HAVEN'T SUBBED HINATA OUT YET?
!
NOT REALLY...
IF THIS WAS A REAL GAME, I MIGHT HAVE. BUT IT'S NOT. THIS GIVES HIM A CHANCE TO FIGURE OUT SOME KIND OF SOLUTION ON HIS OWN.
HOWEVER...
IF IT LOOKS LIKE HE'S GETTING TOO DOWN ABOUT IT, HAVING HIM SIT OUT A FEW RALLIES TO PULL HIMSELF BACK TOGETHER MIGHT BE A GOOD IDEA.

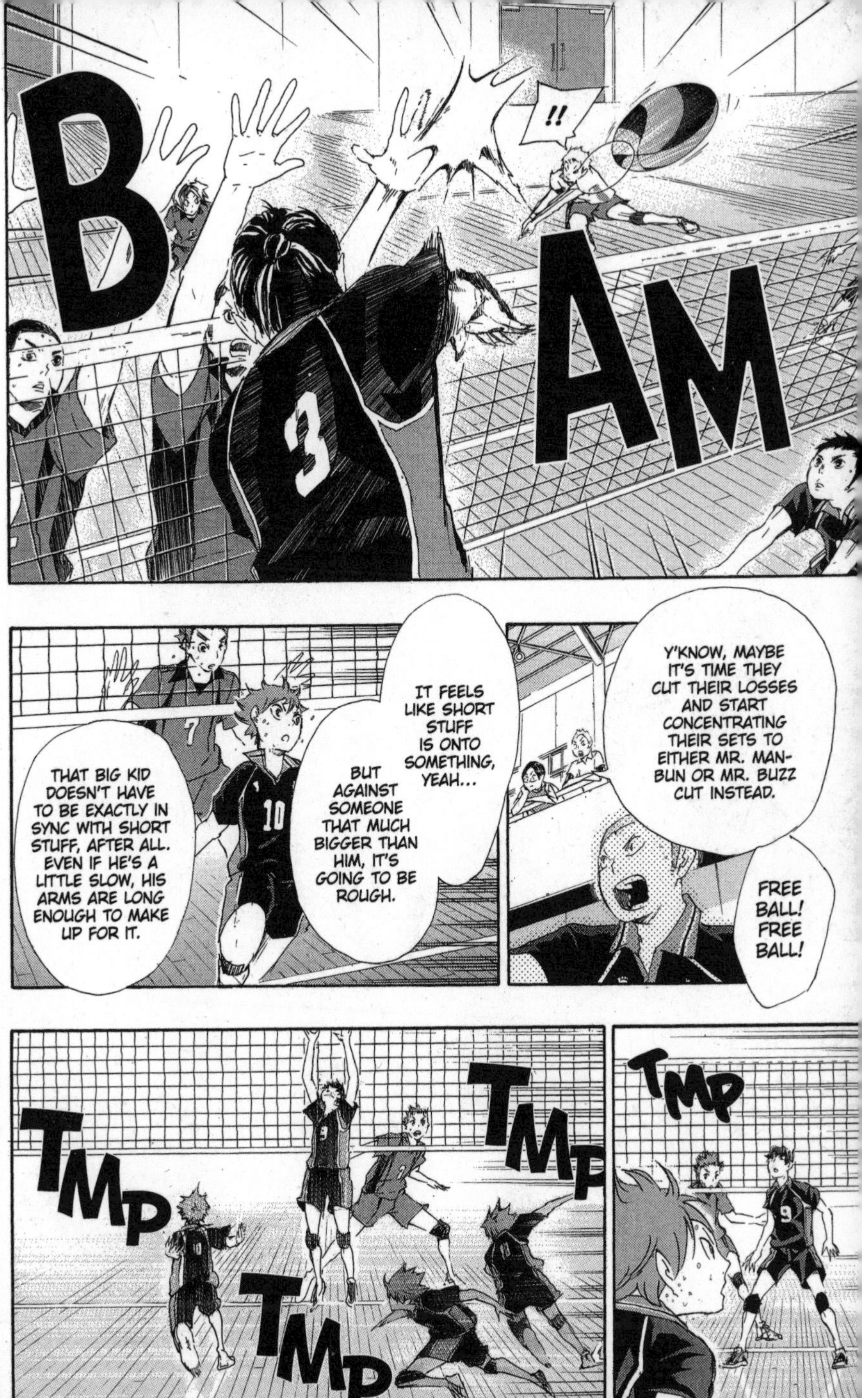
!!
BAM
Y'KNOW, MAYBE IT'S TIME THEY CUT THEIR LOSSES AND START CONCENTRATING THEIR SETS TO EITHER MR. MAN-BUN OR MR. BUZZ CUT INSTEAD.
FREE BALL! FREE BALL!
IT FEELS LIKE SHORT STUFF IS ONTO SOMETHING, YEAH...
BUT AGAINST SOMEONE THAT MUCH BIGGER THAN HIM, IT'S GOING TO BE ROUGH.
THAT BIG KID DOESN'T HAVE TO BE EXACTLY IN SYNC WITH SHORT STUFF, AFTER ALL. EVEN IF HE'S A LITTLE SLOW, HIS ARMS ARE LONG ENOUGH TO MAKE UP FOR IT.
TMP
TMP
TMP
TMP

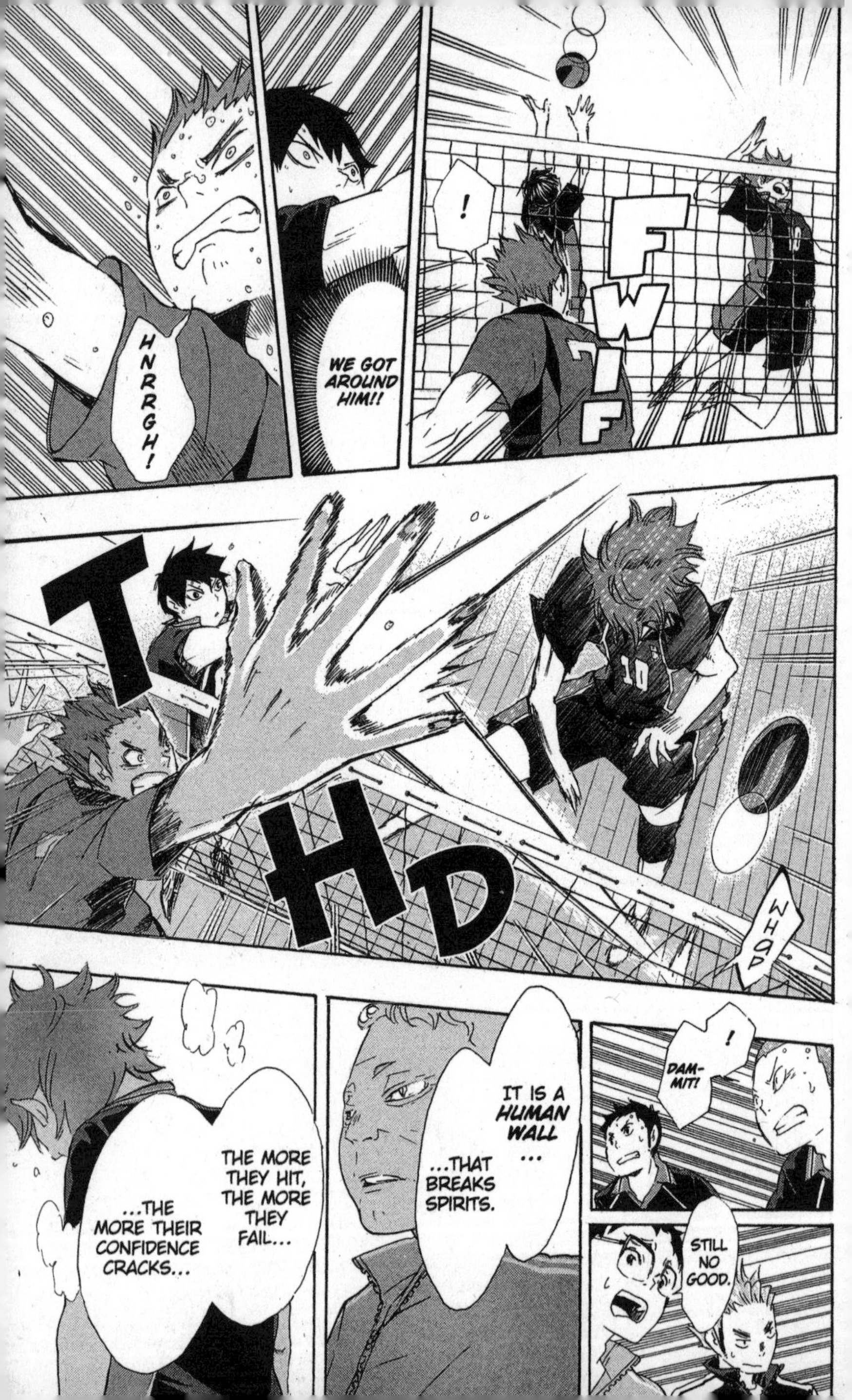
!
FWIF
WE GOT AROUND HIM!!
HNRRGH!
THD
WHAP
!
DAM-MIT!
STILL NO GOOD.
IT IS A *HUMAN WALL*...
...THAT BREAKS SPIRITS.
THE MORE THEY HIT, THE MORE THEY FAIL...
...THE MORE THEIR CONFIDENCE CRACKS...

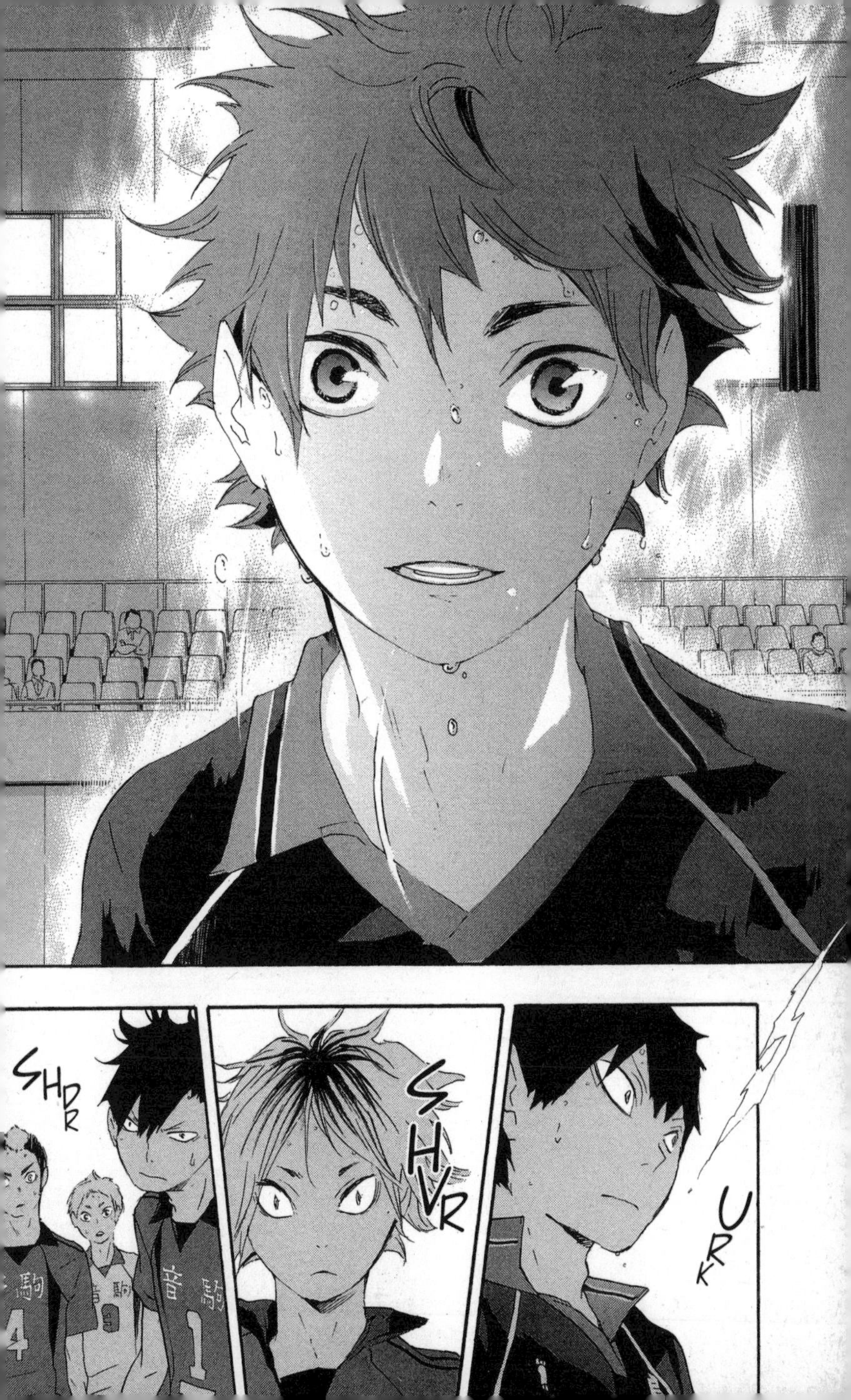
URK
SHVR
SHDR

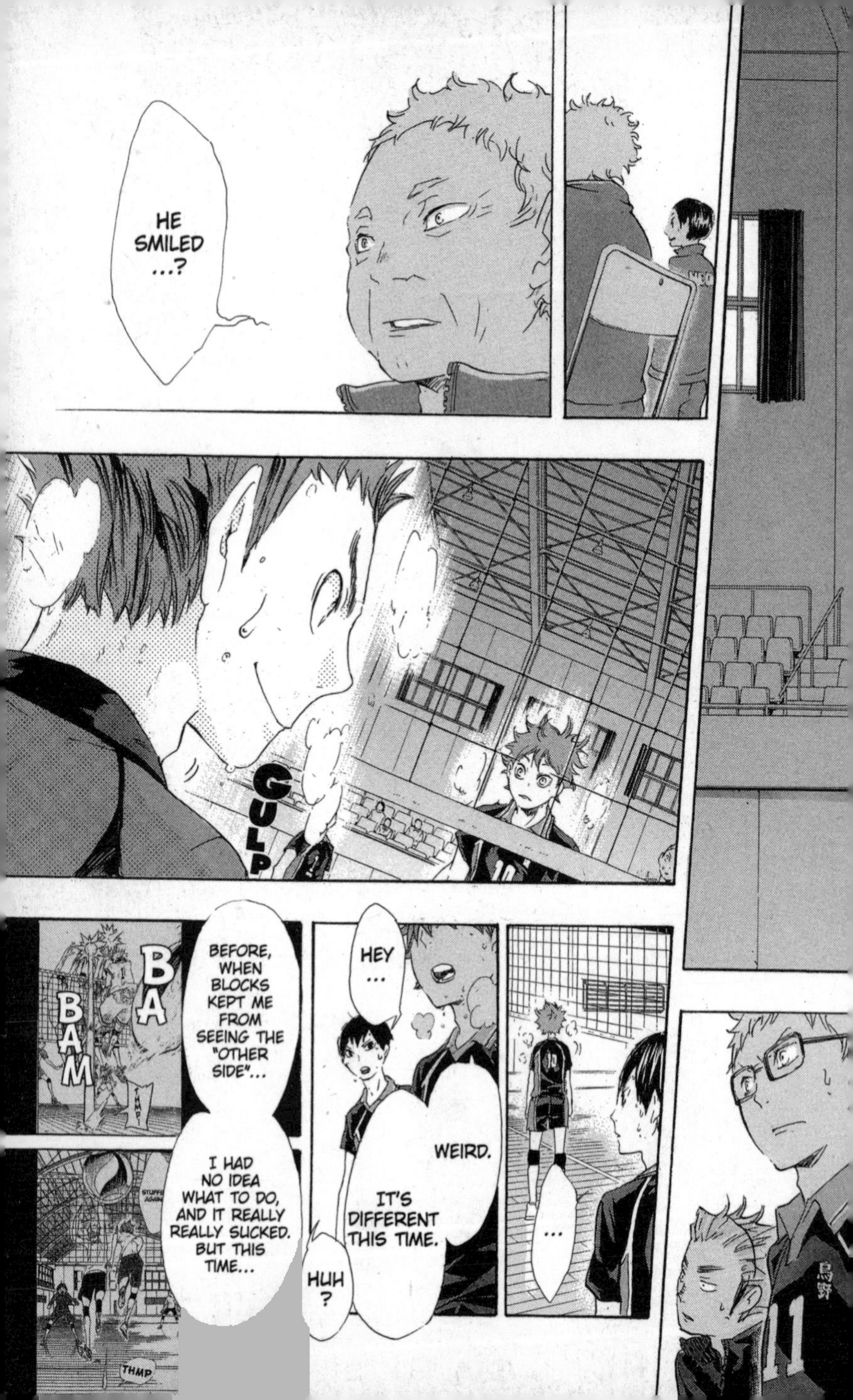
HE SMILED ...?
GULP
...
HEY ...
WEIRD.
IT'S DIFFERENT THIS TIME.
HUH ?
BEFORE, WHEN BLOCKS KEPT ME FROM SEEING THE "OTHER SIDE"...
I HAD NO IDEA WHAT TO DO, AND IT REALLY REALLY SUCKED. BUT THIS TIME...
BA BAM
THMP
THMP

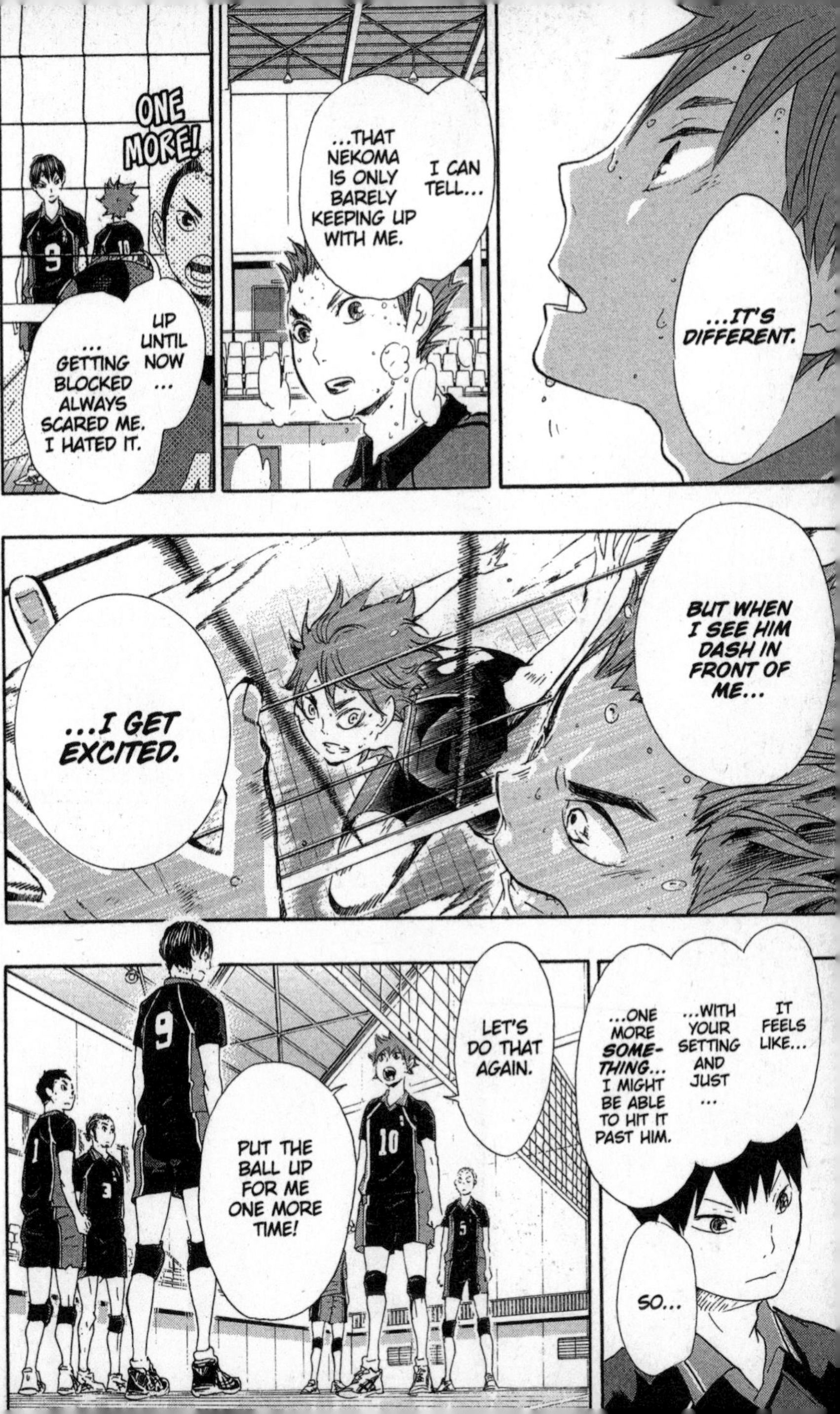
...IT'S DIFFERENT.
I CAN TELL...
...THAT NEKOMA IS ONLY BARELY KEEPING UP WITH ME.
ONE MORE!
UP UNTIL NOW...
...GETTING BLOCKED ALWAYS SCARED ME. I HATED IT.
BUT WHEN I SEE HIM DASH IN FRONT OF ME...
...I GET EXCITED.
IT FEELS LIKE...
...WITH YOUR SETTING AND JUST...
...ONE MORE SOMETHING... I MIGHT BE ABLE TO HIT IT PAST HIM.
SO...
LET'S DO THAT AGAIN.
PUT THE BALL UP FOR ME ONE MORE TIME!

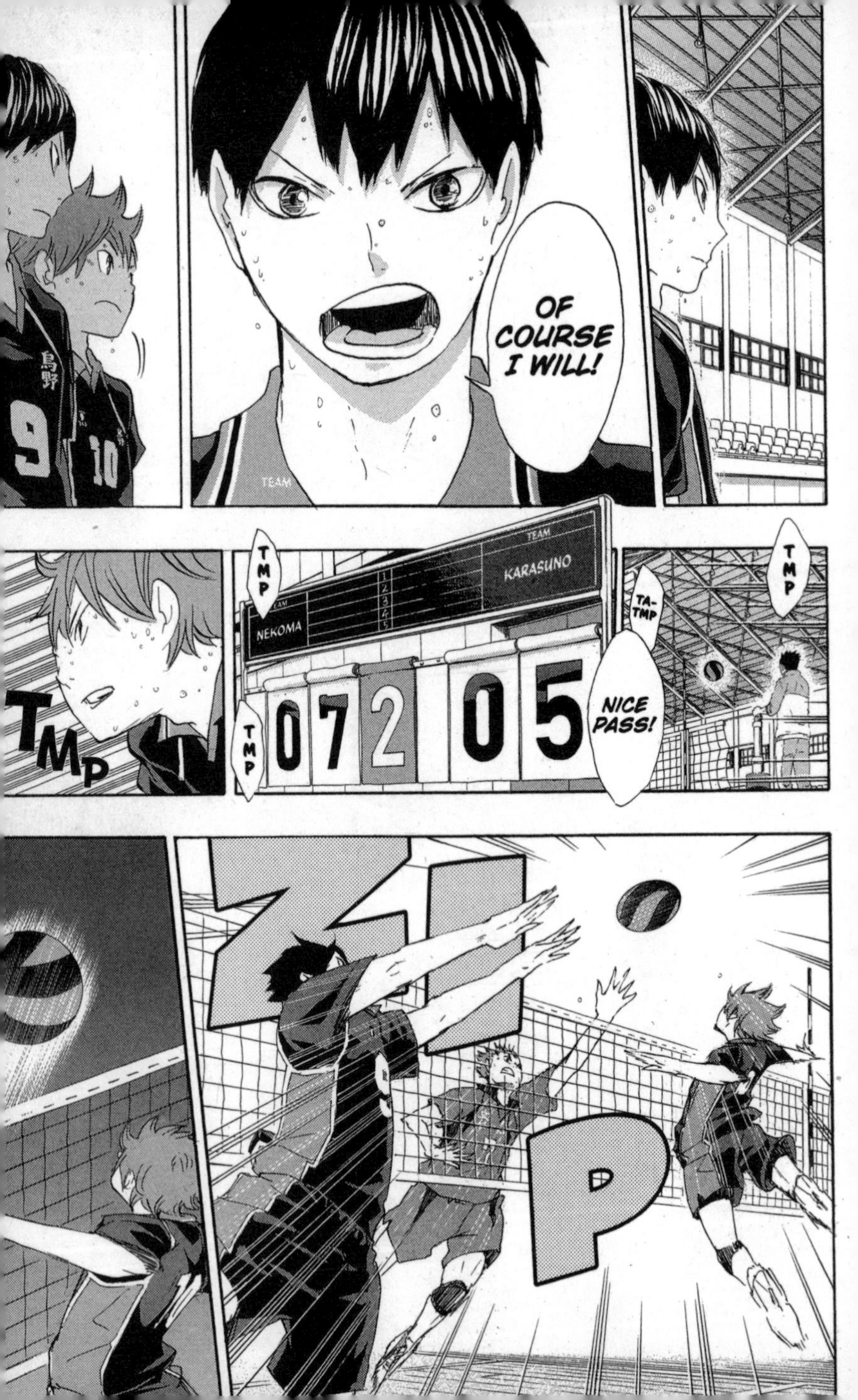
OF COURSE I WILL!
TMP
TA-TMP
NICE PASS!
TMP
TEAM
KARASUNO
NEKOMA
07 2 05
TMP
TMP
ZIP

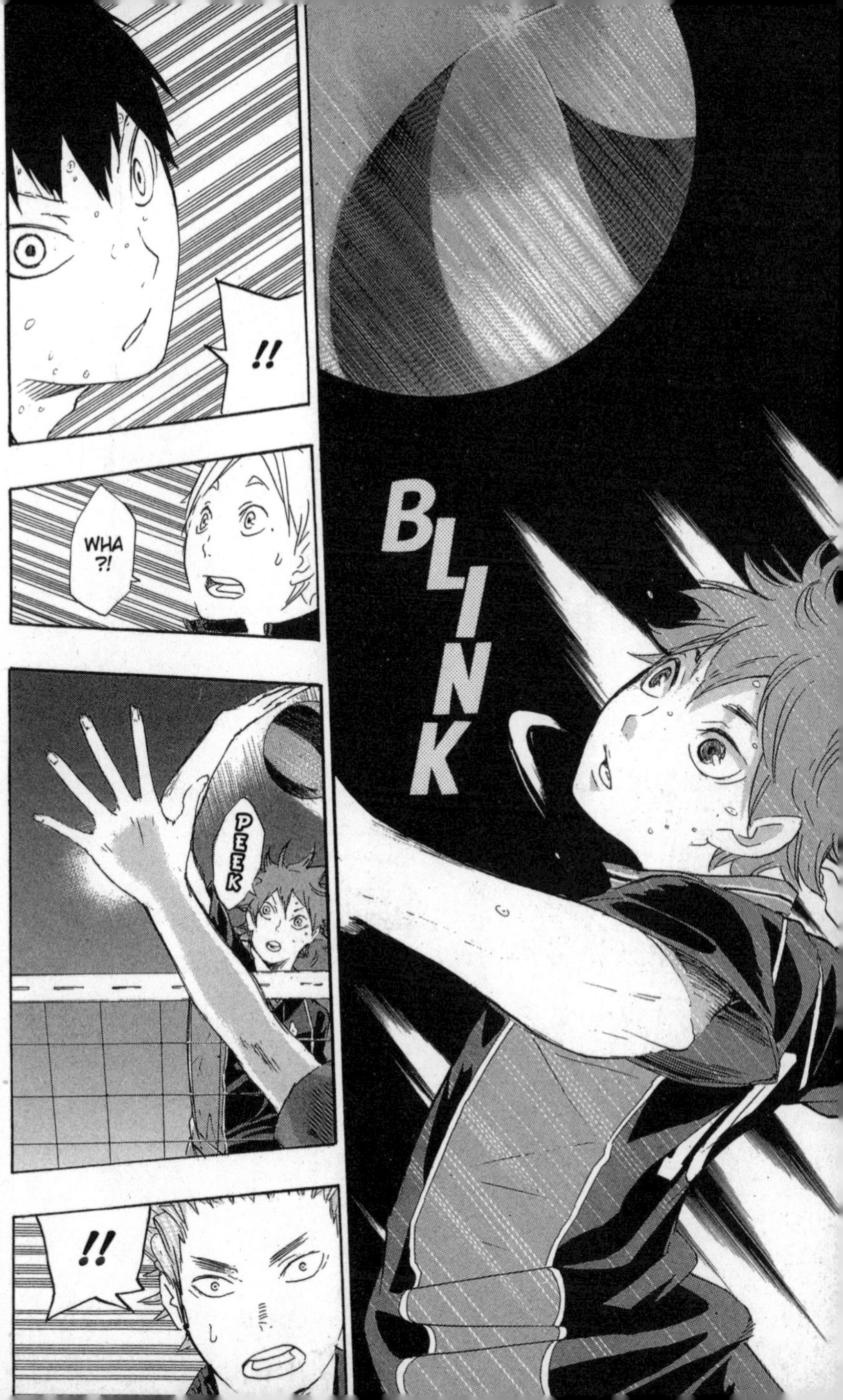
BLINK
!!
WHA ?!
PEEK
!!

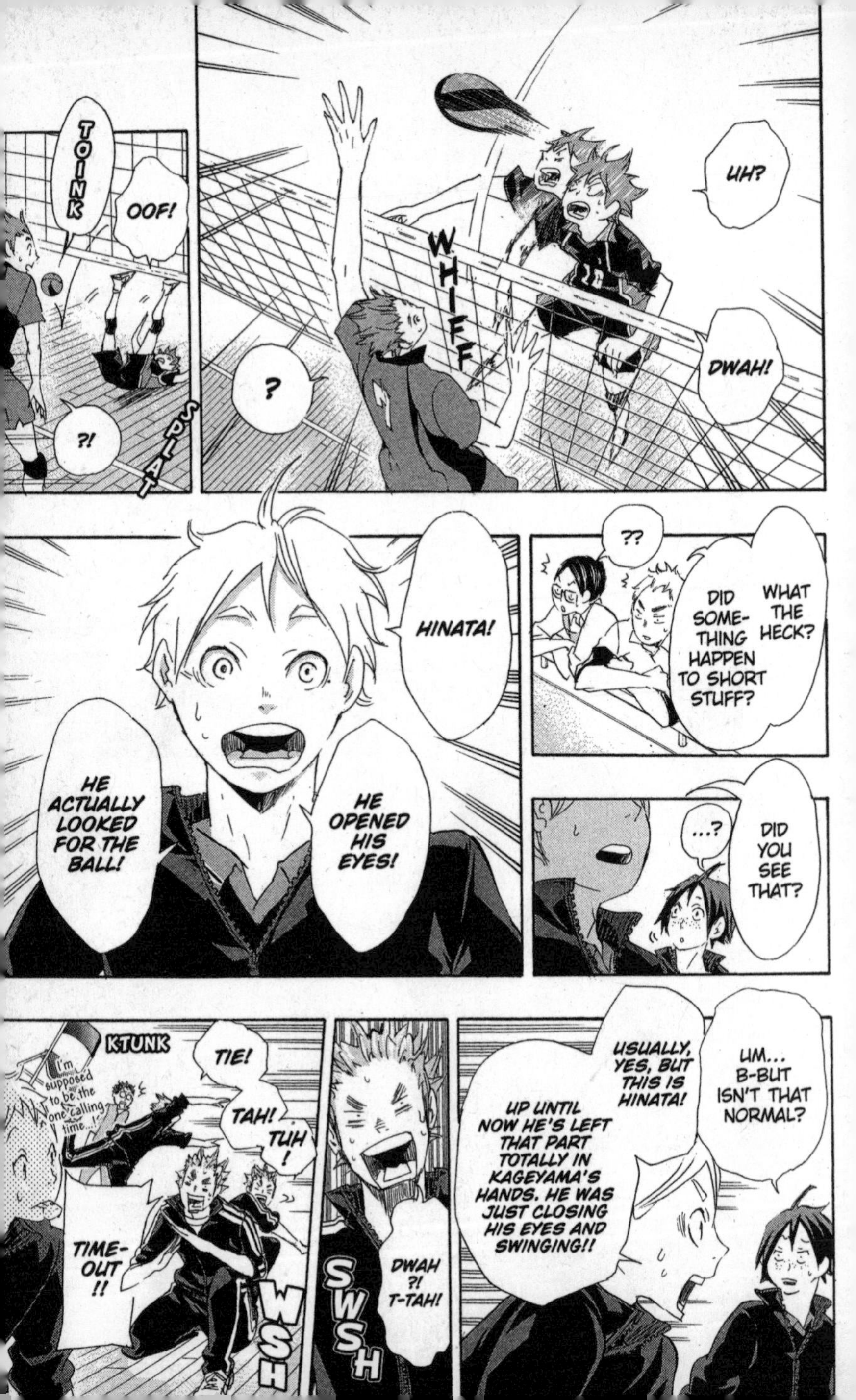
UH?
DWAH!
WHIFF
?
OOF!
TOINK
?!
SPLAT
WHAT THE HECK?
DID SOMETHING HAPPEN TO SHORT STUFF?
??
DID YOU SEE THAT?
...?
HINATA!
HE OPENED HIS EYES!
HE ACTUALLY LOOKED FOR THE BALL!
UM... B-BUT ISN'T THAT NORMAL?
USUALLY, YES, BUT THIS IS HINATA!
UP UNTIL NOW HE'S LEFT THAT PART TOTALLY IN KAGEYAMA'S HANDS. HE WAS JUST CLOSING HIS EYES AND SWINGING!!
DWAH?! T-TAH!
SWSH
TIE!
TAH!
TUH!
KTUNK
I'm supposed to be the one calling time...!
TIME-OUT!!
WSH

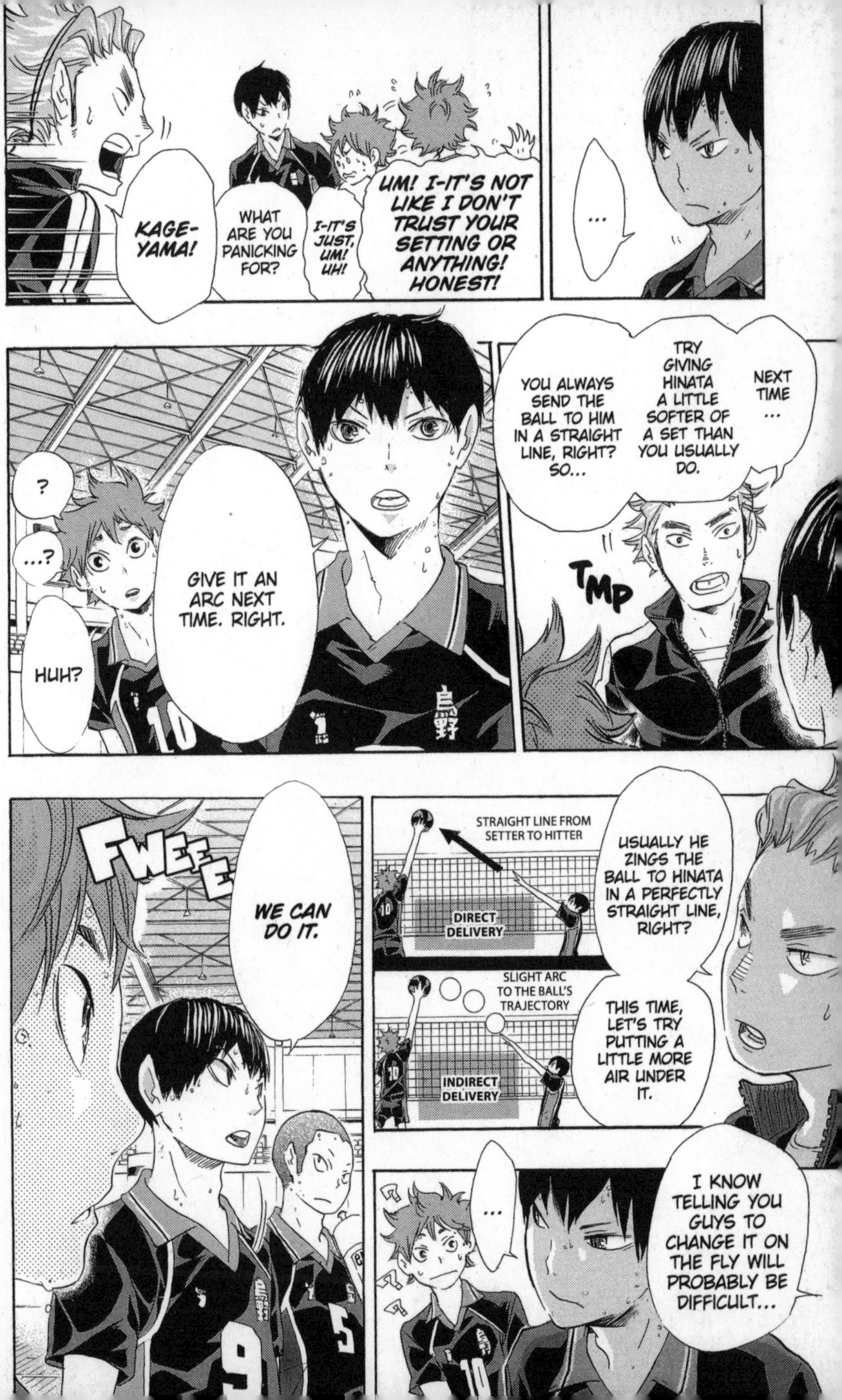
...
UM! I-IT'S NOT LIKE I DON'T TRUST YOUR SETTING OR ANYTHING! HONEST!
I-IT'S JUST, UM! UH!
WHAT ARE YOU PANICKING FOR?
KAGE-YAMA!
NEXT TIME...
TRY GIVING HINATA A LITTLE SOFTER OF A SET THAN YOU USUALLY DO.
YOU ALWAYS SEND THE BALL TO HIM IN A STRAIGHT LINE, RIGHT? SO...
TMP
GIVE IT AN ARC NEXT TIME. RIGHT.
?
...?
HUH?
USUALLY HE ZINGS THE BALL TO HINATA IN A PERFECTLY STRAIGHT LINE, RIGHT?
THIS TIME, LET'S TRY PUTTING A LITTLE MORE AIR UNDER IT.
STRAIGHT LINE FROM SETTER TO HITTER
DIRECT DELIVERY
SLIGHT ARC TO THE BALL'S TRAJECTORY
INDIRECT DELIVERY
I KNOW TELLING YOU GUYS TO CHANGE IT ON THE FLY WILL PROBABLY BE DIFFICULT...
...
WE CAN DO IT.
FWEEE

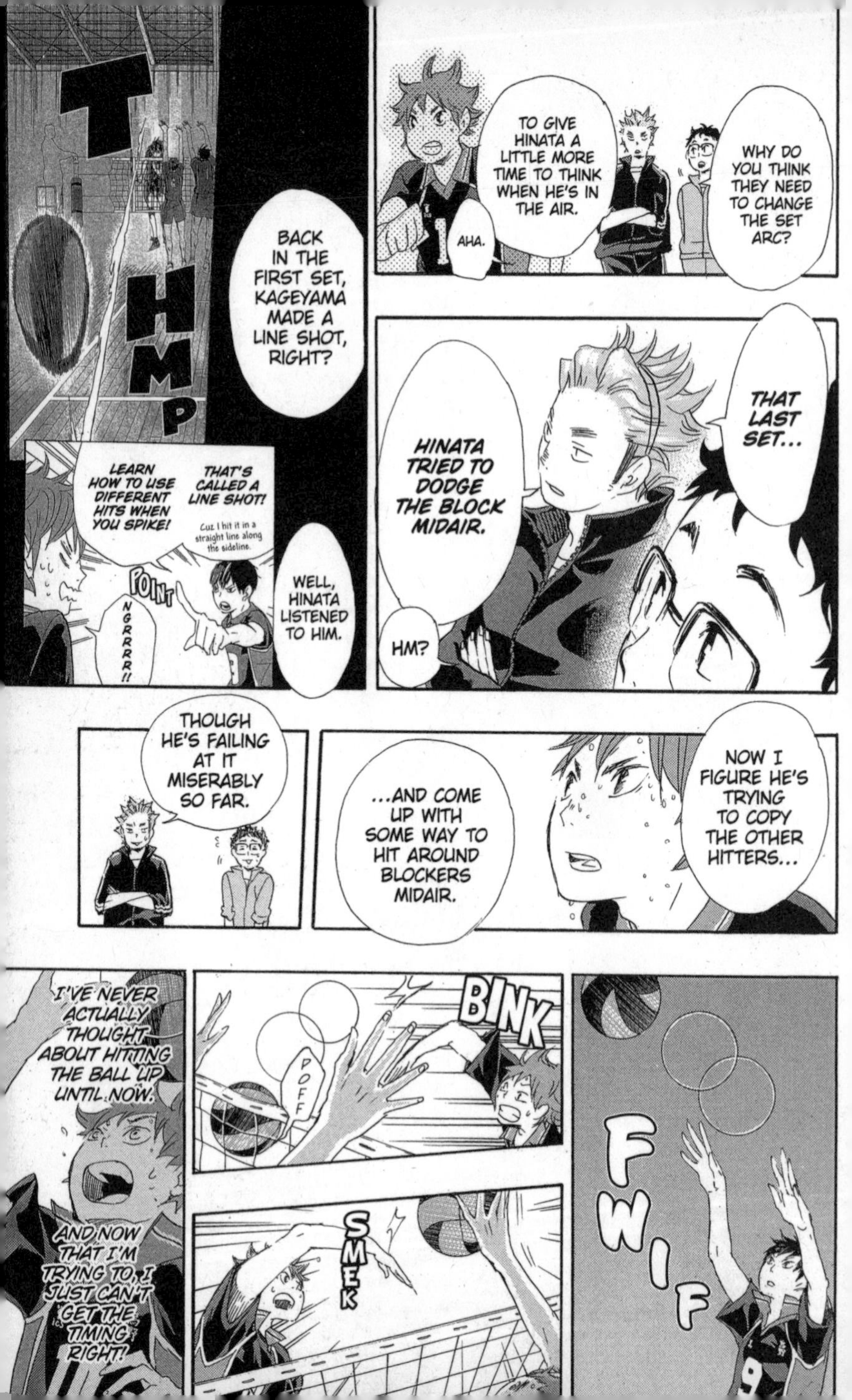
WHY DO YOU THINK THEY NEED TO CHANGE THE SET ARC?
TO GIVE HINATA A LITTLE MORE TIME TO THINK WHEN HE'S IN THE AIR.
AHA.
THAT LAST SET...
HINATA TRIED TO DODGE THE BLOCK MIDAIR.
HM?
THMP
BACK IN THE FIRST SET, KAGEYAMA MADE A LINE SHOT, RIGHT?
THAT'S CALLED A LINE SHOT!
LEARN HOW TO USE DIFFERENT HITS WHEN YOU SPIKE!
Cuz I hit it in a straight line along the sideline.
POINT
NGRRRR!!
WELL, HINATA LISTENED TO HIM.
NOW I FIGURE HE'S TRYING TO COPY THE OTHER HITTERS...
...AND COME UP WITH SOME WAY TO HIT AROUND BLOCKERS MIDAIR.
THOUGH HE'S FAILING AT IT MISERABLY SO FAR.
FWIF
BINK
POFF
SMEK
I'VE NEVER ACTUALLY THOUGHT ABOUT HITTING THE BALL UP UNTIL NOW.
AND NOW THAT I'M TRYING TO, I JUST CAN'T GET THE TIMING RIGHT!

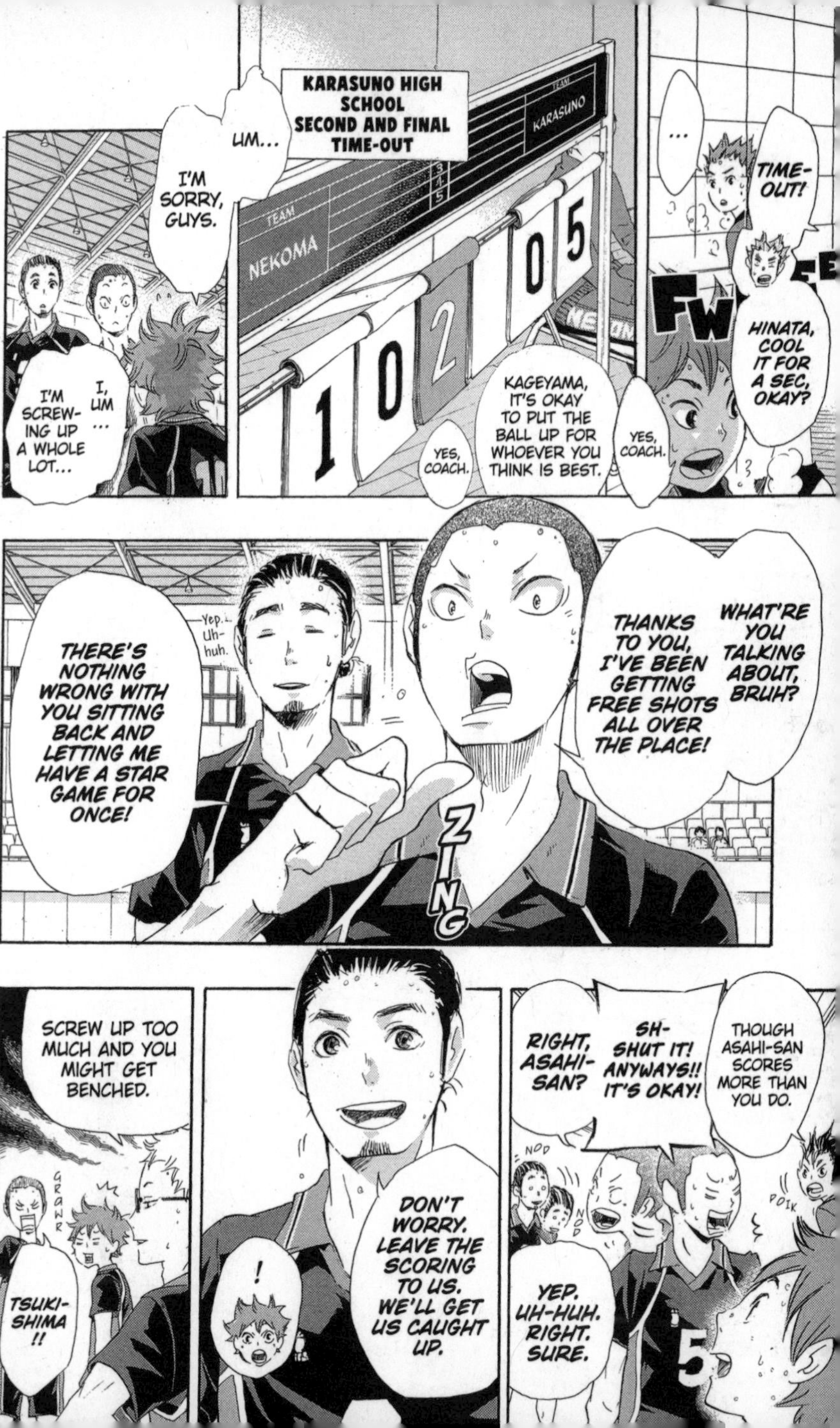

...
TIME-OUT!
FWEE
HINATA, COOL IT FOR A SEC, OKAY?
YES, COACH.
KARASUNO HIGH SCHOOL SECOND AND FINAL TIME-OUT
KARASUNO
NEKOMA
10 2 05
KAGEYAMA, IT'S OKAY TO PUT THE BALL UP FOR WHOEVER YOU THINK IS BEST.
YES, COACH.
UM...
I'M SORRY, GUYS.
I, UM...
I'M SCREWING UP A WHOLE LOT...
WHAT'RE YOU TALKING ABOUT, BRUH?
THANKS TO YOU, I'VE BEEN GETTING FREE SHOTS ALL OVER THE PLACE!
ZING
Yep. Uh-huh.
THERE'S NOTHING WRONG WITH YOU SITTING BACK AND LETTING ME HAVE A STAR GAME FOR ONCE!
THOUGH ASAHI-SAN SCORES MORE THAN YOU DO.
SH-SHUT IT! ANYWAYS!! IT'S OKAY!
RIGHT, ASAHI-SAN?
POIK
NOD
NOD
YEP. UH-HUH. RIGHT. SURE.
DON'T WORRY. LEAVE THE SCORING TO US. WE'LL GET US CAUGHT UP.
!
SCREW UP TOO MUCH AND YOU MIGHT GET BENCHED.
GRAWR
TSUKISHIMA!!

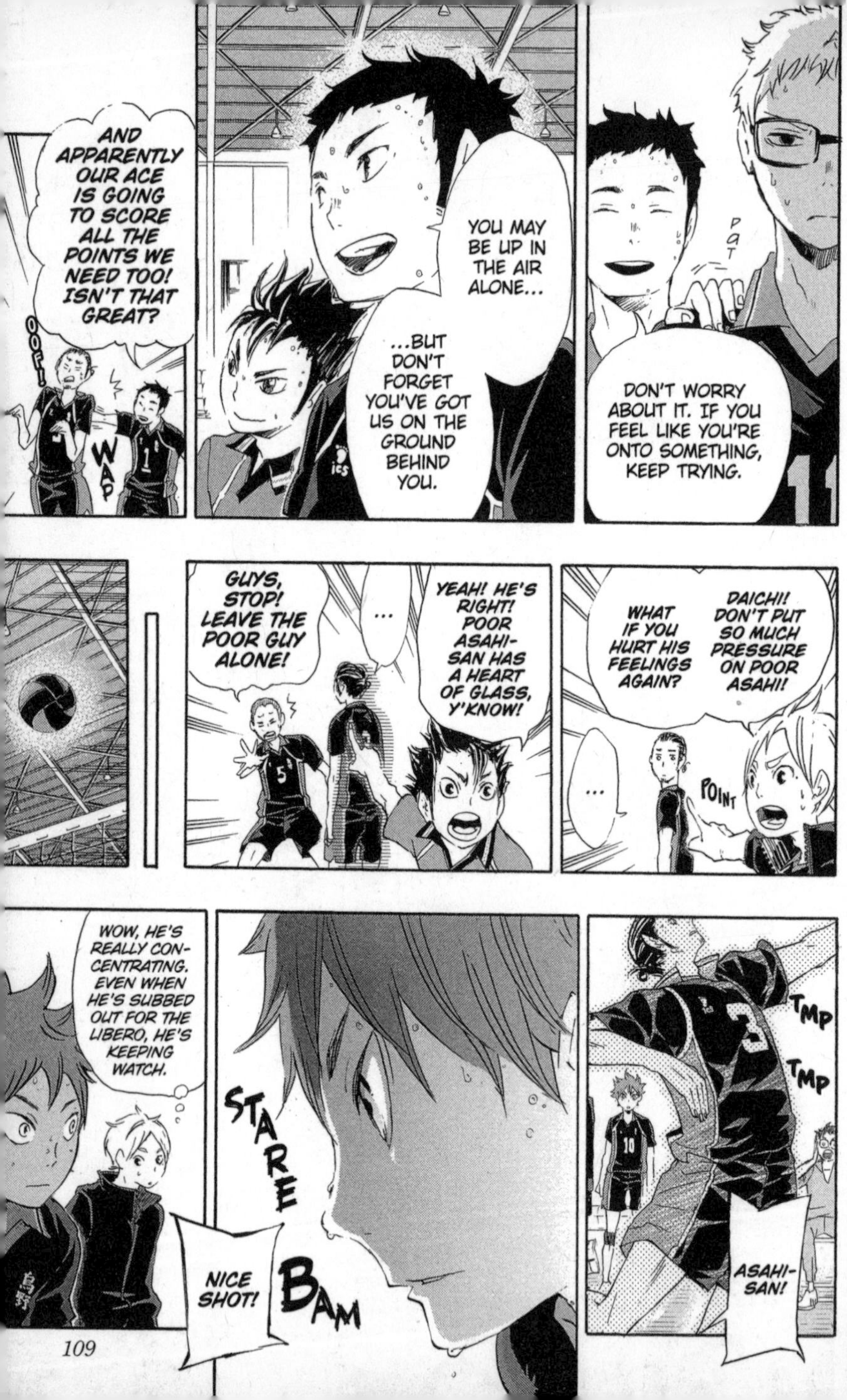
PAT
DON'T WORRY ABOUT IT. IF YOU FEEL LIKE YOU'RE ONTO SOMETHING, KEEP TRYING.
YOU MAY BE UP IN THE AIR ALONE...
...BUT DON'T FORGET YOU'VE GOT US ON THE GROUND BEHIND YOU.
AND APPARENTLY OUR ACE IS GOING TO SCORE ALL THE POINTS WE NEED TOO! ISN'T THAT GREAT?
OOF!
WAP
DAICHI! DON'T PUT SO MUCH PRESSURE ON POOR ASAHI!
WHAT IF YOU HURT HIS FEELINGS AGAIN?
...
POINT
YEAH! HE'S RIGHT! POOR ASAHI-SAN HAS A HEART OF GLASS, Y'KNOW!
...
GUYS, STOP! LEAVE THE POOR GUY ALONE!
TMP
TMP
ASAHI-SAN!
STARE
BAM
NICE SHOT!
WOW, HE'S REALLY CON-CENTRATING. EVEN WHEN HE'S SUBBED OUT FOR THE LIBERO, HE'S KEEPING WATCH.

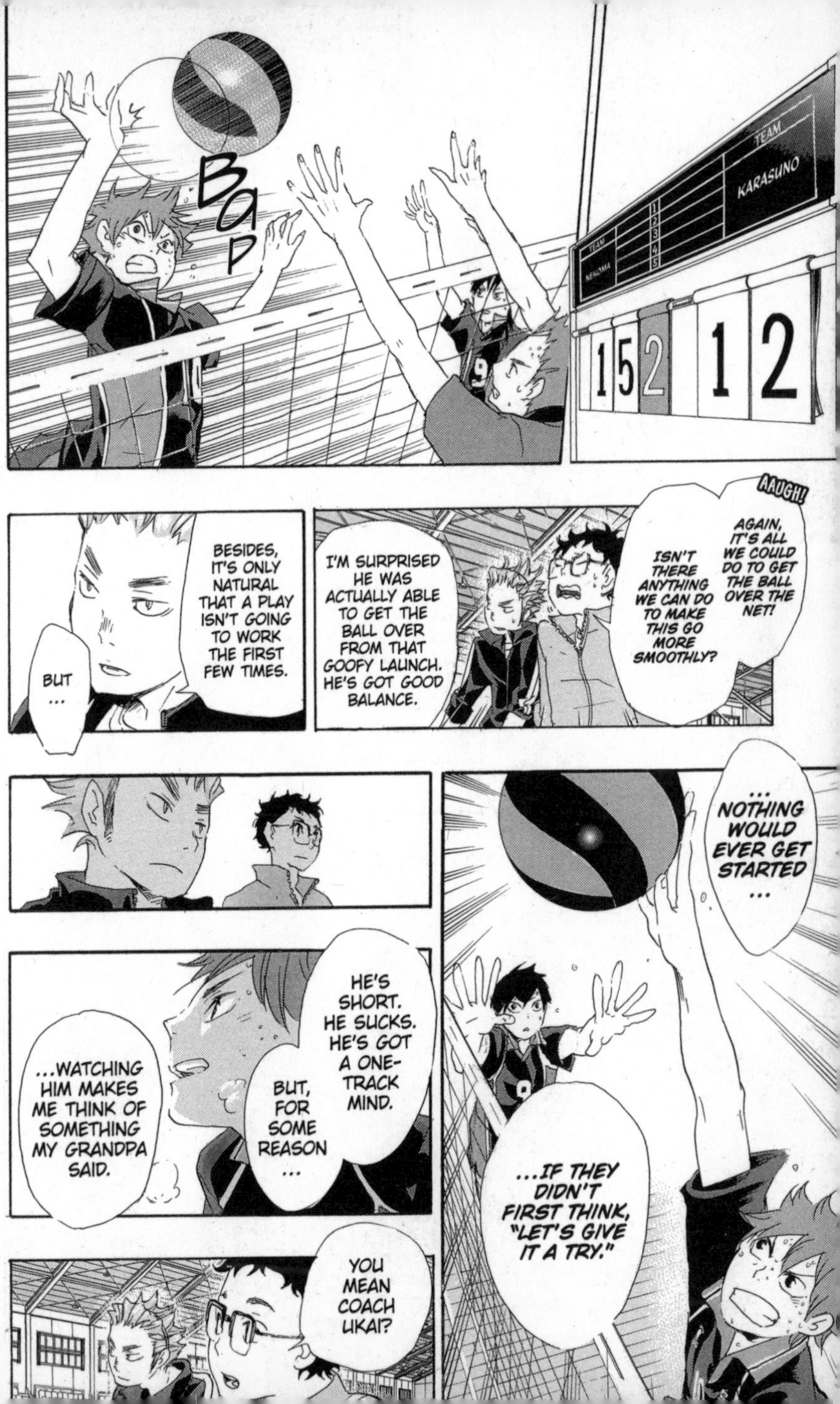
BAP
TEAM
KARASUNO
TEAM
NEKOMA
AAUGH!
AGAIN, IT'S ALL WE COULD DO TO GET THE BALL OVER THE NET!
ISN'T THERE ANYTHING WE CAN DO TO MAKE THIS GO MORE SMOOTHLY?
I'M SURPRISED HE WAS ACTUALLY ABLE TO GET THE BALL OVER FROM THAT GOOFY LAUNCH. HE'S GOT GOOD BALANCE.
BESIDES, IT'S ONLY NATURAL THAT A PLAY ISN'T GOING TO WORK THE FIRST FEW TIMES.
BUT ...
... NOTHING WOULD EVER GET STARTED ...
...IF THEY DIDN'T FIRST THINK, "LET'S GIVE IT A TRY."
HE'S SHORT. HE SUCKS. HE'S GOT A ONE-TRACK MIND.
BUT, FOR SOME REASON ...
...WATCHING HIM MAKES ME THINK OF SOMETHING MY GRANDPA SAID.
YOU MEAN COACH UKAI?

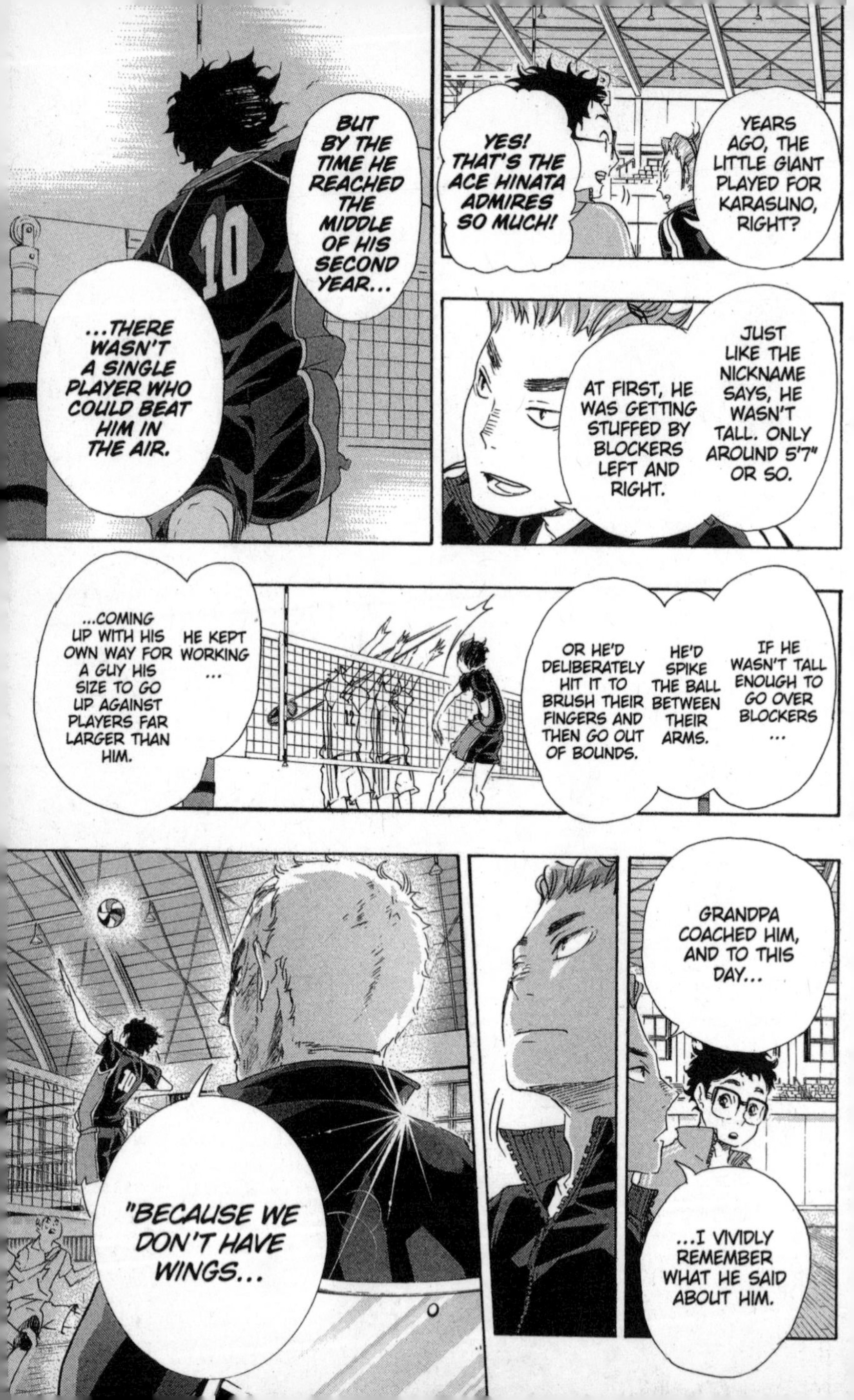
YEARS AGO, THE LITTLE GIANT PLAYED FOR KARASUNO, RIGHT?
YES! THAT'S THE ACE HINATA ADMIRES SO MUCH!
JUST LIKE THE NICKNAME SAYS, HE WASN'T TALL. ONLY AROUND 5'7" OR SO.
AT FIRST, HE WAS GETTING STUFFED BY BLOCKERS LEFT AND RIGHT.
BUT BY THE TIME HE REACHED THE MIDDLE OF HIS SECOND YEAR...
...THERE WASN'T A SINGLE PLAYER WHO COULD BEAT HIM IN THE AIR.
IF HE WASN'T TALL ENOUGH TO GO OVER BLOCKERS...
HE'D SPIKE THE BALL BETWEEN THEIR ARMS.
OR HE'D DELIBERATELY HIT IT TO BRUSH THEIR FINGERS AND THEN GO OUT OF BOUNDS.
HE KEPT WORKING...
...COMING UP WITH HIS OWN WAY FOR A GUY HIS SIZE TO GO UP AGAINST PLAYERS FAR LARGER THAN HIM.
GRANDPA COACHED HIM, AND TO THIS DAY...
...I VIVIDLY REMEMBER WHAT HE SAID ABOUT HIM.
"BECAUSE WE DON'T HAVE WINGS...

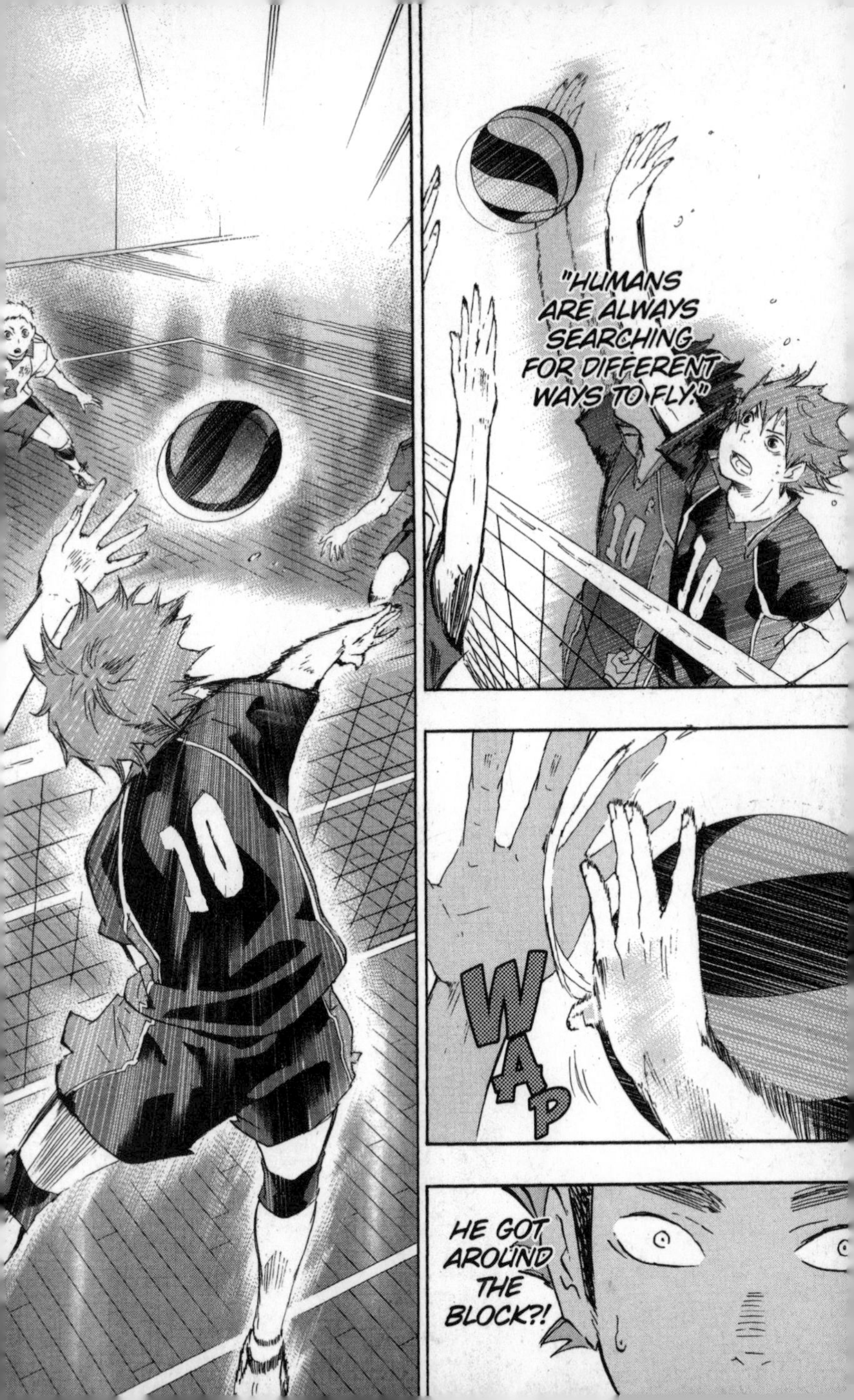

"HUMANS ARE ALWAYS SEARCHING FOR DIFFERENT WAYS TO FLY."
WAP
HE GOT AROUND THE BLOCK?!

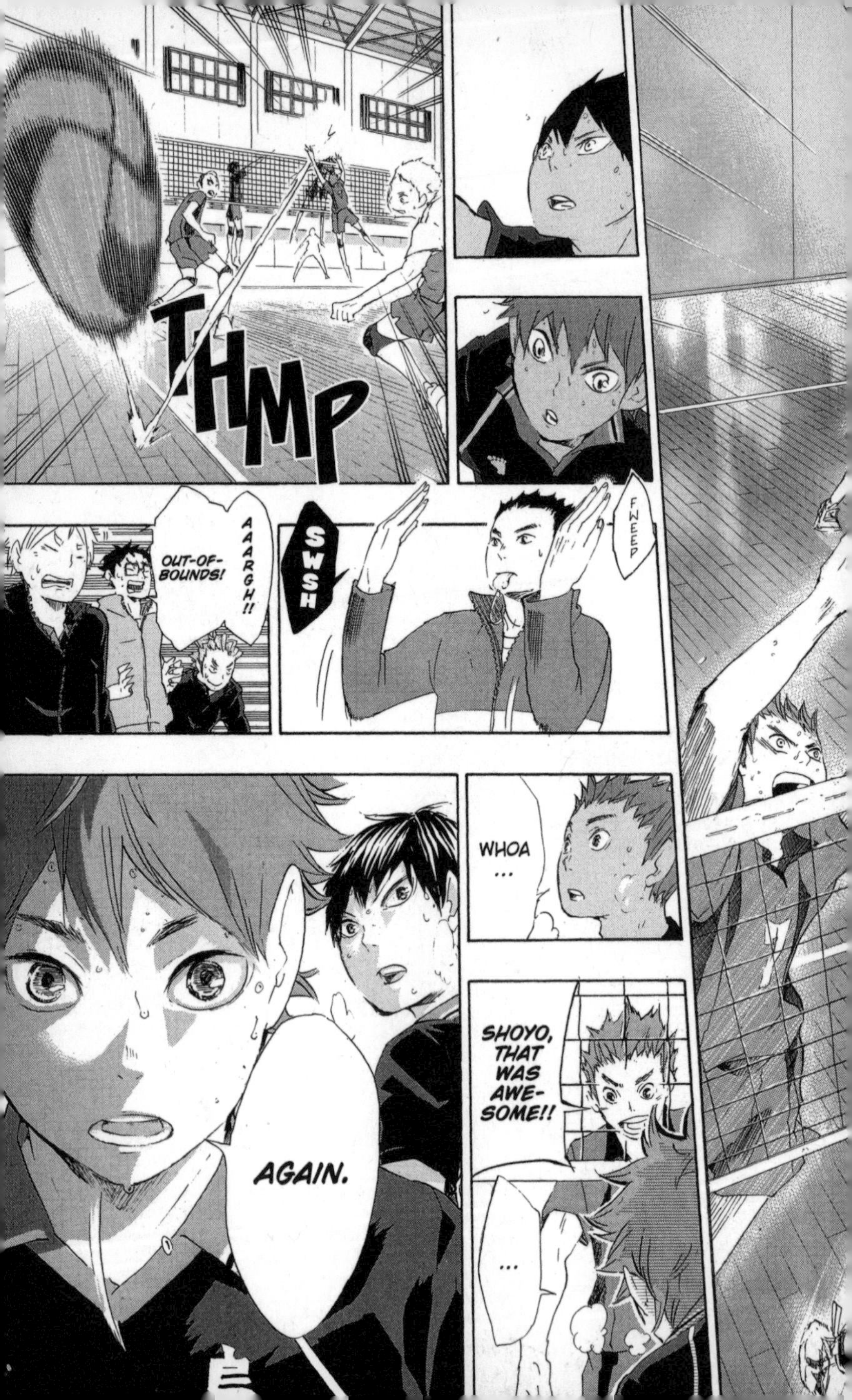
THMP
FWEEP
SWSH
AAAARGH!!
OUT-OF-BOUNDS!
WHOA ...
SHOYO, THAT WAS AWESOME!!
...
AGAIN.

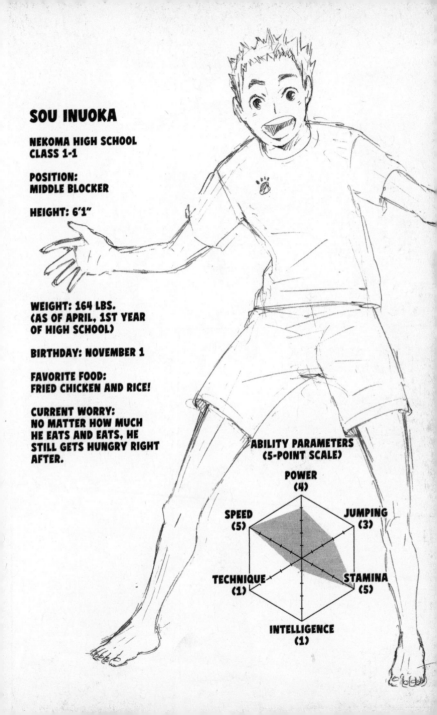

SOU INUOKA

**NEKOMA HIGH SCHOOL
CLASS 1-1**

**POSITION:
MIDDLE BLOCKER**

HEIGHT: 6'1"

**WEIGHT: 164 LBS.
(AS OF APRIL, 1ST YEAR
OF HIGH SCHOOL)**

BIRTHDAY: NOVEMBER 1

**FAVORITE FOOD:
FRIED CHICKEN AND RICE!**

**CURRENT WORRY:
NO MATTER HOW MUCH
HE EATS AND EATS, HE
STILL GETS HUNGRY RIGHT
AFTER.**

**ABILITY PARAMETERS
(5-POINT SCALE)**

POWER
(4)

SPEED
(5)

JUMPING
(3)

TECHNIQUE
(1)

STAMINA
(5)

INTELLIGENCE
(1)

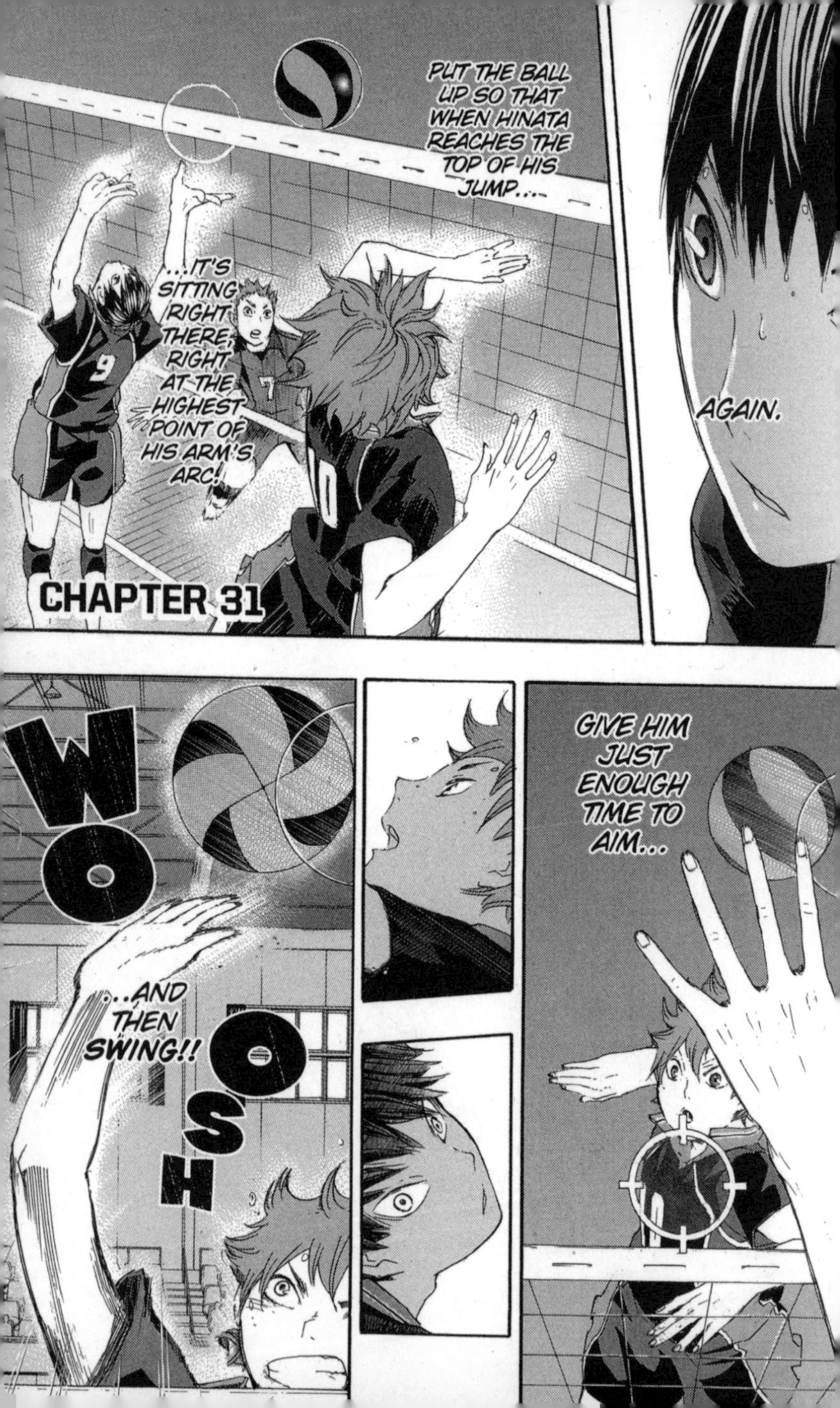
AGAIN.
PUT THE BALL UP SO THAT WHEN HINATA REACHES THE TOP OF HIS JUMP...
...IT'S SITTING RIGHT THERE, RIGHT AT THE HIGHEST POINT OF HIS ARM'S ARC!
CHAPTER 31
GIVE HIM JUST ENOUGH TIME TO AIM...
WHOOSH
...AND THEN SWING!!

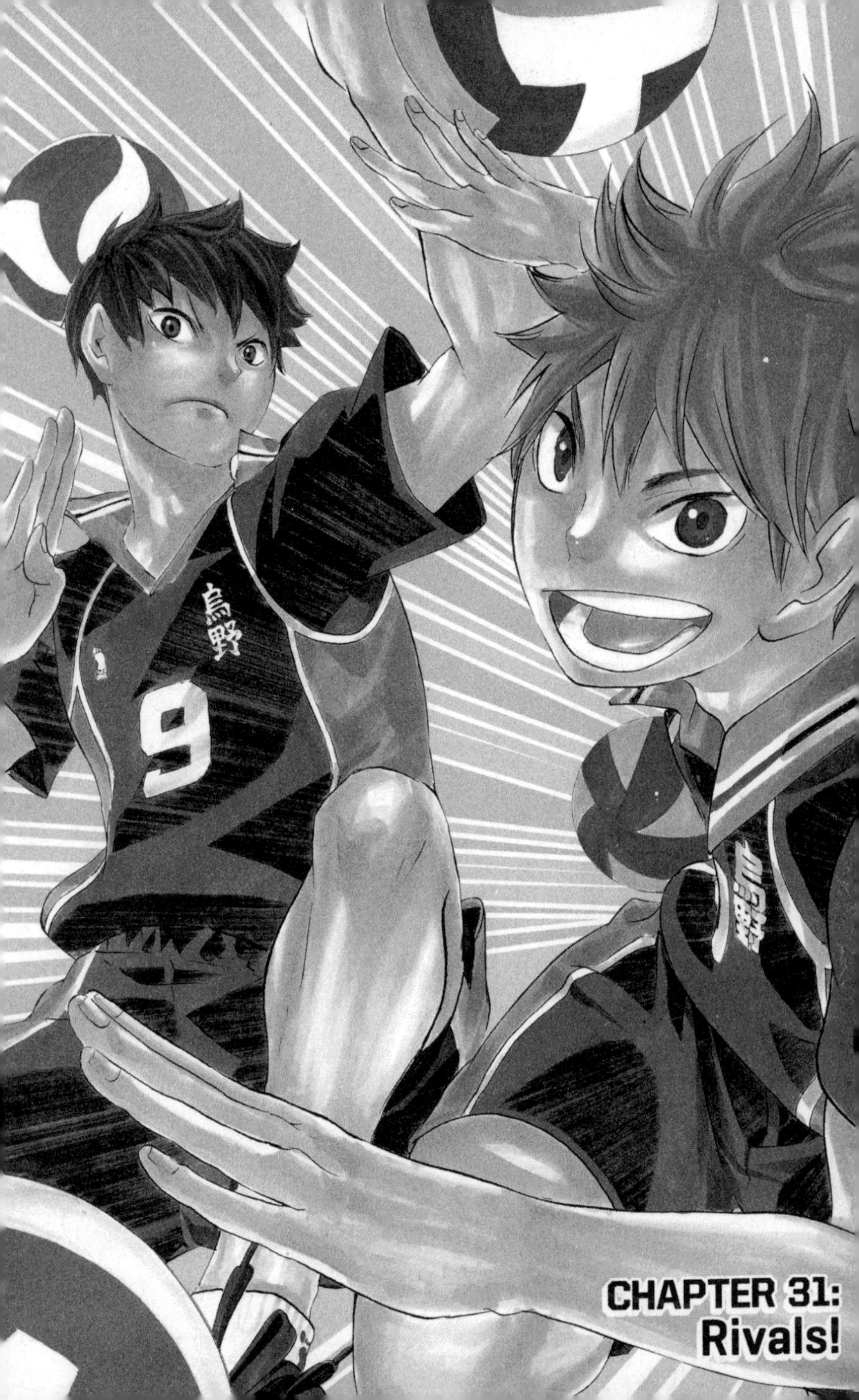

CHAPTER 31: Rivals!

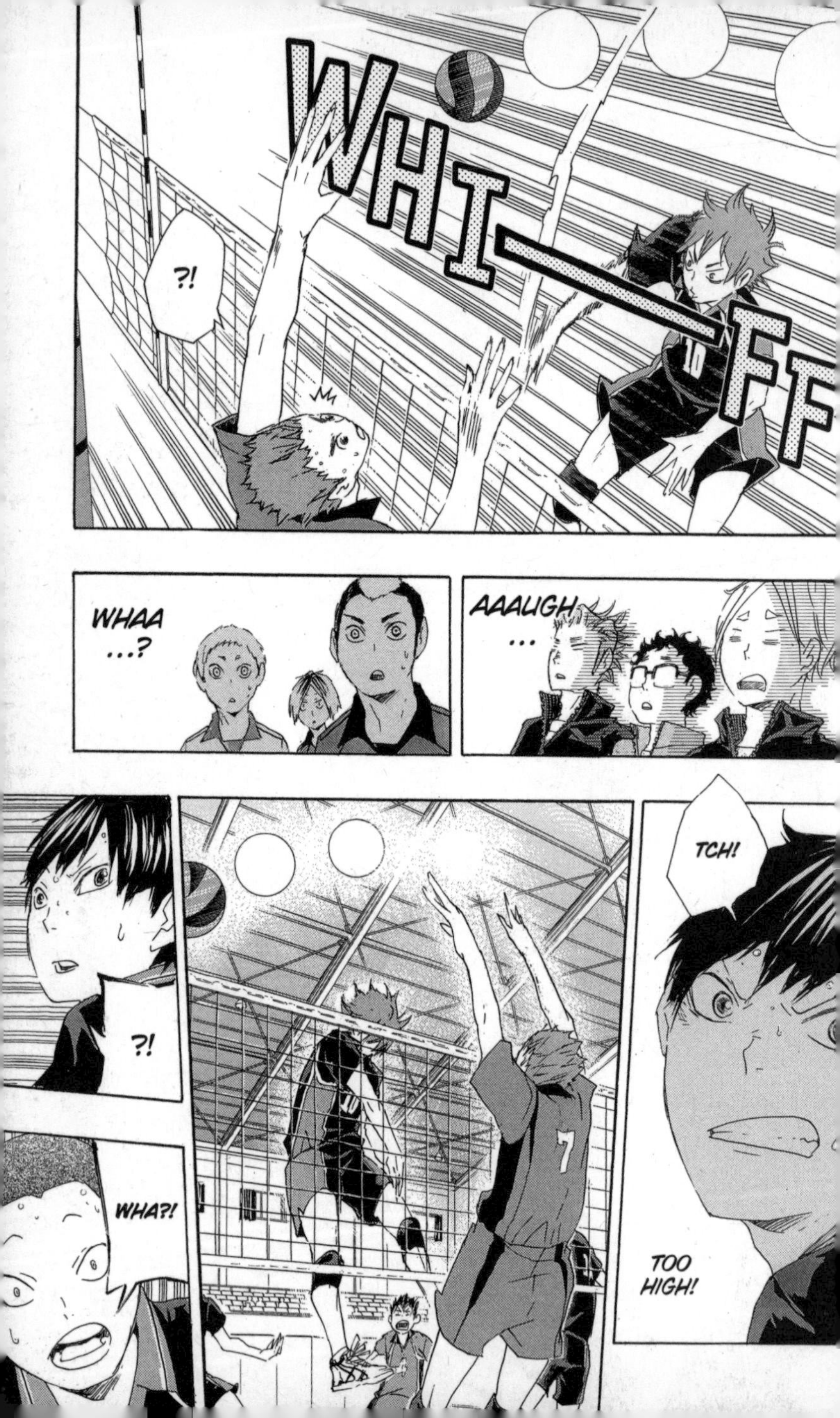
WHI—FF
?!
AAAUGH ...
WHAA ...?
TCH!
TOO HIGH!
?!
WHA?!

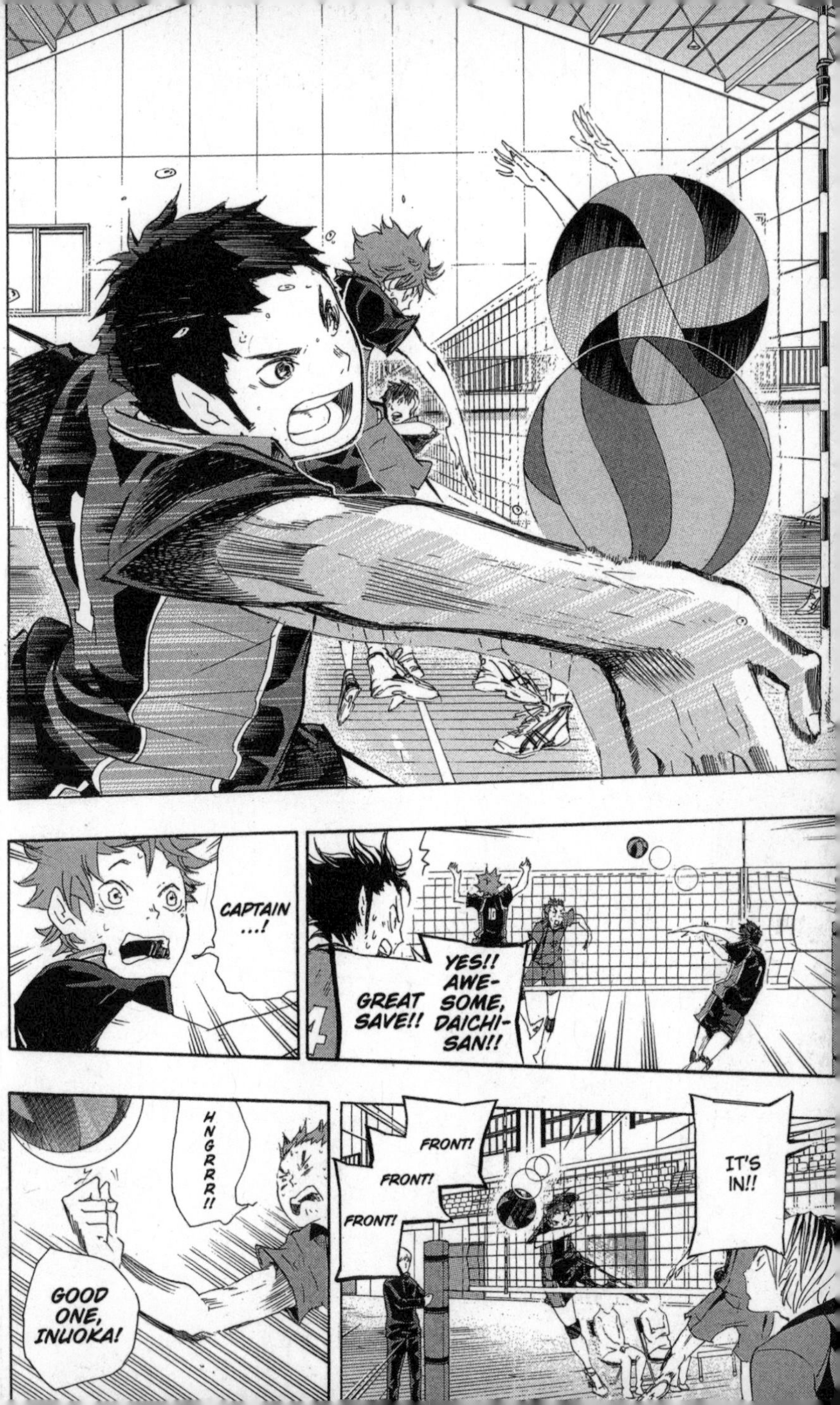
YES!! AWESOME, DAICHI-SAN!!
GREAT SAVE!!
CAPTAIN...!
IT'S IN!!
FRONT!
FRONT!
FRONT!
HNGRRR!!
GOOD ONE, INUOKA!

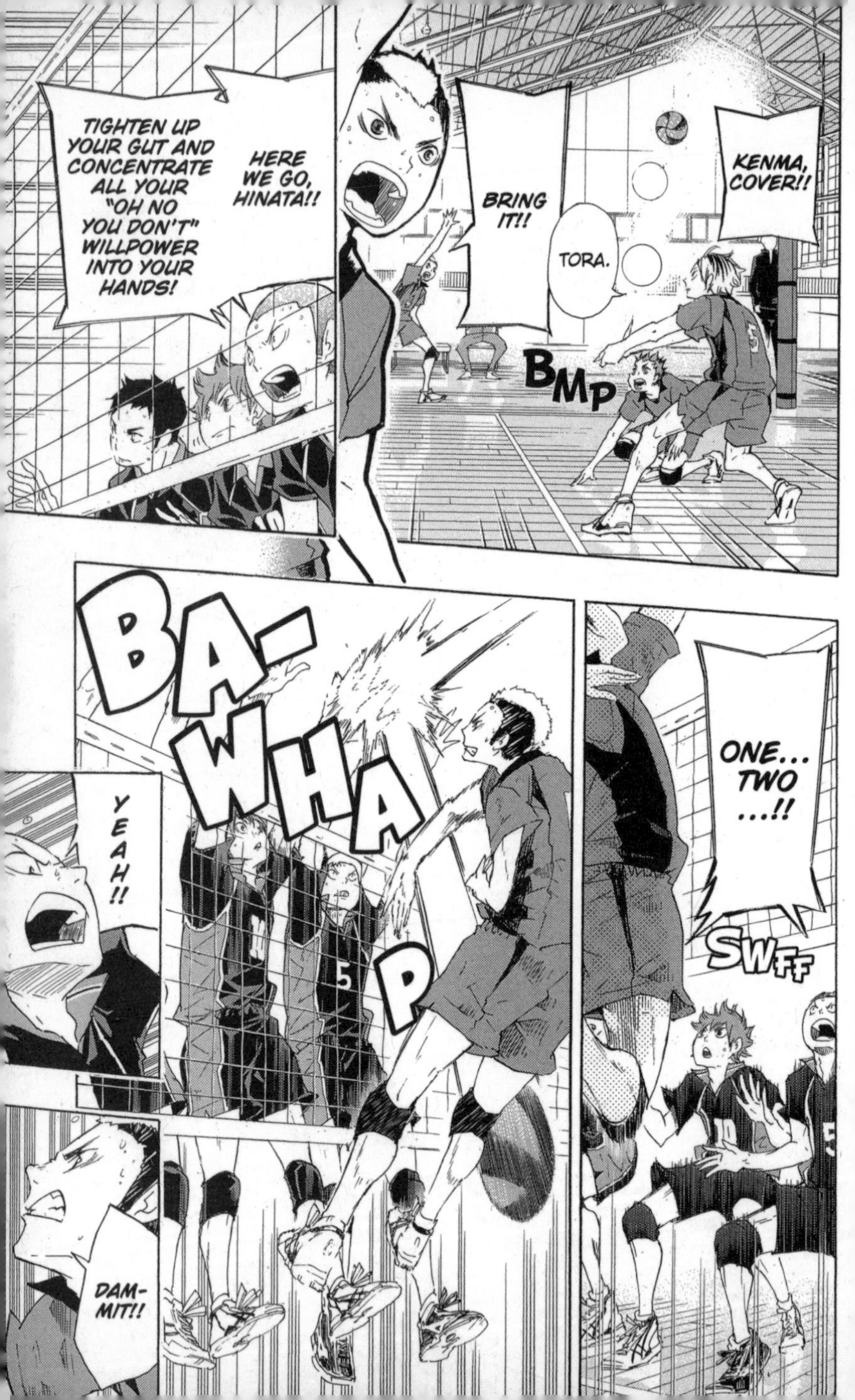
KENMA, COVER!!
TORA.
BRING IT!!
BMP
HERE WE GO, HINATA!!
TIGHTEN UP YOUR GUT AND CONCENTRATE ALL YOUR "OH NO YOU DON'T" WILLPOWER INTO YOUR HANDS!
ONE... TWO ...!!
SWFF
BA-WHAP
YEAH!!
DAM-MIT!!

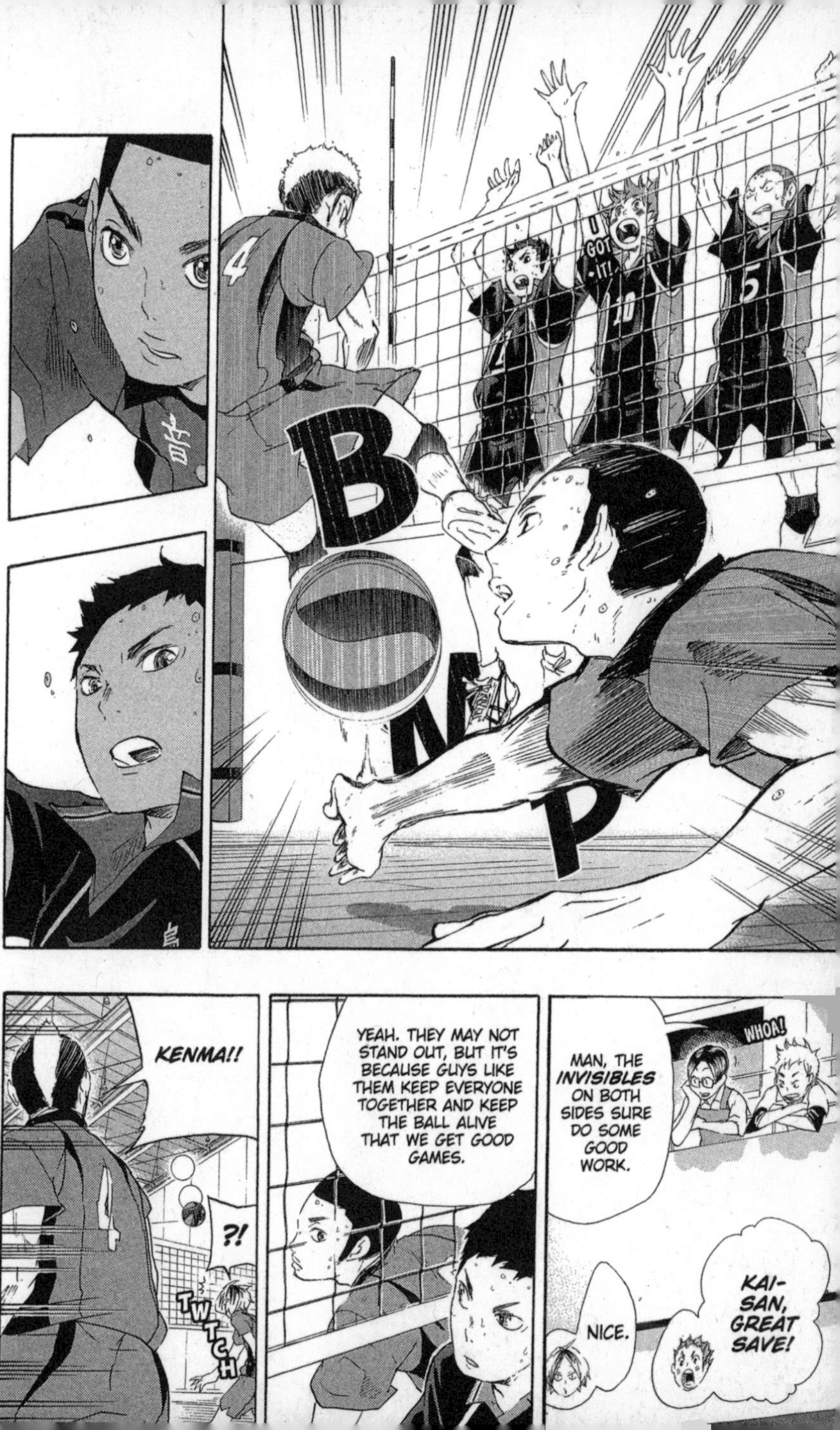
U GOT IT!
BOMP
WHOA!
MAN, THE *INVISIBLES* ON BOTH SIDES SURE DO SOME GOOD WORK.
KAI-SAN, GREAT SAVE!
NICE.
YEAH. THEY MAY NOT STAND OUT, BUT IT'S BECAUSE GUYS LIKE THEM KEEP EVERYONE TOGETHER AND KEEP THE BALL ALIVE THAT WE GET GOOD GAMES.
KENMA!!
?!
TWITCH

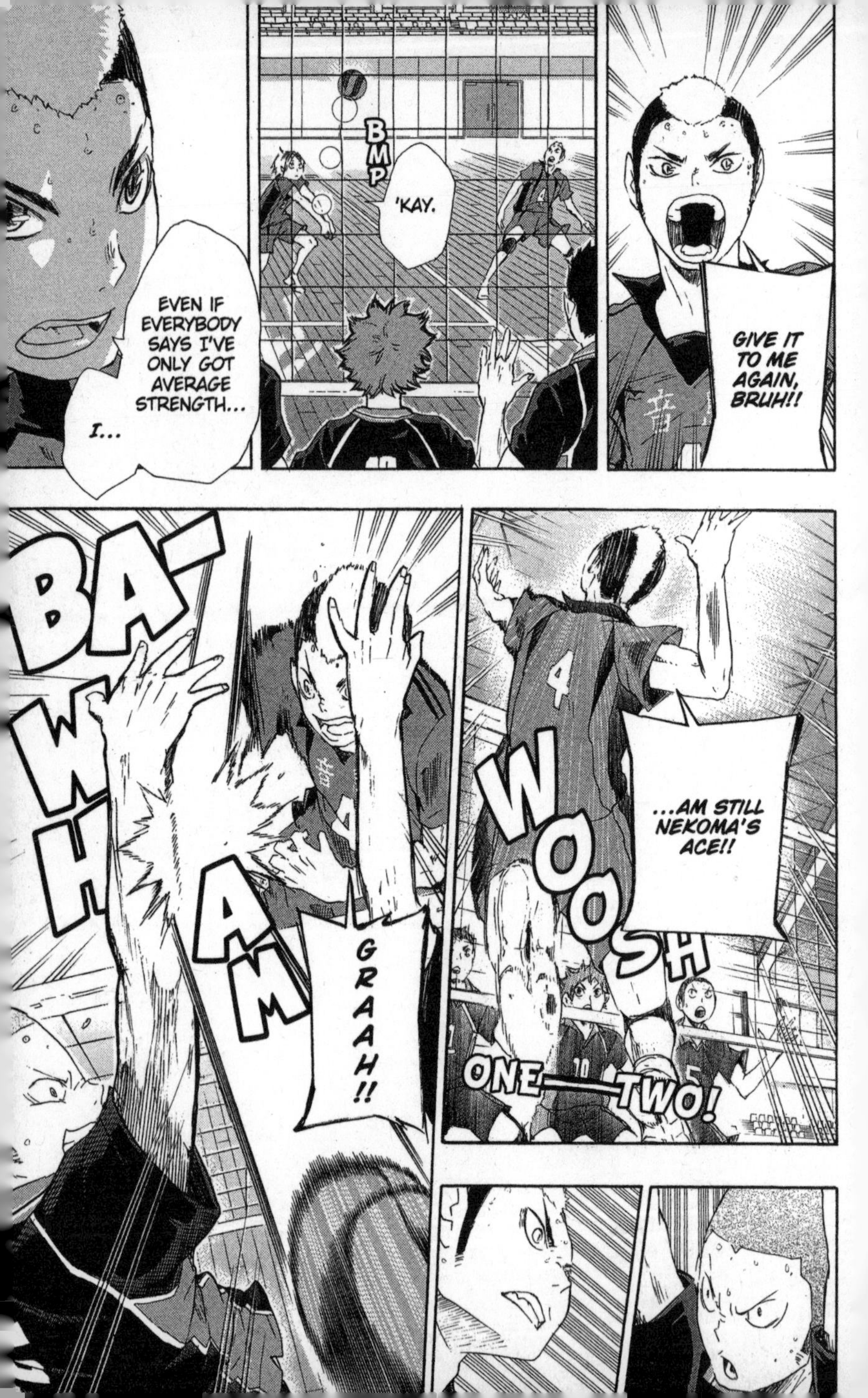
GIVE IT TO ME AGAIN, BRUH!!
BMP
'KAY.
EVEN IF EVERYBODY SAYS I'VE ONLY GOT AVERAGE STRENGTH...
I...
...AM STILL NEKOMA'S ACE!!
WOOSH
ONE—TWO!
BA-WHAM
GRAAH!!

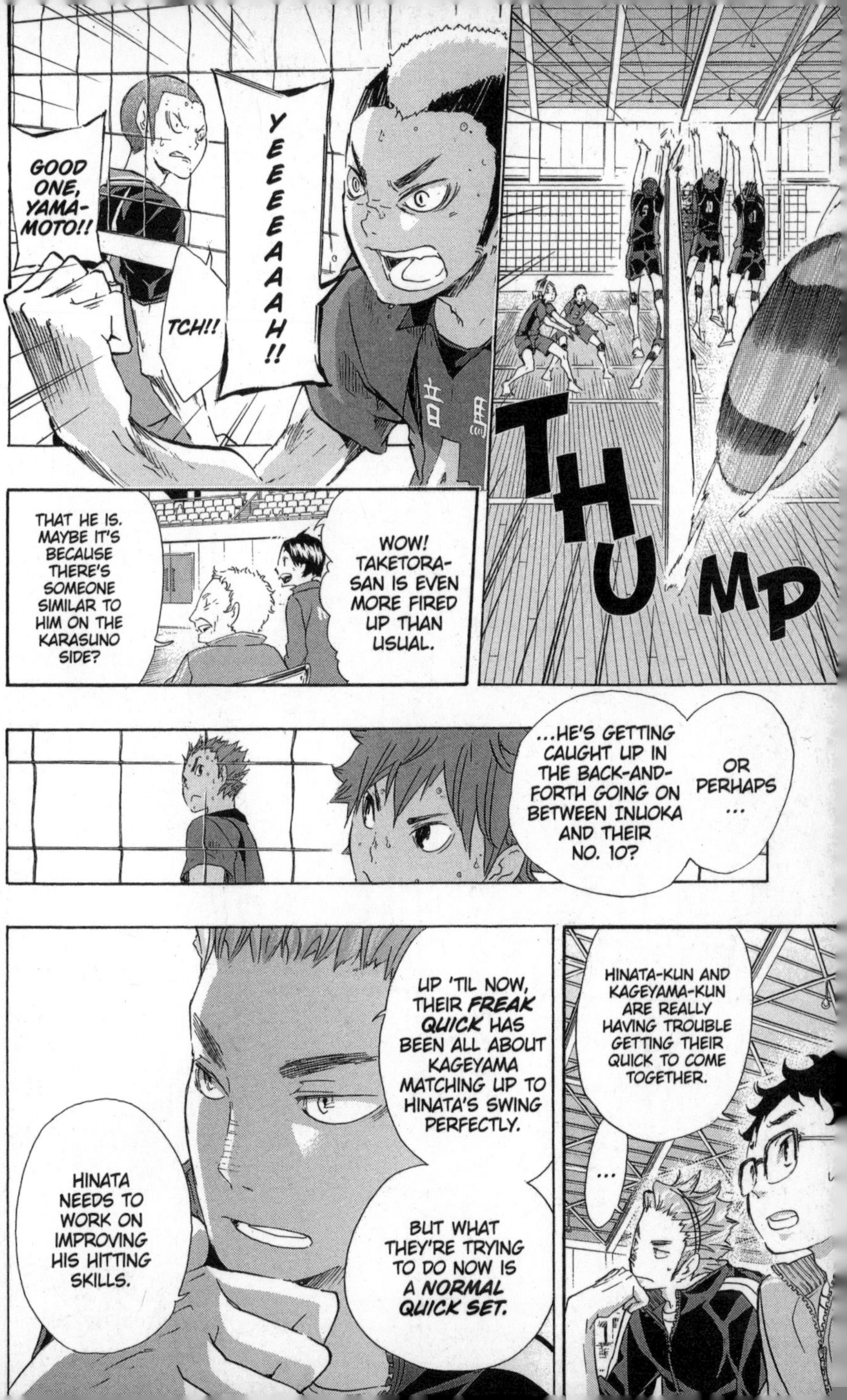
THUMP
YEEEEAAAAH!!
GOOD ONE, YAMAMOTO!!
TCH!!
WOW! TAKETORA-SAN IS EVEN MORE FIRED UP THAN USUAL.
THAT HE IS. MAYBE IT'S BECAUSE THERE'S SOMEONE SIMILAR TO HIM ON THE KARASUNO SIDE?
OR PERHAPS...
...HE'S GETTING CAUGHT UP IN THE BACK-AND-FORTH GOING ON BETWEEN INUOKA AND THEIR NO. 10?
HINATA-KUN AND KAGEYAMA-KUN ARE REALLY HAVING TROUBLE GETTING THEIR QUICK TO COME TOGETHER.
...
UP 'TIL NOW, THEIR FREAK QUICK HAS BEEN ALL ABOUT KAGEYAMA MATCHING UP TO HINATA'S SWING PERFECTLY.
BUT WHAT THEY'RE TRYING TO DO NOW IS A NORMAL QUICK SET.
HINATA NEEDS TO WORK ON IMPROVING HIS HITTING SKILLS.

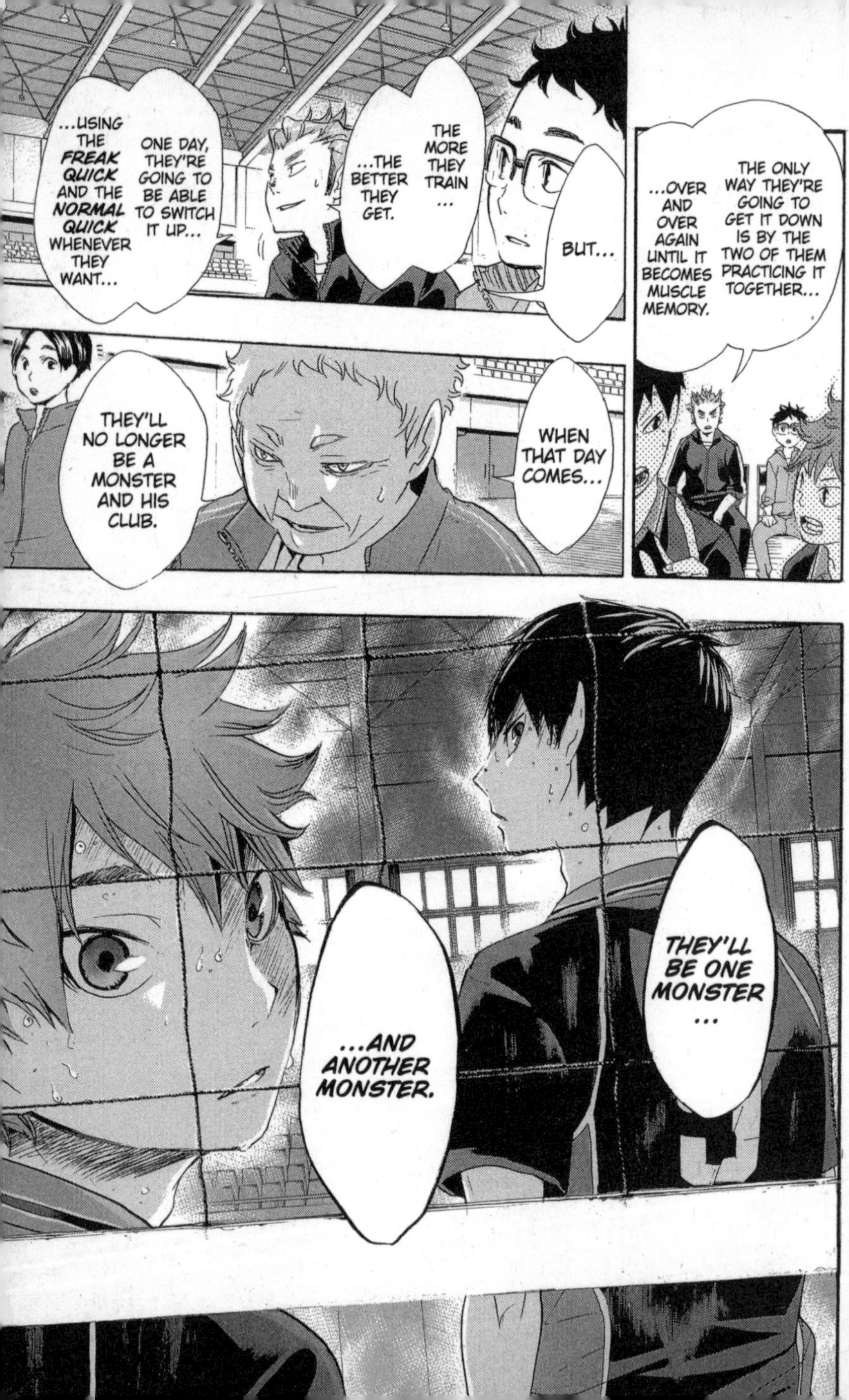
THE ONLY WAY THEY'RE GOING TO GET IT DOWN IS BY THE TWO OF THEM PRACTICING IT TOGETHER...
...OVER AND OVER AGAIN UNTIL IT BECOMES MUSCLE MEMORY.
BUT...
THE MORE THEY TRAIN...
...THE BETTER THEY GET.
ONE DAY, THEY'RE GOING TO BE ABLE TO SWITCH IT UP...
...USING THE FREAK QUICK AND THE NORMAL QUICK WHENEVER THEY WANT...
WHEN THAT DAY COMES...
THEY'LL NO LONGER BE A MONSTER AND HIS CLUB.
THEY'LL BE ONE MONSTER...
...AND ANOTHER MONSTER.

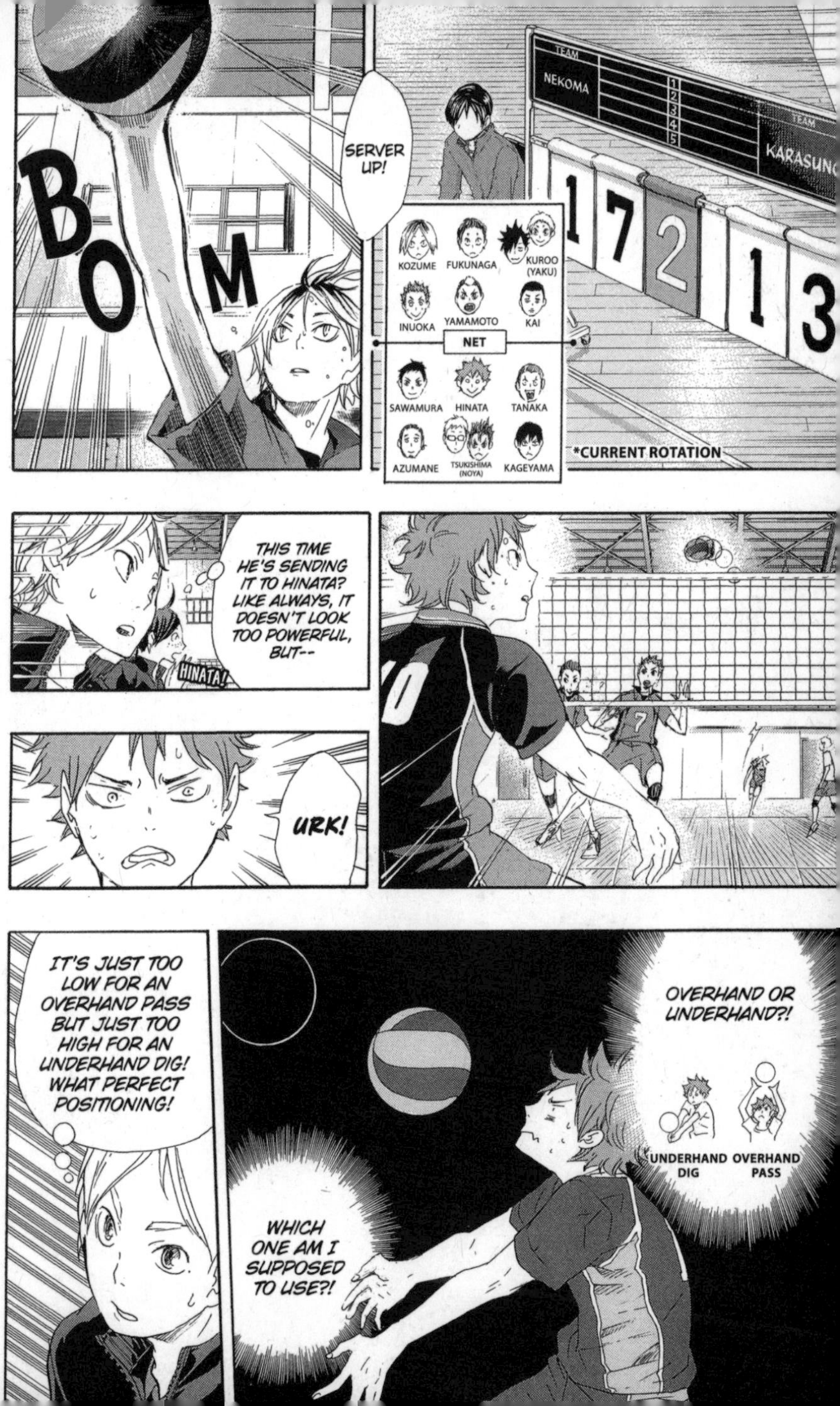
TEAM
NEKOMA
1
2
3
4
5
TEAM
KARASUN
17
2
13
KOZUME
FUKUNAGA
KUROO (YAKU)
INUOKA
YAMAMOTO
KAI
NET
SAWAMURA
HINATA
TANAKA
AZUMANE
TSUKISHIMA (NOYA)
KAGEYAMA
*CURRENT ROTATION
SERVER UP!
BOM
THIS TIME HE'S SENDING IT TO HINATA? LIKE ALWAYS, IT DOESN'T LOOK TOO POWERFUL, BUT--
HINATA!
URK!
OVERHAND OR UNDERHAND?!
UNDERHAND DIG
OVERHAND PASS
WHICH ONE AM I SUPPOSED TO USE?!
IT'S JUST TOO LOW FOR AN OVERHAND PASS BUT JUST TOO HIGH FOR AN UNDERHAND DIG! WHAT PERFECT POSITIONING!

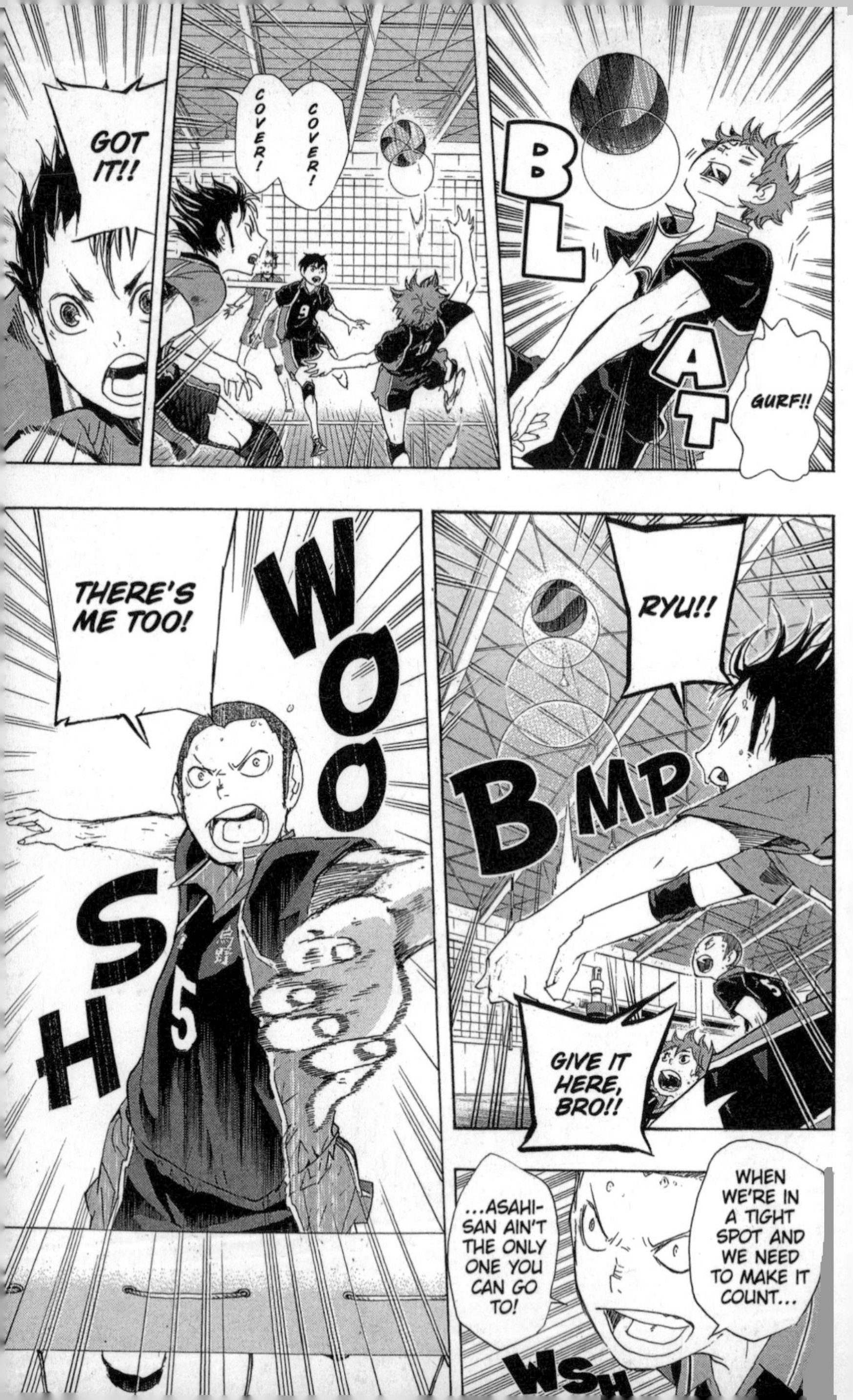
BLAT
GURF!!
COVER!
COVER!
GOT IT!!
RYU!!
BMP
GIVE IT HERE, BRO!!
WHEN WE'RE IN A TIGHT SPOT AND WE NEED TO MAKE IT COUNT...
...ASAHI-SAN AIN'T THE ONLY ONE YOU CAN GO TO!
WSH
THERE'S ME TOO!
WOOSH

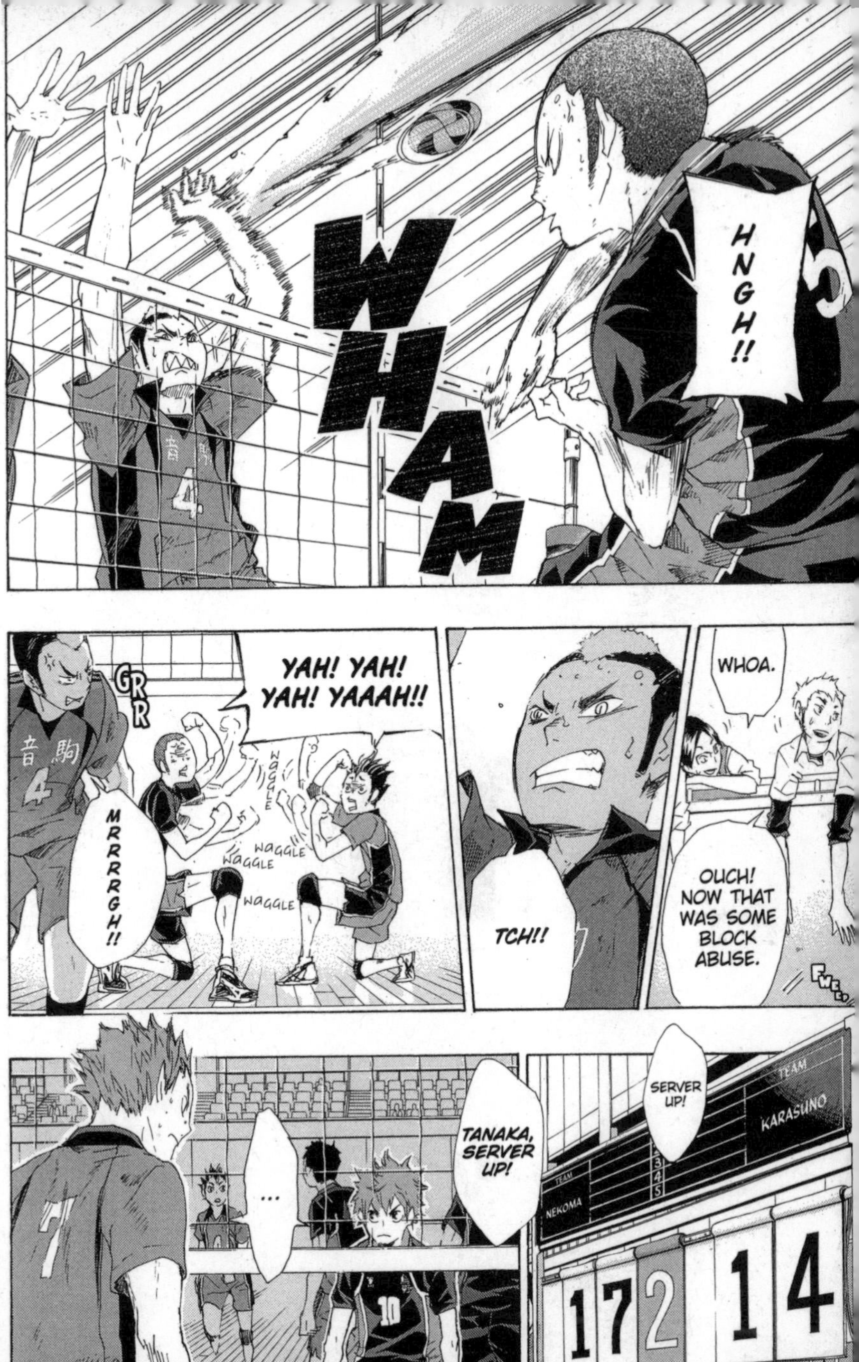
HNGH!!
WHAM
WHOA.
OUCH! NOW THAT WAS SOME BLOCK ABUSE.
FWEE
TCH!!
YAH! YAH! YAH! YAAAH!!
WAGGLE
WAGGLE
WAGGLE
WAGGLE
GRR
MRRRRGH!!
SERVER UP!
TEAM
KARASUNO
TEAM
NEKOMA
17
2
14
TANAKA, SERVER UP!
...

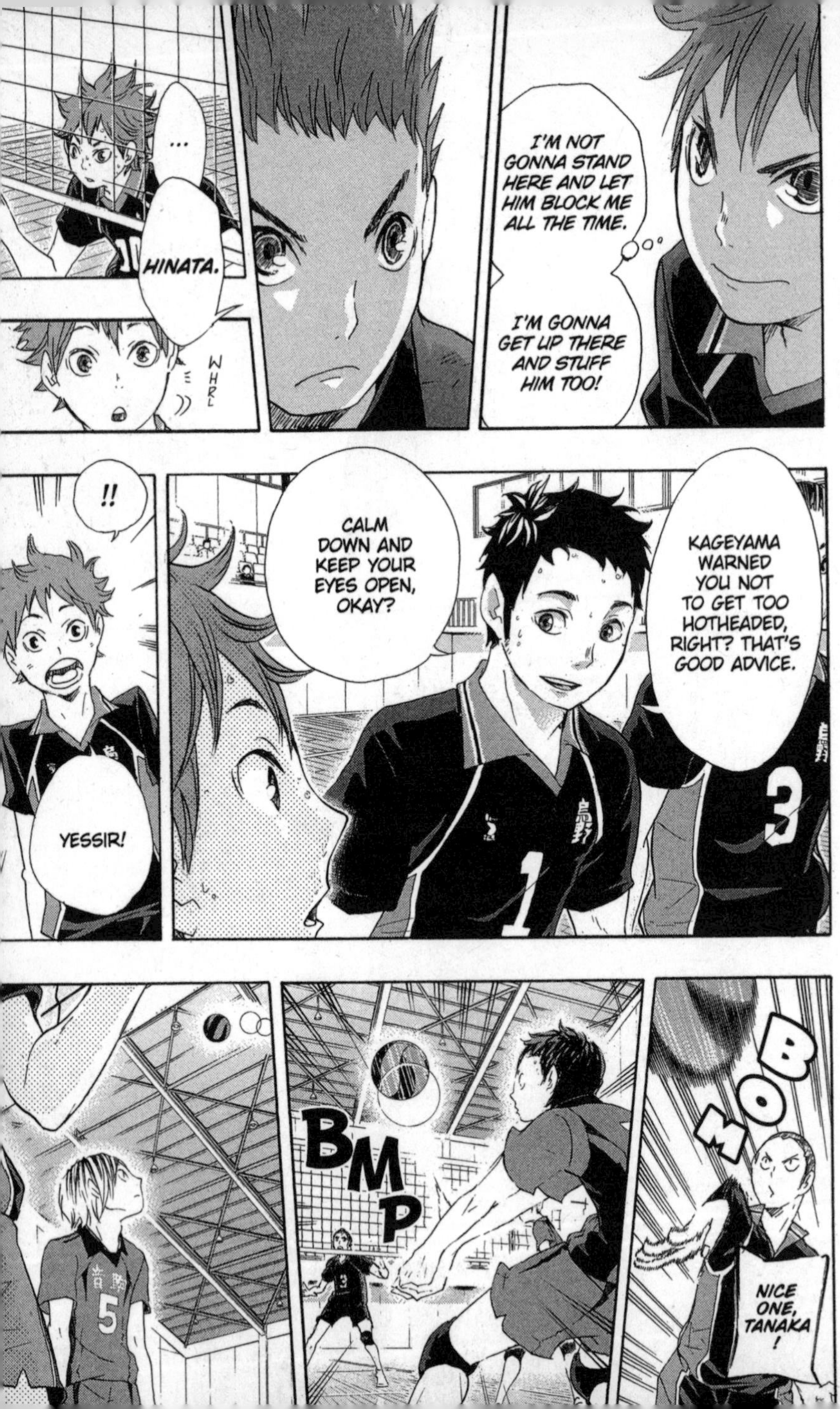
I'M NOT GONNA STAND HERE AND LET HIM BLOCK ME ALL THE TIME.
I'M GONNA GET UP THERE AND STUFF HIM TOO!
...
HINATA.
WHRL
KAGEYAMA WARNED YOU NOT TO GET TOO HOTHEADED, RIGHT? THAT'S GOOD ADVICE.
CALM DOWN AND KEEP YOUR EYES OPEN, OKAY?
!!
YESSIR!
BOOM
NICE ONE, TANAKA!
BMP

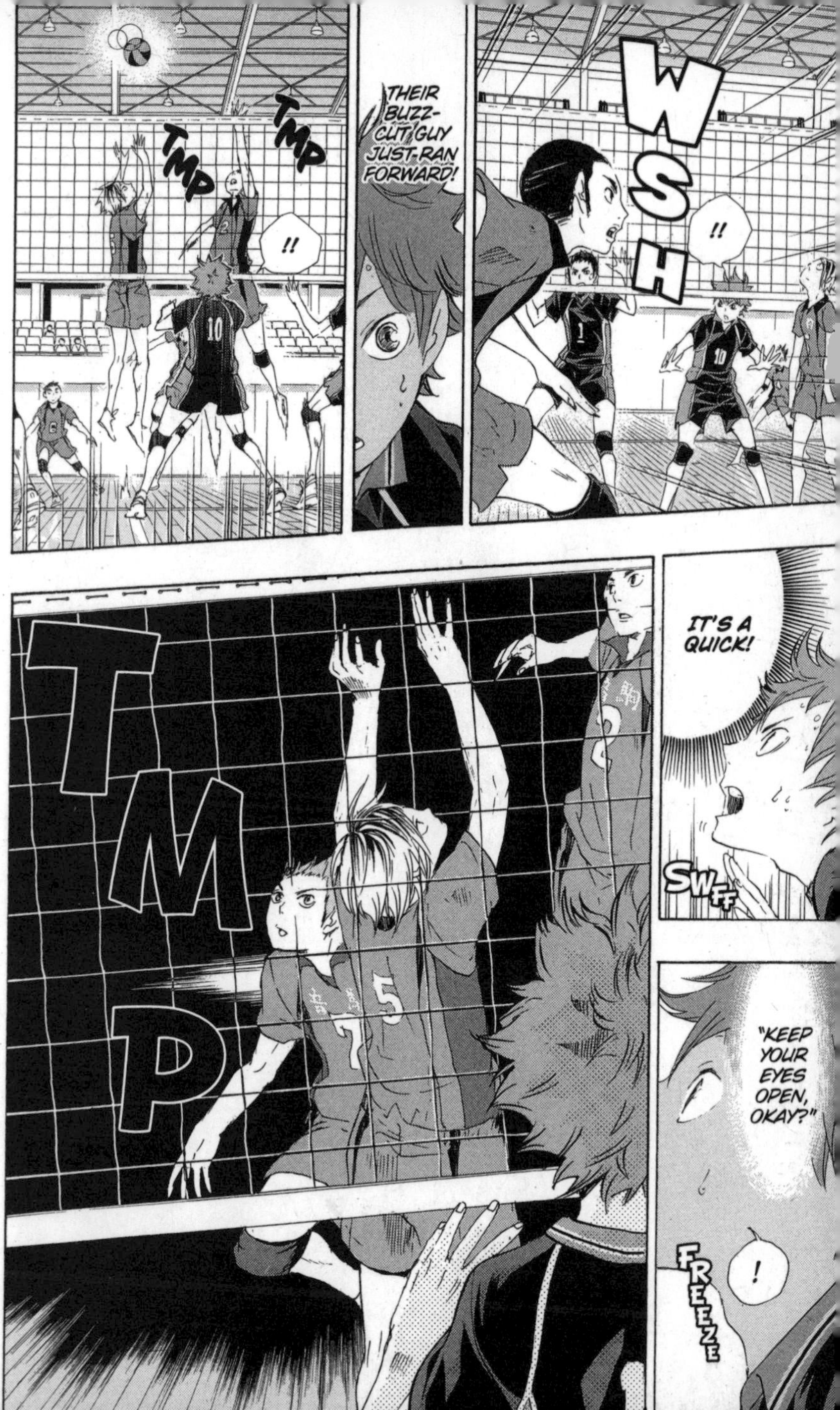
WSH
!!
THEIR BUZZ-CUT GUY JUST RAN FORWARD!
TMP
TMP
!!
IT'S A QUICK!
SWFF
"KEEP YOUR EYES OPEN, OKAY?"
FREEZE
!
TMP

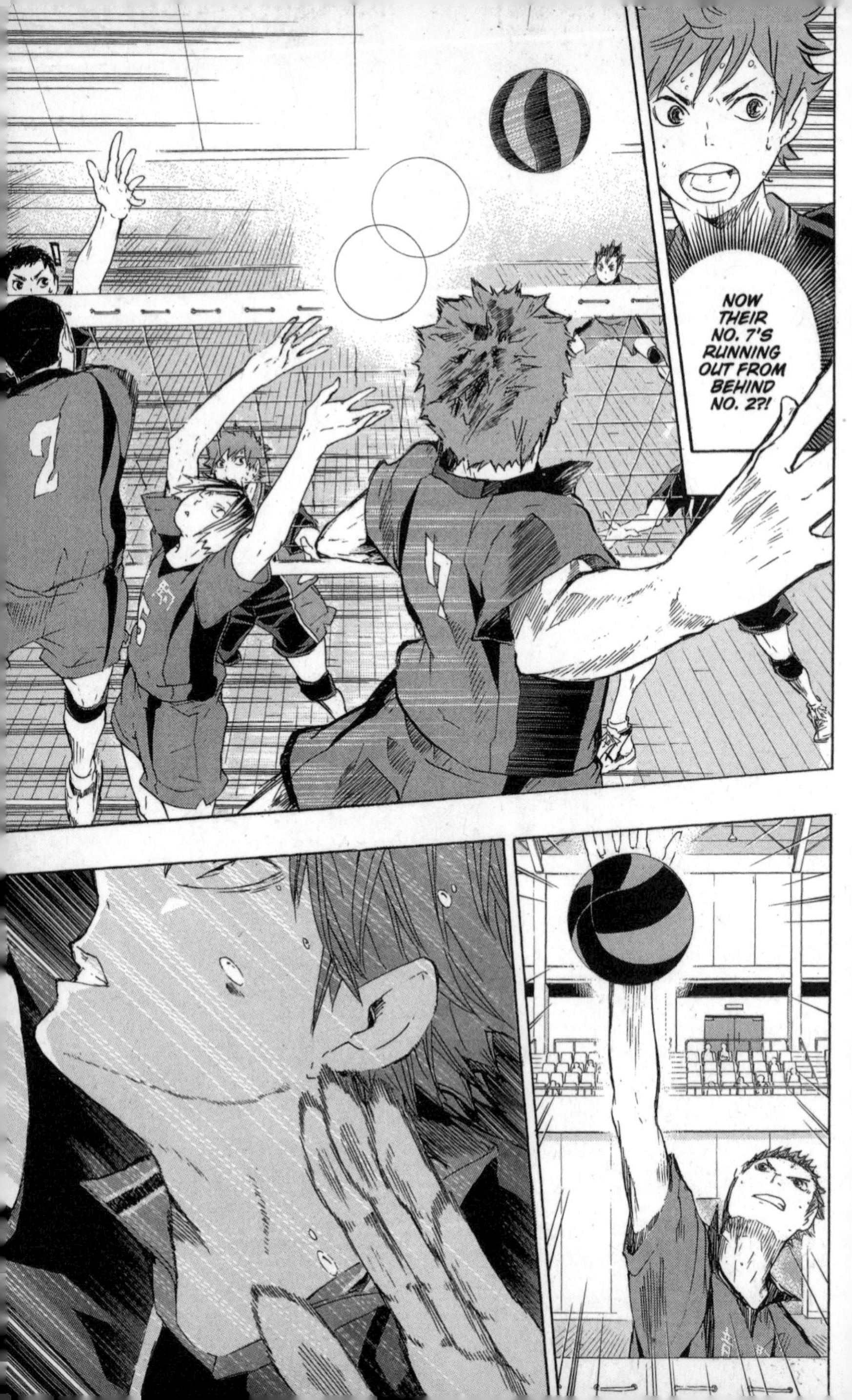
NOW THEIR NO. 7'S RUNNING OUT FROM BEHIND NO. 2?!

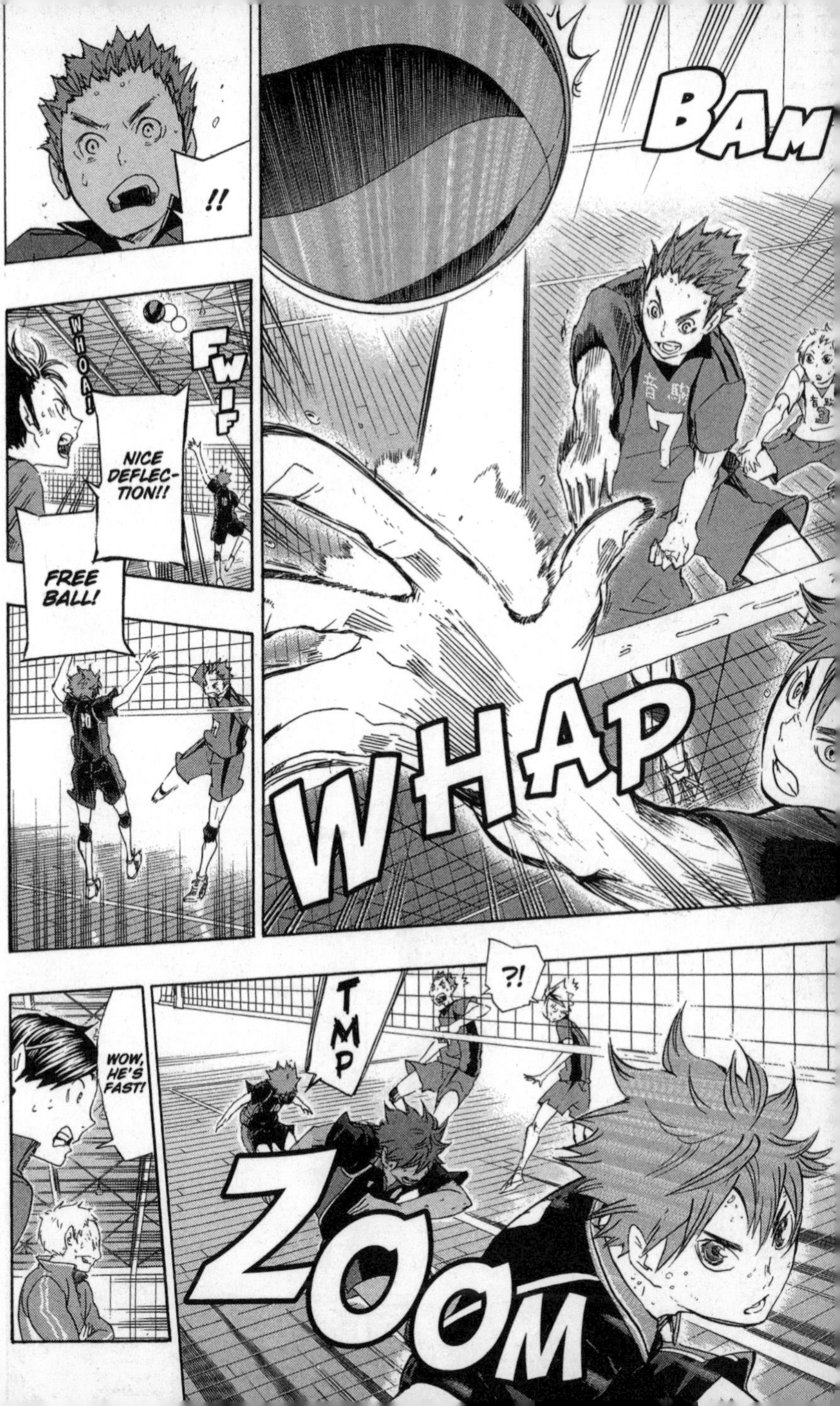
BAM
WHAP
!!
FWIF
WHOA!
NICE DEFLECTION!!
FREE BALL!
?!
TMP
ZOOM
WOW, HE'S FAST!

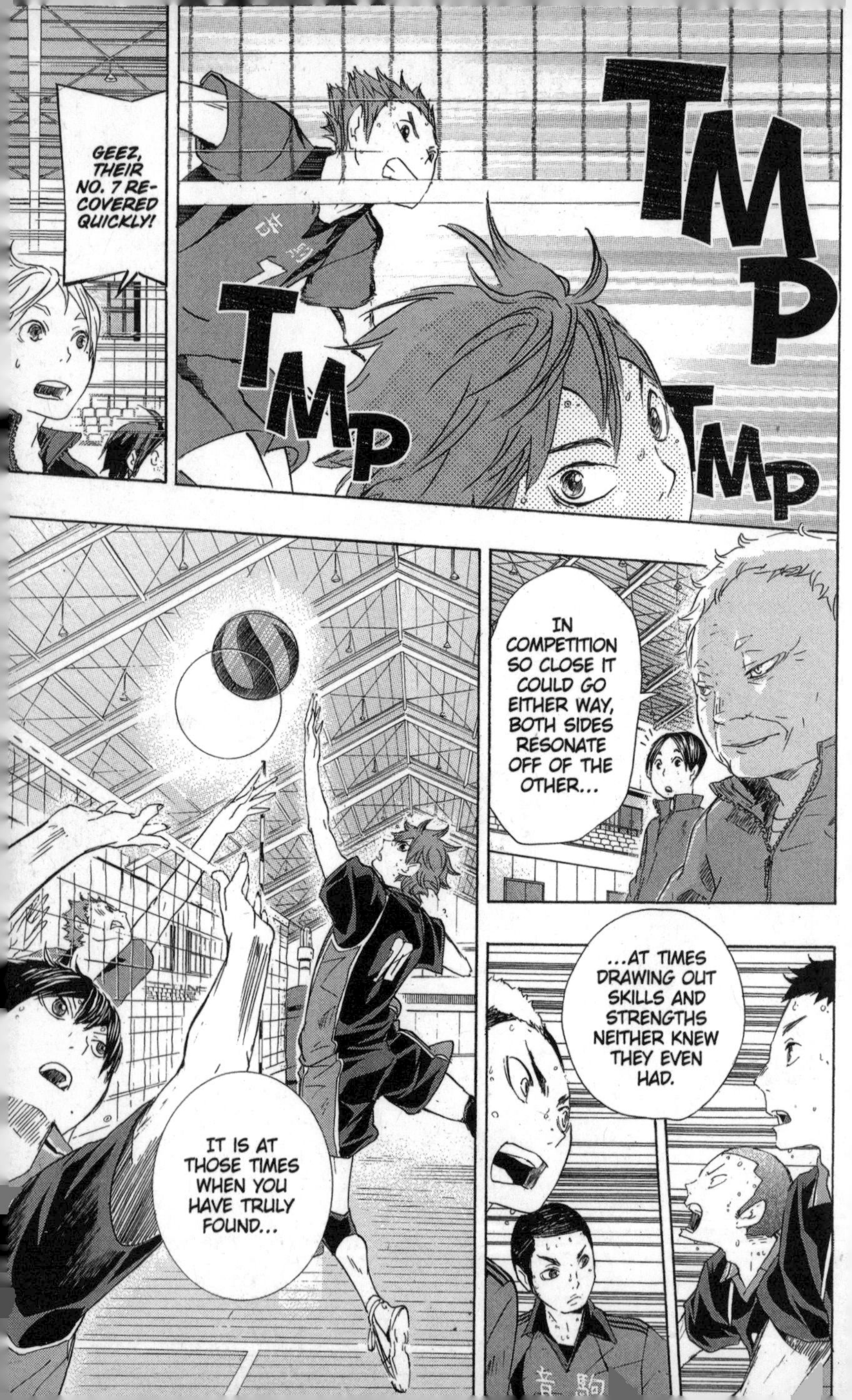
TMP
TMP
TMP
GEEZ, THEIR NO. 7 RE-COVERED QUICKLY!
IN COMPETITION SO CLOSE IT COULD GO EITHER WAY, BOTH SIDES RESONATE OFF OF THE OTHER...
...AT TIMES DRAWING OUT SKILLS AND STRENGTHS NEITHER KNEW THEY EVEN HAD.
IT IS AT THOSE TIMES WHEN YOU HAVE TRULY FOUND...

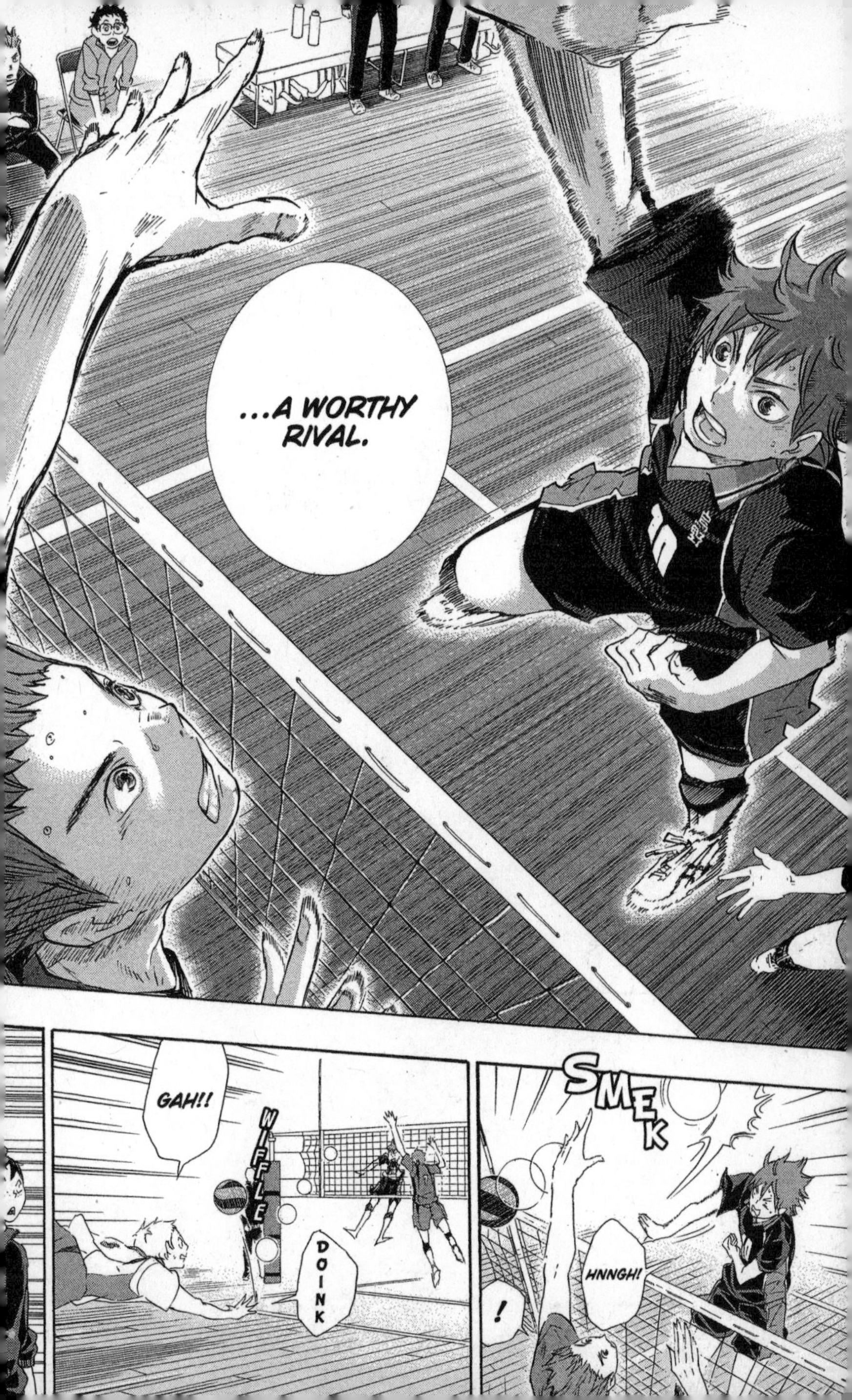
...A WORTHY RIVAL.
SMEK
HNNGH!
!
WIFFLE
GAH!!
DOINK

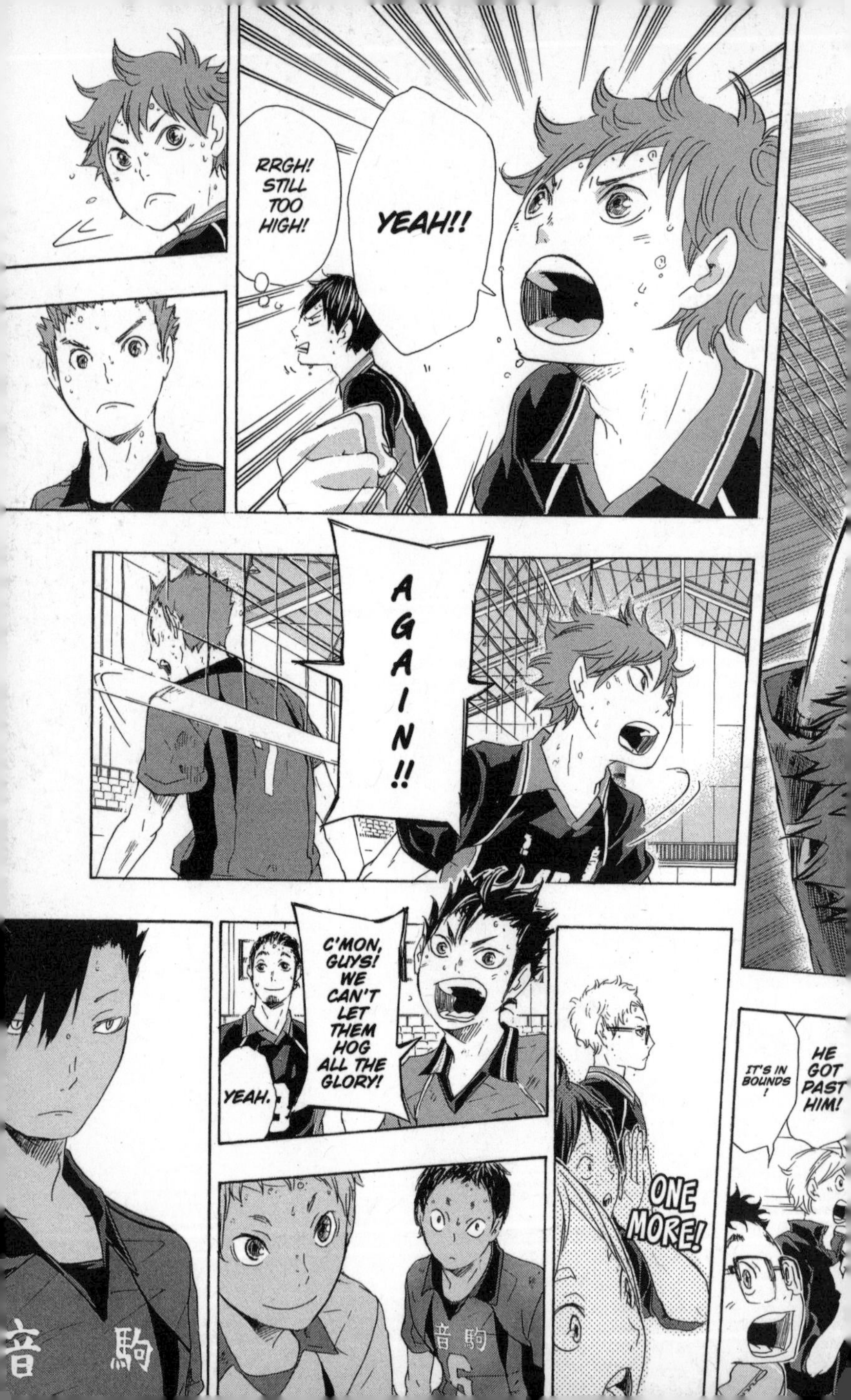
YEAH!!
RRGH! STILL TOO HIGH!
AGAIN!!
HE GOT PAST HIM!
IT'S IN BOUNDS!
ONE MORE!
C'MON, GUYS! WE CAN'T LET THEM HOG ALL THE GLORY!
YEAH.

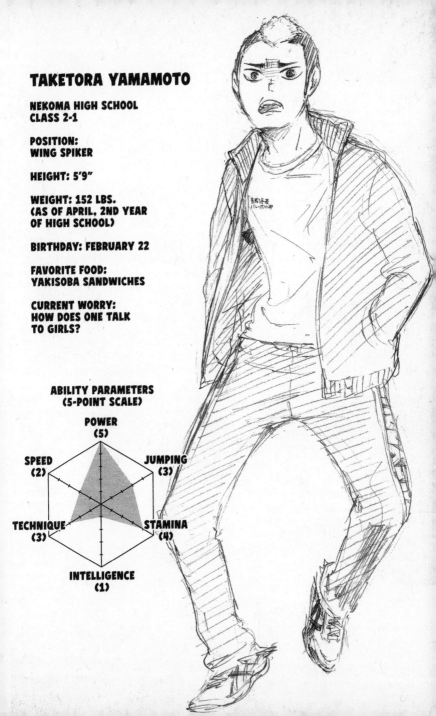

TAKETORA YAMAMOTO

NEKOMA HIGH SCHOOL
CLASS 2-1

POSITION:
WING SPIKER

HEIGHT: 5’9”

WEIGHT: 152 LBS.
(AS OF APRIL, 2ND YEAR
OF HIGH SCHOOL)

BIRTHDAY: FEBRUARY 22

FAVORITE FOOD:
YAKISOBA SANDWICHES

CURRENT WORRY:
HOW DOES ONE TALK
TO GIRLS?

ABILITY PARAMETERS
(5-POINT SCALE)

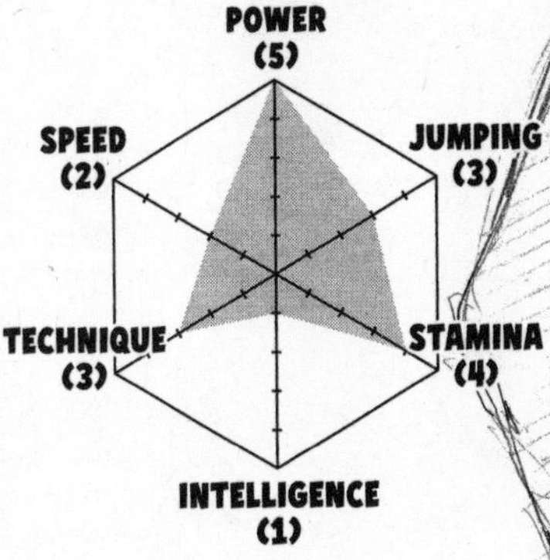
POWER
(5)
JUMPING
(3)
STAMINA
(4)
INTELLIGENCE
(1)
TECHNIQUE
(3)
SPEED
(2)

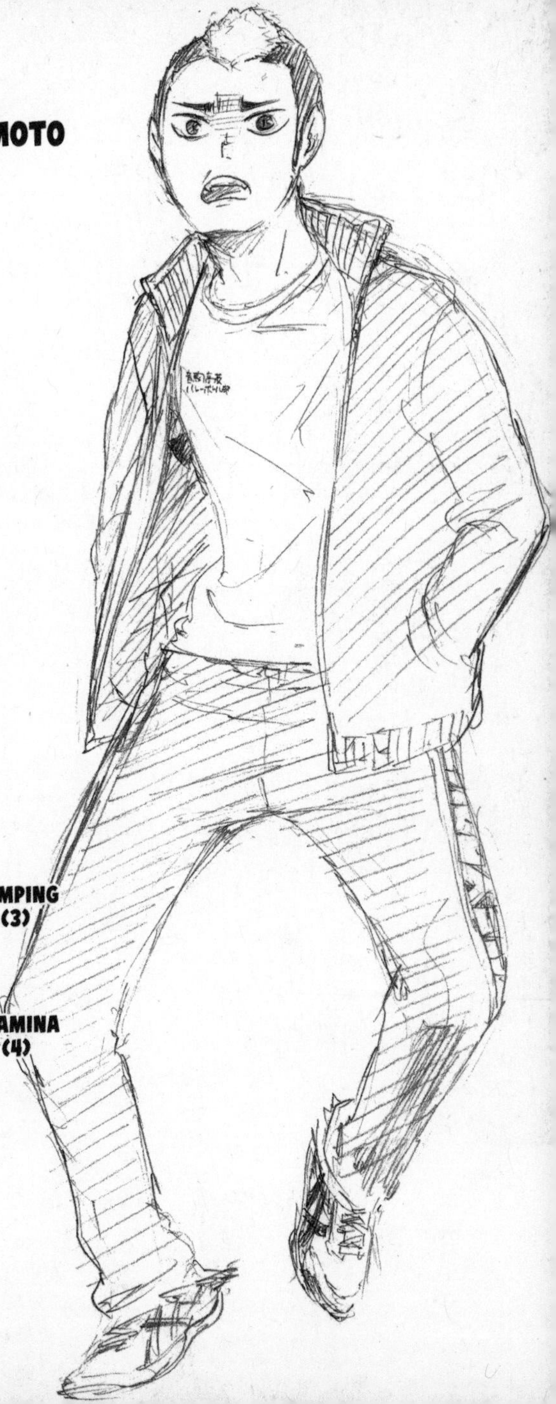

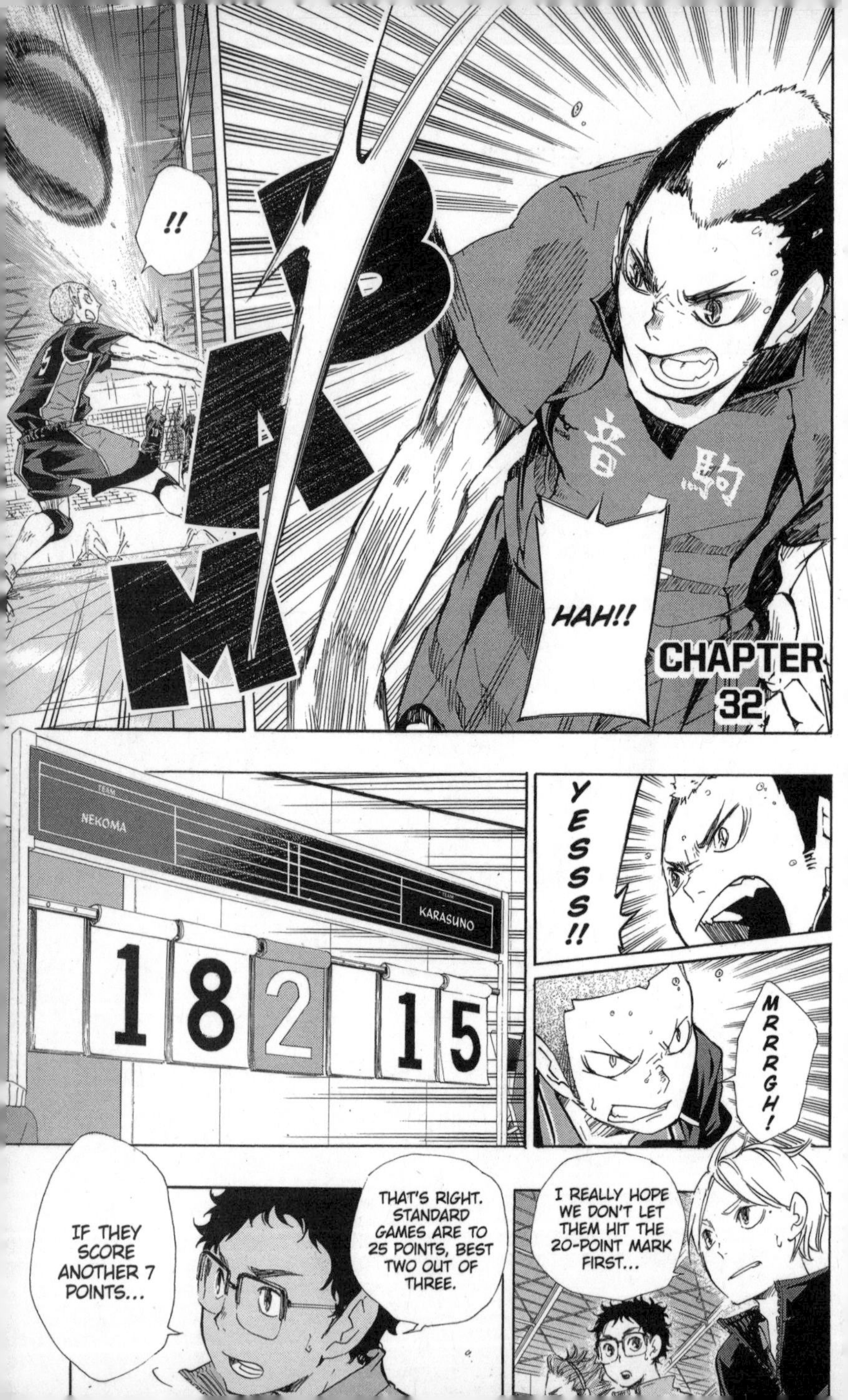
HAH!!
CHAPTER 32
BAM
!!
YESSS!!
MRRRGH!
NEKOMA
KARASUNO
18 2 15
I REALLY HOPE WE DON'T LET THEM HIT THE 20-POINT MARK FIRST...
THAT'S RIGHT. STANDARD GAMES ARE TO 25 POINTS, BEST TWO OUT OF THREE.
IF THEY SCORE ANOTHER 7 POINTS...

WE LOSE.

CHAPTER 32:
Grown Cat vs. Baby Crow

*CURRENT ROTATION

INUOKA (YAKU) | KOZUME | FUKUNAGA
YAMAMOTO | KAI | KUROO

NET

AZUMANE | SAWAMURA | HINATA
TSUKISHIMA (NOYA) | KAGEYAMA | TANAKA

INUOKA, YOUR SERVE!

'KAY!

TMP

YOU'RE UP!

SERVER UP!

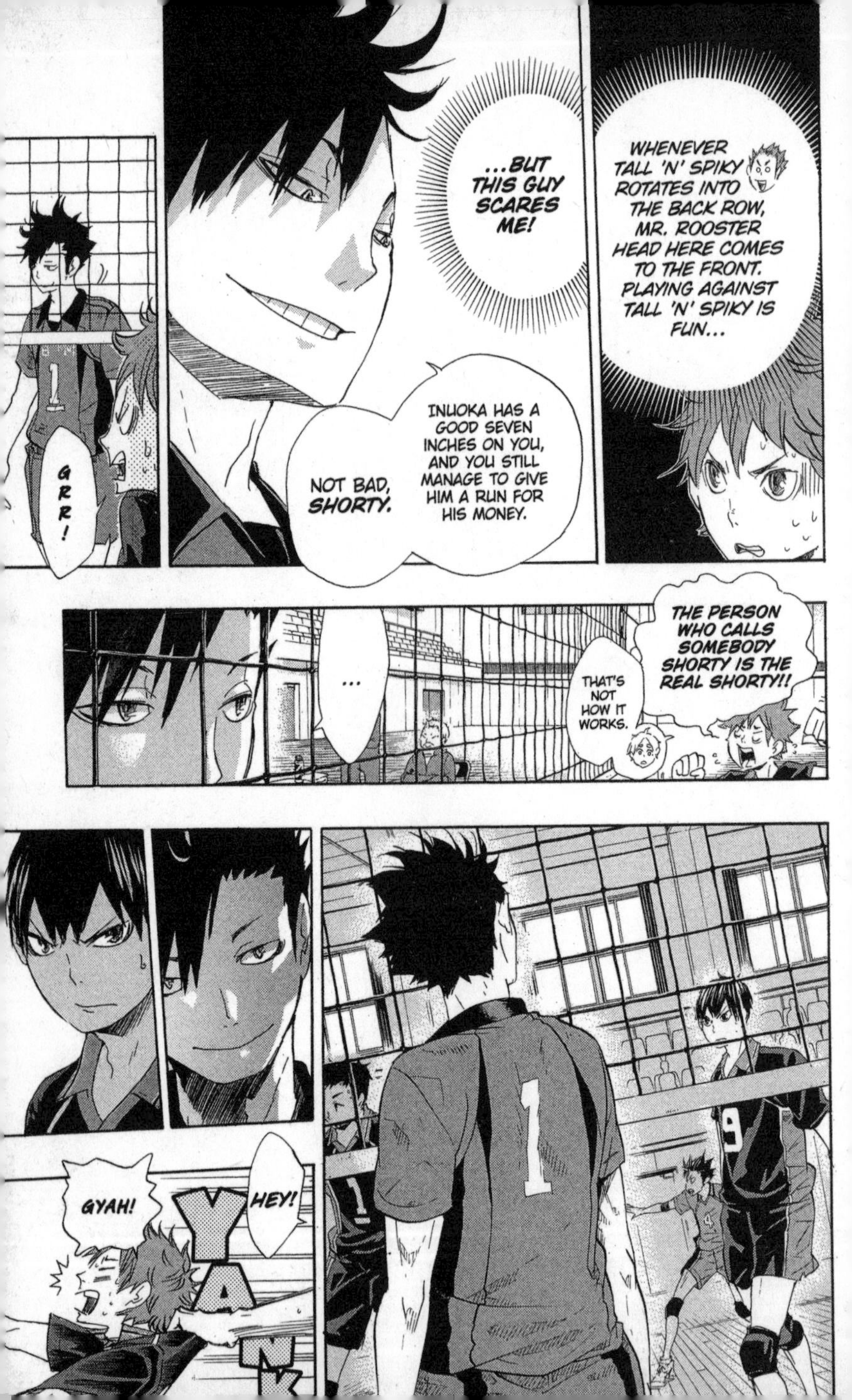
WHENEVER TALL 'N' SPIKY ROTATES INTO THE BACK ROW, MR. ROOSTER HEAD HERE COMES TO THE FRONT. PLAYING AGAINST TALL 'N' SPIKY IS FUN...
...BUT THIS GUY SCARES ME!
INUOKA HAS A GOOD SEVEN INCHES ON YOU, AND YOU STILL MANAGE TO GIVE HIM A RUN FOR HIS MONEY.
NOT BAD, SHORTY.
GRR!
THE PERSON WHO CALLS SOMEBODY SHORTY IS THE REAL SHORTY!!
THAT'S NOT HOW IT WORKS.
...
HEY!
GYAH!
YANK

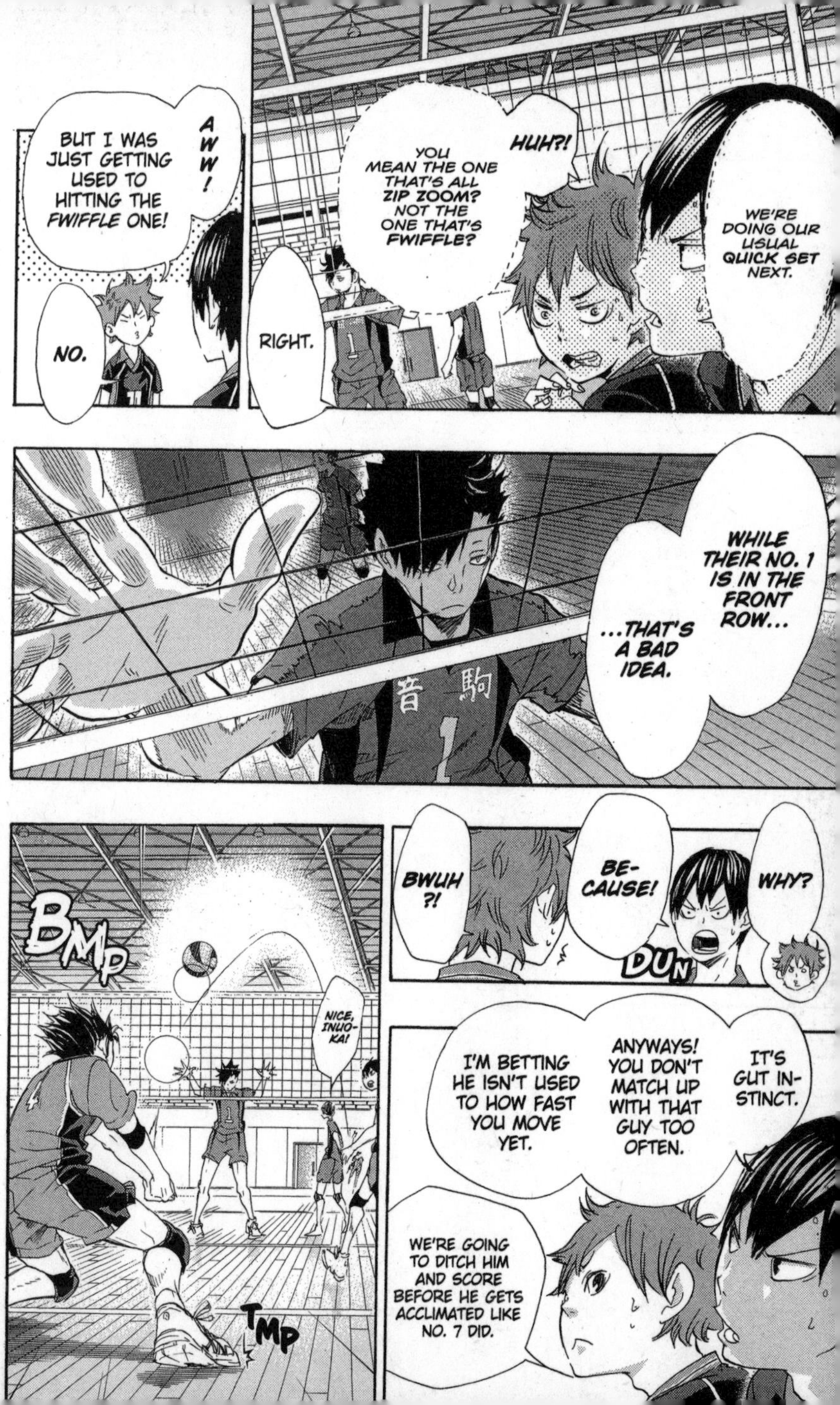
WE'RE DOING OUR USUAL QUICK SET NEXT.
HUH?!
YOU MEAN THE ONE THAT'S ALL ZIP ZOOM? NOT THE ONE THAT'S FWIFFLE?
RIGHT.
AWW!
BUT I WAS JUST GETTING USED TO HITTING THE FWIFFLE ONE!
NO.
WHILE THEIR NO. 1 IS IN THE FRONT ROW...
...THAT'S A BAD IDEA.
音 駒
WHY?
BE-CAUSE!
DUN
BWUH?!
IT'S GUT IN-STINCT.
ANYWAYS! YOU DON'T MATCH UP WITH THAT GUY TOO OFTEN.
I'M BETTING HE ISN'T USED TO HOW FAST YOU MOVE YET.
WE'RE GOING TO DITCH HIM AND SCORE BEFORE HE GETS ACCLIMATED LIKE NO. 7 DID.
BMP
NICE, INUOKA!
TMP

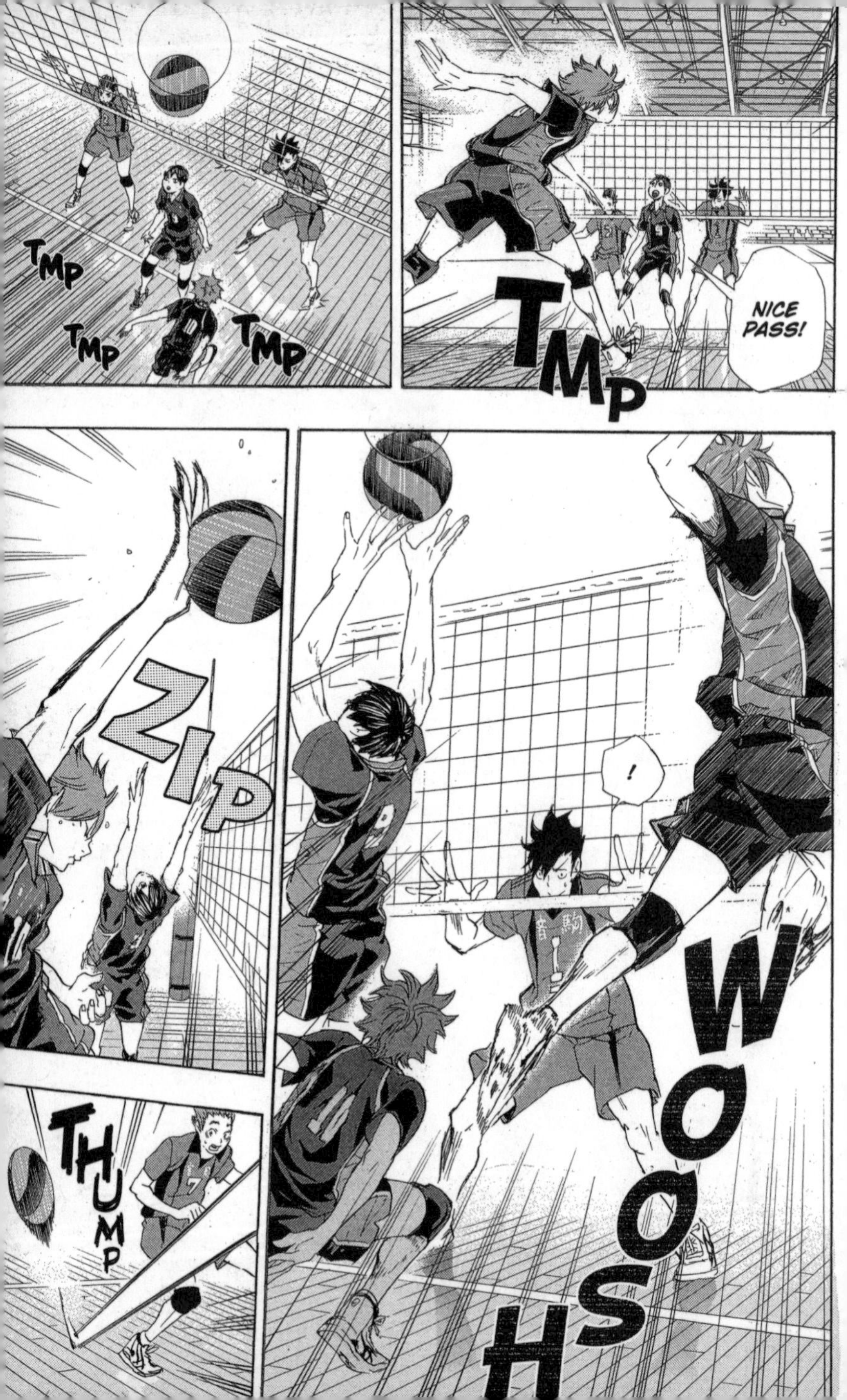
NICE PASS!
TMP
TMP
TMP
TMP
!
WHOOSH
ZIP
THUMP

OOH! I SERVE NEXT!

THAT WAS A GOOD CHOICE.

HM?

YES!

STING STING STING

WOO!!

YESSSS!! THIS FEELING IS THE BEST!!

NEKOMA	KARASUNO
18	16

THAT GUY IS OBVIOUSLY A VETERAN. IT'S LIKELY HE HAS A LOT OF EXPERIENCE WITH STOPPING A NORMAL QUICK SET.

I AGREE WITH HIM. RIGHT NOW, AGAINST THAT BIG THIRD-YEAR MIDDLE BLOCKER, THE FREAK QUICK IS PROBABLY THE MORE EFFECTIVE OPTION.

HINATA SERVE

NISHINOYA OUT

TSUKI-SHIMA IN

HINATA, SERVER UP!

LET'S GO GET THAT BALL BACK.

I GUESS THAT'S WHAT PEOPLE MEAN WHEN THEY CALL SOMEONE "SUPER-HUMAN."

MAN, THEY'RE AMAZ-ING.

...

WELL THEN...

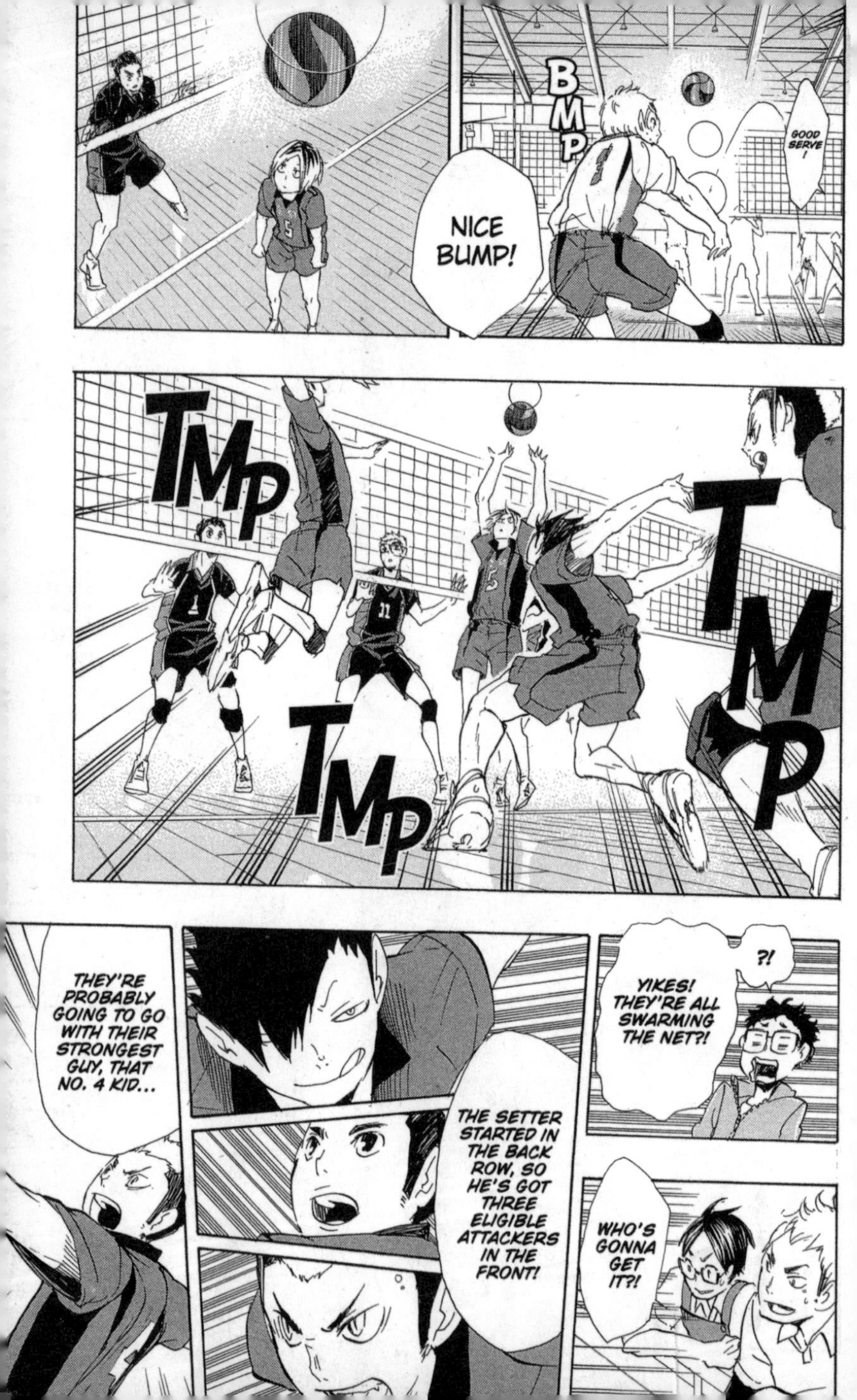
BMP
GOOD SERVE!
NICE BUMP!
TMP
TMP
TMP
?!
YIKES! THEY'RE ALL SWARMING THE NET?!
WHO'S GONNA GET IT?!
THE SETTER STARTED IN THE BACK ROW, SO HE'S GOT THREE ELIGIBLE ATTACKERS IN THE FRONT!
THEY'RE PROBABLY GOING TO GO WITH THEIR STRONGEST GUY, THAT NO. 4 KID...

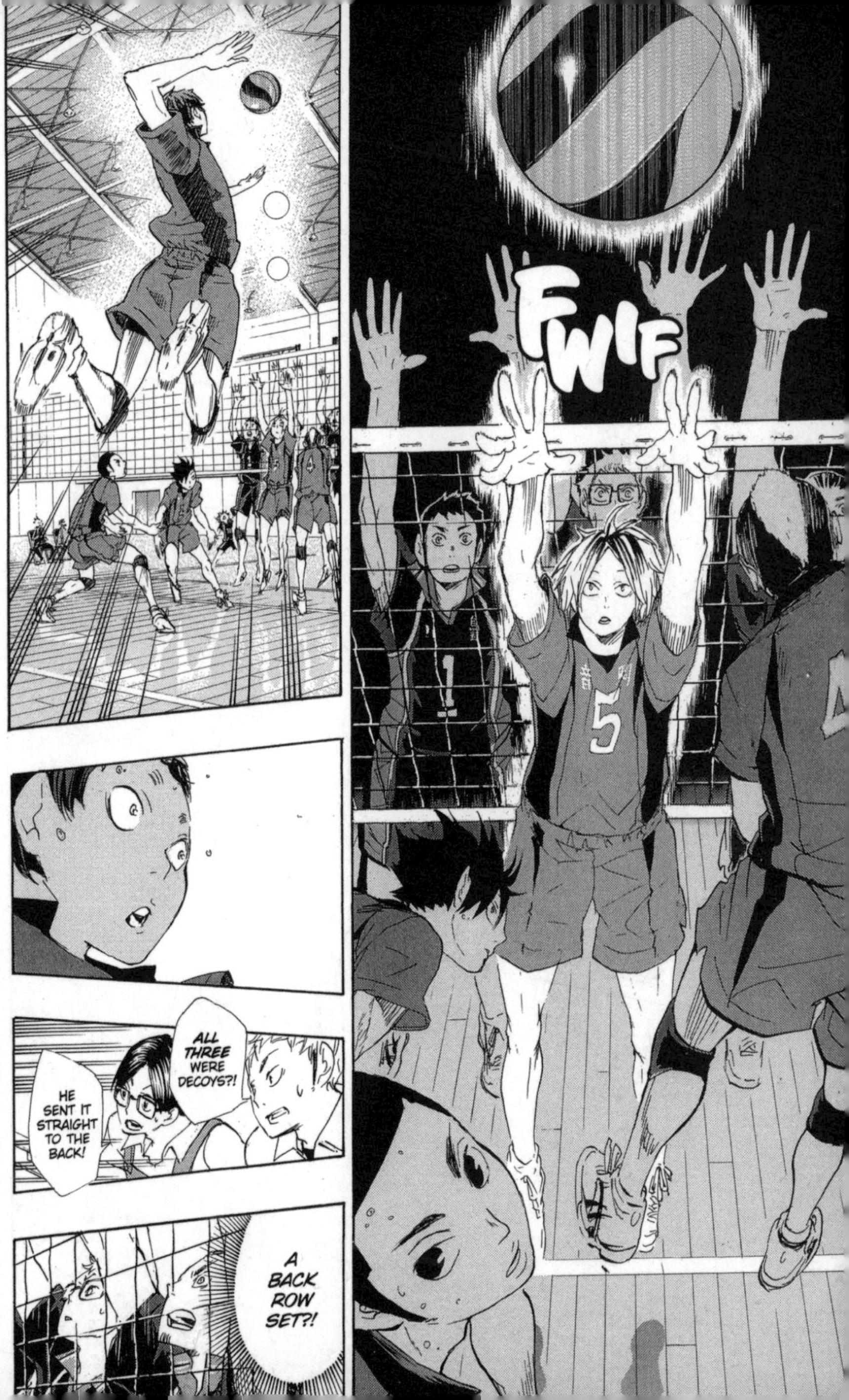
FWIF
ALL THREE WERE DECOYS?!
HE SENT IT STRAIGHT TO THE BACK!
A BACK ROW SET?!

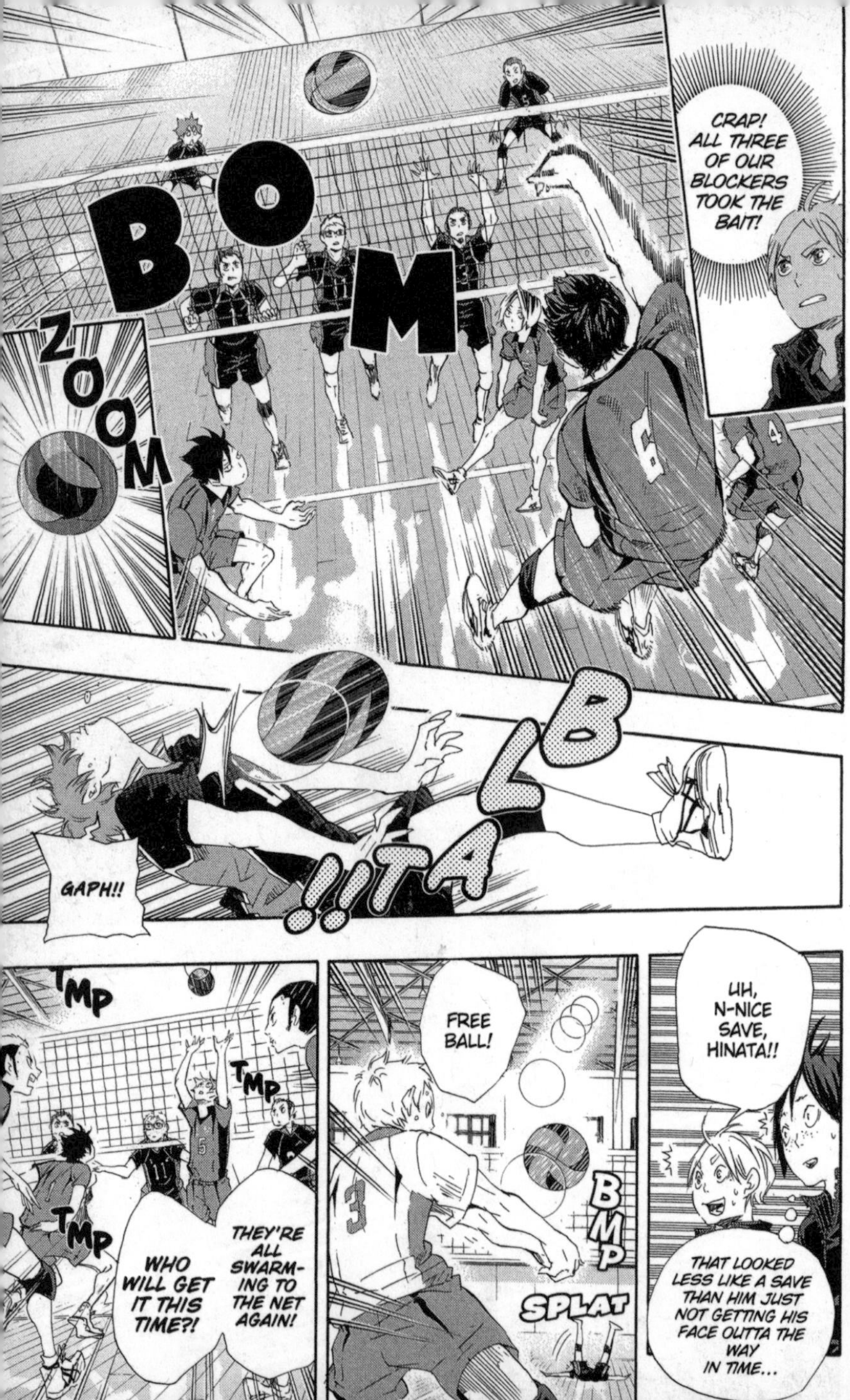
CRAP! ALL THREE OF OUR BLOCKERS TOOK THE BAIT!
BOOM
ZOOM
BLAT!!
GAPH!!
UH, N-NICE SAVE, HINATA!!
THAT LOOKED LESS LIKE A SAVE THAN HIM JUST NOT GETTING HIS FACE OUTTA THE WAY IN TIME...
FREE BALL!
BMP
SPLAT
TMP
TMP
TMP
THEY'RE ALL SWARMING TO THE NET AGAIN!
WHO WILL GET IT THIS TIME?!

BAM

THMP

FWIF

A QUICK?!

THIS TIME THEY WENT WITH A **QUICK**.

GEEZ, THAT WAS FAST!

NICE SERVE, YAMA-MOTO!

HUP!

BOM

NEKOMA	KARASUNO
19	16

MAYBE IT'S JUST BECAUSE I'VE GOTTEN USED TO WATCHING TOO MANY LAST-SECOND CRAZY ONES FROM HINATA, BUT...

THEIR ATTACKS, ESPECIALLY THAT QUICK SET, HAVE A REAL STABLE FEELING TO THEM.

Y'KNOW...

144

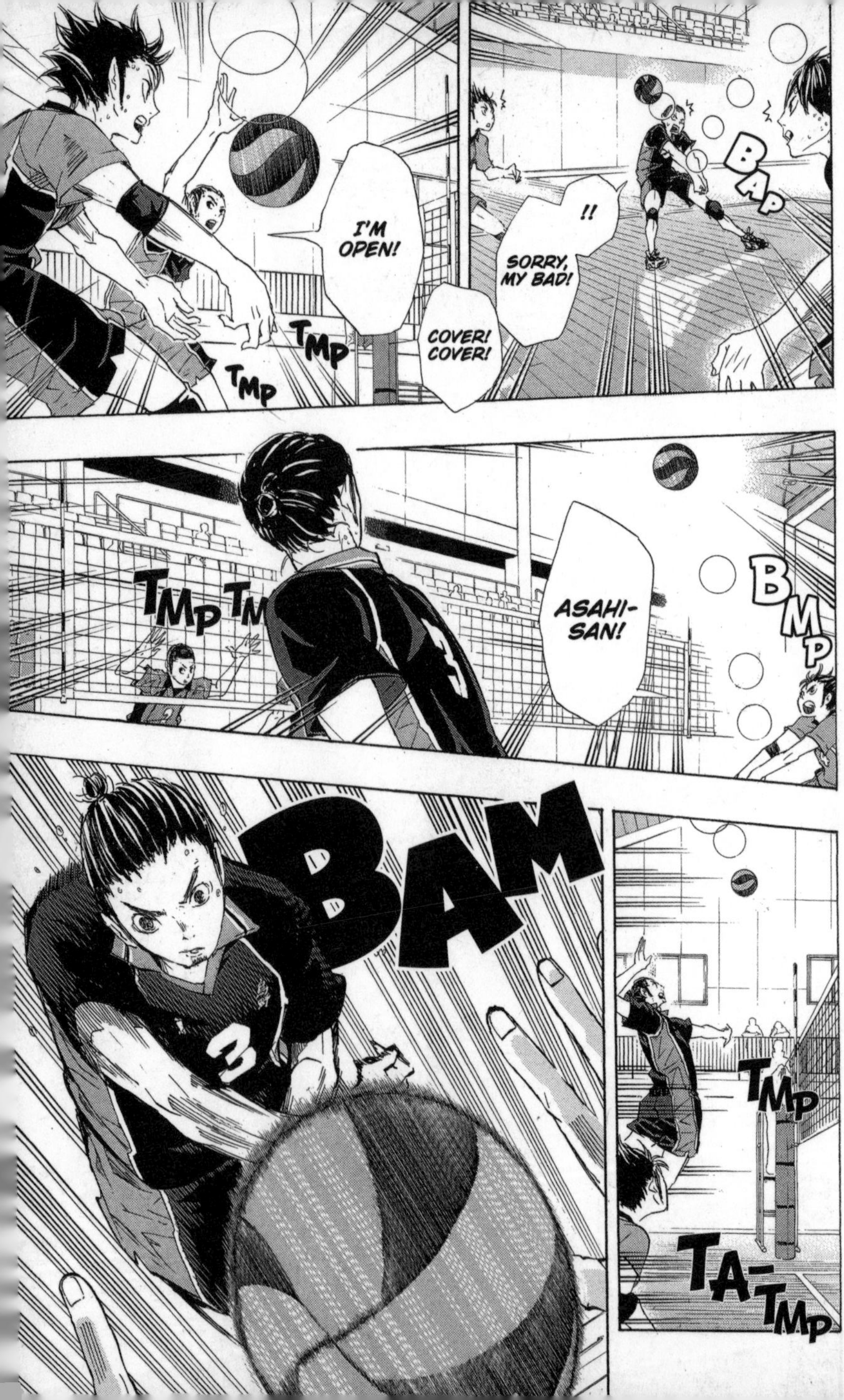
BAP
!!
SORRY, MY BAD!
COVER! COVER!
I'M OPEN!
TMP
TMP
BMP
ASAHI-SAN!
TMP TM
TMP
TA-TMP
BAM

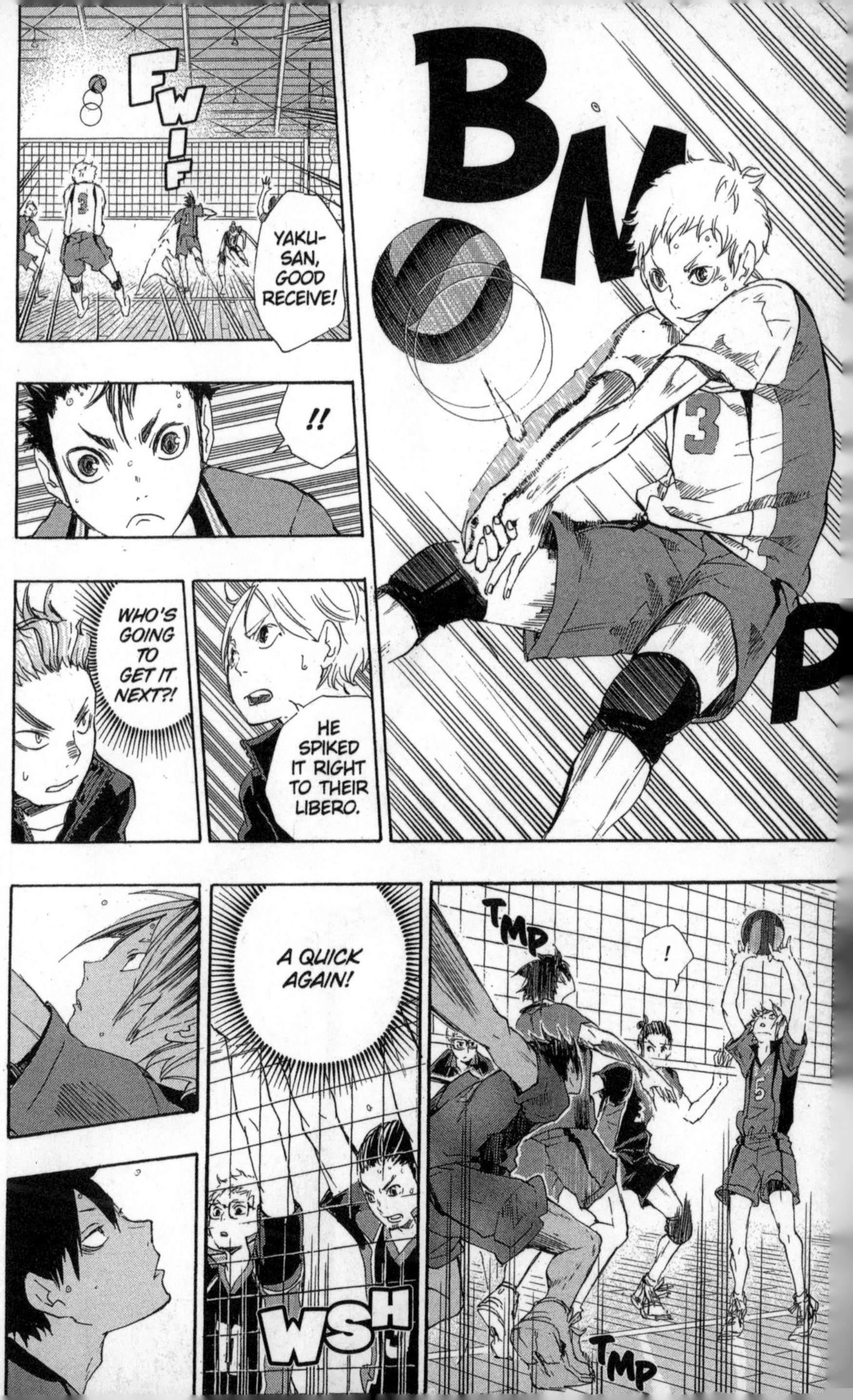
BMP
FWIF
YAKU-SAN, GOOD RECEIVE!
!!
HE SPIKED IT RIGHT TO THEIR LIBERO.
WHO'S GOING TO GET IT NEXT?!
TMP
!
TMP
A QUICK AGAIN!
WSH

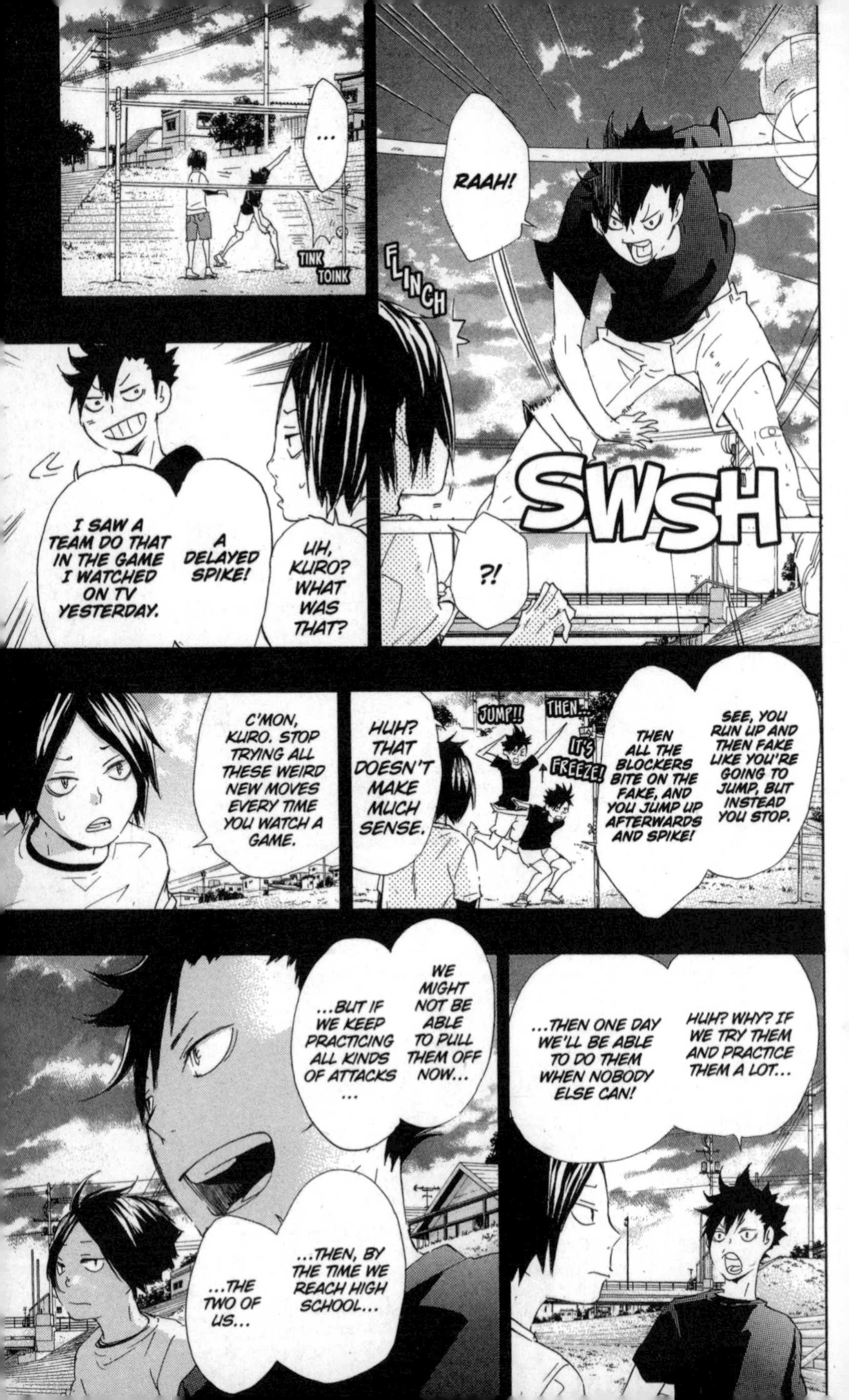
RAAH!
FLINCH
SWSH
?!
...
TINK TOINK
UH, KURO? WHAT WAS THAT?
A DELAYED SPIKE!
I SAW A TEAM DO THAT IN THE GAME I WATCHED ON TV YESTERDAY.
SEE, YOU RUN UP AND THEN FAKE LIKE YOU'RE GOING TO JUMP, BUT INSTEAD YOU STOP.
THEN ALL THE BLOCKERS BITE ON THE FAKE, AND YOU JUMP UP AFTERWARDS AND SPIKE!
THEN...
JUMP!!
IT'S FREEZE!
HUH? THAT DOESN'T MAKE MUCH SENSE.
C'MON, KURO. STOP TRYING ALL THESE WEIRD NEW MOVES EVERY TIME YOU WATCH A GAME.
HUH? WHY? IF WE TRY THEM AND PRACTICE THEM A LOT...
...THEN ONE DAY WE'LL BE ABLE TO DO THEM WHEN NOBODY ELSE CAN!
WE MIGHT NOT BE ABLE TO PULL THEM OFF NOW...
...BUT IF WE KEEP PRACTICING ALL KINDS OF ATTACKS...
...THEN, BY THE TIME WE REACH HIGH SCHOOL...
...THE TWO OF US...

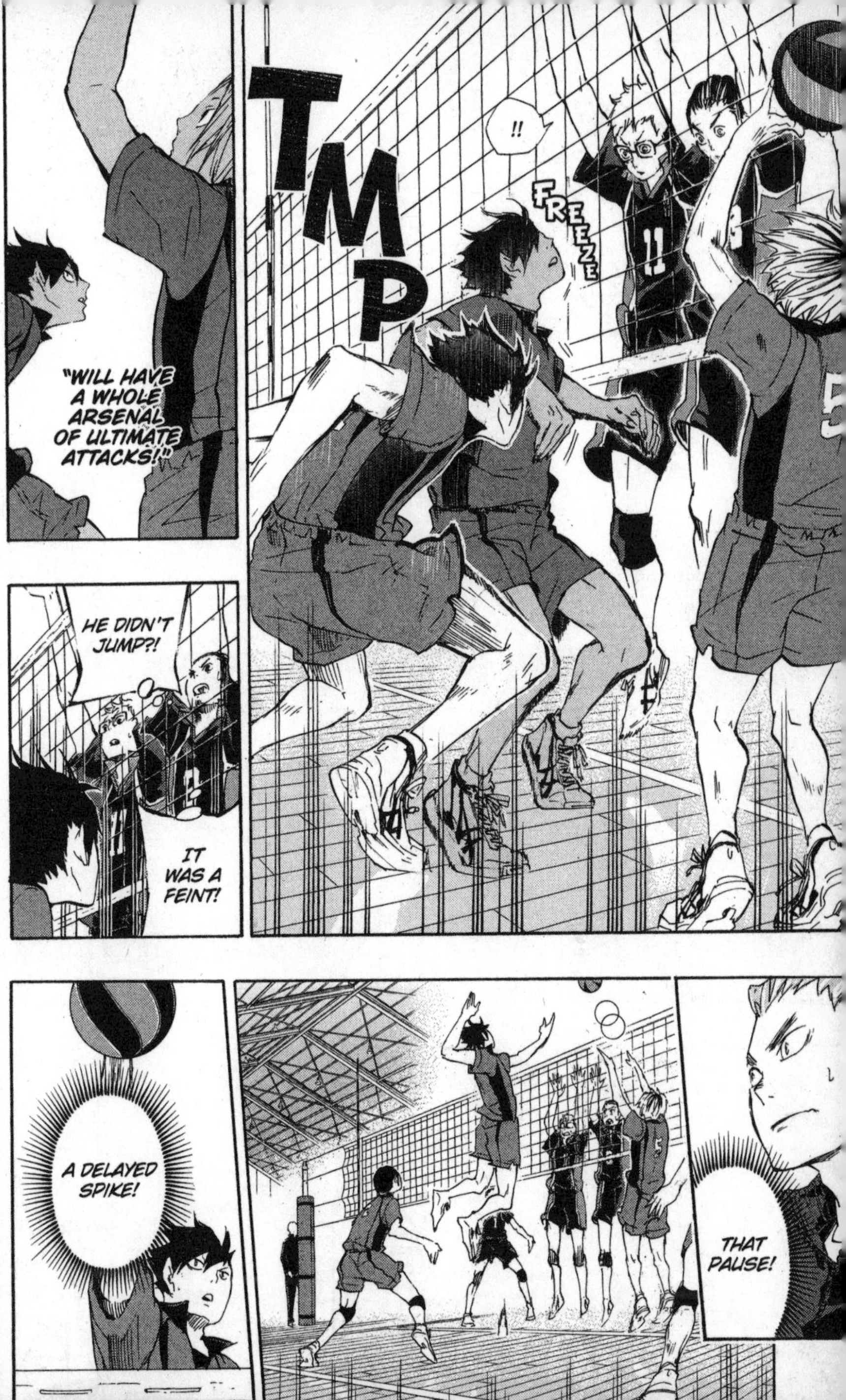
TMP
!!
FREEZE
"WILL HAVE A WHOLE ARSENAL OF ULTIMATE ATTACKS!"
HE DIDN'T JUMP?!
IT WAS A FEINT!
THAT PAUSE!
A DELAYED SPIKE!

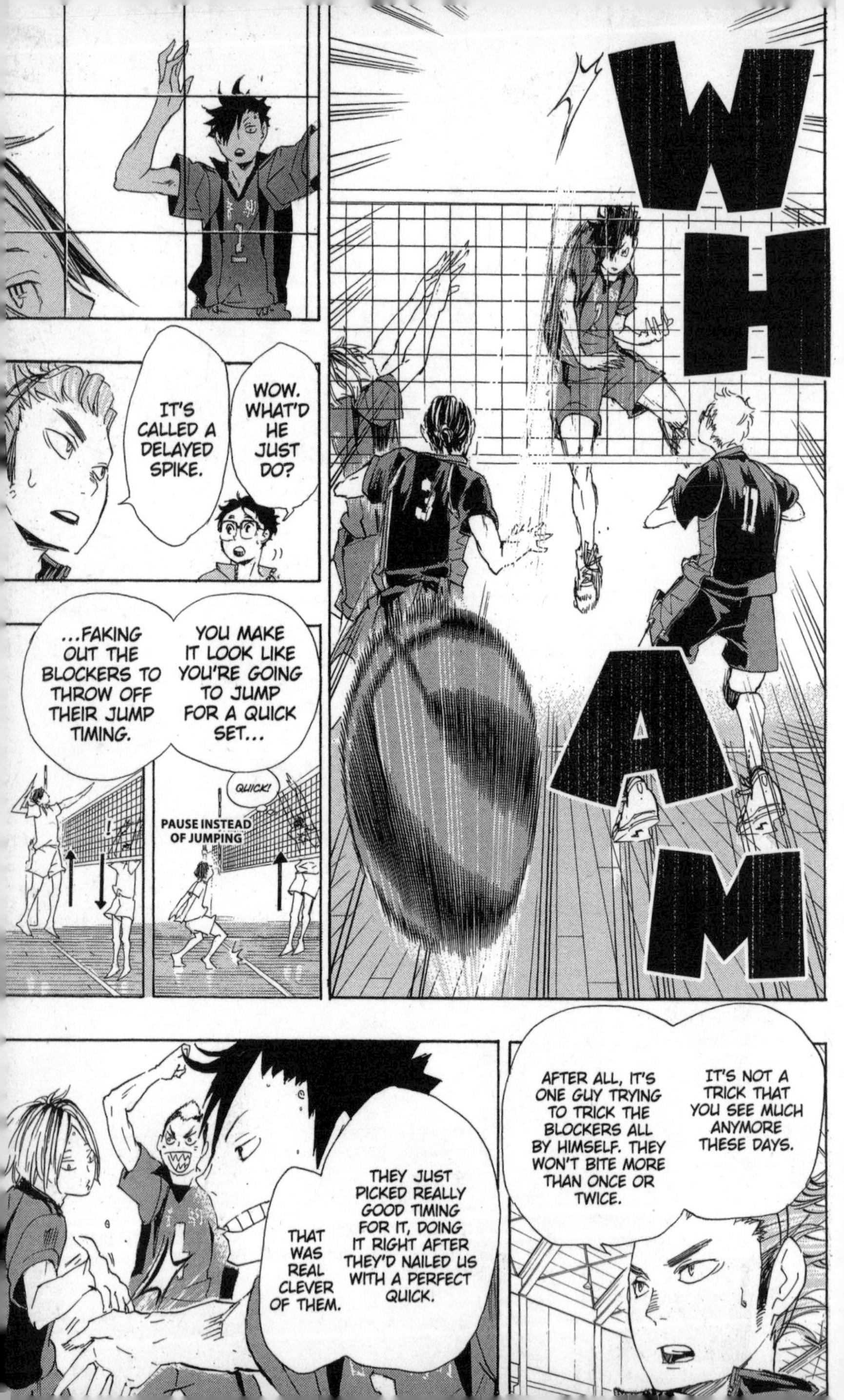
WHAM
WOW. WHAT'D HE JUST DO?
IT'S CALLED A DELAYED SPIKE.
YOU MAKE IT LOOK LIKE YOU'RE GOING TO JUMP FOR A QUICK SET...
...FAKING OUT THE BLOCKERS TO THROW OFF THEIR JUMP TIMING.
QUICK!
PAUSE INSTEAD OF JUMPING
IT'S NOT A TRICK THAT YOU SEE MUCH ANYMORE THESE DAYS.
AFTER ALL, IT'S ONE GUY TRYING TO TRICK THE BLOCKERS ALL BY HIMSELF. THEY WON'T BITE MORE THAN ONCE OR TWICE.
THEY JUST PICKED REALLY GOOD TIMING FOR IT, DOING IT RIGHT AFTER THEY'D NAILED US WITH A PERFECT QUICK.
THAT WAS REAL CLEVER OF THEM.

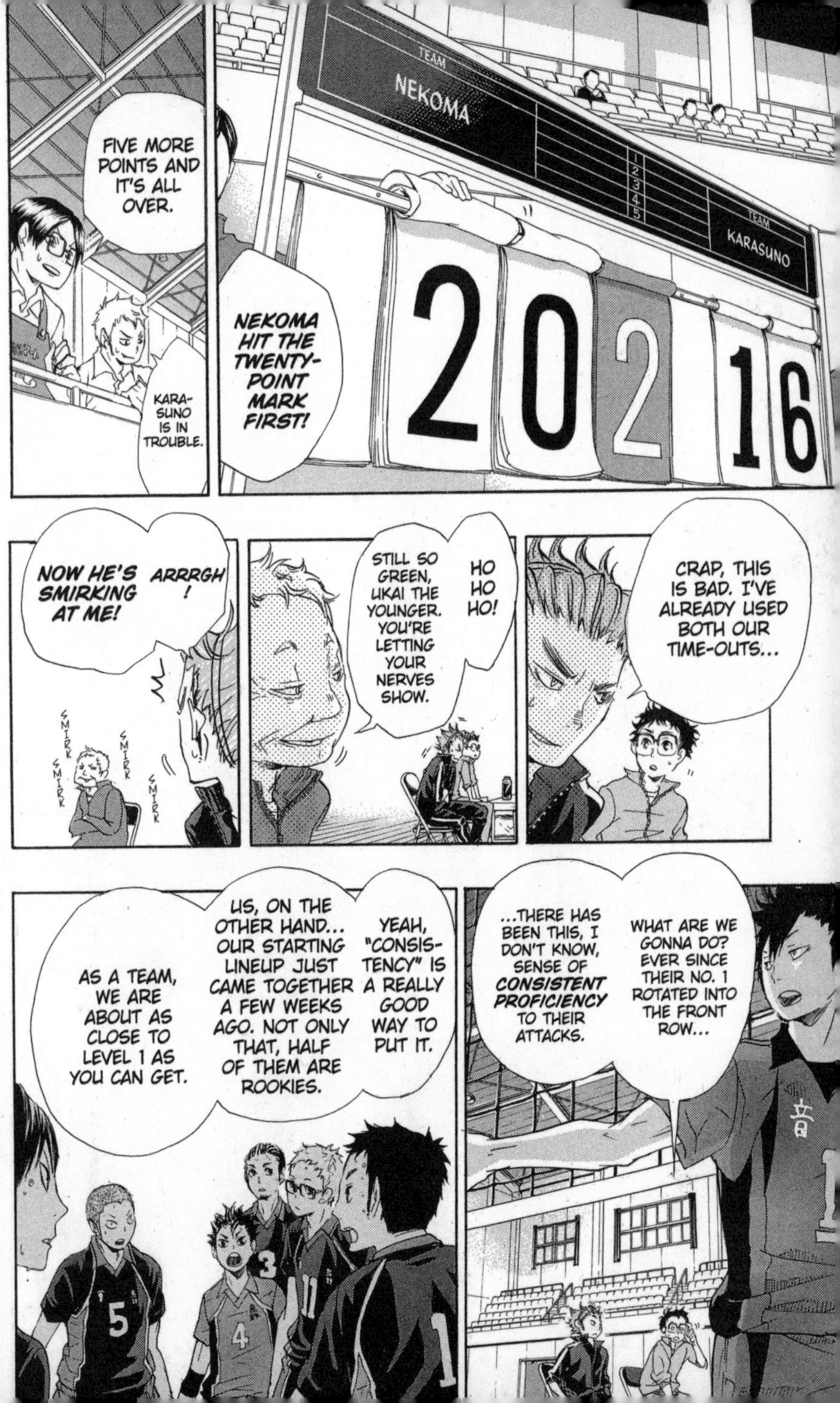
TEAM
NEKOMA
1 2 3 4 5
TEAM
KARASUNO
20 2 16
NEKOMA HIT THE TWENTY-POINT MARK FIRST!
FIVE MORE POINTS AND IT'S ALL OVER.
KARA-SUNO IS IN TROUBLE.
CRAP, THIS IS BAD. I'VE ALREADY USED BOTH OUR TIME-OUTS...
HO HO HO!
STILL SO GREEN, UKAI THE YOUNGER. YOU'RE LETTING YOUR NERVES SHOW.
ARRRGH!
NOW HE'S SMIRKING AT ME!
SMIRK
SMIRK
SMIRK
SMIRK
WHAT ARE WE GONNA DO? EVER SINCE THEIR NO. 1 ROTATED INTO THE FRONT ROW...
...THERE HAS BEEN THIS, I DON'T KNOW, SENSE OF CONSISTENT PROFICIENCY TO THEIR ATTACKS.
YEAH, "CONSIS-TENCY" IS A REALLY GOOD WAY TO PUT IT.
US, ON THE OTHER HAND... OUR STARTING LINEUP JUST CAME TOGETHER A FEW WEEKS AGO. NOT ONLY THAT, HALF OF THEM ARE ROOKIES.
AS A TEAM, WE ARE ABOUT AS CLOSE TO LEVEL 1 AS YOU CAN GET.

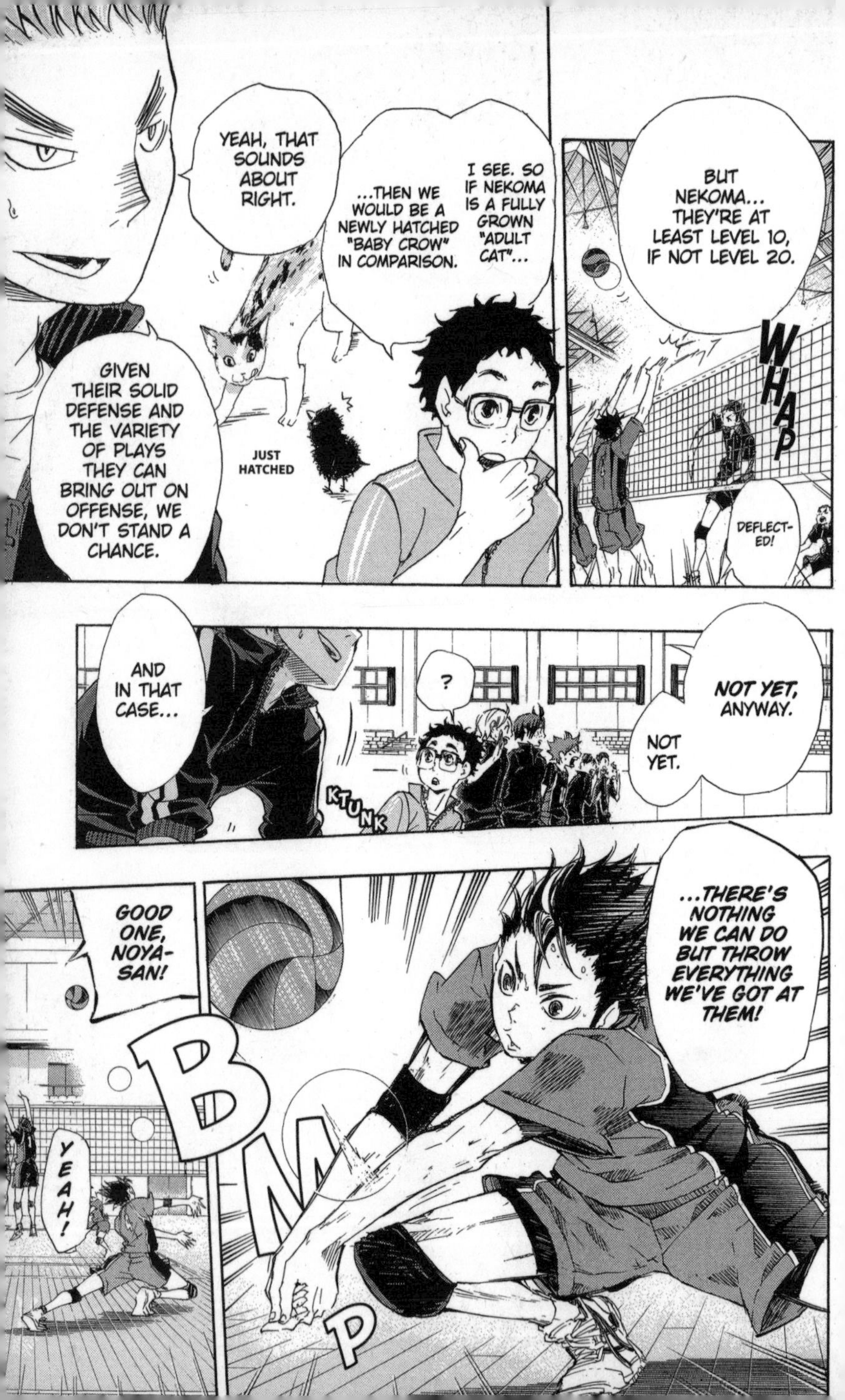
BUT NEKOMA... THEY'RE AT LEAST LEVEL 10, IF NOT LEVEL 20.
WHAP
DEFLECTED!
I SEE. SO IF NEKOMA IS A FULLY GROWN "ADULT CAT"...
...THEN WE WOULD BE A NEWLY HATCHED "BABY CROW" IN COMPARISON.
JUST HATCHED
YEAH, THAT SOUNDS ABOUT RIGHT.
GIVEN THEIR SOLID DEFENSE AND THE VARIETY OF PLAYS THEY CAN BRING OUT ON OFFENSE, WE DON'T STAND A CHANCE.
NOT YET, ANYWAY.
NOT YET.
?
KTUNK
AND IN THAT CASE...
...THERE'S NOTHING WE CAN DO BUT THROW EVERYTHING WE'VE GOT AT THEM!
BAMP
GOOD ONE, NOYA-SAN!
YEAH!

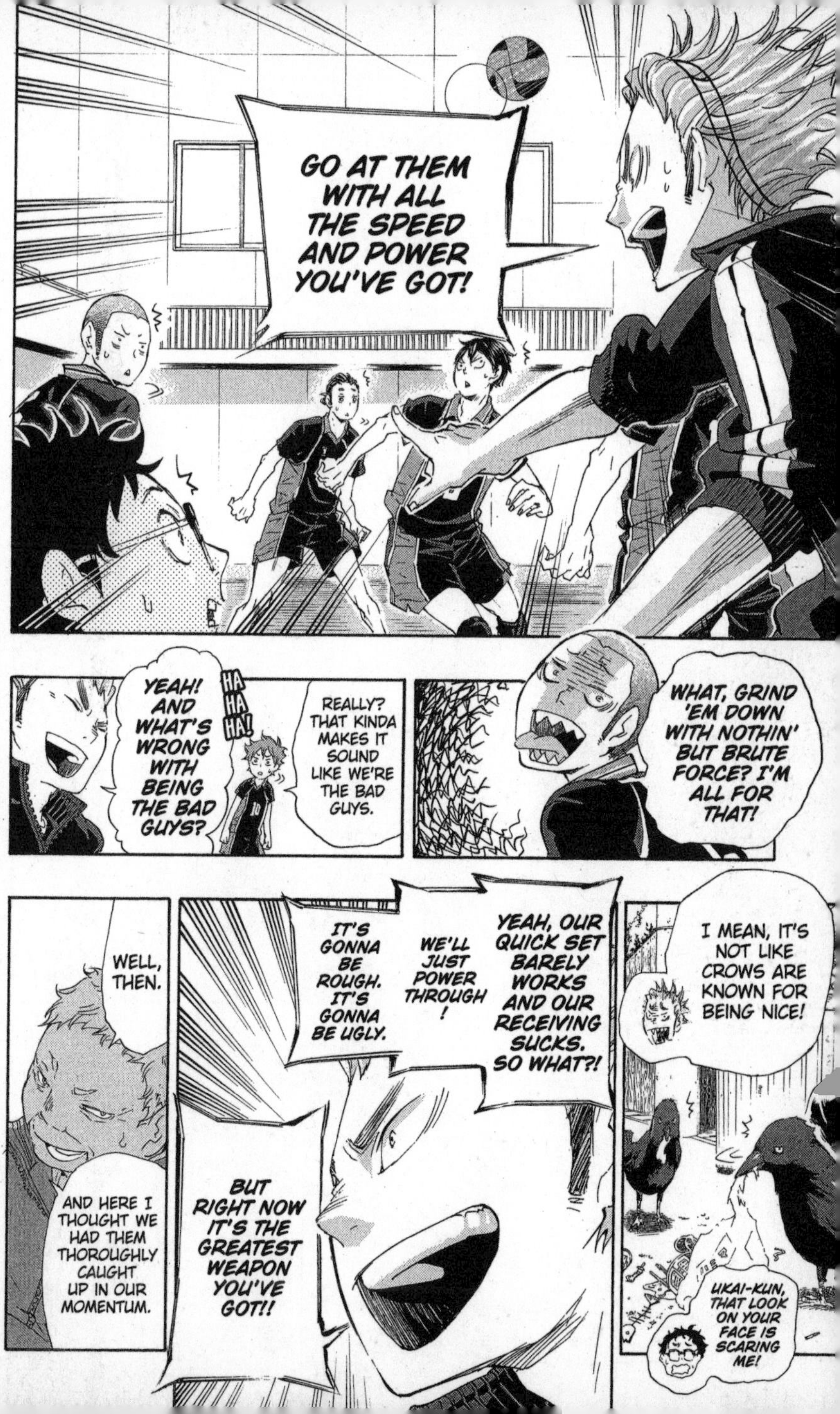
GO AT THEM WITH ALL THE SPEED AND POWER YOU'VE GOT!
WHAT, GRIND 'EM DOWN WITH NOTHIN' BUT BRUTE FORCE? I'M ALL FOR THAT!
REALLY? THAT KINDA MAKES IT SOUND LIKE WE'RE THE BAD GUYS.
HA HA HA!
YEAH! AND WHAT'S WRONG WITH BEING THE BAD GUYS?
I MEAN, IT'S NOT LIKE CROWS ARE KNOWN FOR BEING NICE!
UKAI-KUN, THAT LOOK ON YOUR FACE IS SCARING ME!
YEAH, OUR QUICK SET BARELY WORKS AND OUR RECEIVING SUCKS. SO WHAT?!
WE'LL JUST POWER THROUGH!
IT'S GONNA BE ROUGH. IT'S GONNA BE UGLY.
BUT RIGHT NOW IT'S THE GREATEST WEAPON YOU'VE GOT!!
WELL, THEN.
AND HERE I THOUGHT WE HAD THEM THOROUGHLY CAUGHT UP IN OUR MOMENTUM.

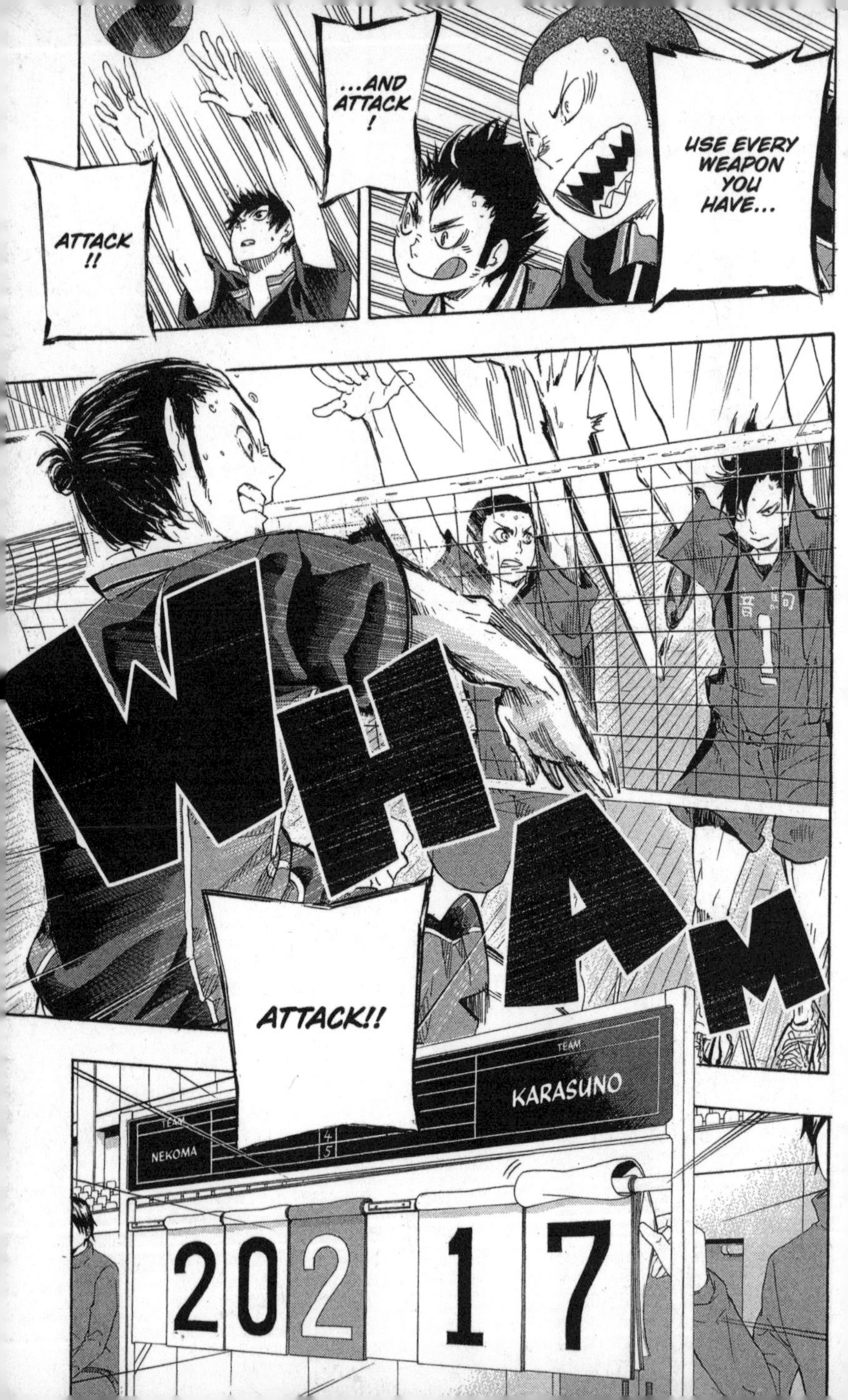
USE EVERY WEAPON YOU HAVE...
...AND ATTACK!
ATTACK!!
WHAM
ATTACK!!
TEAM
KARASUNO
TEAM
NEKOMA
4
5
20
2
17

TETSURO KUROO (PRONOUNCED "KOO-ROH-OH")

NEKOMA HIGH SCHOOL
CLASS 3-5
VOLLEYBALL CLUB CAPTAIN

POSITION:
MIDDLE BLOCKER

HEIGHT: 6'2"

WEIGHT: 166 LBS.
(AS OF APRIL, 3RD YEAR OF HIGH SCHOOL)

BIRTHDAY: NOVEMBER 17

FAVORITE FOOD:
SALT-GRILLED PIKE

CURRENT WORRY:
HE CAN'T SEEM TO GET RID OF HIS BED-HEAD HAIR.

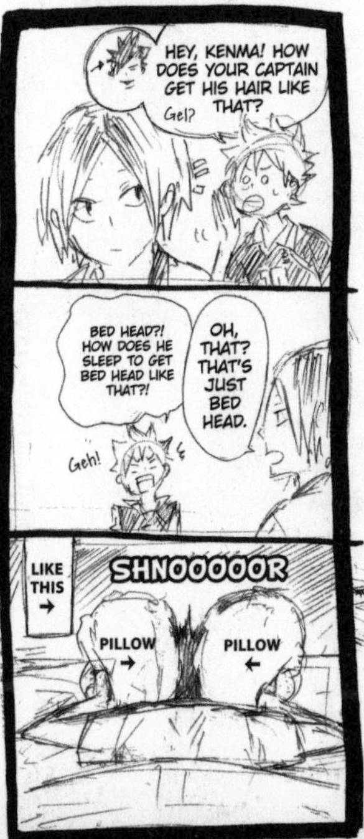
HEY, KENMA! HOW DOES YOUR CAPTAIN GET HIS HAIR LIKE THAT?
Gel?
OH, THAT? THAT'S JUST BED HEAD.
BED HEAD?! HOW DOES HE SLEEP TO GET BED HEAD LIKE THAT?!
Geh!
SHNOOOOOR
LIKE THIS →
PILLOW ←
PILLOW →

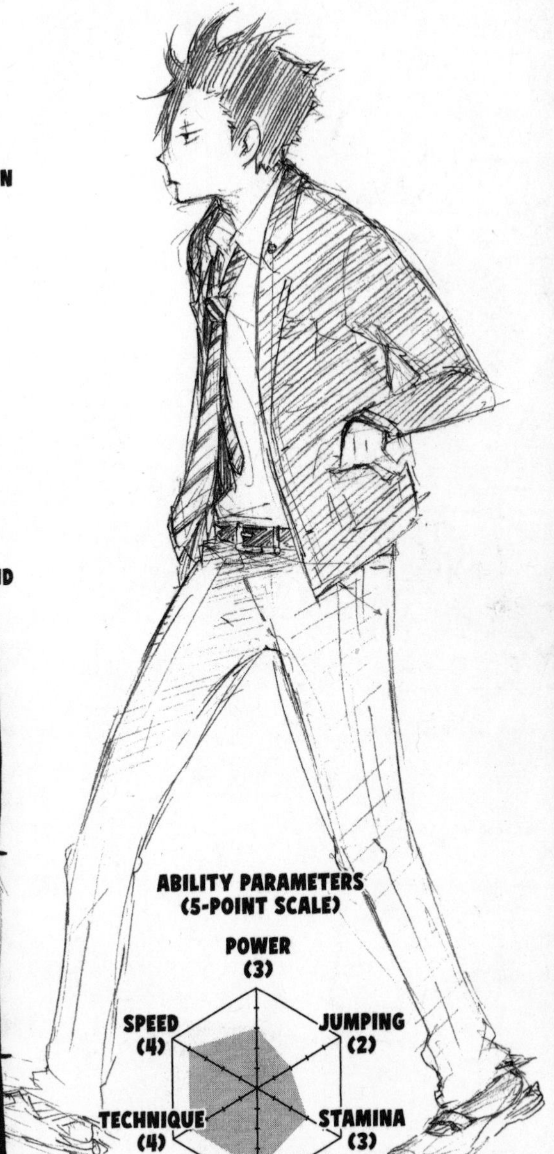
ABILITY PARAMETERS (5-POINT SCALE)
POWER (3)
JUMPING (2)
STAMINA (3)
INTELLIGENCE (4)
TECHNIQUE (4)
SPEED (4)

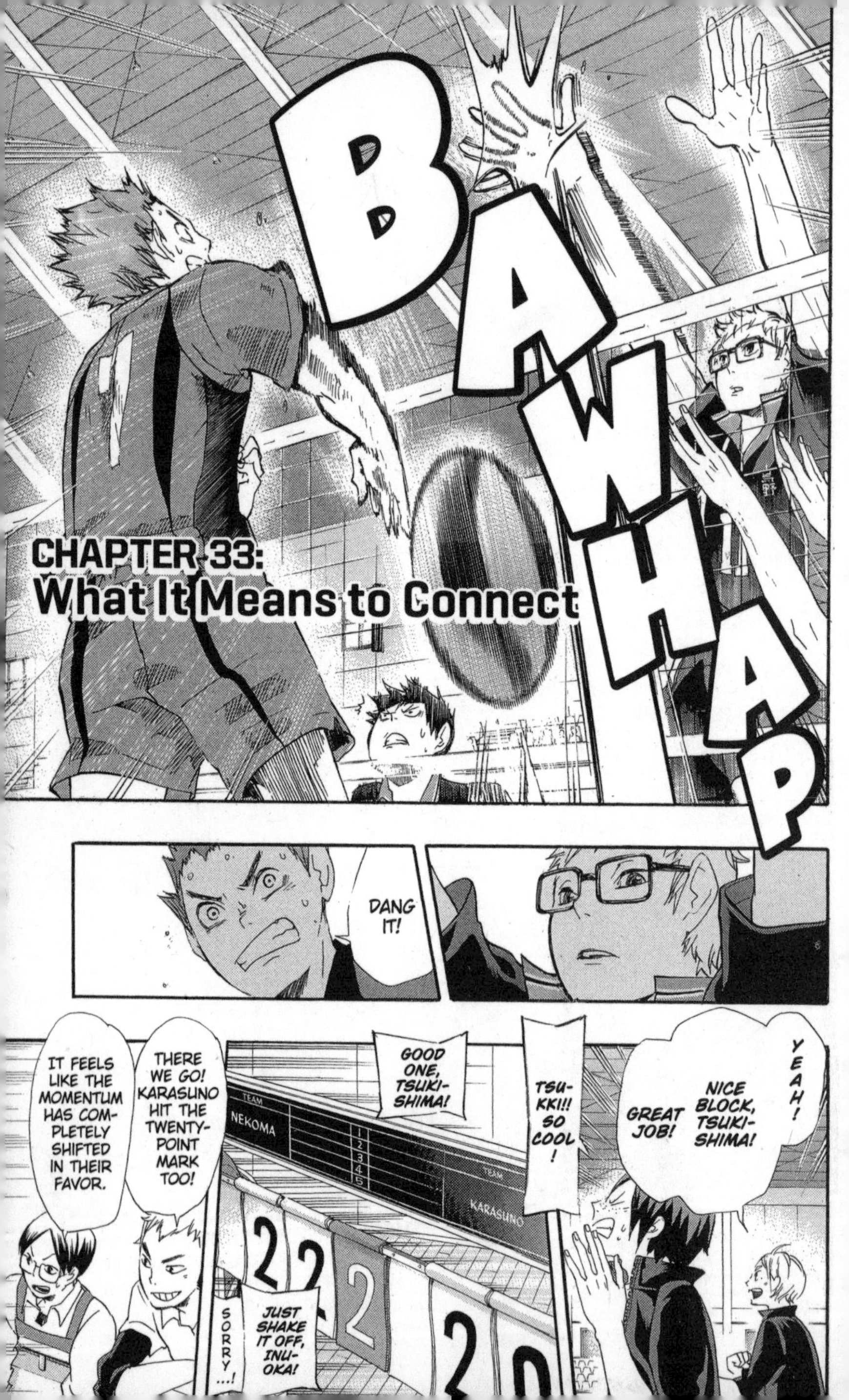
BAWHAP
CHAPTER 33:
What It Means to Connect
DANG IT!
YEAH!
NICE BLOCK, TSUKI-SHIMA!
GREAT JOB!
TSU-KKI!!! SO COOL!
GOOD ONE, TSUKI-SHIMA!
JUST SHAKE IT OFF, INU-OKA!
SORRY...!
TEAM
NEKOMA
TEAM
KARASUNO
THERE WE GO! KARASUNO HIT THE TWENTY-POINT MARK TOO!
IT FEELS LIKE THE MOMENTUM HAS COM-PLETELY SHIFTED IN THEIR FAVOR.

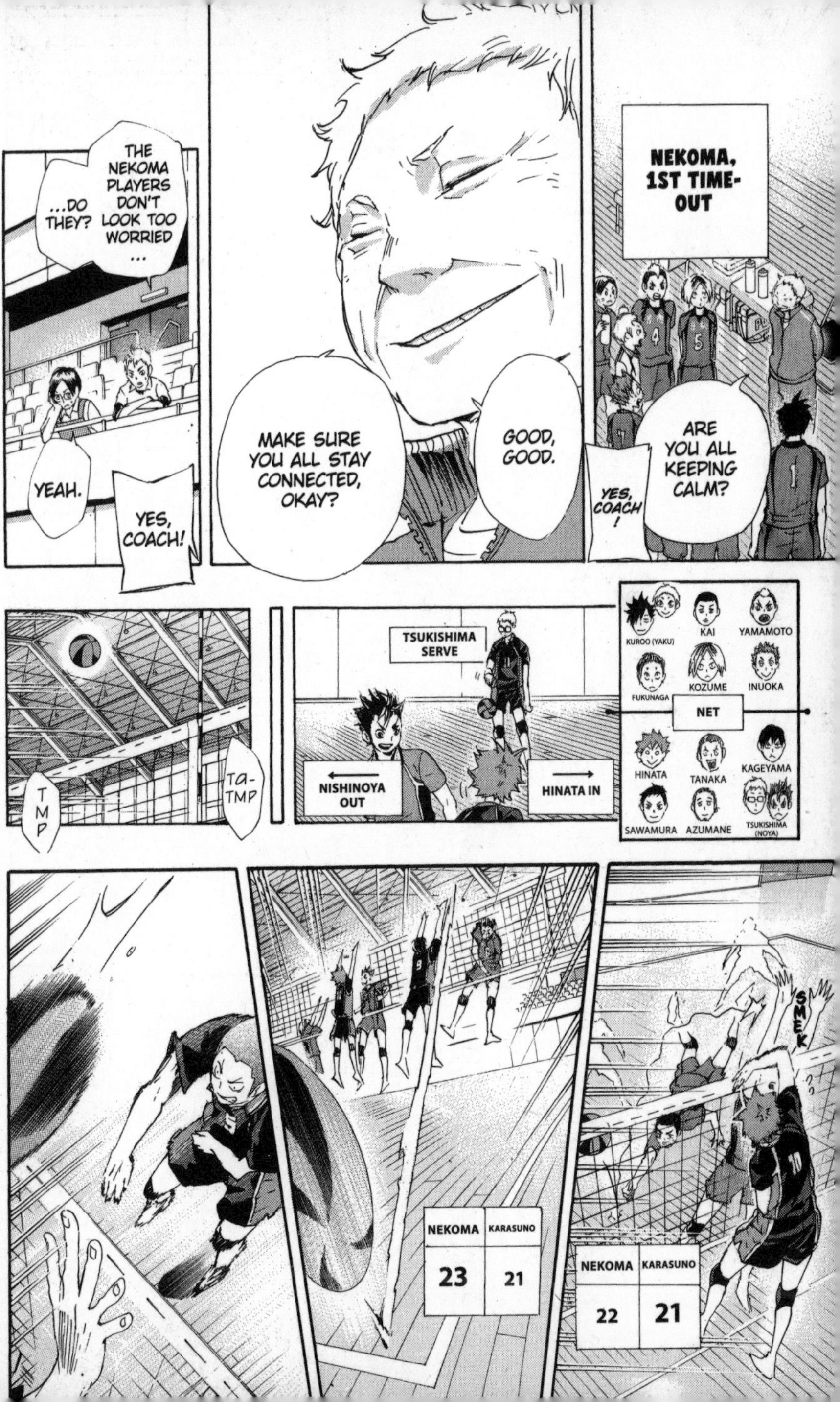
NEKOMA, 1ST TIME-OUT
ARE YOU ALL KEEPING CALM?
YES, COACH!
GOOD, GOOD.
MAKE SURE YOU ALL STAY CONNECTED, OKAY?
THE NEKOMA PLAYERS DON'T LOOK TOO WORRIED...
...DO THEY?
YES, COACH!
YEAH.
KUROO (YAKU)
KAI
YAMAMOTO
FUKUNAGA
KOZUME
INUOKA
NET
HINATA
TANAKA
KAGEYAMA
SAWAMURA
AZUMANE
TSUKISHIMA (NOYA)
TSUKISHIMA SERVE
HINATA IN
NISHINOYA OUT
TA-TMP
TMP
SMEK
NEKOMA 22
KARASUNO 21
NEKOMA 23
KARASUNO 21

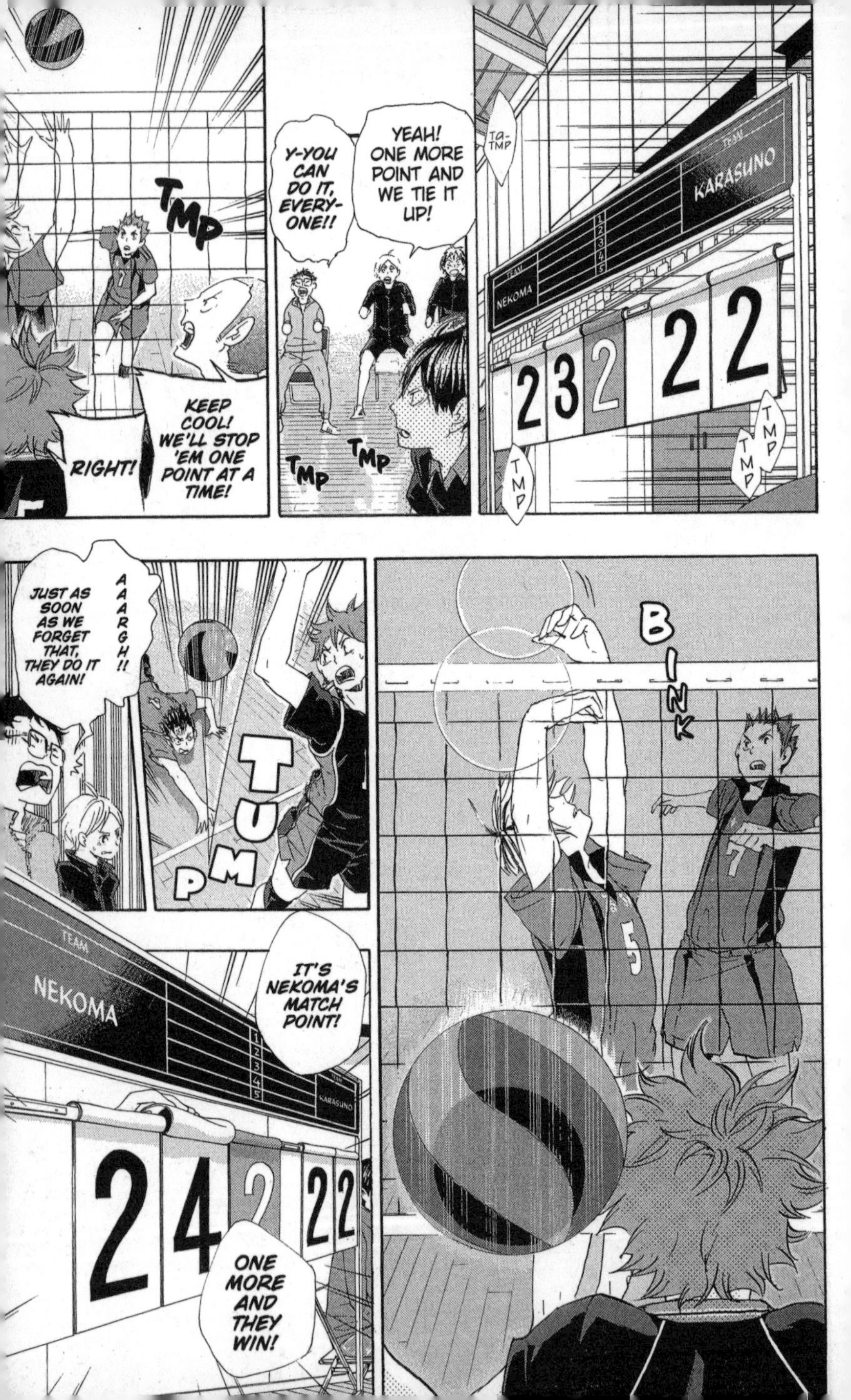
Ta-TMP
KARASUNO
NEKOMA
TMP TMP
TMP
YEAH! ONE MORE POINT AND WE TIE IT UP!
Y-YOU CAN DO IT, EVERYONE!!
TMP
TMP
TMP
KEEP COOL! WE'LL STOP 'EM ONE POINT AT A TIME!
RIGHT!
BINK
TUMP
AAARGH!!
JUST AS SOON AS WE FORGET THAT, THEY DO IT AGAIN!
NEKOMA
KARASUNO
IT'S NEKOMA'S MATCH POINT!
ONE MORE AND THEY WIN!

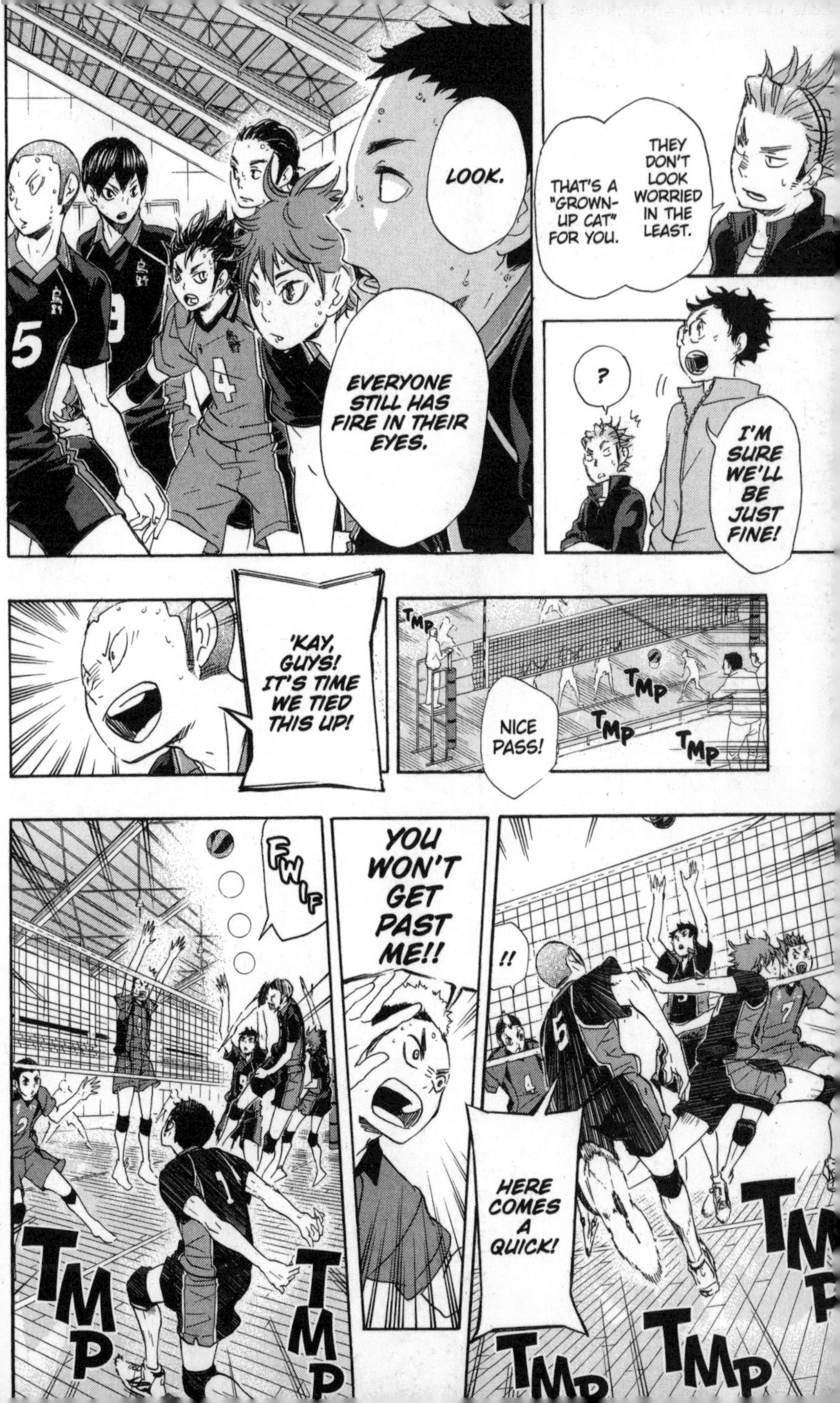
THEY DON'T LOOK WORRIED IN THE LEAST.
THAT'S A "GROWN-UP CAT" FOR YOU.
I'M SURE WE'LL BE JUST FINE!
?
LOOK.
EVERYONE STILL HAS FIRE IN THEIR EYES.
TMP
TMP
TMP
TMP
NICE PASS!
'KAY, GUYS! IT'S TIME WE TIED THIS UP!
!!
HERE COMES A QUICK!
TMP
TMP
TMP
TMP
YOU WON'T GET PAST ME!!
FWIF
TMP
TMP

YES!!

AWW-RIIIGHT!

BAM

KARASUNO

24 2 | 23

NOW THAT FULL-GROWN ADULT THEY CALL A HIGH SCHOOLER HAS ROTATED TO THE FRONT.

TANAKA-SAN!

SERVER UP!

KOZUME | FUKUNAGA | KURO O (YAKU)

INUOKA | YAMAMOTO | KAI

NET

AZUMANE | SAWAMURA | HINATA

TSUKISHIMA (NOYA) | KAGEYAMA | TANAKA

THIS IS THE BEST CHANCE WE'VE GOT TO PULL OFF A COMEBACK!

BOTH OF THEM IN THE FRONT ROW AT THE SAME TIME PUTS US IN OUR BEST OFFENSIVE ROTATION.

AND RIGHT NOW, AZUMANE IS THE STRONGEST SINGLE HITTER ON THE WHOLE COURT.

HINATA FORCES NEKOMA TO SPLIT UP THEIR BLOCKING TO ACCOUNT FOR HIM. AND EVEN WHEN HE'S NOT A DECOY, HE STILL HAS THE POTENTIAL TO GET AROUND THEIR BLOCKS AND SCORE.

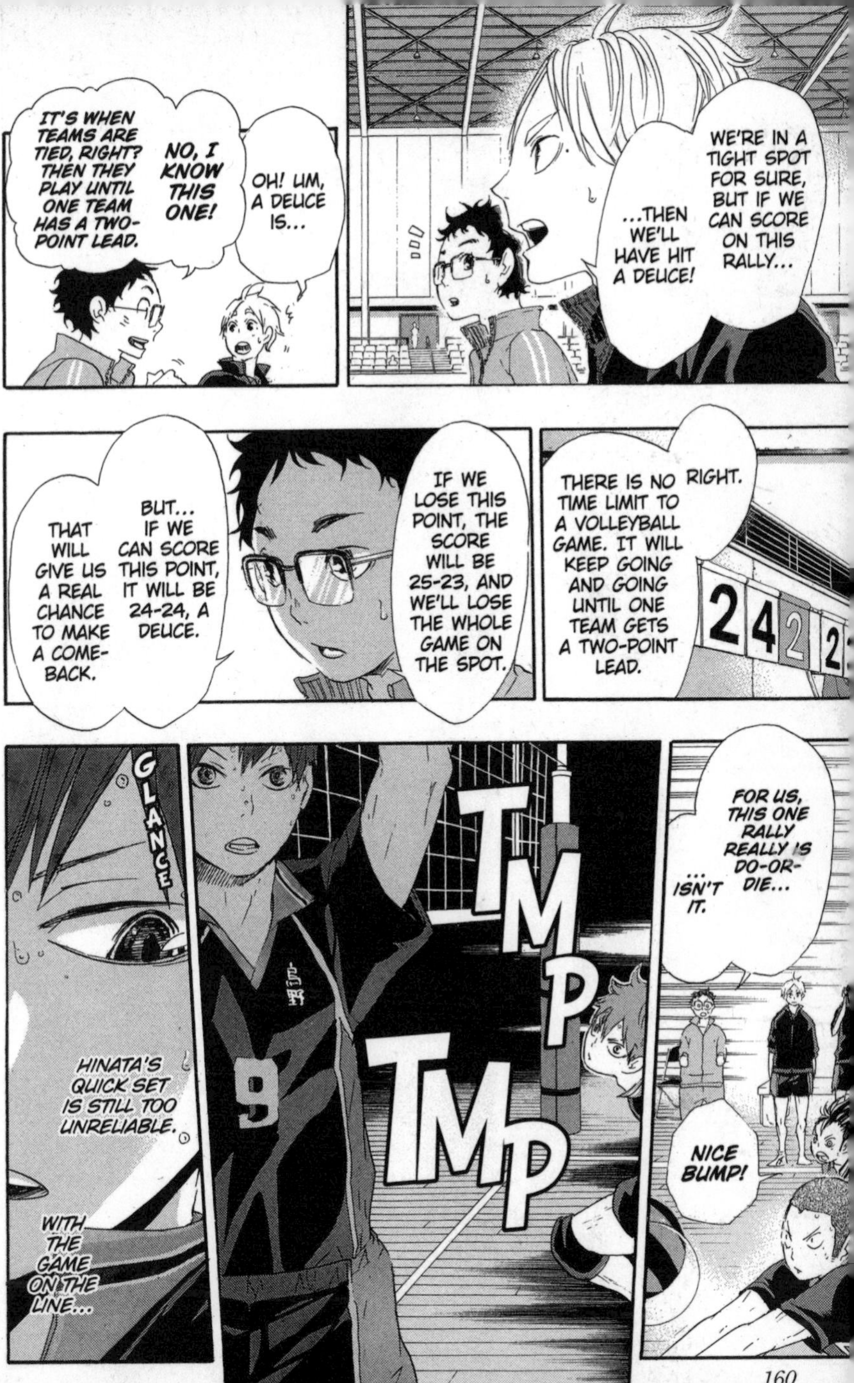
WE'RE IN A TIGHT SPOT FOR SURE, BUT IF WE CAN SCORE ON THIS RALLY...
...THEN WE'LL HAVE HIT A DEUCE!
OH! UM, A DEUCE IS...
NO, I KNOW THIS ONE!
IT'S WHEN TEAMS ARE TIED, RIGHT? THEN THEY PLAY UNTIL ONE TEAM HAS A TWO-POINT LEAD.
RIGHT.
THERE IS NO TIME LIMIT TO A VOLLEYBALL GAME. IT WILL KEEP GOING AND GOING UNTIL ONE TEAM GETS A TWO-POINT LEAD.
IF WE LOSE THIS POINT, THE SCORE WILL BE 25-23, AND WE'LL LOSE THE WHOLE GAME ON THE SPOT.
BUT... IF WE CAN SCORE THIS POINT, IT WILL BE 24-24, A DEUCE.
THAT WILL GIVE US A REAL CHANCE TO MAKE A COME-BACK.
FOR US, THIS ONE RALLY REALLY IS DO-OR-DIE...
...ISN'T IT.
NICE BUMP!
TMP
TMP
GLANCE
HINATA'S QUICK SET IS STILL TOO UNRELIABLE.
WITH THE GAME ON THE LINE...

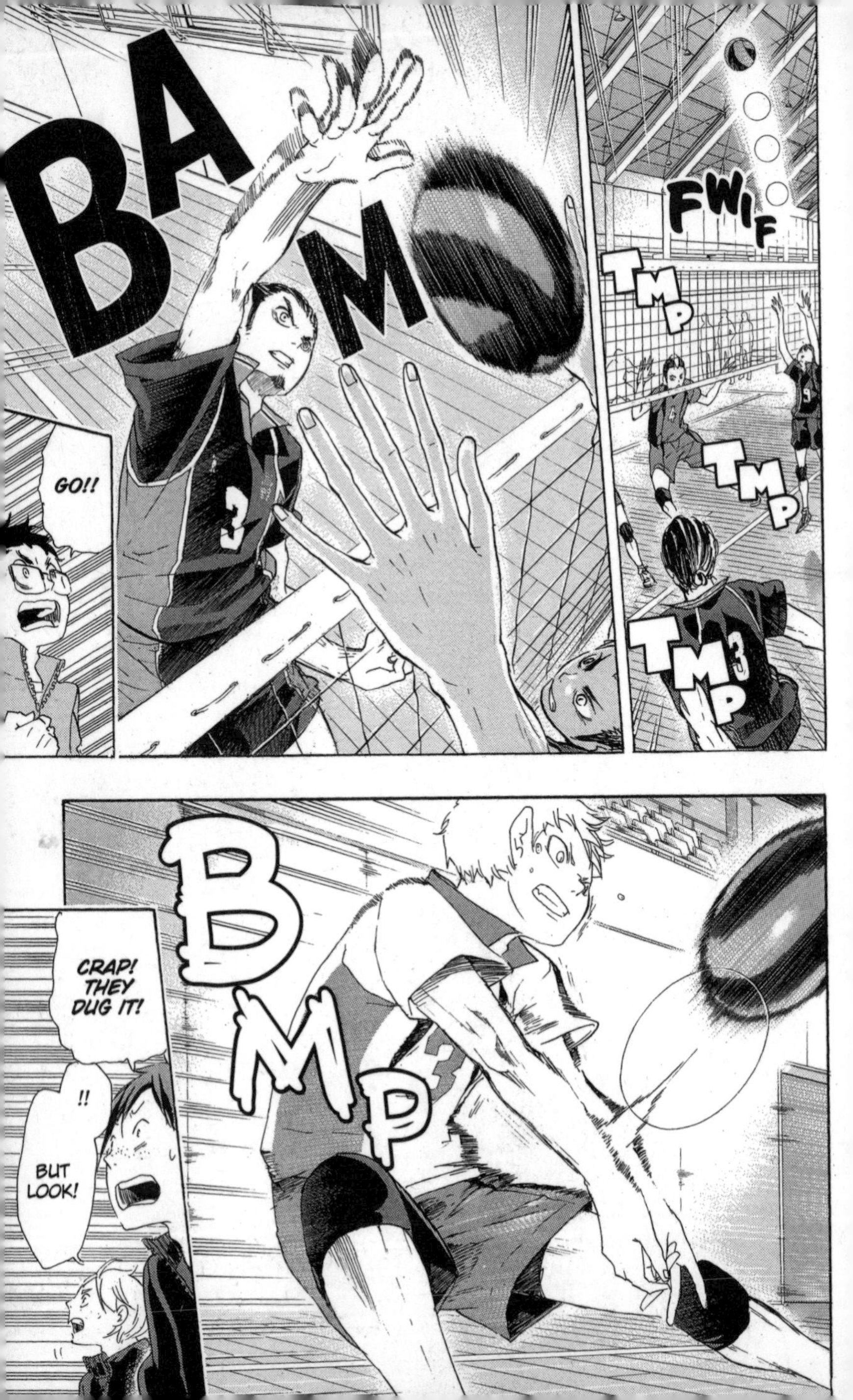
FWIF
TMP
TMP
TMP
BAM
GO!!
BMP
CRAP! THEY DUG IT!
!!
BUT LOOK!

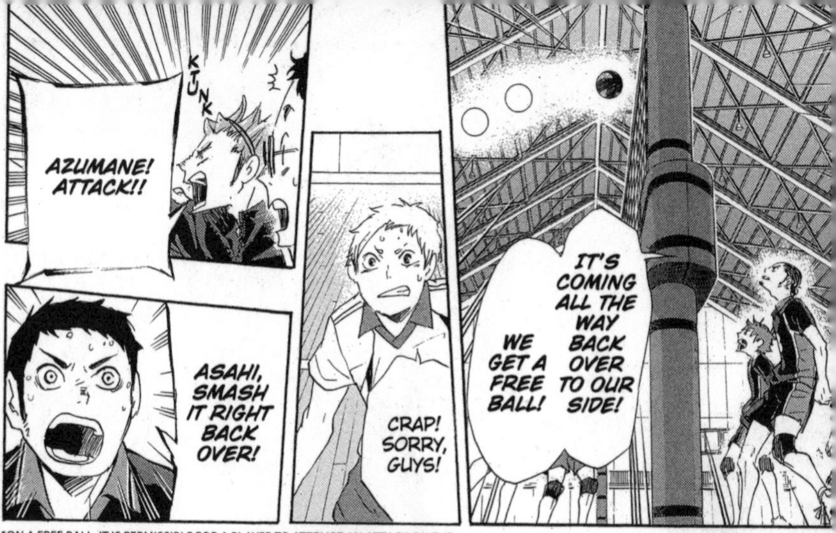
IT'S COMING ALL THE WAY BACK OVER TO OUR SIDE!
WE GET A FREE BALL!
CRAP! SORRY, GUYS!
KTUNK
AZUMANE! ATTACK!!
ASAHI, SMASH IT RIGHT BACK OVER!

*ON A FREE BALL, IT IS PERMISSIBLE FOR A PLAYER TO ATTEMPT AN ATTACK ON THE FIRST TOUCH RATHER THAN USE THE STANDARD PASS-SET-ATTACK THREE TOUCHES.

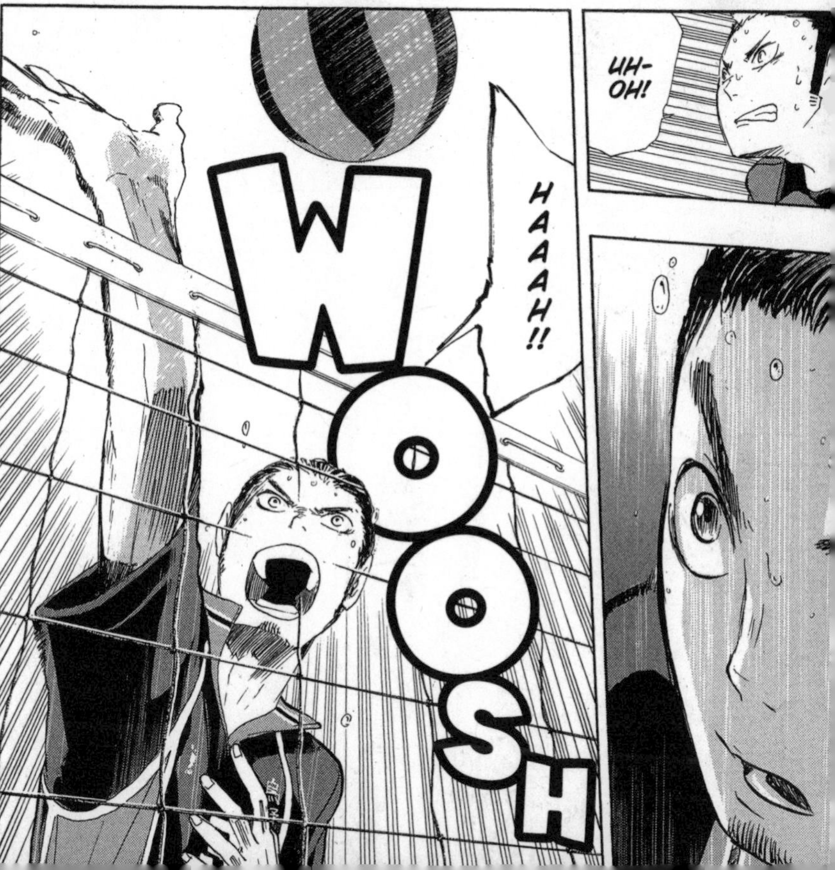
UH-OH!
HAAAAH!!
WOOOSH

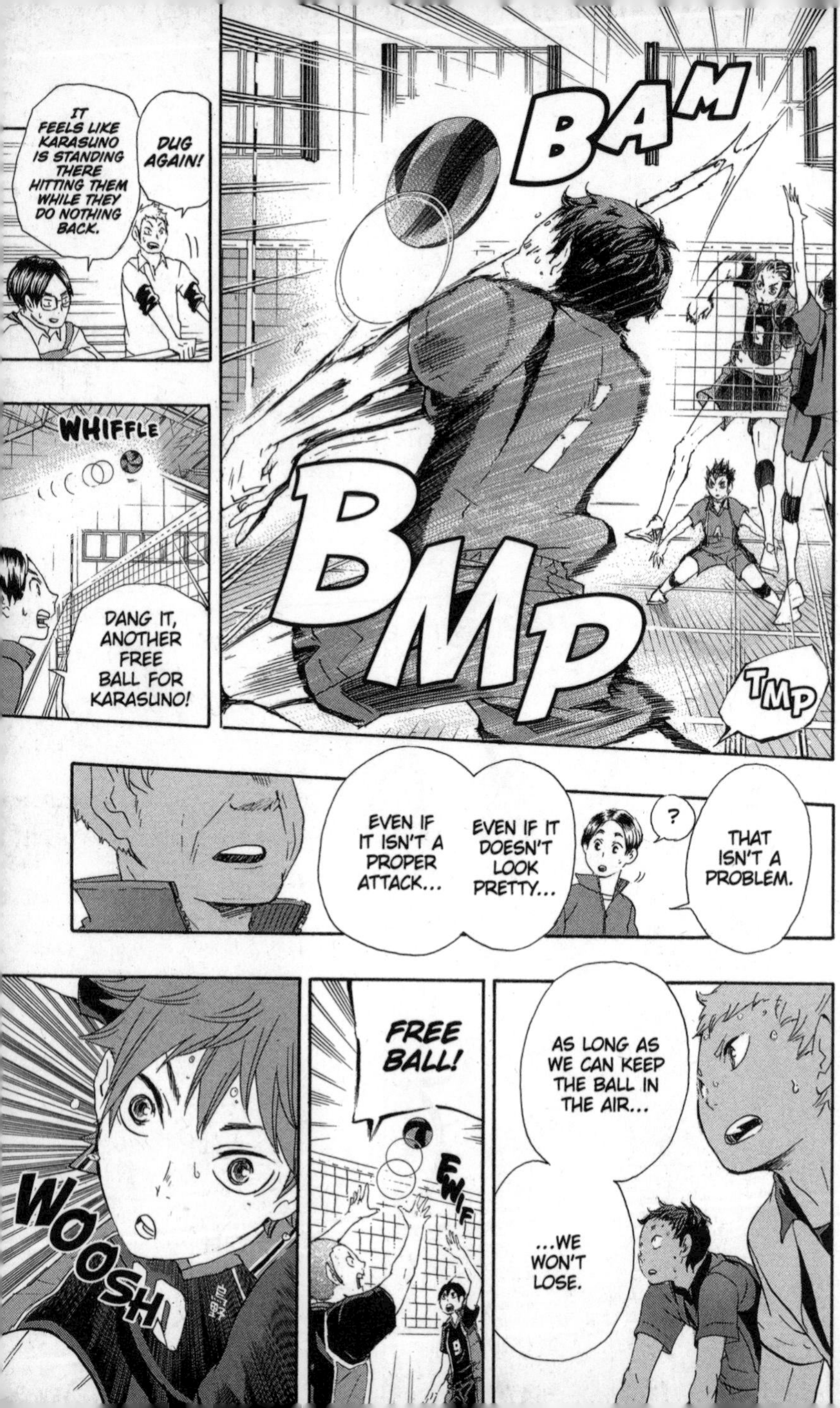
BAM
BMP
TMP
DUG AGAIN!
IT FEELS LIKE KARASUNO IS STANDING THERE HITTING THEM WHILE THEY DO NOTHING BACK.
WHIFFLE
DANG IT, ANOTHER FREE BALL FOR KARASUNO!
THAT ISN'T A PROBLEM.
?
EVEN IF IT DOESN'T LOOK PRETTY...
EVEN IF IT ISN'T A PROPER ATTACK...
AS LONG AS WE CAN KEEP THE BALL IN THE AIR...
...WE WON'T LOSE.
FREE BALL!
FWIF
WOOSH

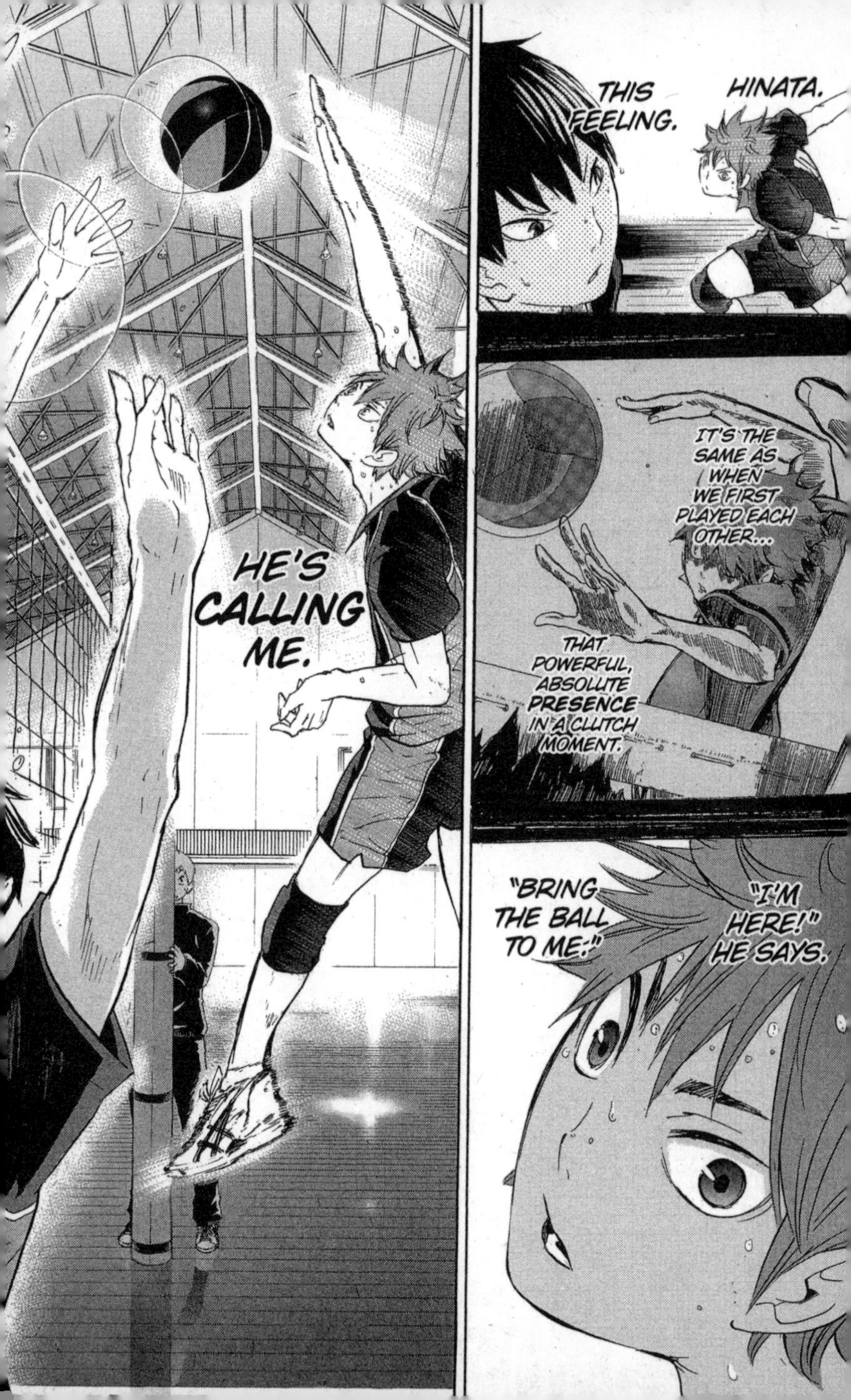
HINATA.
THIS FEELING.
IT'S THE SAME AS WHEN WE FIRST PLAYED EACH OTHER...
THAT POWERFUL, ABSOLUTE PRESENCE IN A CLUTCH MOMENT.
"I'M HERE!" HE SAYS.
"BRING THE BALL TO ME."
HE'S CALLING ME.

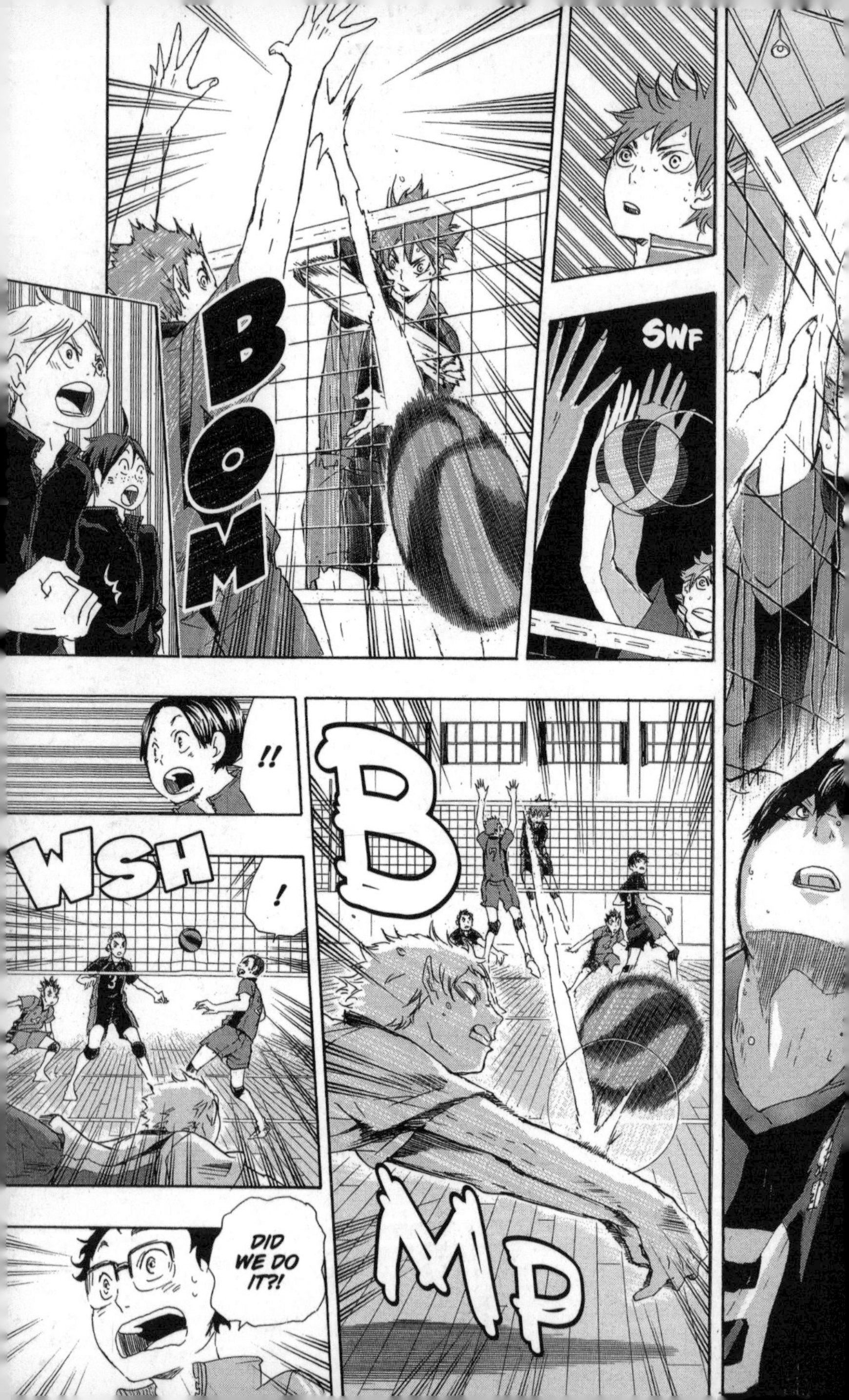
SWF
BOOM
BMP
!!
WSH
!
DID WE DO IT?!

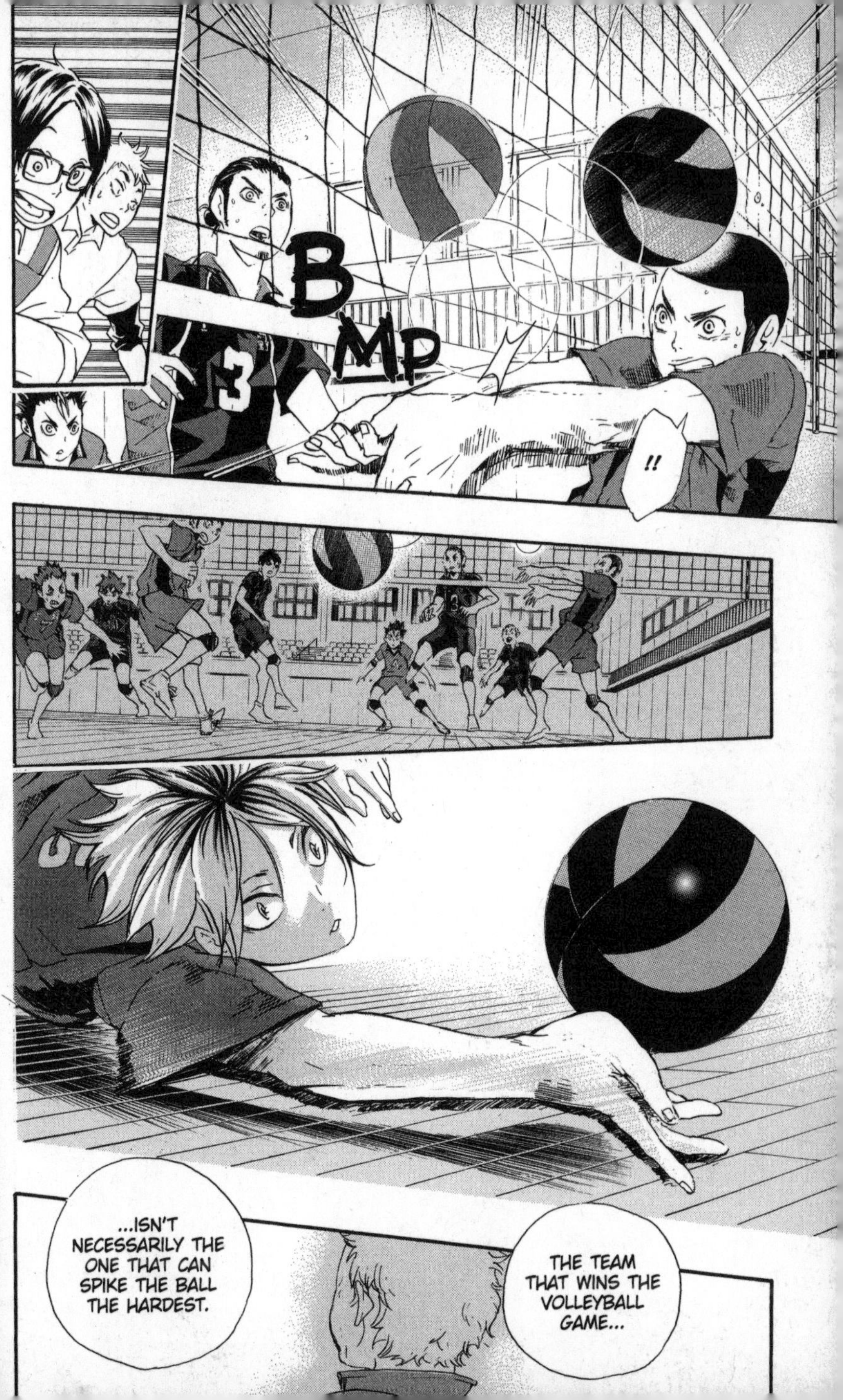
BMP
!!
THE TEAM THAT WINS THE VOLLEYBALL GAME...
...ISN'T NECESSARILY THE ONE THAT CAN SPIKE THE BALL THE HARDEST.

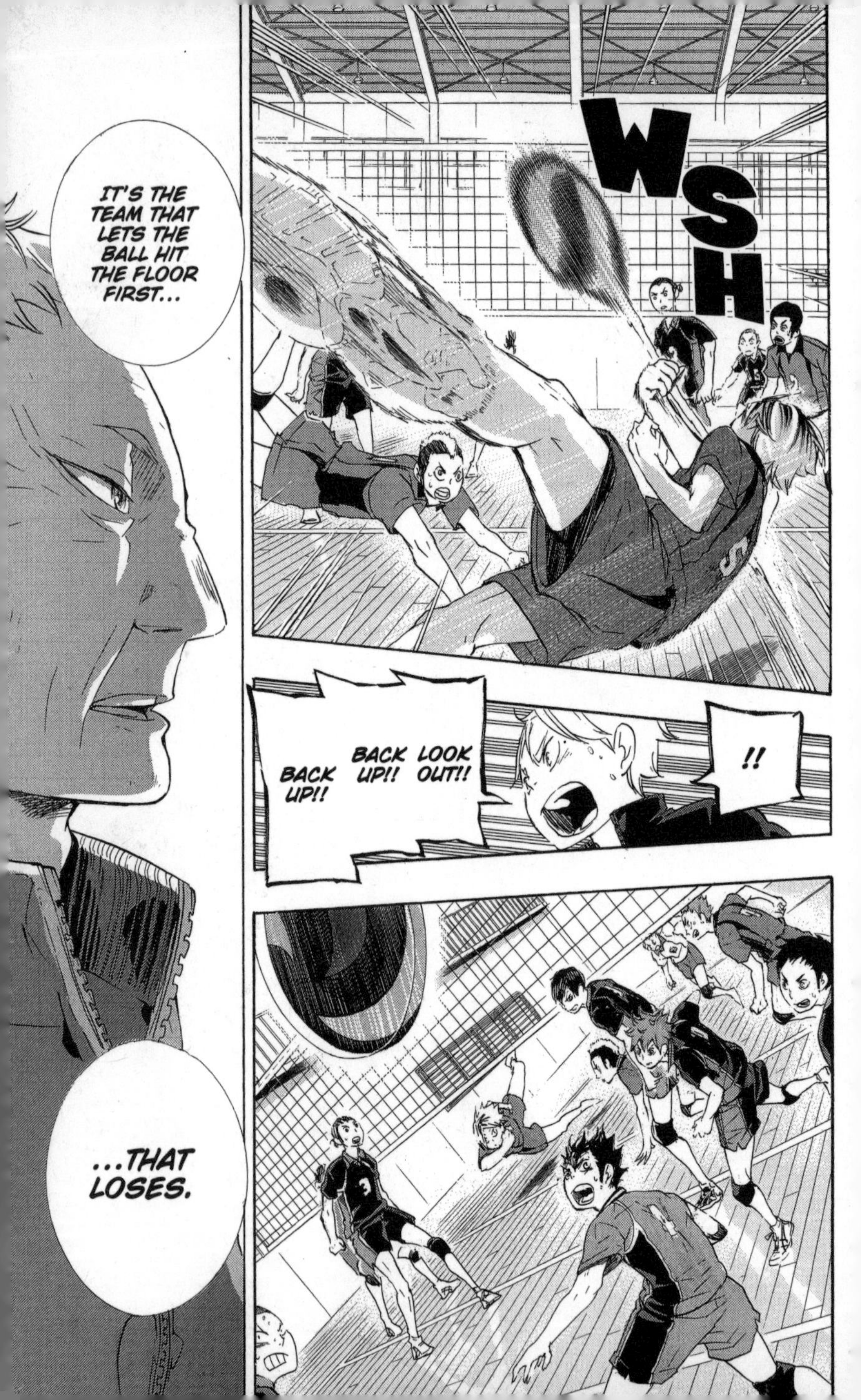
WSH
!!
LOOK OUT!!
BACK UP!!
BACK UP!!
IT'S THE TEAM THAT LETS THE BALL HIT THE FLOOR FIRST...
...THAT LOSES.

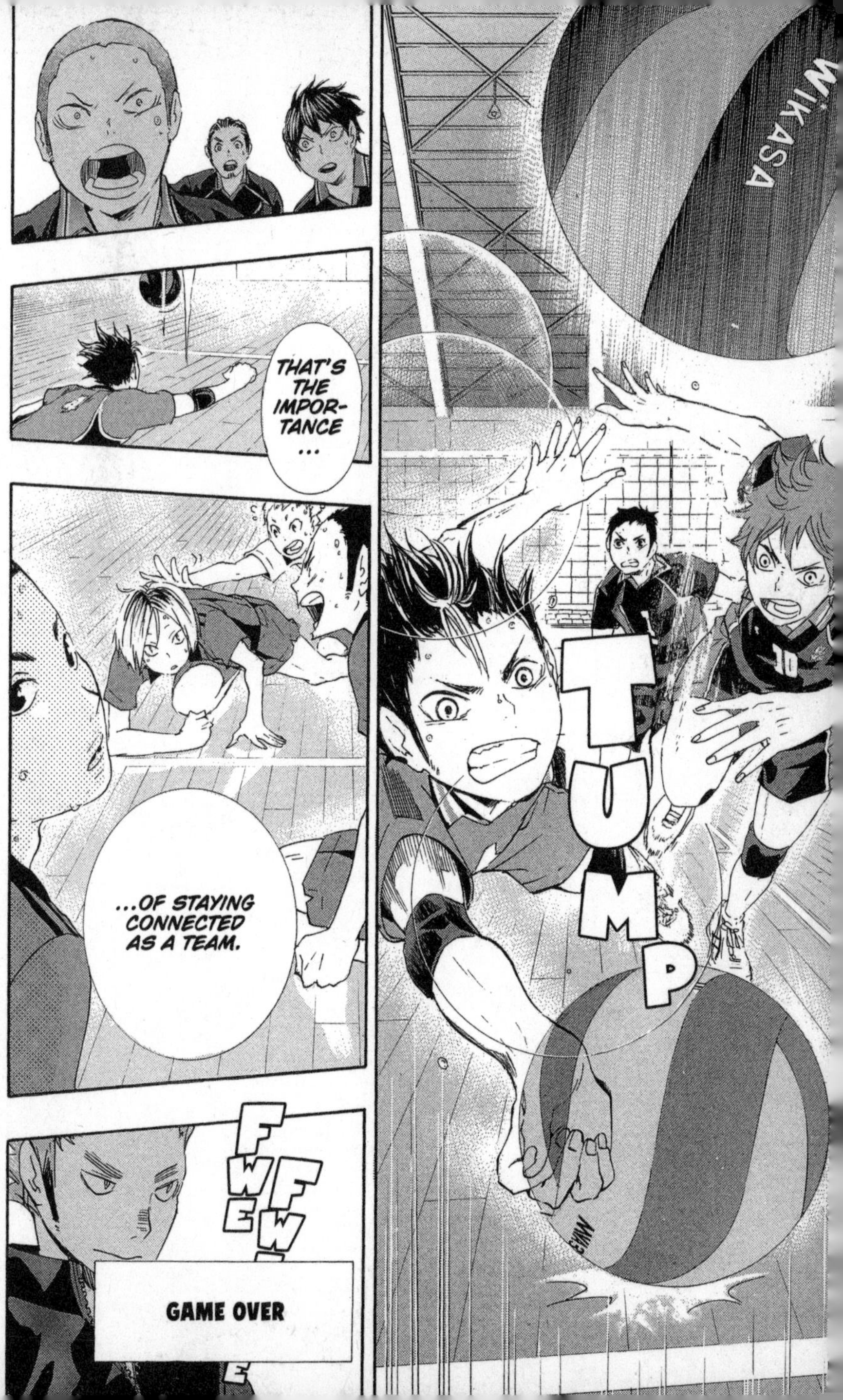

TUMP
THAT'S THE IMPORTANCE...
...OF STAYING CONNECTED AS A TEAM.
FWE
FWE
GAME OVER

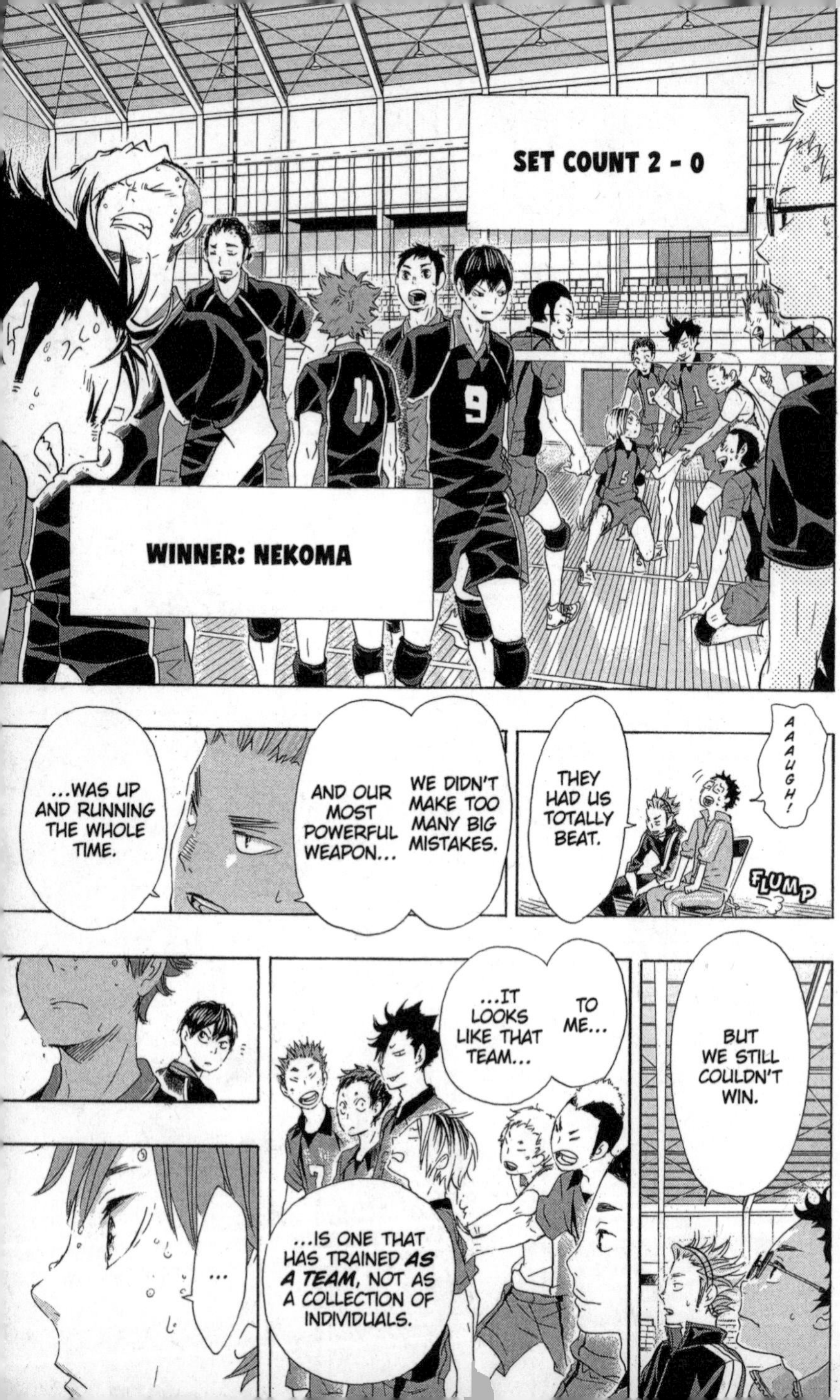
SET COUNT 2 - 0
WINNER: NEKOMA
AAAAUGH!
THEY HAD US TOTALLY BEAT.
FLUMP
WE DIDN'T MAKE TOO MANY BIG MISTAKES.
AND OUR MOST POWERFUL WEAPON...
...WAS UP AND RUNNING THE WHOLE TIME.
BUT WE STILL COULDN'T WIN.
TO ME...
...IT LOOKS LIKE THAT TEAM...
...IS ONE THAT HAS TRAINED *AS A TEAM*, NOT AS A COLLECTION OF INDIVIDUALS.
...

!!

THE GAME'S OVER--

LET'S DO THAT AGAIN!!

PRACTICE MEANS YOU GET TO DO IT AGAIN AND AGAIN.

AFTER ALL, THIS IS A PRACTICE GAME.

!!

OF COURSE!

THAT'S EXACTLY WHAT WE PLAN TO DO.

...

KARASUNO	GAME 2	NEKOMA
	22 - 25	
	24 - 26	

KARASUNO	GAME 3	NEKOMA
	25 - 27	
	30 - 32	

TMP

TMP

AGAIN!

SERVER UP!

TA-TMP

TMP

TMP

TMP

BAM

TMP

TMP

TMP

NICE SHOT!!

AWWW....!!

HOLD IT RIGHT THERE! ENOUGH IS ENOUGH. BESIDES, THEY HAVE A TRAIN TO CATCH.

YOU HAVE BEEN RUNNING AROUND LIKE A MANIAC THIS WHOLE TIME! HOW CAN YOU HAVE ANY ENERGY LEFT?!

WHAAA?!

AGAIN!!

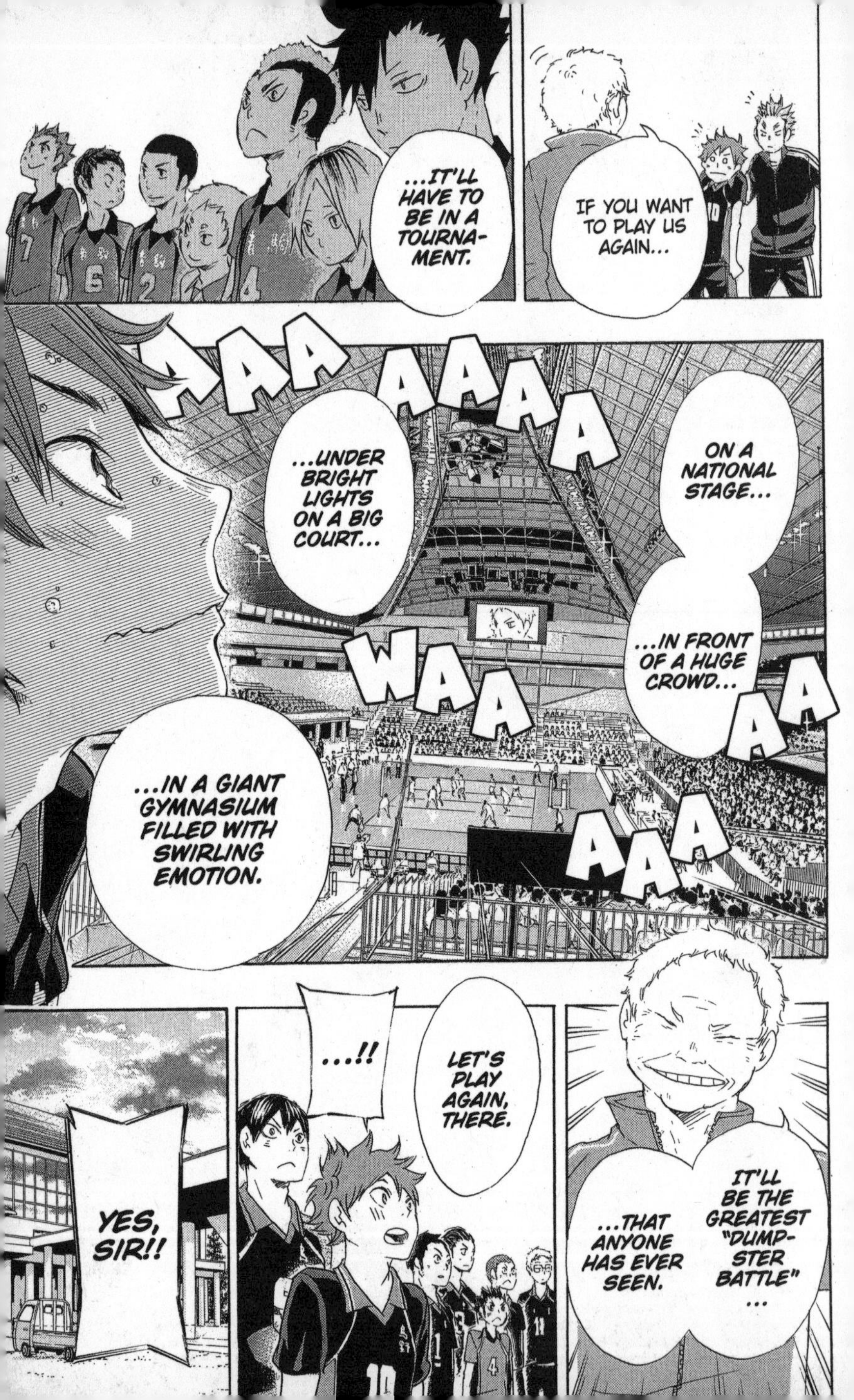
IF YOU WANT TO PLAY US AGAIN...
...IT'LL HAVE TO BE IN A TOURNAMENT.
AAAAAAAA
ON A NATIONAL STAGE...
...IN FRONT OF A HUGE CROWD...
...UNDER BRIGHT LIGHTS ON A BIG COURT...
WAAAAAAA
...IN A GIANT GYMNASIUM FILLED WITH SWIRLING EMOTION.
IT'LL BE THE GREATEST "DUMPSTER BATTLE"...
...THAT ANYONE HAS EVER SEEN.
LET'S PLAY AGAIN, THERE.
...!!
YES, SIR!!

MORISUKE YAKU

**NEKOMA HIGH SCHOOL
CLASS 3-5**

**POSITION:
LIBERO**

HEIGHT: 5'5"

**WEIGHT: 133 LBS.
(AS OF APRIL, 3RD YEAR
OF HIGH SCHOOL)**

BIRTHDAY: AUGUST 8

**FAVORITE FOOD:
STIR-FRY VEGETABLES**

**CURRENT WORRY:
THERE'S JUST SOMETHING
KINDA OFF ABOUT SOME OF
HIS JUNIORS ON THE TEAM.**

**ABILITY PARAMETERS
(5-POINT SCALE)**

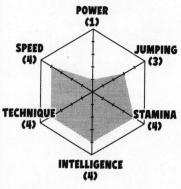

POWER
(1)

SPEED
(4)

JUMPING
(3)

TECHNIQUE
(4)

STAMINA
(4)

INTELLIGENCE
(4)

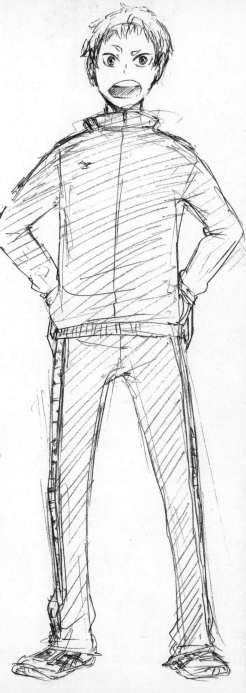

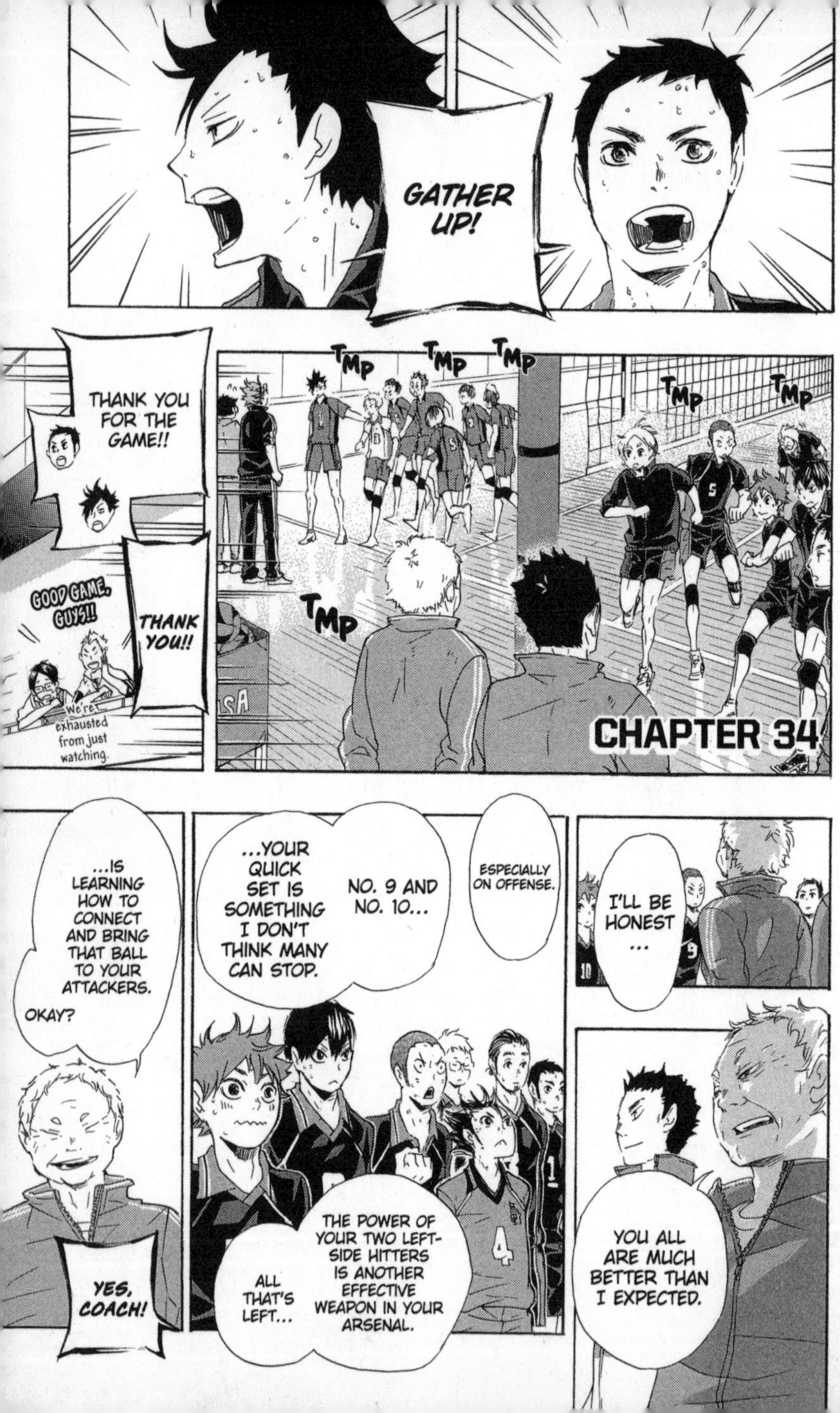
GATHER UP!
TMP
TMP
TMP
TMP
TMP
TMP
CHAPTER 34
THANK YOU FOR THE GAME!!
THANK YOU!!
GOOD GAME, GUYS!!
We're exhausted from just watching.
I'LL BE HONEST...
YOU ALL ARE MUCH BETTER THAN I EXPECTED.
ESPECIALLY ON OFFENSE.
NO. 9 AND NO. 10...
...YOUR QUICK SET IS SOMETHING I DON'T THINK MANY CAN STOP.
THE POWER OF YOUR TWO LEFT-SIDE HITTERS IS ANOTHER EFFECTIVE WEAPON IN YOUR ARSENAL.
ALL THAT'S LEFT...
...IS LEARNING HOW TO CONNECT AND BRING THAT BALL TO YOUR ATTACKERS.
OKAY?
YES, COACH!

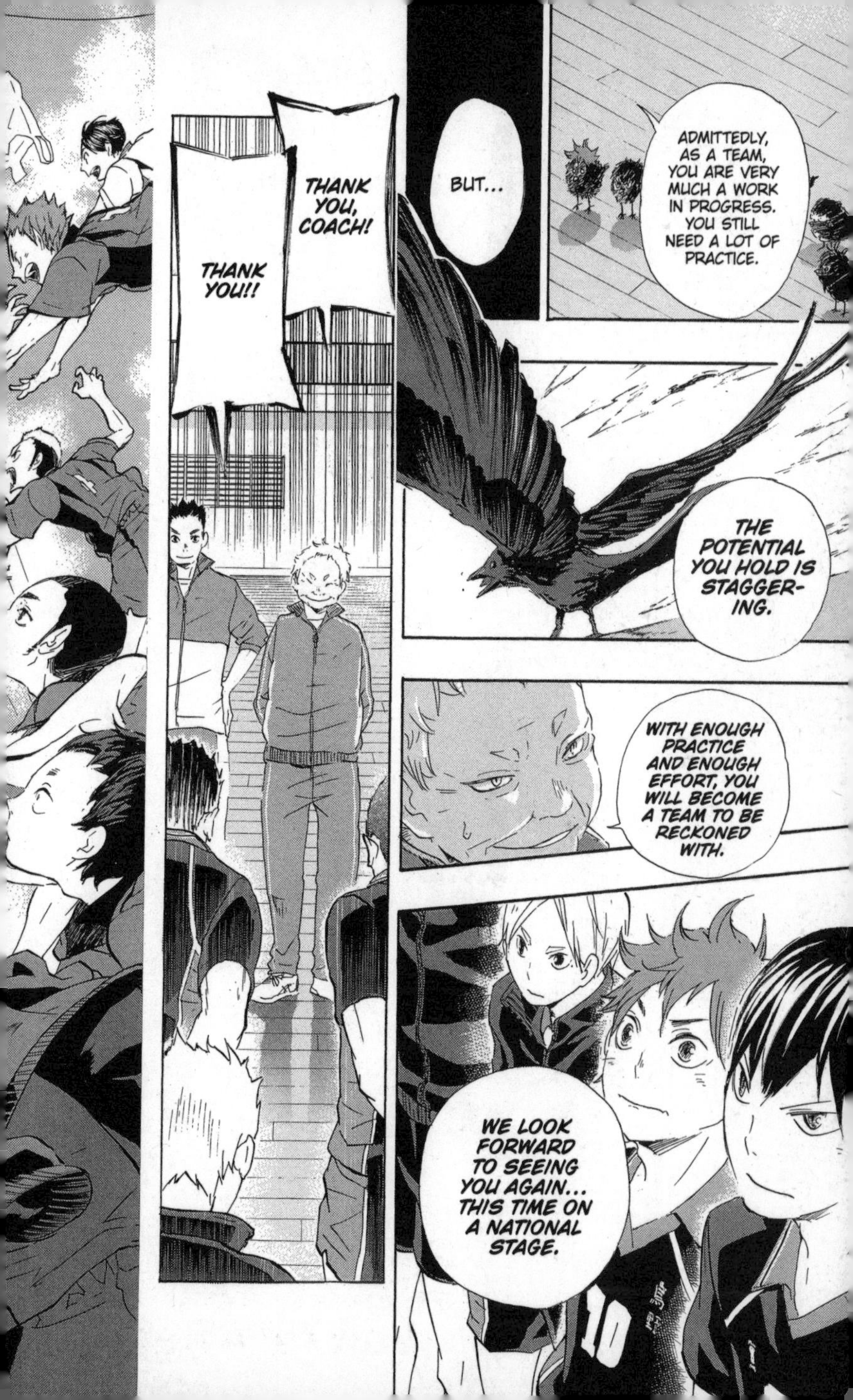
ADMITTEDLY, AS A TEAM, YOU ARE VERY MUCH A WORK IN PROGRESS. YOU STILL NEED A LOT OF PRACTICE.
BUT...
THE POTENTIAL YOU HOLD IS STAGGER-ING.
WITH ENOUGH PRACTICE AND ENOUGH EFFORT, YOU WILL BECOME A TEAM TO BE RECKONED WITH.
WE LOOK FORWARD TO SEEING YOU AGAIN... THIS TIME ON A NATIONAL STAGE.
THANK YOU, COACH!
THANK YOU!!

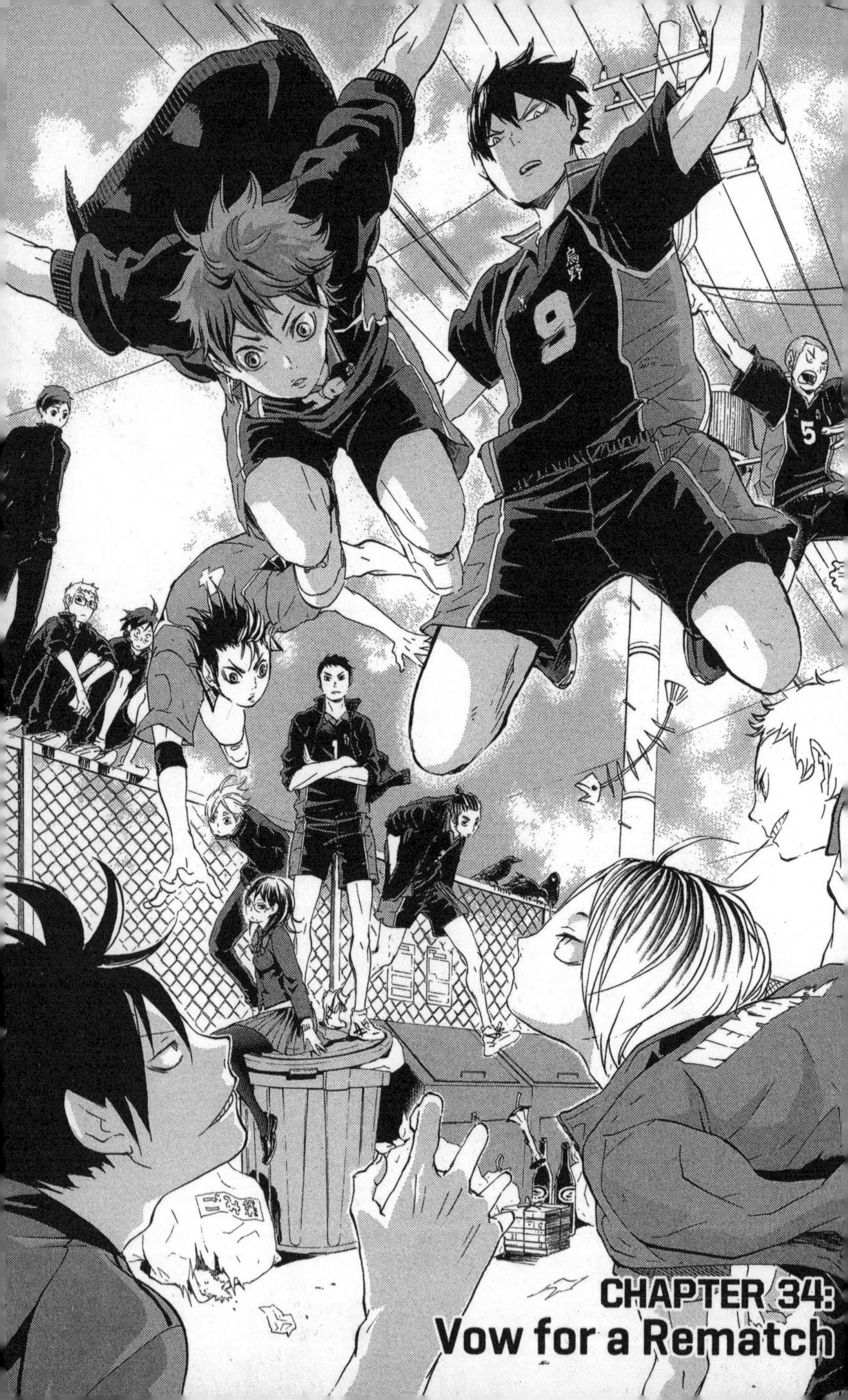

CHAPTER 34: Vow for a Rematch

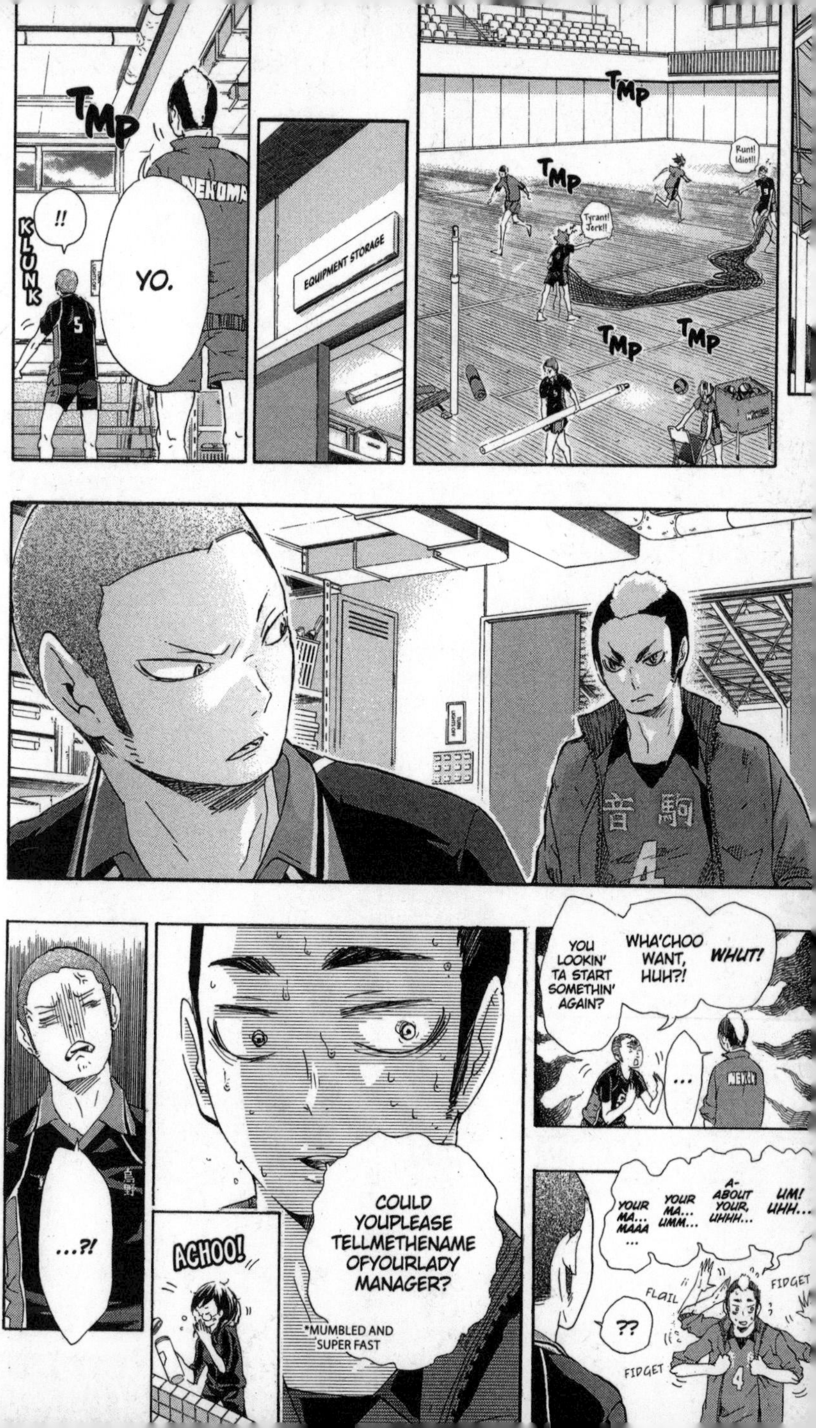
TMP
Runt! Idiot!!
TMP
Tyrant! Jerk!!
TMP
TMP
EQUIPMENT STORAGE
TMP
YO.
!!
KLUNK
WHUT!
WHA'CHOO WANT, HUH?!
YOU LOOKIN' TA START SOMETHIN' AGAIN?
...
UM! UHH...
A-ABOUT YOUR, UHHH...
YOUR MA... UMM...
YOUR MA... MAAA ...
FIDGET
FLAIL
??
FIDGET
COULD YOUPLEASE TELLMETHENAME OFYOURLADY MANAGER?
*MUMBLED AND SUPER FAST
ACHOO!
...?!

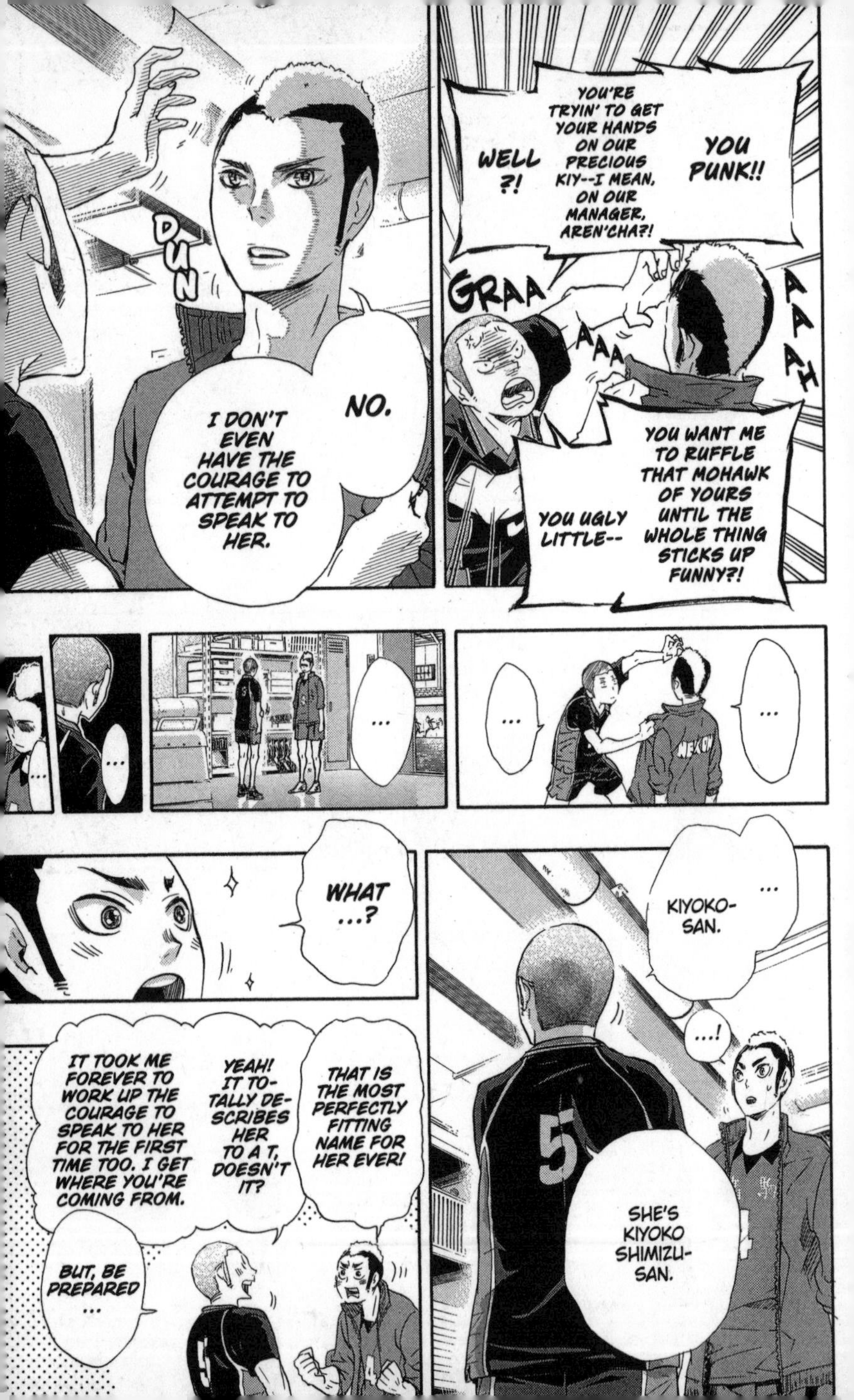
WELL ?!
YOU'RE TRYIN' TO GET YOUR HANDS ON OUR PRECIOUS KIY--I MEAN, ON OUR MANAGER, AREN'CHA?!
YOU PUNK!!
GRAA
AAAA
AAAAH
YOU WANT ME TO RUFFLE THAT MOHAWK OF YOURS UNTIL THE WHOLE THING STICKS UP FUNNY?!
YOU UGLY LITTLE--
DUN
NO.
I DON'T EVEN HAVE THE COURAGE TO ATTEMPT TO SPEAK TO HER.
...
...
...
...
...
...
KIYOKO-SAN.
...!
SHE'S KIYOKO SHIMIZU-SAN.
WHAT ...?
THAT IS THE MOST PERFECTLY FITTING NAME FOR HER EVER!
YEAH! IT TOTALLY DESCRIBES HER TO A T, DOESN'T IT?
IT TOOK ME FOREVER TO WORK UP THE COURAGE TO SPEAK TO HER FOR THE FIRST TIME TOO. I GET WHERE YOU'RE COMING FROM.
BUT, BE PREPARED ...

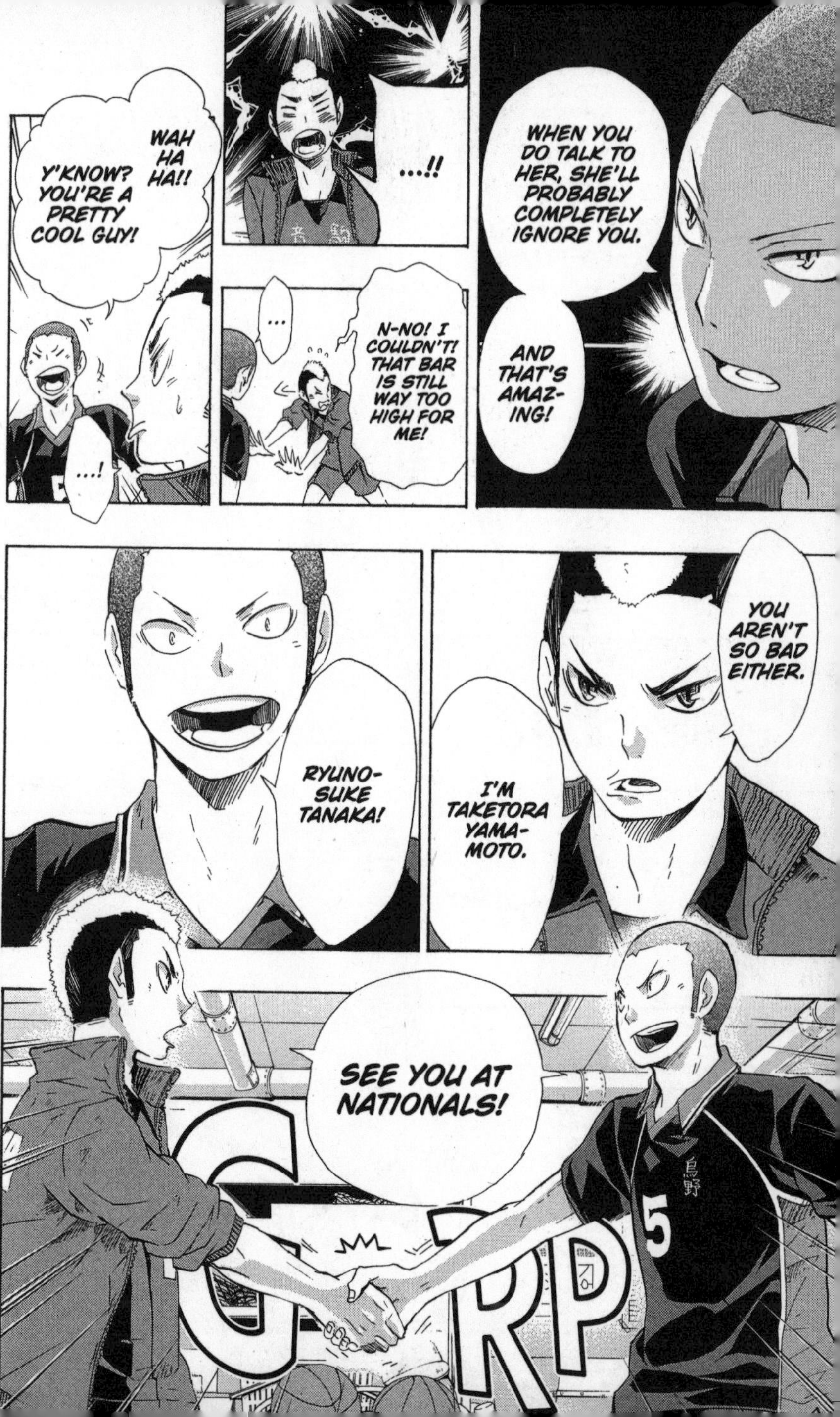
WHEN YOU DO TALK TO HER, SHE'LL PROBABLY COMPLETELY IGNORE YOU.
AND THAT'S AMAZ-ING!
...!!
N-NO! I COULDN'T! THAT BAR IS STILL WAY TOO HIGH FOR ME!
...
WAH HA HA!!
Y'KNOW? YOU'RE A PRETTY COOL GUY!
...!
YOU AREN'T SO BAD EITHER.
I'M TAKETORA YAMA-MOTO.
RYUNO-SUKE TANAKA!
SEE YOU AT NATIONALS!

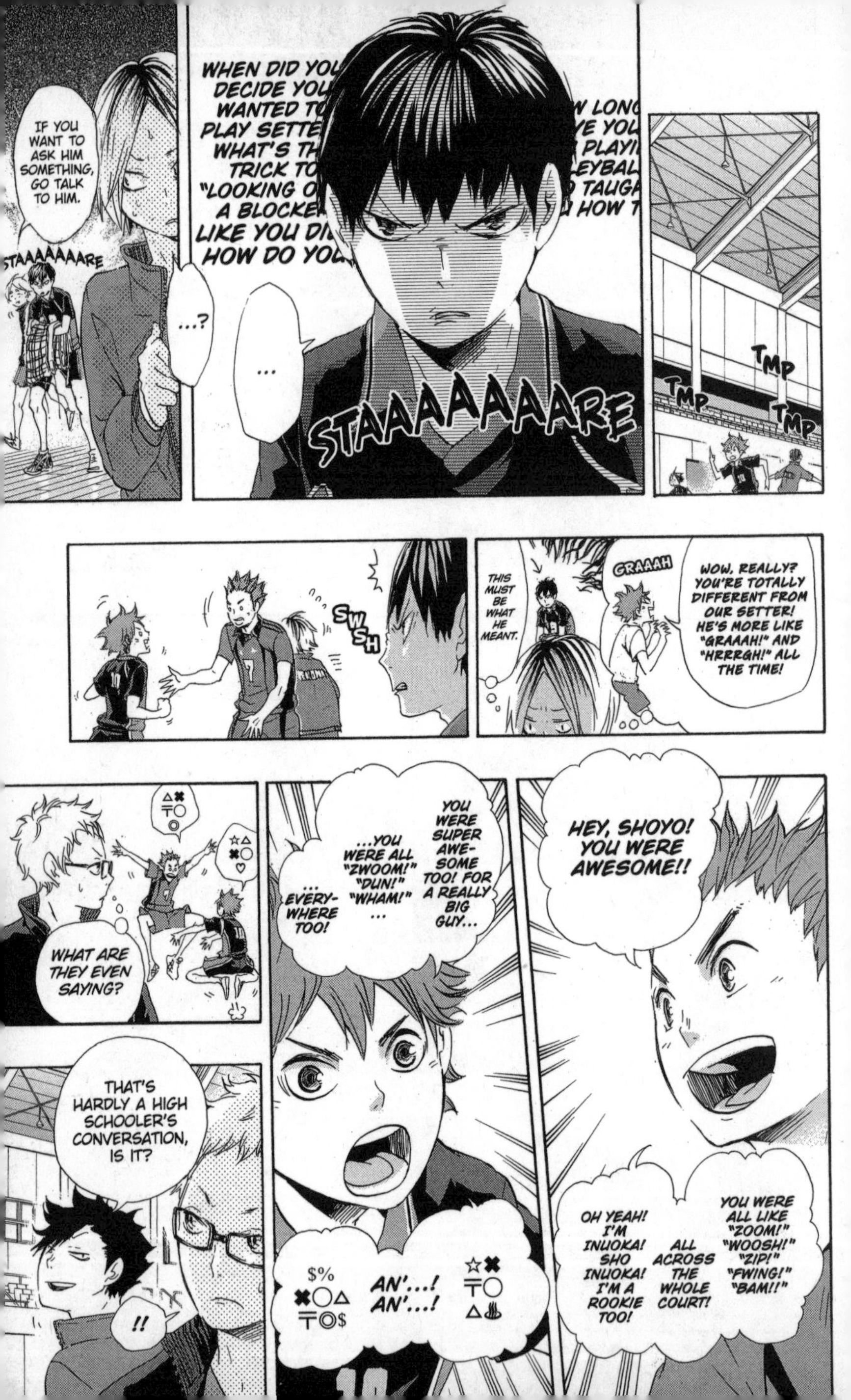
TMP
TMP
TMP
W LONG VE YOU PLAYI EYBAL D TAUGH HOW T
WHEN DID YOU DECIDE YOU WANTED TO PLAY SETTE WHAT'S TH TRICK TO "LOOKING O A BLOCKE LIKE YOU DI HOW DO YOU
...
STAAAAAAAARE
IF YOU WANT TO ASK HIM SOMETHING, GO TALK TO HIM.
...?
STAAAAAAAARE
GRAAAH
WOW, REALLY? YOU'RE TOTALLY DIFFERENT FROM OUR SETTER! HE'S MORE LIKE "GRAAAH!" AND "HRRRGH!" ALL THE TIME!
THIS MUST BE WHAT HE MEANT.
SWSH
HEY, SHOYO! YOU WERE AWESOME!!
YOU WERE ALL LIKE "ZOOM!" "WOOSH!" "ZIP!" "FWING!" "BAM!!"
ALL ACROSS THE WHOLE COURT!
OH YEAH! I'M INUOKA! SHO INUOKA! I'M A ROOKIE TOO!
YOU WERE SUPER AWE-SOME TOO! FOR A REALLY BIG GUY...
...YOU WERE ALL "ZWOOM!" "DUN!" "WHAM!" ...
...EVERY-WHERE TOO!
☆✖ 〒○ △♨
AN'...! AN'...!
$% ✖○△ 〒◎$
△✖ 〒○ ◎
☆△ ✖○ ♡
WHAT ARE THEY EVEN SAYING?
THAT'S HARDLY A HIGH SCHOOLER'S CONVERSATION, IS IT?
!!

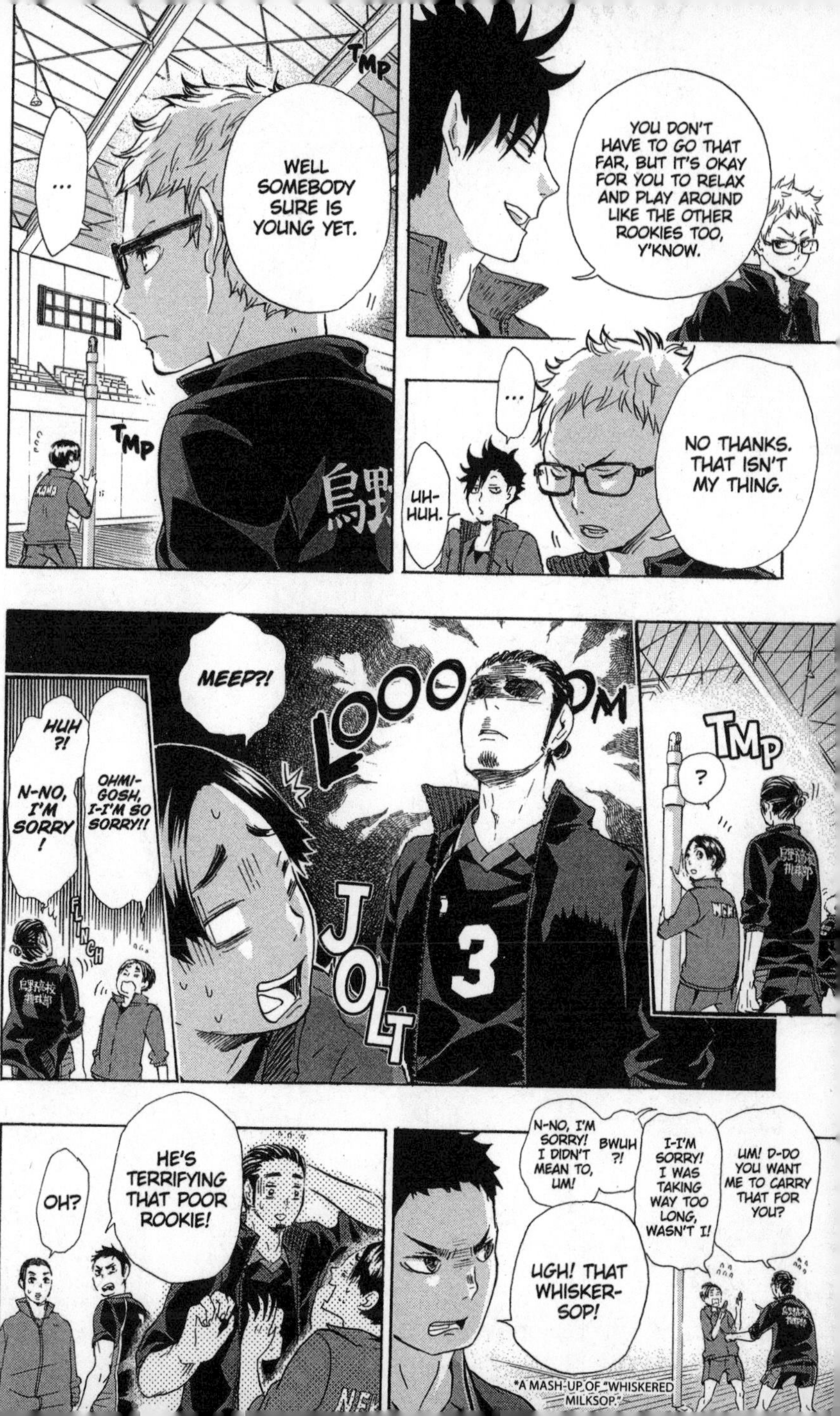
YOU DON'T HAVE TO GO THAT FAR, BUT IT'S OKAY FOR YOU TO RELAX AND PLAY AROUND LIKE THE OTHER ROOKIES TOO, Y'KNOW.
NO THANKS. THAT ISN'T MY THING.
...
UH-HUH.
TMP
WELL SOMEBODY SURE IS YOUNG YET.
...
TMP
TMP
?
LOOOOOM
MEEP?!
JOLT
OHMI-GOSH, I-I'M SO SORRY!!
HUH?!
N-NO, I'M SORRY!
FLINCH
UM! D-DO YOU WANT ME TO CARRY THAT FOR YOU?
I-I'M SORRY! I WAS TAKING WAY TOO LONG, WASN'T I!
BWUH?!
N-NO, I'M SORRY! I DIDN'T MEAN TO, UM!
UGH! THAT WHISKER-SOP!
*A MASH-UP OF "WHISKERED MILKSOP."
HE'S TERRIFYING THAT POOR ROOKIE!
OH?

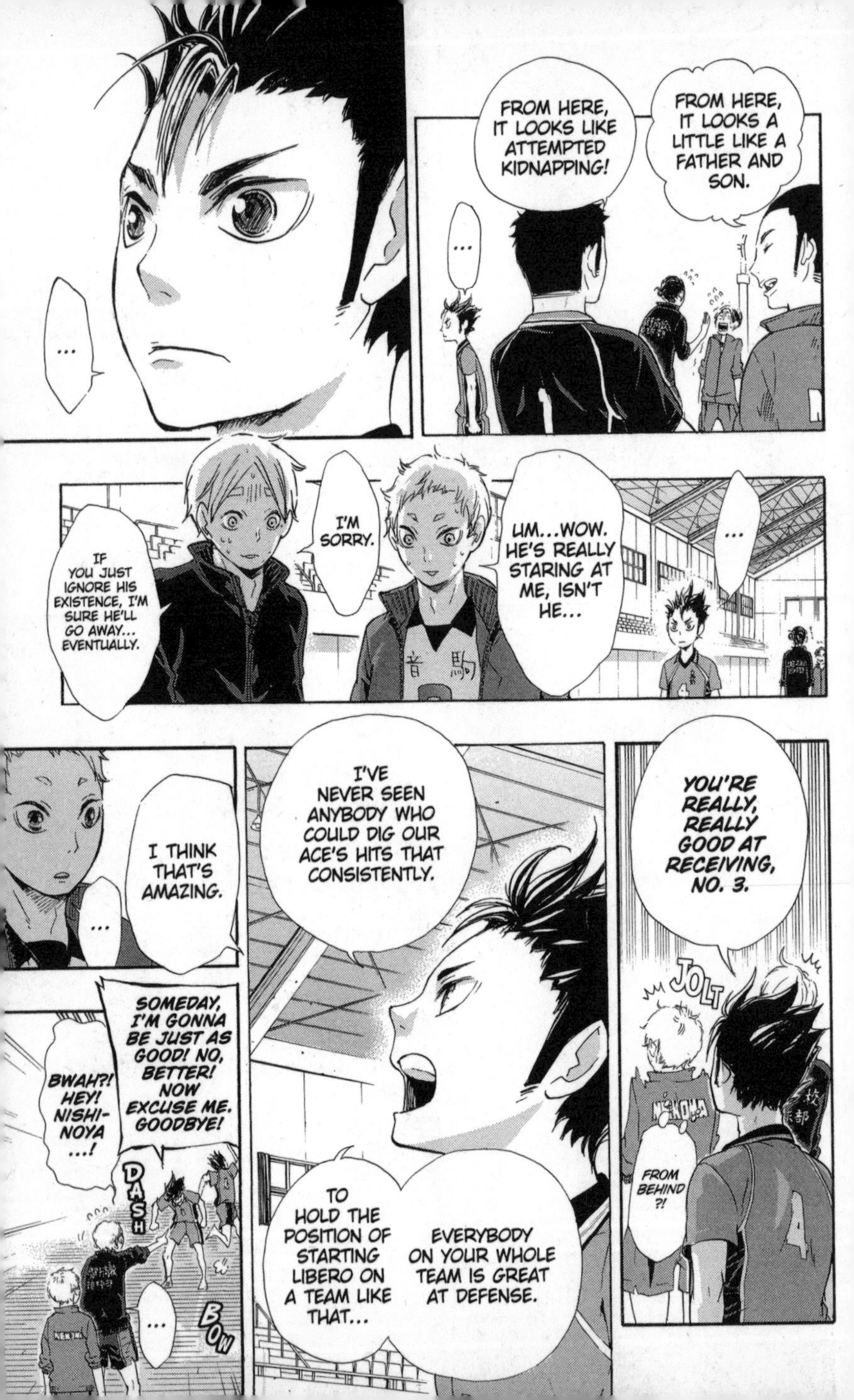
FROM HERE, IT LOOKS A LITTLE LIKE A FATHER AND SON.
FROM HERE, IT LOOKS LIKE ATTEMPTED KIDNAPPING!
...
...
...
UM...WOW. HE'S REALLY STARING AT ME, ISN'T HE...
I'M SORRY.
IF YOU JUST IGNORE HIS EXISTENCE, I'M SURE HE'LL GO AWAY... EVENTUALLY.
YOU'RE REALLY, REALLY GOOD AT RECEIVING, NO. 3.
JOLT
FROM BEHIND ?!
I'VE NEVER SEEN ANYBODY WHO COULD DIG OUR ACE'S HITS THAT CONSISTENTLY.
EVERYBODY ON YOUR WHOLE TEAM IS GREAT AT DEFENSE.
TO HOLD THE POSITION OF STARTING LIBERO ON A TEAM LIKE THAT...
I THINK THAT'S AMAZING.
...
SOMEDAY, I'M GONNA BE JUST AS GOOD! NO, BETTER! NOW EXCUSE ME. GOODBYE!
BWAH?! HEY! NISHINOYA ...!
DASH
...
BOW

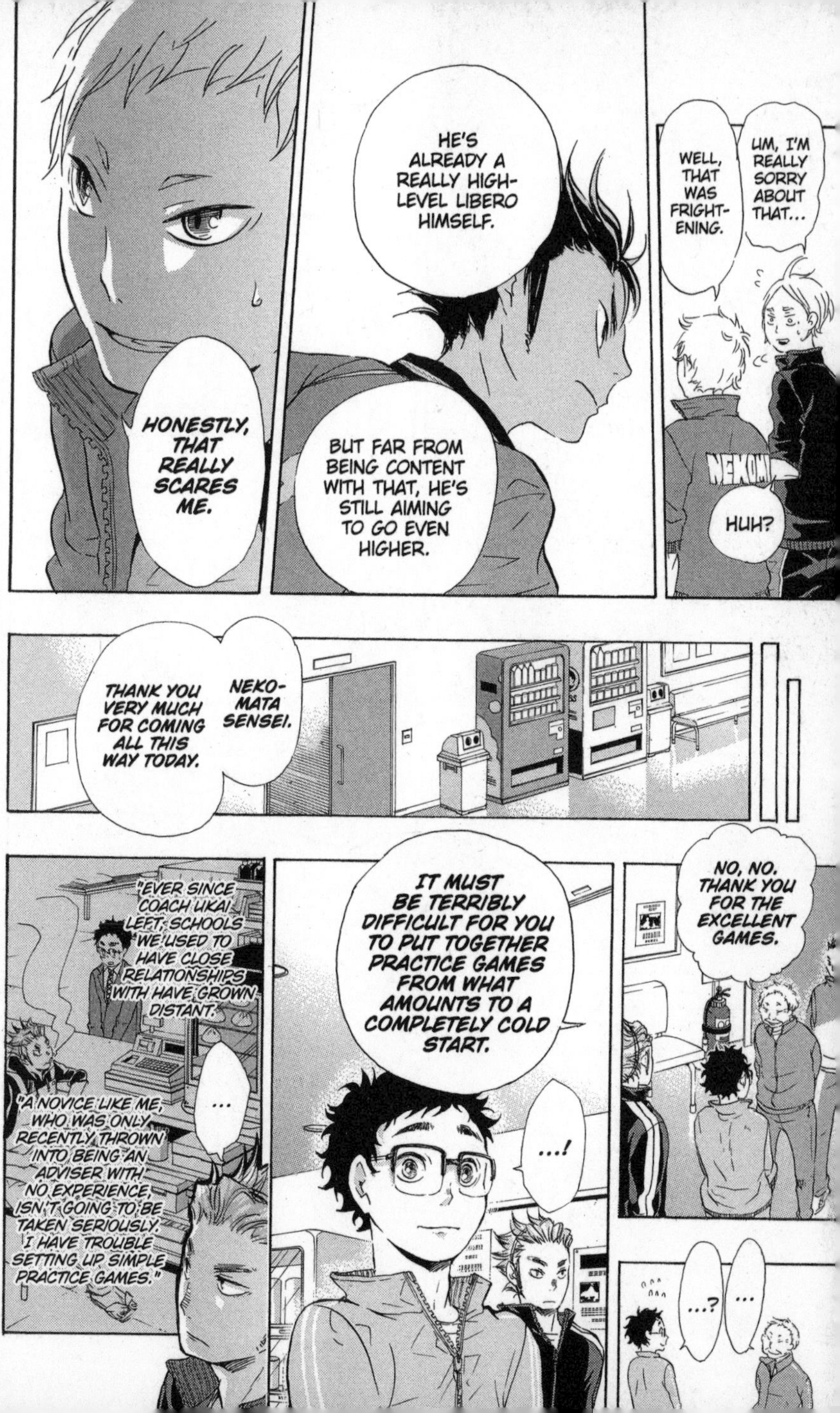
UM, I'M REALLY SORRY ABOUT THAT...
WELL, THAT WAS FRIGHT-ENING.
HUH?
HE'S ALREADY A REALLY HIGH-LEVEL LIBERO HIMSELF.
BUT FAR FROM BEING CONTENT WITH THAT, HE'S STILL AIMING TO GO EVEN HIGHER.
HONESTLY, THAT REALLY SCARES ME.
NEKO-MATA SENSEI.
THANK YOU VERY MUCH FOR COMING ALL THIS WAY TODAY.
NO, NO. THANK YOU FOR THE EXCELLENT GAMES.
...
...?
IT MUST BE TERRIBLY DIFFICULT FOR YOU TO PUT TOGETHER PRACTICE GAMES FROM WHAT AMOUNTS TO A COMPLETELY COLD START.
...!
"EVER SINCE COACH UKAI LEFT, SCHOOLS WE USED TO HAVE CLOSE RELATIONSHIPS WITH HAVE GROWN DISTANT."
...
"A NOVICE LIKE ME, WHO WAS ONLY RECENTLY THROWN INTO BEING AN ADVISER WITH NO EXPERIENCE, ISN'T GOING TO BE TAKEN SERIOUSLY. I HAVE TROUBLE SETTING UP SIMPLE PRACTICE GAMES."

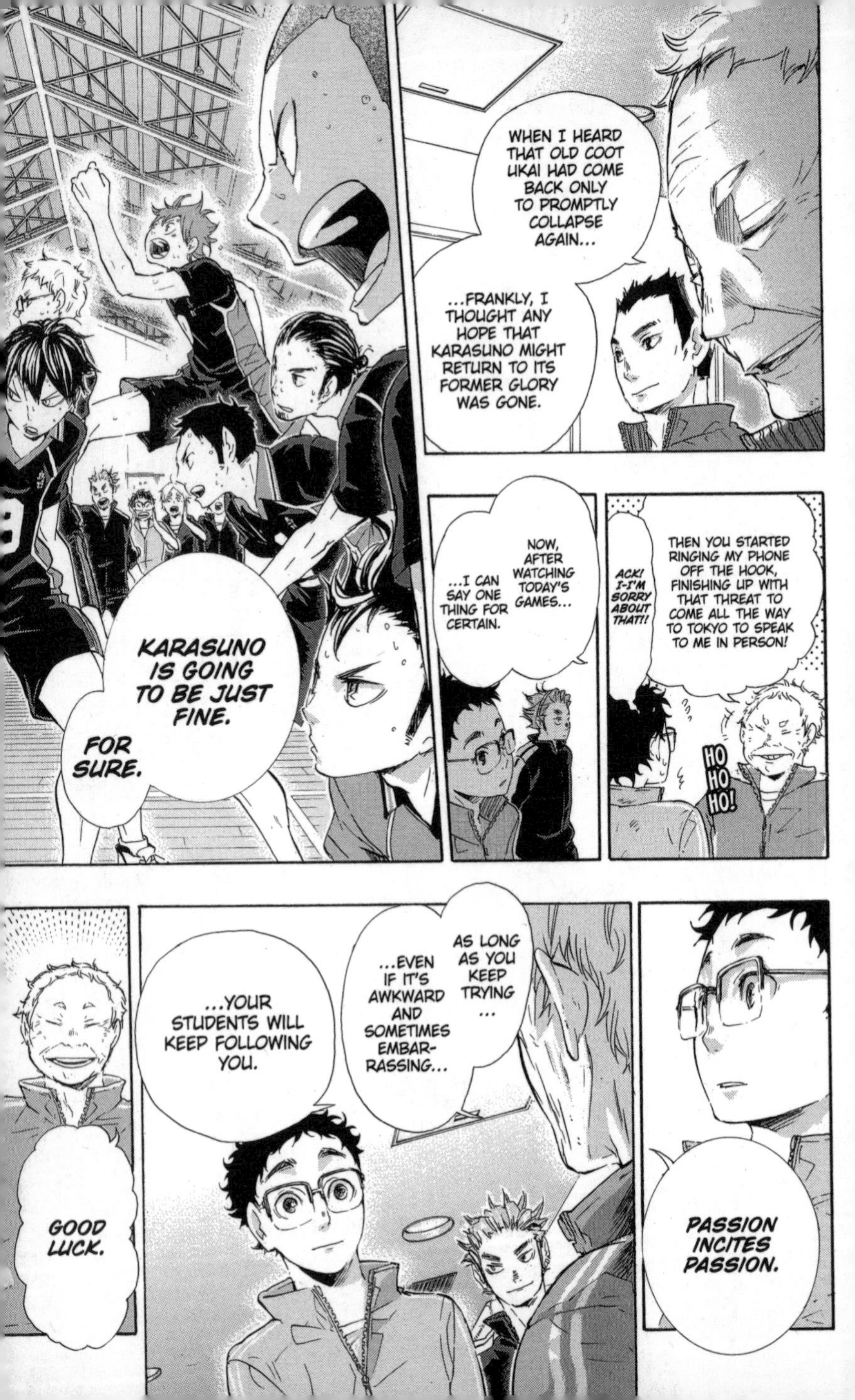
WHEN I HEARD THAT OLD COOT UKAI HAD COME BACK ONLY TO PROMPTLY COLLAPSE AGAIN...
...FRANKLY, I THOUGHT ANY HOPE THAT KARASUNO MIGHT RETURN TO ITS FORMER GLORY WAS GONE.
THEN YOU STARTED RINGING MY PHONE OFF THE HOOK, FINISHING UP WITH THAT THREAT TO COME ALL THE WAY TO TOKYO TO SPEAK TO ME IN PERSON!
ACK! I-I'M SORRY ABOUT THAT!!
HO HO HO!
NOW, AFTER WATCHING TODAY'S GAMES...
...I CAN SAY ONE THING FOR CERTAIN.
KARASUNO IS GOING TO BE JUST FINE.
FOR SURE.
PASSION INCITES PASSION.
AS LONG AS YOU KEEP TRYING...
...EVEN IF IT'S AWKWARD AND SOMETIMES EMBAR-RASSING...
...YOUR STUDENTS WILL KEEP FOLLOWING YOU.
GOOD LUCK.

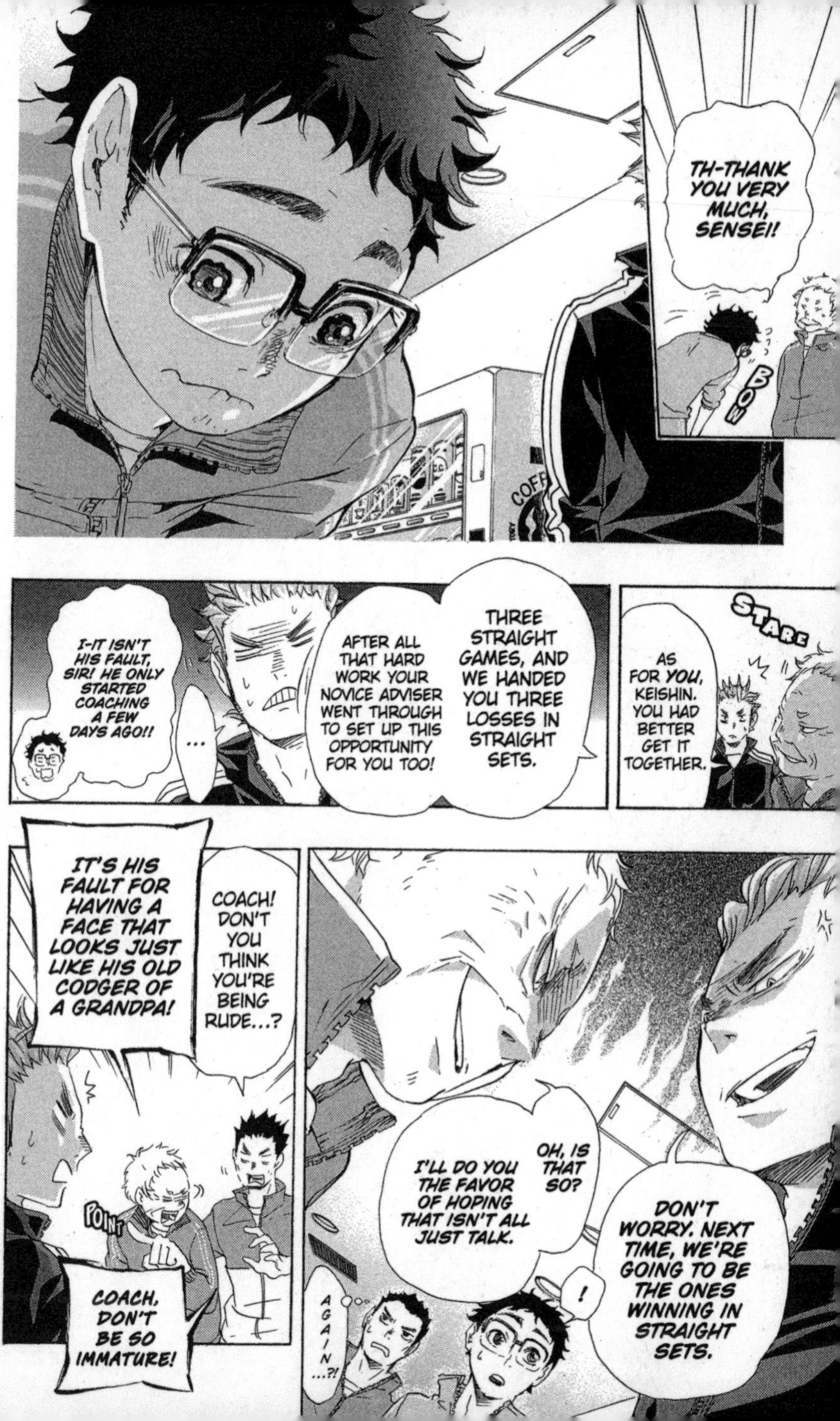
TH-THANK YOU VERY MUCH, SENSEI!
BOW
STARE
AS FOR YOU, KEISHIN. YOU HAD BETTER GET IT TOGETHER.
THREE STRAIGHT GAMES, AND WE HANDED YOU THREE LOSSES IN STRAIGHT SETS.
AFTER ALL THAT HARD WORK YOUR NOVICE ADVISER WENT THROUGH TO SET UP THIS OPPORTUNITY FOR YOU TOO!
...
I-IT ISN'T HIS FAULT, SIR! HE ONLY STARTED COACHING A FEW DAYS AGO!!
DON'T WORRY. NEXT TIME, WE'RE GOING TO BE THE ONES WINNING IN STRAIGHT SETS.
OH, IS THAT SO?
I'LL DO YOU THE FAVOR OF HOPING THAT ISN'T ALL JUST TALK.
!
AGAIN...?!
COACH! DON'T YOU THINK YOU'RE BEING RUDE...?
IT'S HIS FAULT FOR HAVING A FACE THAT LOOKS JUST LIKE HIS OLD CODGER OF A GRANDPA!
POINT
COACH, DON'T BE SO IMMATURE!

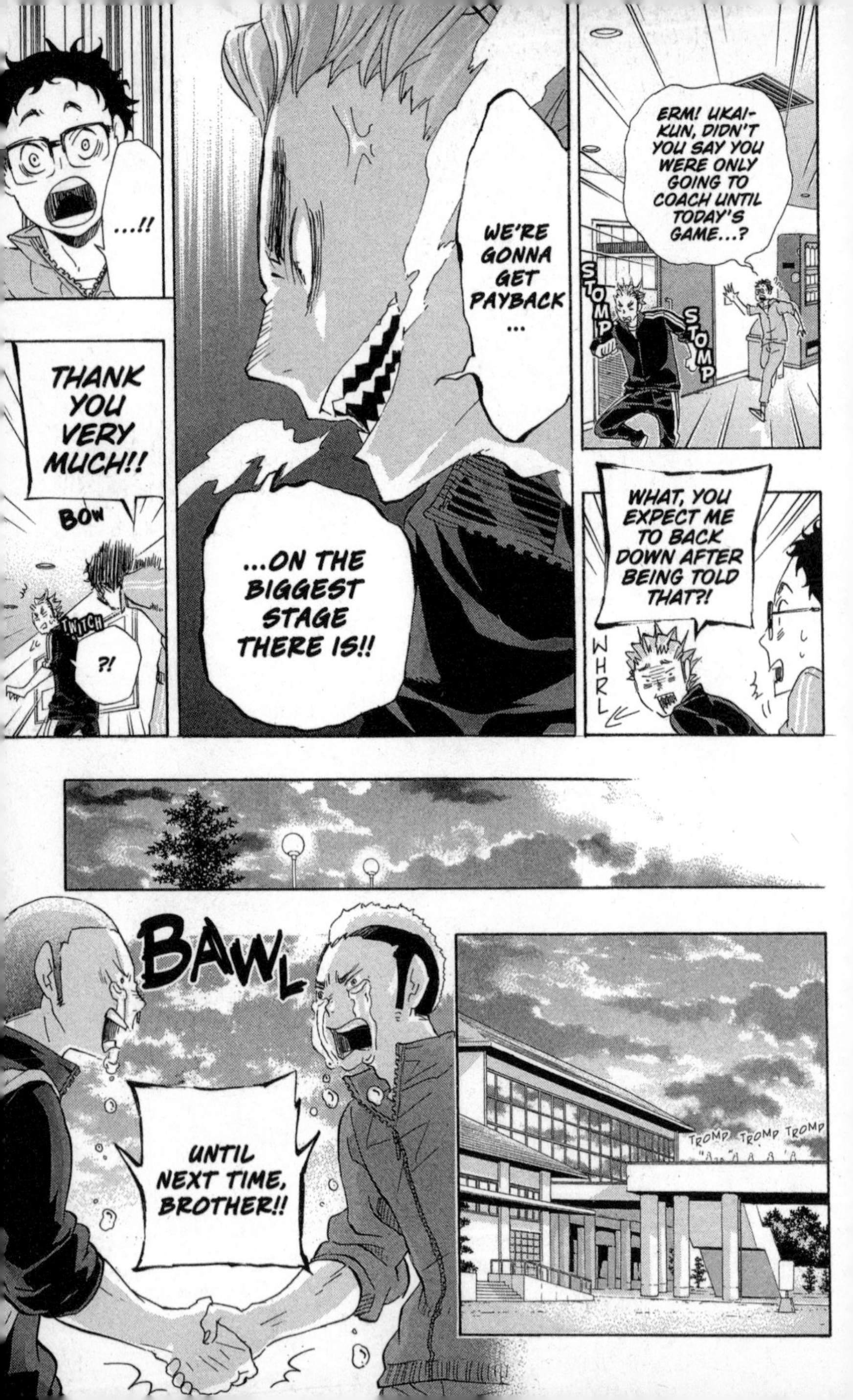
ERM! UKAI-KUN, DIDN'T YOU SAY YOU WERE ONLY GOING TO COACH UNTIL TODAY'S GAME...?
STOMP
STOMP
WHAT, YOU EXPECT ME TO BACK DOWN AFTER BEING TOLD THAT?!
WHRL
WE'RE GONNA GET PAYBACK...
...ON THE BIGGEST STAGE THERE IS!!
...!!
THANK YOU VERY MUCH!!
BOW
TWITCH
?!
TROMP TROMP TROMP
BAWL
UNTIL NEXT TIME, BROTHER!!

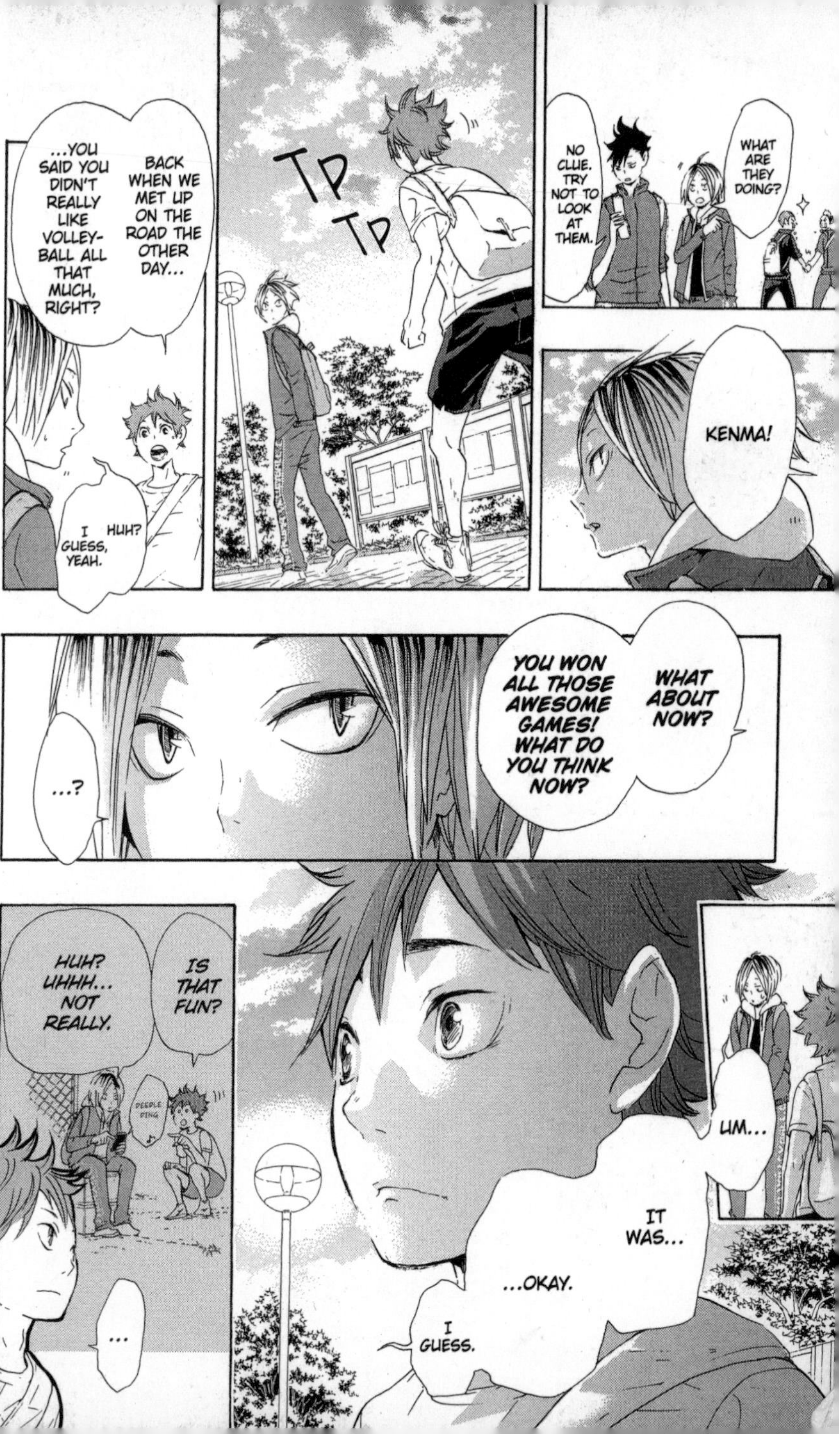
WHAT ARE THEY DOING?
NO CLUE. TRY NOT TO LOOK AT THEM.
KENMA!
Tp Tp
BACK WHEN WE MET UP ON THE ROAD THE OTHER DAY...
...YOU SAID YOU DIDN'T REALLY LIKE VOLLEY-BALL ALL THAT MUCH, RIGHT?
HUH? I GUESS, YEAH.
WHAT ABOUT NOW?
YOU WON ALL THOSE AWESOME GAMES! WHAT DO YOU THINK NOW?
...?
UM...
IT WAS...
...OKAY.
I GUESS.
IS THAT FUN?
HUH? UHHH... NOT REALLY.
PEEPLE DING
...

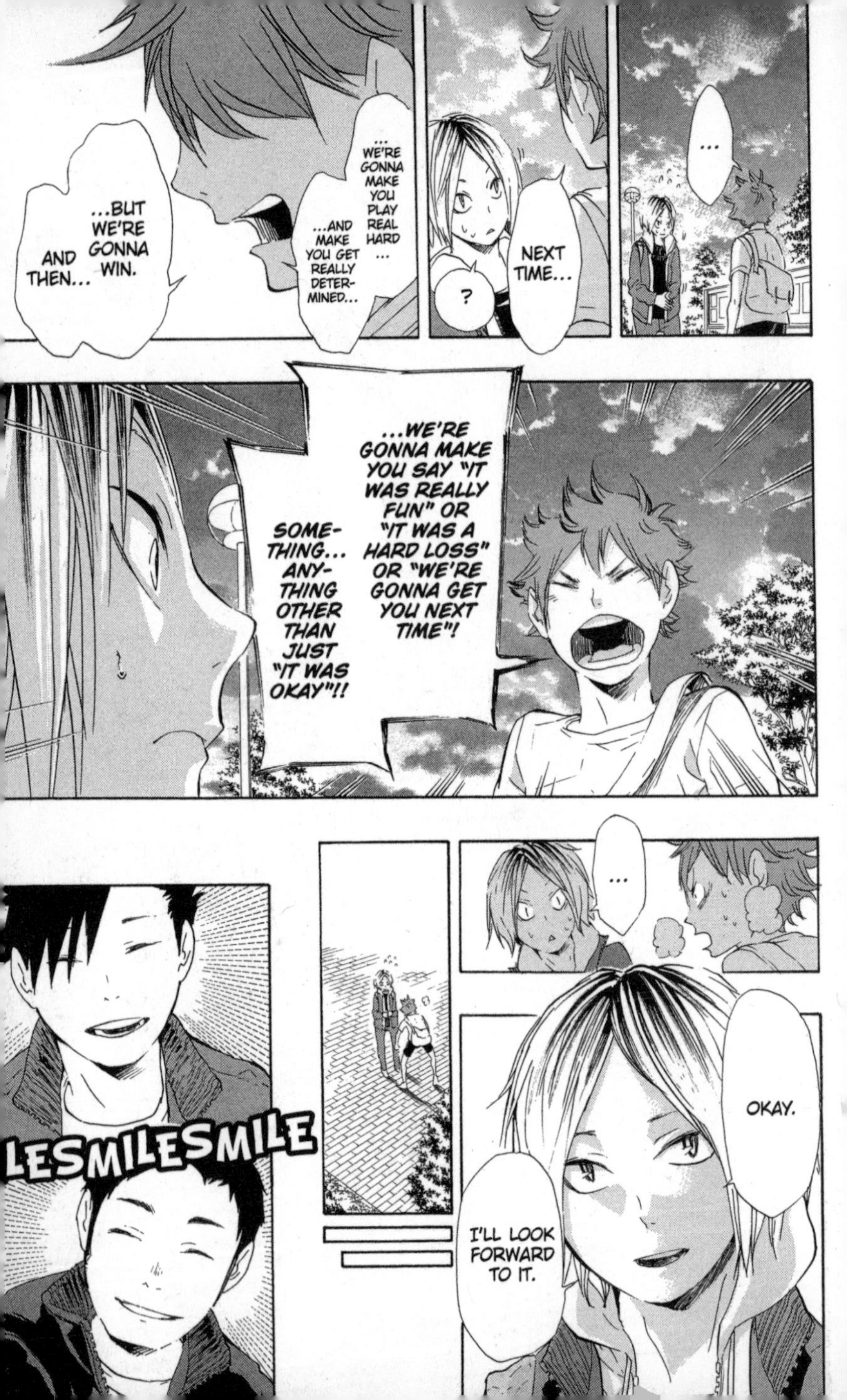
...
NEXT TIME...
?
...WE'RE GONNA MAKE YOU PLAY REAL HARD...
...AND MAKE YOU GET REALLY DETERMINED...
...BUT WE'RE GONNA WIN.
AND THEN...
...WE'RE GONNA MAKE YOU SAY "IT WAS REALLY FUN" OR "IT WAS A HARD LOSS" OR "WE'RE GONNA GET YOU NEXT TIME"!
SOMETHING... ANYTHING OTHER THAN JUST "IT WAS OKAY"!!
...
OKAY.
I'LL LOOK FORWARD TO IT.
LESMILESMILE

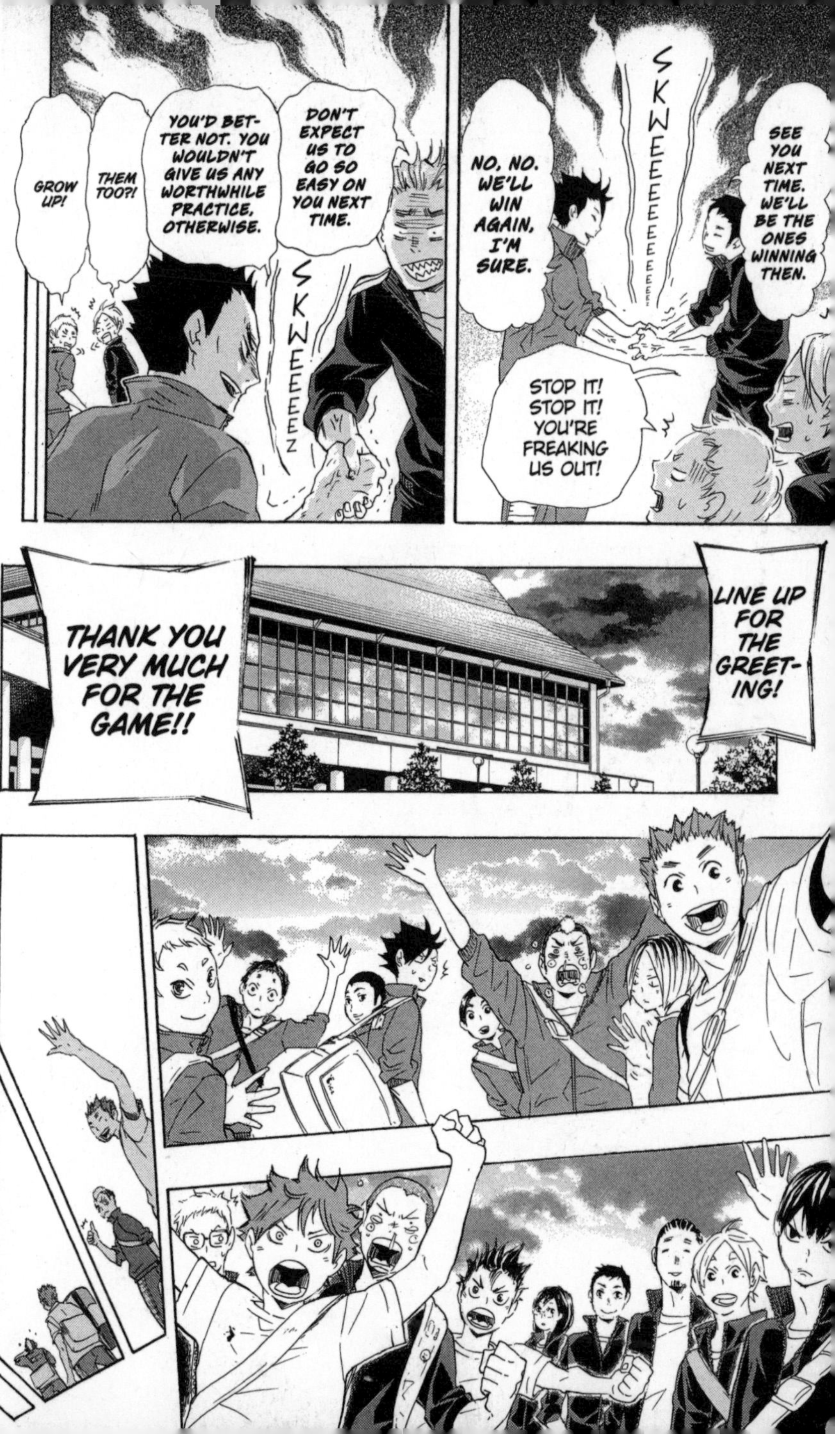
SEE YOU NEXT TIME. WE'LL BE THE ONES WINNING THEN.
SKWEEEEEEEEEEE
NO, NO. WE'LL WIN AGAIN, I'M SURE.
STOP IT! STOP IT! YOU'RE FREAKING US OUT!
DON'T EXPECT US TO GO SO EASY ON YOU NEXT TIME.
SKWEEEEEZ
YOU'D BETTER NOT. YOU WOULDN'T GIVE US ANY WORTHWHILE PRACTICE, OTHERWISE.
THEM TOO?!
GROW UP!
LINE UP FOR THE GREETING!
THANK YOU VERY MUCH FOR THE GAME!!

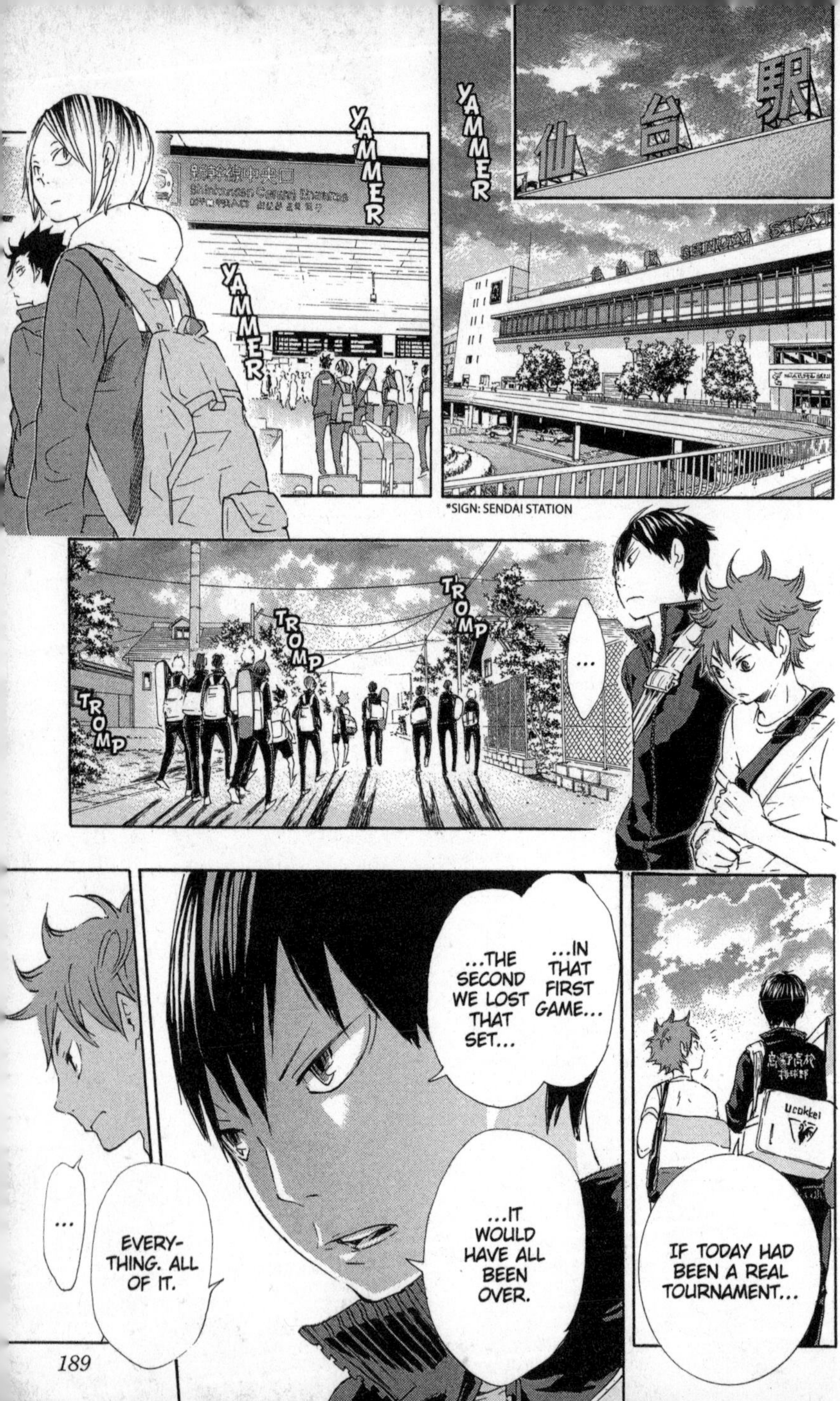

仙台駅
YAMMER
*SIGN: SENDAI STATION
YAMMER
YAMMER
...
TROMP
TROMP
TROMP
IF TODAY HAD BEEN A REAL TOURNAMENT...
...IN THAT FIRST GAME...
...THE SECOND WE LOST THAT SET...
...IT WOULD HAVE ALL BEEN OVER.
EVERY-THING. ALL OF IT.
...

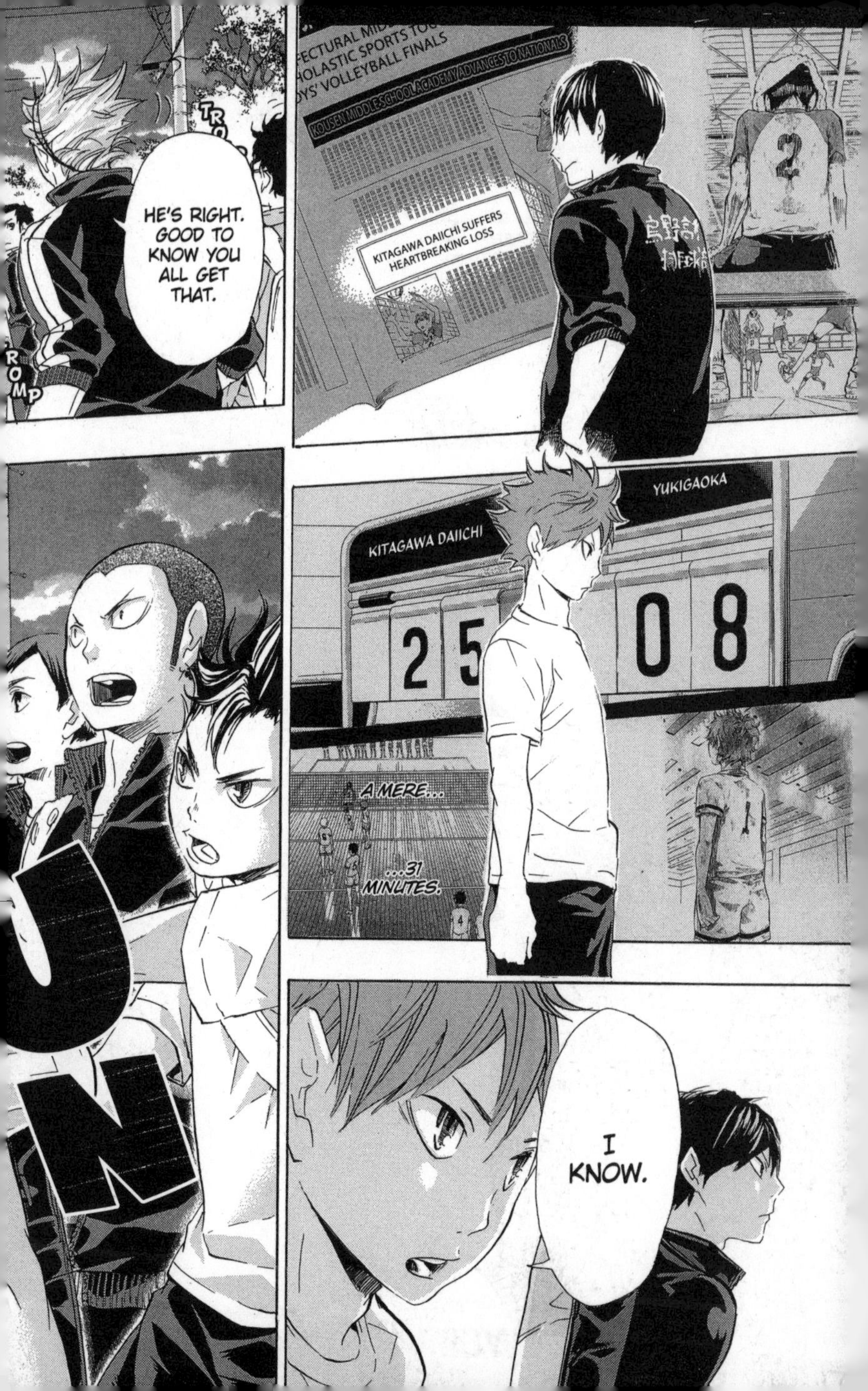
FECTURAL MID
HOLASTIC SPORTS TOU
YS' VOLLEYBALL FINALS
KOUSEN MIDDLE SCHOOL ACADEMY ADVANCES TO NATIONALS
KITAGAWA DAIICHI SUFFERS HEARTBREAKING LOSS
TRO
HE'S RIGHT. GOOD TO KNOW YOU ALL GET THAT.
ROMP
YUKIGAOKA
KITAGAWA DAIICHI
25
08
A MERE...
...31 MINUTES.
I KNOW.
UN

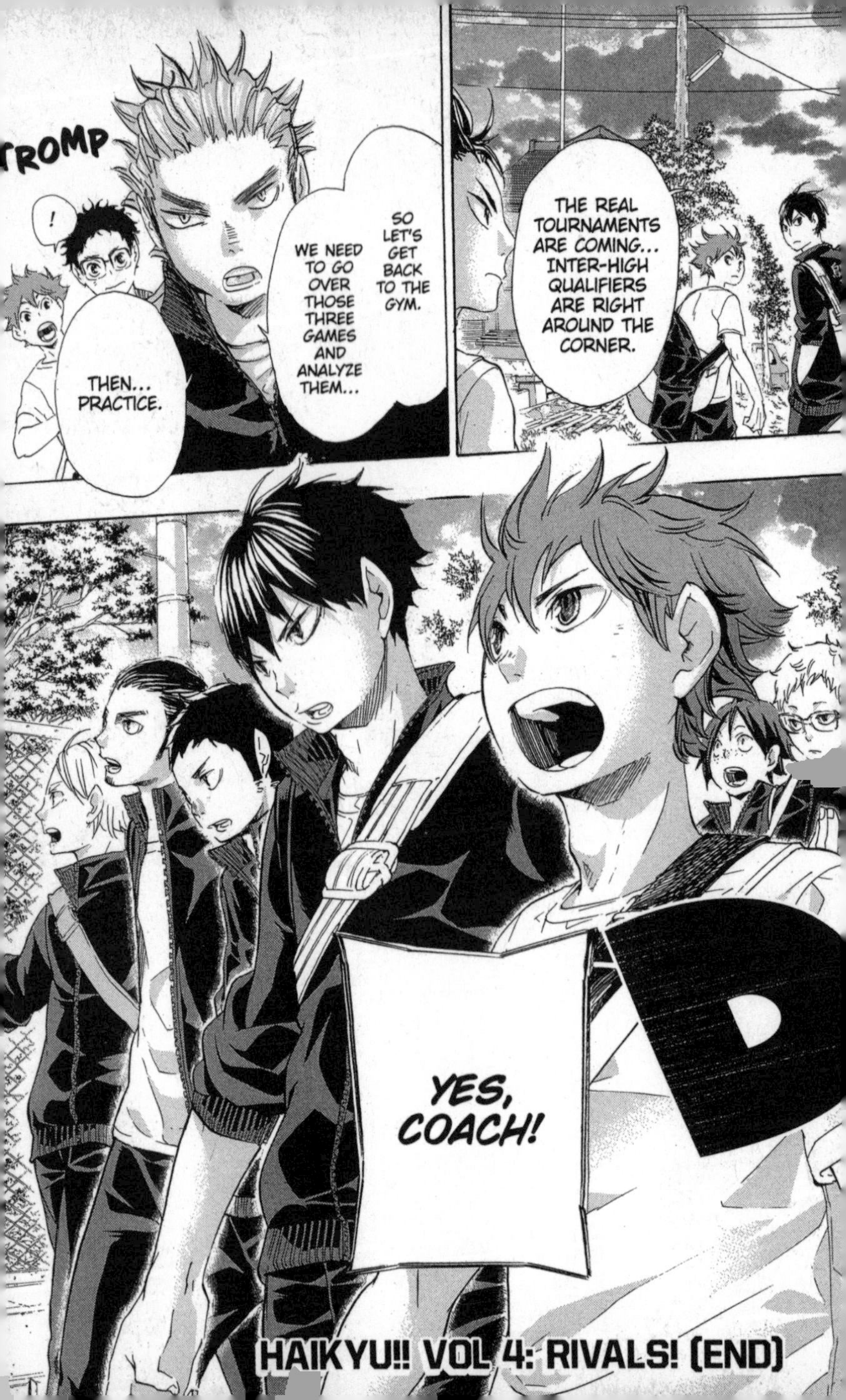
THE REAL TOURNAMENTS ARE COMING... INTER-HIGH QUALIFIERS ARE RIGHT AROUND THE CORNER.
WE NEED TO GO OVER THOSE THREE GAMES AND ANALYZE THEM...
SO LET'S GET BACK TO THE GYM.
TROMP
!
THEN... PRACTICE.
YES, COACH!
HAIKYU!! VOL 4: RIVALS! (END)

NOBUYUKI KAI

**NEKOMA HIGH SCHOOL
CLASS 3-4**

**POSITION:
WING SPIKER**

HEIGHT: 5'9"

**WEIGHT: 152 LBS.
(AS OF APRIL, 3RD YEAR
OF HIGH SCHOOL)**

BIRTHDAY: APRIL 8

**FAVORITE FOOD:
SEA GRAPES**

**CURRENT WORRY: LIFE DOES
HAVE ITS UPS AND DOWNS,
BUT AS LONG AS YOU
KEEP LIVING AND TRYING,
EVERYTHING WILL WORK
OUT.**

**ABILITY PARAMETERS
(5-POINT SCALE)**

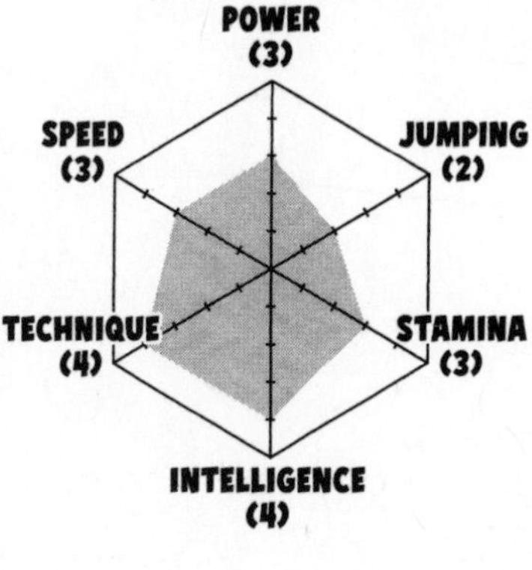
POWER (3)
JUMPING (2)
STAMINA (3)
INTELLIGENCE (4)
TECHNIQUE (4)
SPEED (3)

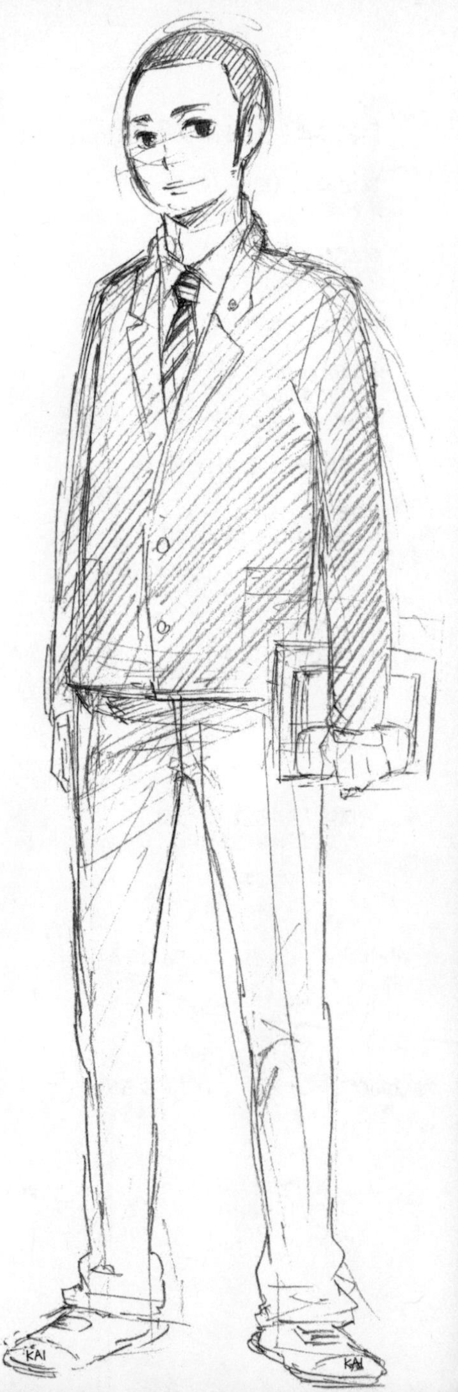
KAI
KAI

SHOHEI FUKUNAGA

NEKOMA HIGH SCHOOL
CLASS 2-2

POSITION:
WING SPIKER

HEIGHT: 5'10"

WEIGHT: 151 LBS.
(AS OF APRIL, 2ND YEAR
OF HIGH SCHOOL)

BIRTHDAY: SEPTEMBER 29

FAVORITE FOOD:
DRIED SHREDDED SQUID

CURRENT WORRY:
YAMAMOTO KEEPS
PESTERING HIM TO TALK
MORE.

ABILITY PARAMETERS
(5-POINT SCALE)

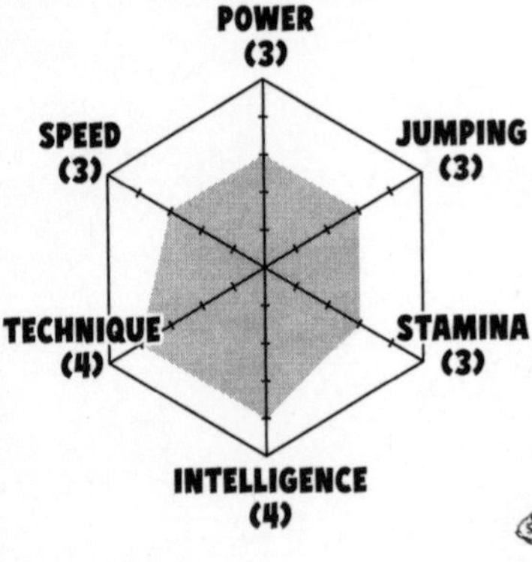
POWER
(3)
JUMPING
(3)
STAMINA
(3)
INTELLIGENCE
(4)
TECHNIQUE
(4)
SPEED
(3)

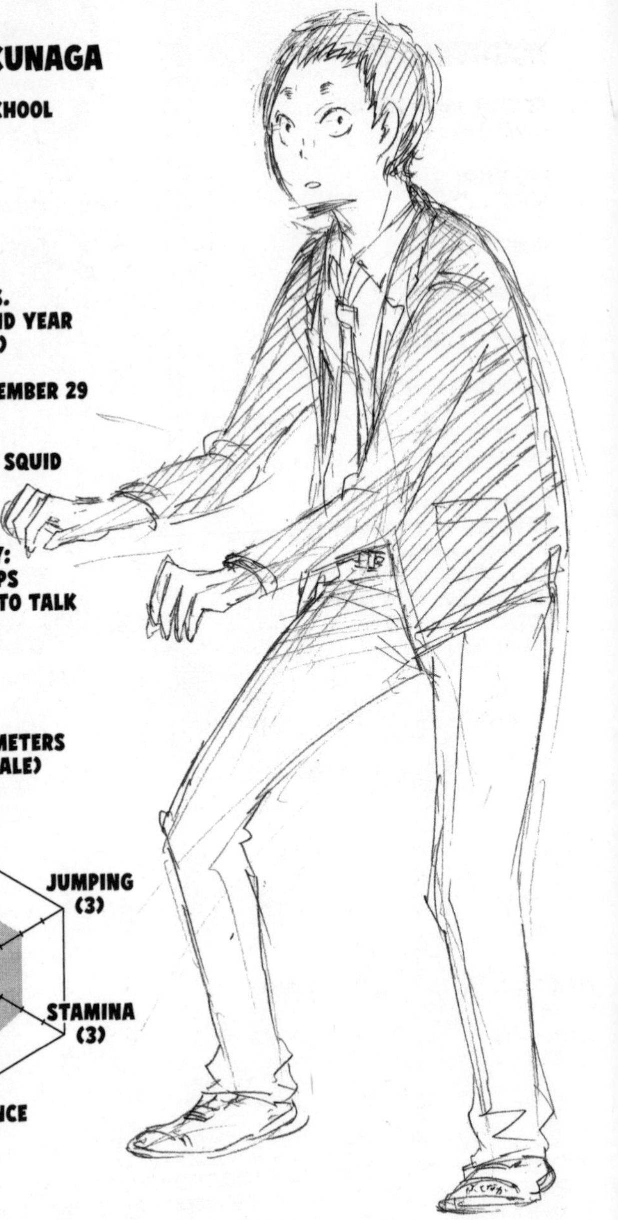

YUKI SHIBAYAMA

**NEKOMA HIGH SCHOOL
CLASS 1-4**

**POSITION:
LIBERO**

HEIGHT: 5'4"

**WEIGHT: 118 LBS.
(AS OF APRIL, 2ND YEAR
OF HIGH SCHOOL)**

BIRTHDAY: DECEMBER 16

**FAVORITE FOOD:
OMELET RICE**

**CURRENT WORRY:
EVERYONE IS SO GOOD AT
DEFENSE THAT HE HAS NO
IDEA HOW HE'S GOING TO
KEEP UP, BUT HE'S GOING
TO KEEP PRACTICING
REALLY HARD.**

**ABILITY PARAMETERS
(5-POINT SCALE)**

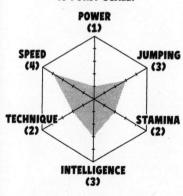

POWER
(1)

SPEED
(4)

JUMPING
(3)

TECHNIQUE
(2)

STAMINA
(2)

INTELLIGENCE
(3)

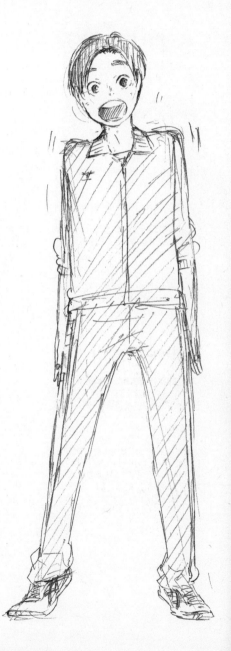

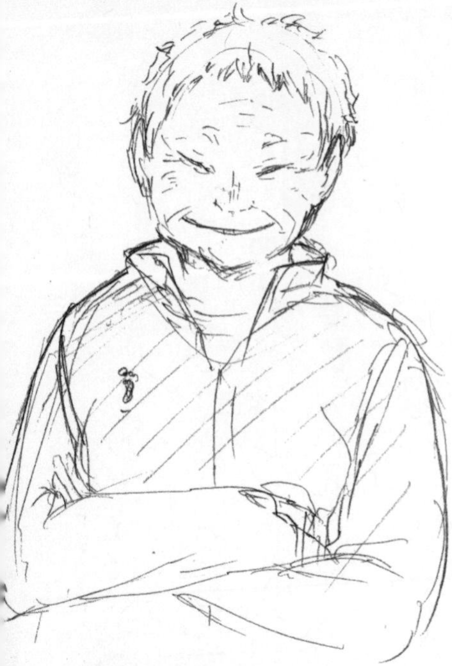

YASUFUMI NEKOMATA

NEKOMA HIGH SCHOOL

VOLLEYBALL CLUB HEAD COACH

AGE: 68

CURRENT WORRY:
NAOI IS A BORE TO GO DRINKING WITH BECAUSE HE'S TOO EASY TO DRINK UNDER THE TABLE.

MANABU NAOI

NEKOMA HIGH SCHOOL

VOLLEYBALL CLUB COACH

AGE: 26

CURRENT WORRY:
PEOPLE KEEP TELLING HIM THAT HE CAN'T HOLD HIS LIQUOR AS WELL AS THEY EXPECTED.

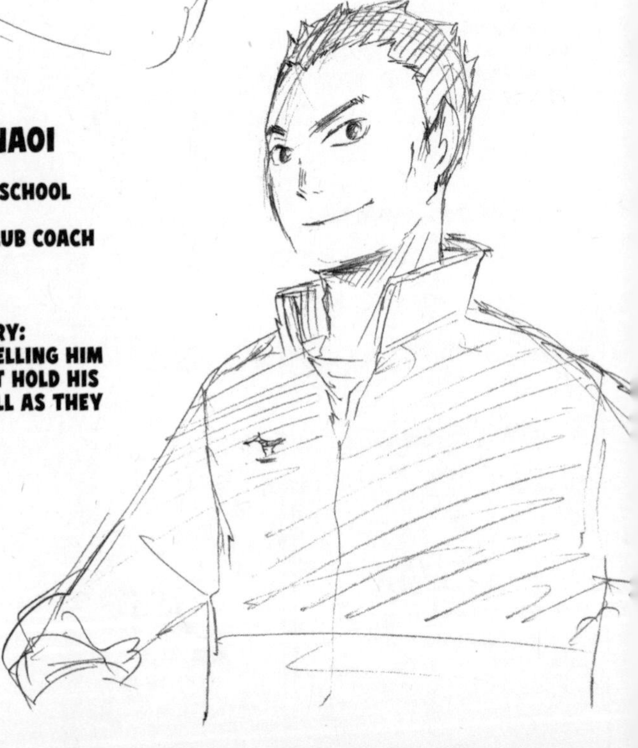

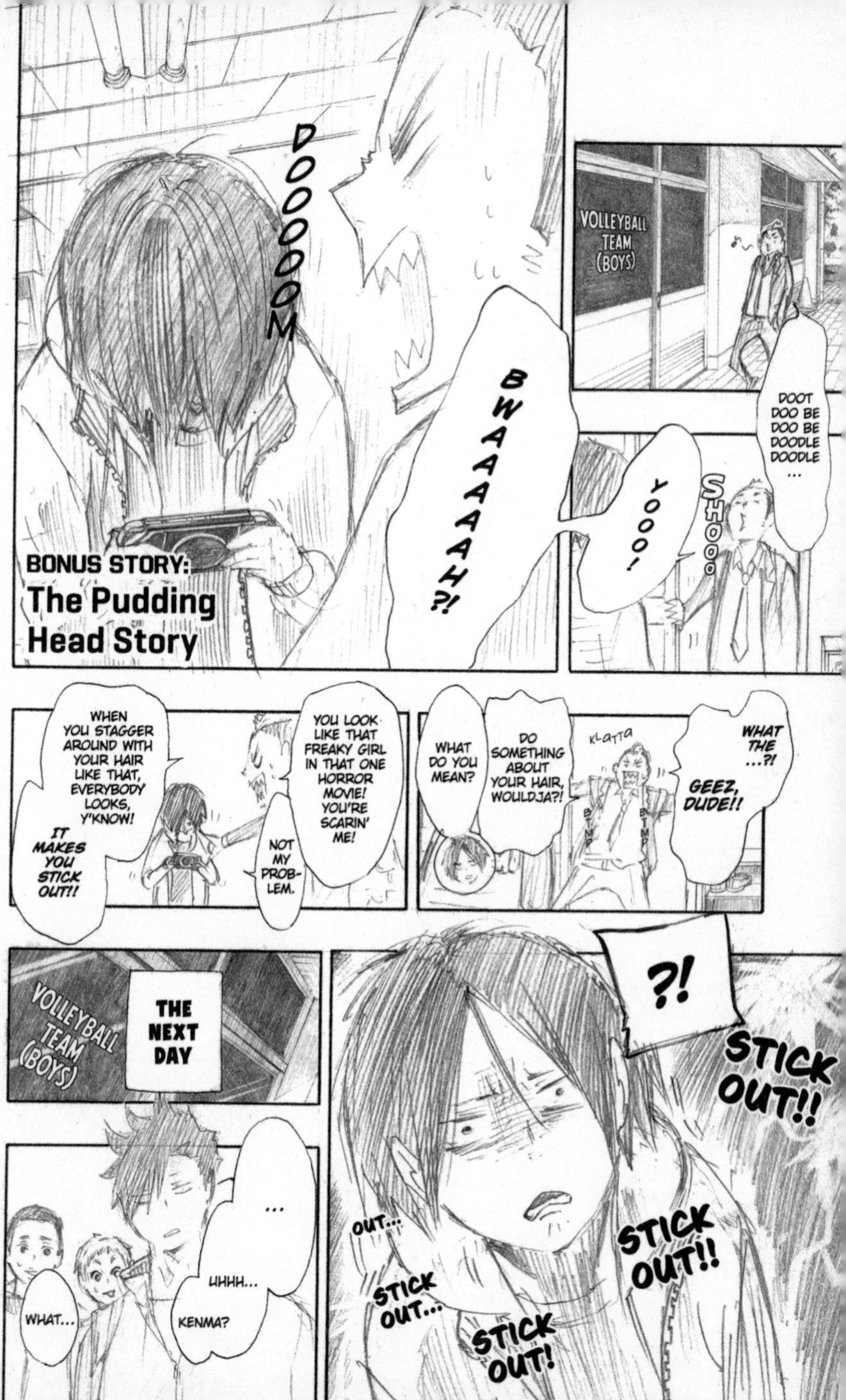
VOLLEYBALL TEAM (BOYS)
DOOT DOO BE DOO BE DOODLE DOODLE ...
SHOOO
YOOOO!
BWAAAAAAAH?!
DOOOOOOOM
BONUS STORY:
The Pudding Head Story
WHAT THE ...?!
GEEZ, DUDE!!
KLATTA
BTMP
BTMP
DO SOMETHING ABOUT YOUR HAIR, WOULDJA?!
WHAT DO YOU MEAN?
YOU LOOK LIKE THAT FREAKY GIRL IN THAT ONE HORROR MOVIE! YOU'RE SCARIN' ME!
NOT MY PROB-LEM.
WHEN YOU STAGGER AROUND WITH YOUR HAIR LIKE THAT, EVERYBODY LOOKS, Y'KNOW!
IT MAKES YOU STICK OUT!!
?!
STICK OUT!!
STICK OUT!!
OUT...
STICK OUT...
STICK OUT!
VOLLEYBALL TEAM (BOYS)
THE NEXT DAY
...
UHHH...
KENMA?
WHAT...

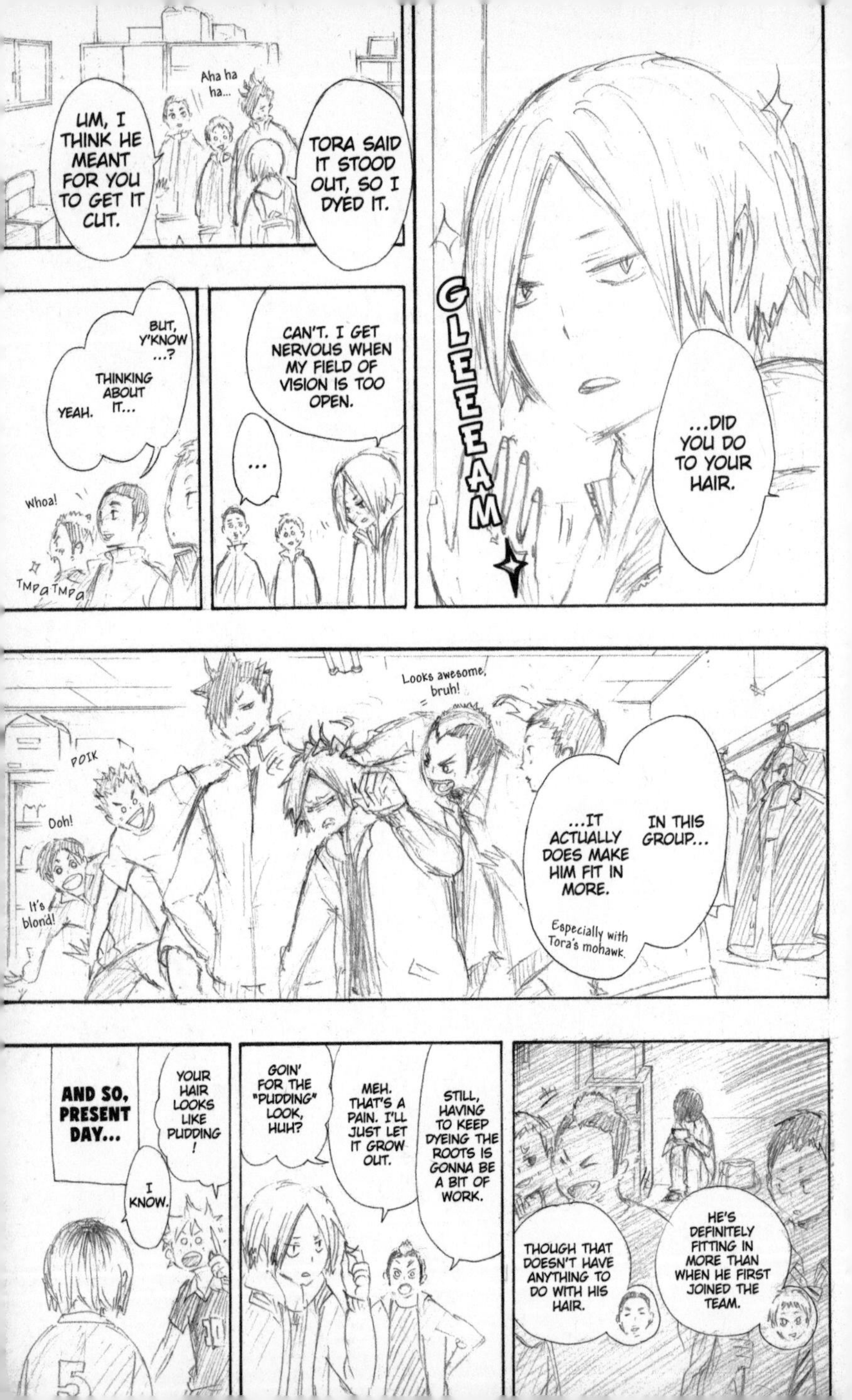
GLEEEEAM
...DID YOU DO TO YOUR HAIR.
TORA SAID IT STOOD OUT, SO I DYED IT.
Aha ha ha...
UM, I THINK HE MEANT FOR YOU TO GET IT CUT.
CAN'T. I GET NERVOUS WHEN MY FIELD OF VISION IS TOO OPEN.
...
BUT, Y'KNOW ...?
THINKING ABOUT IT...
YEAH.
Whoa!
TMPa TMPa
Looks awesome, bruh!
POIK
Ooh!
It's blond!
IN THIS GROUP...
...IT ACTUALLY DOES MAKE HIM FIT IN MORE.
Especially with Tora's mohawk.
HE'S DEFINITELY FITTING IN MORE THAN WHEN HE FIRST JOINED THE TEAM.
THOUGH THAT DOESN'T HAVE ANYTHING TO DO WITH HIS HAIR.
STILL, HAVING TO KEEP DYEING THE ROOTS IS GONNA BE A BIT OF WORK.
MEH. THAT'S A PAIN. I'LL JUST LET IT GROW OUT.
GOIN' FOR THE "PUDDING" LOOK, HUH?
AND SO, PRESENT DAY...
YOUR HAIR LOOKS LIKE PUDDING!
I KNOW.

EDITOR'S NOTES

The English edition of Haikyu!! maintains the honorifics used in the original Japanese version. For those of you who are new to these terms, here's a brief explanation to help with your reading experience!

When saying someone's name in Japanese, a suffix is often attached to indicate how familiar the speaker is with the person. Some are more polite and respectful, while others are endearing.

1. **-kun** is often used for young men or boys, usually someone you are familiar with.

2. **-chan** is used for young children and can be used as a term of endearment.

3. **-san** is used for someone you respect or are not close to, or to be polite.

4. **Senpai** is used for someone who is older than you or in a higher position or grade in school.

5. **Kohai** is used for someone who is younger than you or in a lower position or grade in school.

6. **Sensei** means teacher.

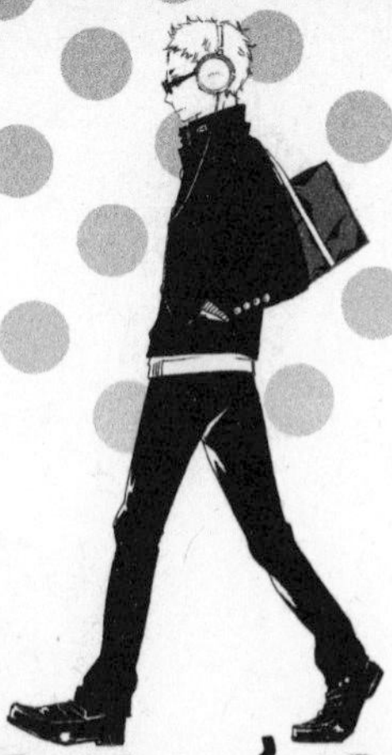

You're Reading the WRONG WAY!

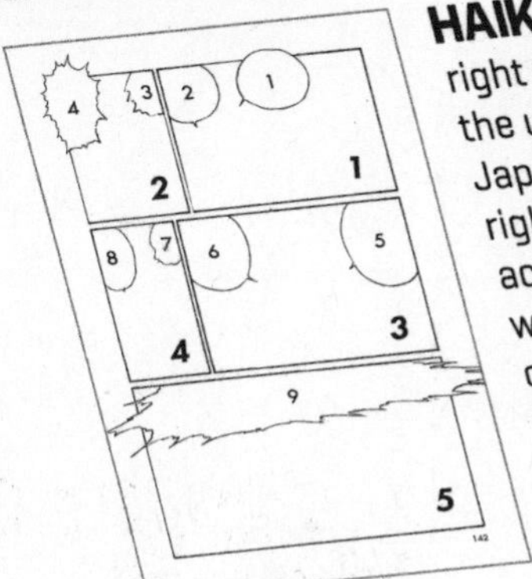
1
2
3
4
1
2
5
6
7
8
3
4
9
5
142

HAIKYU!! reads from right to left, starting in the upper-right corner. Japanese is read from right to left, meaning that action, sound effects and word-balloon order are completely reversed from English order.

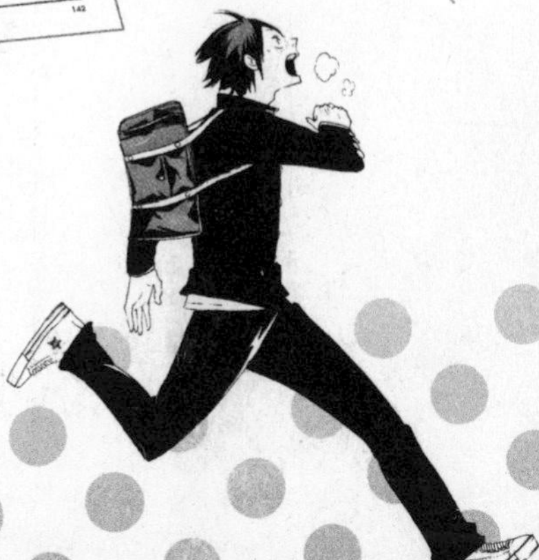